The Odyssey of the
Abraham Lincoln Brigade

The *Odyssey* of the *Abraham Lincoln Brigade*

Americans in the Spanish Civil War

Peter N. Carroll

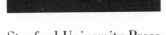

Stanford University Press
Stanford, California • 1994

Stanford University Press

Stanford, California

© 1994 by the Board of Trustees of the

Leland Stanford Junior University

Printed in the United States of America

CIP data appear at the end of the book

Stanford University Press publications are distributed exclusively by
Stanford University Press within the United States, Canada, and
Mexico; they are distributed exclusively by Cambridge University
Press throughout the rest of the world.

For my friend

MICHAEL BATINSKI,

ever wise, ever wacko

Preface

The history of the Spanish civil war is consumed by mythology and legend, so much so that it is extremely difficult to separate fact from fiction. Nearly everything written about the war has generated controversy. Even the title of this book will raise eyebrows, for there was no Lincoln "brigade," per se. The first of the 2,800 Americans who fought to defend the Spanish Republic against the insurrection led by General Francisco Franco named themselves the Abraham Lincoln *battalion*, which was part of the Fifteenth International Brigade. But since many American volunteers served with other battalions and military groups, it has proven convenient to call them all members of the Lincoln brigade. The political basis of this technical argument is discussed elsewhere in these pages.

Indeed, politics and ideology lie at the core of many controversies involving the American volunteers. Some observers have questioned whether they were "volunteers" at all, arguing that those who went to Spain were merely following the orders of the Communist party. Others have claimed that the Communist leadership imposed a reign of terror in the brigade and forced the Americans into battle against their will. Under the guise of military necessity, it is alleged, Communists executed those who disagreed with the party line. Are these charges true? And outsiders, such as the novelist Ernest Hemingway, who dared to criticize Communist control became enemies of the brigade. Why, we may ask, did the Spanish war veterans condemn his novel, *For Whom the Bell Tolls*?

Such political quarrels dogged the Lincoln veterans after Spain. They were criticized at the beginning of World War II for following the Communist line "The Yanks are not coming!" Yet few realize how some of the Lincolns secretly violated the Communist policy of opposing U.S. intervention and provided crucial assistance to British intelligence and to the American Office of Strategic Services, the predecessor of the CIA. Their ambiguous relationship to the U.S. military during the Second World War nonetheless proved a harbinger of postwar problems.

Amid the anti-Communist hysteria of the 1940's and 1950's, the Lincoln brigade became a prominent target for harassment and political persecution. But were the Veterans of the Abraham Lincoln Brigade part of a Communist conspiracy? We may also wonder about the impact of these ideological conflicts on the careers of the intellectuals and creative artists who had served in the Lincoln brigade. How did politics affect their writing and their art?

Five and a half decades after the Spanish war, the Lincoln brigade has not quite passed into history. What happened to these old soldiers? Have the old radicals of the 1930's grown sour with age? And how have they responded to the momentous changes of their lifetimes? To what extent, in short, have they maintained the commitments of their youth?

Many of these questions can now, finally, be laid to rest. With the collapse of the Soviet Union, most Communists and ex-Communists have agreed to address issues that hitherto have been obscured by fetishes of privacy and an understandable fear of persecution. The aging of the Lincoln veterans has also played a role in opening the historical record. Of the two-hundred-odd who survive, the youngest are in their mid-seventies. Most well understand the importance of preserving their history as truthfully as possible.

In the course of writing this book, I have benefited enormously from the cooperation of Lincoln veterans and their families and friends. The research commenced nearly two decades ago as I interviewed individual veterans about their personal lives and their role in the larger history that surrounded them.

In the beginning, these oral histories served limited purposes: to satisfy the curiosity of a prying historian. But as I came to know the veterans better—and they came to trust my purposes—these conversations and interviews became more systematic and thorough. I accumulated a private archive of information, much of it otherwise unavailable and unknown. To facilitate my work, the northern California veterans elected me their historian. Needless to say—but I will say it anyway—there were no strings attached.

Oral histories have inevitable limitations, ranging from the participants' poor memories to their occasional outright fabrications. Only in very few cases did I settle for one person's account of a particular issue, and then only out of necessity. Such exceptions are clearly acknowledged in the text. About most historical problems, however, there exists abundant supporting material to explain and justify my conclusions. The same factors that have encouraged a concern for historical accuracy—the diminishing importance of partisan controversies and the aging of the Lincolns—have produced a wealth of new archival material. As the veterans or their survivors clear out closets and basements, they have uncovered a tremendous number of documents, many of them unread for decades. These sources provide the backbone of this book. Whether quoting from unknown Hemingway letters, speeches of his opponents, or previously unused government records, I have allowed the original words to assume priority over the retrospective memories and belated analyses. But, in fact, the oral testimony and the written record reveal few contradictions. Usually the one amplifies and corroborates the other.

The availability of these new sources facilitates what might be called a third generation of writing about the Lincoln brigade. The first consisted of accounts by the participants: Edwin Rolfe's *The Lincoln Battalion* and Alvah Bessie's *Men in Battle*, both published in 1939, and Art Landis's *The Abraham Lincoln Brigade*, based on the collective memories of the volunteers and published in 1968. The second generation, written by academic scholars, showed the limitations of the available evidence as well as the continuation of partisan disputes. Cecil Eby's *Between the Bullet and the Lie* (1969) is fraught with political bias and innumerable errors. Robert Rosenstone's *Crusade of the Left* (1969) accepted the limited scope demanded by the paucity of evidence. John Gerassi's *Premature Antifascists* (1986) too readily takes the Lincolns at their word.

This book, by contrast, endeavors to assess the divergence of opinions fairly and forthrightly. The bottom line, as it were, remains the historical sources. Unlike earlier studies of the Lincoln volunteers, moreover, this book expands the scope of inquiry to include the entire lifetime of the participants. For most of the men and women who went to Spain, that experience constituted merely one chapter of a longer and more elaborate story. By placing the Spanish war within the context of lifelong commitments, we can better understand the motives and expectations, the values and beliefs, of those who put their lives on the line when they volunteered to fight against fascism in Spain. No less important has been the war's legacy in their lives. The ordeal of Spain, the loss of so many friends and comrades, inevitably followed the veterans long after they had returned home. For most of the Lincolns, commitments made in the 1930's persisted through the remainder of their lives. However one may judge the wisdom of their convictions—and surely they remain open to criticism—their political passion has given meaning both to their own lives and to their times.

Some books walk through the front door. Although I had been intrigued about writing a history of the Lincoln volunteers since I first interviewed novelist-veteran Alvah Bessie in 1975, it was not until Milton Wolff, last commander of the brigade, literally dropped three heavy cartons of his personal papers in my living room thirteen years later that I felt sufficiently confident about the value of the historical material I had accumulated. Only then did I realize that the preciousness of my archive—interviews, oral histories, a variety of unpublished sources—obliged me to undertake this project. To be slightly immodest, if I did not write this history probably no one else would have been able to assemble the necessary information.

As I turned seriously to this book, I benefited further from the extraordinary generosity of the Lincoln veterans, their families, and their friends. Not only did most of those I contacted agree to speak with me about their lives and adventures, but many spontaneously provided additional source material—letters, diaries, news clippings, and a multitude of historical paraphernalia. Often, too, they fed me and gave me a place to sleep.

The following is a list of those participants who answered my questions, often more than once, though a few have asked to remain anonymous:

Mel Anderson, Bill Bailey, Barney Baley, Reuben Barr, Vita Barsky, Edward Bender, James Benét, Jenny Berman, Alvah Bessie, Jack Bjoze, Esther

Silverstein Blanc, Vernon Bown, Joseph Brandt, Moishe Brier, Archie Brown, Esther "Hon" Brown, Charles Burley, Paul Burns, Joe Cobert, Morris Cohen, Robert Colodny, Maury Colow, Rudy Corbin, Ruth Davidow, George Draper, Rebecca Durem, Ralph Fasanella, Harry Fisher, Bernard Fishman, Moe Fishman, John Gates, Carl Geiser, John Gerlach, Howard Goddard, Irving Goff, Sana Goldblatt, Ben Goldring, Sam Gonshak, Al Gottlieb, Manny Harriman, William Herrick, Hy Hersh, Harry K. Hubbard, Leo Hurwitz, Dolores Ibarruri, John Jacobs, Irving Jenkins, James M. Jones, Stan Junas, Sid Kaufman, George Kaye, Fred Keller, Al Koslow, Leonard Lamb, Edward Lending, Leonard Levenson, Sid Levine, Vaughn Love, Jack Lucid, Percy Ludwich, Don MacLeod, Eluard Luchelle McDaniels, William Miller, John Murra, Conlon Nancarrow, Steve Nelson, Marion Noble, Hela Norman, Charles Nusser, Leonard Olsen, Michael O'Riordan, Abe Osheroff, Norman Perlman, William Pike, Sophie Pitney, Albert Prago, Bob Reed, Michelle Reichman, Al Richmond, Hilda Roberts, Mary Rolfe, Herman Rosenstein, Hy Rosner, Adolph Ross, John Rosser, Viola Schuetrum, James Schuyler, William Sennett, Elman Service, Jack Shafran, Mildred Rackley Simon, Ruth Simon, David Smith, Abe Smorodin, Irene Goldin Spiegel, Mark Strauss, William Susman, Alfred Tanz, Robert Taylor, Millie Thayer, Nate Thornton, John Tisa, Anthony Toney, Dorothy Tucker, Mary Tyler, Ted Veltfort, Joseph Vogel, Marion Merriman Wachtel, George Watt, Milton Weiner, Irving Weissman, Saul Wellman, Bill Wheeler, Milton Wolff, and James Yates.

Recent changes in the international climate also enabled me, as a representative of the Abraham Lincoln Brigade Archives, to examine the extensive Spanish civil war archives in Moscow, which previously had not been available to Western historians. These records, which had been shipped hastily to the Soviet Union as Franco was conquering Republican Spain in 1939, provide detailed documentation of the military and political activities within the International Brigades. They have helped resolve many ambiguities created by the unfortunate dispersal of the official records of the Lincoln brigade. In particular, I would like to thank Oleg Naumov, Andrei Doronin, Eleanora Shakhnazarova, and Svetlana Rosenthal for innumerable courtesies while I conducted research at the Russian Center for the Preservation and Study of Recent Historical Documents. My steadfast interpreter, translator, and guide was Galina Khartulary.

In addition, I was able to conduct two lengthy interviews in Moscow with one of the more notorious Lincoln veterans, the former Soviet agent Morris Cohen, for which I would like to thank Boris N. Labusov, press officer of the Russian Intelligence Service. And a Soviet veteran of the Fifteenth Brigade, Percy Ludwich, provided fresh information about the political and military history of the American volunteers.

I would also like to acknowledge those who gave me access to privately held primary sources: Sylviane Bessie, Joseph Brandt, Esther Brown, Lillian Chodorow, Eleanor Friede, Muriel Goldring, Ernest Goodman, John Jacobs, Alice Josephs, Adelmo Lo Presto, Mary Rolfe, Jeff Wachtel, and David Wills.

My research was assisted greatly by the willingness of other researchers to share information and sources: Charles Amirkhanian, Maria Brooks, Jim Carriger, Tom Entwhistle, Martha Evans, Jerry Fischman, Kyle Gann, Maurice Isserman, Barbara Head Millstein, Gerald Monroe, Judy Montell, Cary Nelson, Frances Patai, Eva Soltes, William B. Watson, and Robert Whealey.

My thanks to the many archivists who have gone out of their way to assist my efforts: at Brandeis University, Charles Cutter, John Favorman, and Victor Berch (who deserves a medal for building the Spanish civil war collection there); at the Bancroft Library in Berkeley, California, Nicole Bouchét; at the Hoover Institution at Stanford University, Marjorie Rauen; at Adelphi University, Erika Doctorow; and at the Niebyl-Proctor Library in Berkeley, Jane Hodes.

For help with translations, I am grateful to Victoria Parraga and Lenore Veltfort.

And for a multitude of favors and courtesies, I thank Richard Bermack, Danny Duncan Collum, Deirdre Cossman, Brandon Cushing, Susan Falb, Earl Harju, Tom Sarbaugh, and Sue Thrasher. I would like to acknowledge a Travel-to-Collections grant from the National Endowment for the Humanities. This work has benefited from the care and attention of Laura Bloch, Karen Brown Davison, Jan Johnson, and Norris Pope of Stanford University Press.

My friends and family, as always, went the extra mile with me. Michael Batinski, Fred Hill, and Jules Tygiel made numerous suggestions for improving the early drafts. Two good kids, Matthew and Natasha, lightened my days. Jeannette Ferrary, who gave endless support, I will speak to privately.

P.N.C.

Contents

xiv   Contents

Photographs follow p. 5

Military Chronology

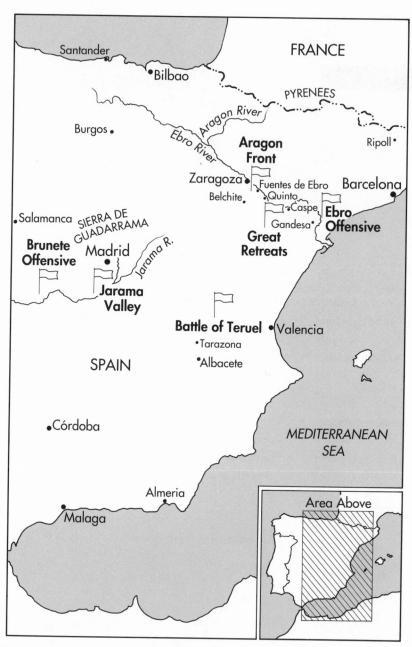

Military Actions of the Lincoln Brigade

The Odyssey of the
Abraham Lincoln Brigade

Prologue: What They Dared

Irving Weissman was over 60 years old in the mid-1970's when he left his home in New York City and traveled back to Spain, a land of his youth. Soon he was heading toward Tarazona de la Mancha, the dry, dusty town where he had trained as a soldier in the Lincoln brigade during the summer of 1937. Trees and hedges outlined the town square, where four companies of his battalion had stood in formation on the morning before they moved toward the front lines. Weissman remembered the women of the town, all dressed in black, coming to these foreign soldiers with goatskins of wine and water. "They did not smile and they did not cry," he recalled. "Their own sons and husbands were long gone." Weissman remembered the thirst of that morning, and now, forty years later, he entered a small shop to purchase a bottle of water and a package of hazelnuts. An older woman at the counter instantly recognized him as a North American; she had seen so many in that town long before. And while Weissman stood speechless she spontaneously lifted a necklace from inside her dress, revealing a small tin whistle given to her by one of those Americans who had come to help the Republic. Weissman fingered the trinket, feeling the warmth from the woman's bosom. In his mind he could still see the face of the battalion postman who blew through its aperture to announce the mail. Weissman looked into the expectant eyes of this Spanish woman, and he told her with certainty that her American friend had been killed in battle several months after leaving behind his souvenir.

Spain had gnawed on Weissman's conscience. As he drove into the Aragon region, he remembered the battles of 1937—Quinto, Belchite, Fuentes de Ebro—that the American battalions had fought in the futile effort to advance toward the fascist-held Zaragoza. Each landmark held memories of valor and death, hope and its extinction. But it was at Belchite, amidst the remaining ruins of the devastated city—Franco's "necropolis," as Weissman called it—that the visitor could still glimpse the everlasting agony of the war. The broken walls served now as an unsubtle reminder to those who might dare to rebel against the Franco regime. Weissman held no illusions about the possibility of revolt. He studied the crumbled buildings for what they evoked about comrades long dead, and he found himself staring in awe at a black wrought-iron cross that was, he said, "a witness of the desolation of soul and earth that is the real victor in war." Weissman stood there with his memories, wondering at his own survival. He felt the hot Spanish sun press against his skin, a warmth that had shaped his identity for all those intervening years. And then, like virtually every other veteran of the Lincoln brigade who returned to Spain to bear witness and pay homage, Irving Weissman began to weep.

Those were the tears of a lifetime—grief, surely, for those who had fallen in Spain, but also an outpouring of desperation for the living. History had not vindicated the Lincoln brigade. For forty years, from the time the first American volunteers had journeyed to Spain in December 1936, they had stood outside the mainstream of society. At a time when American ideals seemed imperiled by the rise of fascism abroad, they had taken a bold stand, put their lives in place of words, and embarked to fight the enemy with bullets and guns. In Spain, these anti-fascists saw a chance to stop aggression before the world tumbled into another global war. Many Americans felt as they did about fascism, similarly deploring its racism, militarization, and brutality. But of the 125 million Americans who answered the census polls of the 1930's, fewer than 3,000 dared to risk their lives to help the Spanish people.

Those who responded to the crisis acted primarily from political motives.

Most were Communists; nearly all accepted the leadership of the Communist party, at least for the war's duration. Such attachments need to be understood in historical context. What did it mean to be a Communist in the 1930's? During that tumultuous decade, anti-Communists objected bitterly to the dogmatism of the party's ideology and attacked the authoritarianism of its leadership. Subsequently, revelations of Communist totalitarianism challenged the party's claim to idealistic principles. More recently, the collapse of Communist regimes in the Soviet Union and eastern Europe testifies to the disastrous failure of the movement's theory and practice. It is easy, therefore, to dismiss those who followed the Communist standard as blind, malevolent, and dangerous.

In assessing the men and women who served in the Abraham Lincoln brigade, however, there are other considerations to remember. During America's political struggles in the 1930's, Communist dogmatism proved a great asset in winning economic benefits for the unemployed and the homeless. In addition, Communists established a fine and honorable record of opposing racial injustice; the party was virtually the only white political organization of its time to accept blacks on equal terms. Communist principles thus meshed with a practical agenda. Cynics, hypocrites, and manipulators may indeed have joined the party, but the great lure of communism was its idealism. The American volunteers who went to Spain saw themselves as liberators, not oppressors, and gave generously whatever they had—their time, their lives, and their hope.

The war experience consequently reinforced a special identity. "Because of the intensity of the experience," recalled Don MacLeod, who left his undergraduate studies at Berkeley to drive trucks across the plains and mountains of Spain, "you got to know everybody so deeply and so quickly, so intimately, that they made . . . indelible impressions." Surrounded by enormous casualties—one-third of the American volunteers would be buried in Spanish earth—the Lincolns endured a collective ordeal that separated them from those who had stayed at home. Spain drew them together emotionally, politically, spiritually. "We, all of us here," wrote the poet Edwin Rolfe from Barcelona in 1938, "date a certain birth of ourselves to our arrival here, and since we didn't, most of us, know each other at home, all that we have in common is Spain."

The survivors returned from the war marked men. Friends and comrades idealized their courage; the FBI promptly put them under surveillance. But the legacy of Spain was etched even deeper. For Spain under the victorious Franco remained, as Albert Camus put it, "a bad wound" in the heart, ever a reminder "that one can be right and yet be vanquished, that force can subdue the spirit, that there are times when courage does not have its reward. It is this, no doubt," he said, "which explains why so many men all over the world feel the Spanish drama as a personal tragedy."

It was a tragedy, however, that the Lincoln volunteers refused to accept. Famous as "fighting anti-fascists," they continued to challenge the legitimacy of the Franco government, taking on in the process a multitude of other enemies—the U.S. Department of State, the American army, the witch-hunting anti-Communists—who opposed their efforts to overthrow the Franco dictatorship. Indeed, struggle became a way of life—a procession of causes and commitments that would eventually link the veterans of the Spanish war with a variety of social and political issues during the next half-century.

The experience was reminiscent of the baseball pitcher who held a ball in his hand for most of his adult life only to discover that the ball was holding him. Battle after battle, protest after protest, the Lincoln veterans emerged, to their surprise, as elder statesmen of dissent, the radicals' American Legion. But it was not old wars that they fought. To the contrary, the Lincolns built bridges to a younger generation of political activists. "We were naive," the 70-year-old Don MacLeod would admit of his decision to go to Spain in 1937, "but it's the kind of naiveté that the world needs and will always find somewhere, among the youth especially."

"If you lose [a war]," the great American novelist of the Spanish civil war, Ernest Hemingway, exclaimed in 1939, "you lose everything and your ideology won't save you." The Lincoln volunteers—whom Hemingway disparaged as the "ideology boys"—clung to the opposite view. Although they "lost the war," their last commander, Milton Wolff, insisted that "neither the Spaniards nor the [international volunteers], nor anti-fascists of any mettle, lost their ideology, much less 'everything.'" To Wolff, writing twenty years after Hemingway's suicide, it was precisely ideology that had "saved us. And may yet save the world." Indeed, it was this spirit of commitment—an unyielding optimism in the face of defeat—that distinguished the Lincoln veterans. For them, Spain lived not as the landscape for a novel or as a place of metaphysical inspiration. "Spain"—the word, the country, the cause—embodied ideology and political passion, anguish and hope; the ordeal of Spain became the essential continuity of their lives.

Anticipating this half-century's commitment, the poet Genevieve Taggard composed "To the Veterans of the Abraham Lincoln Brigade" in 1941:

> Say of them,
> They are no longer young, they never learned
> The arts, the stealth of peace, this peace, the tricks of fear;
> And what they knew, they know
> And what they dared they dare.

To protest the 1936 Olympic Games in Nazi Germany, amateur athletes from around the world organized a counter-Olympics in Barcelona. Five members of the American team—from left to right, Charles Burley, Irving Jenkins, Dorothy Tucker, Myron Dickes, and Frank Payton—pose for snapshots en route to Spain. The outbreak of war on July 18, 1936, prevented the staging of the sports competition. (Author's collection)

Edward Bender (*left*), an early organizer of the American volunteers in New York, stands in front of a camouflaged vehicle with Dr. Irving Busch, one of the physicians sent to Spain by the American Medical Bureau to Aid Spanish Democracy. (Author's collection)

Right: While fewer than 3,000 Americans volunteered to serve in Spain, nationwide appeals for financial assistance for the Spanish Republic were successful. Among the most valuable donations were ambulances, which were sponsored by a variety of organizations. (Author's collection)

Below: The Spanish civil war attracted the interest of writers and intellectuals from around the world. The American novelist Ernest Hemingway went to Spain four times during the war to support the Republican government. Here he stands with officers of the International Brigades. (Author's collection)

Robert Hale Merriman, a graduate student in economics at the University of California at Berkeley, led the Lincoln battalion into action at Jarama, where he was wounded in the left shoulder. After recovering, he became chief of staff of the Fifteenth Brigade. (Author's collection)

Lincoln battalion commissar Fred Lutz gives a political lecture during training. The commissars kept the soldiers informed about political events around the world, explained the reasons for military strategy, and served as morale officers. (Author's collection)

Otto Reeves (*left*), son of an African American storefront preacher from Cleveland, and Morris Brier, a New York Jew, peer over a trench parapet near Teruel. During the disastrous retreats of 1938, Reeves volunteered to find ammunition for his besieged company and disappeared, presumably killed by the advancing fascists. (Author's collection)

Members of the first company of the George Washington battalion pause during their preparations for the battle of Brunete. American losses were so high that the Washingtons and Lincolns were subsequently merged into a single battalion, officially known as the Lincoln-Washington. (Author's collection)

Sight again

Taking Care
Of the Wounded

Soup's on!

The American volunteers in the International Brigades typically had much less military experience than other foreign volunteers, who had fought in World War I or served in the conscripted armies of Europe. The lack of training initially caused serious military mistakes, but after their baptism in combat the Lincolns learned their trade. (Author's collection)

Commissar Steve Nelson (*right*) and Doug Roach, a native of Provincetown, Rhode Island, prepare for action on the Brunete front in July 1937. Nelson's resourcefulness in solving personnel problems won the admiration and love of the volunteers. (Author's collection/ Adelphi University Library)

Responsible for American personnel in Spain were three experienced Communist organizers, (*left to right*) Edward Bender, Harry Haywood, and Bill Lawrence. Haywood's ineptness led his colleagues to demand his return to the U.S. (Author's collection)

The Tom Mooney machine gun company, named after a labor organizer imprisoned in California, takes a respite behind the lines at Jarama. David Smith (*right, in light shirt*) holds the flag. (Author's collection)

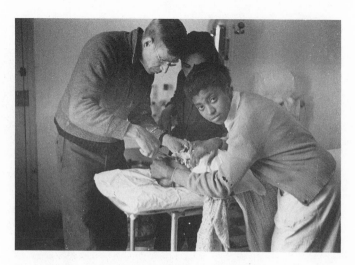

Salaria Kee, the only African American woman to serve in the Spanish war, helps treat a child injured in a fascist attack. (Author's collection)

The poets Langston Hughes (*left*) and Edwin Rolfe renewed their friendship in Spain. As editor of the brigade's newspaper, *Volunteer for Liberty*, Rolfe published Hughes's anti-fascist writings to inspire the soldiers. (Author's collection/ Bancroft Library)

Left: William Aalto, one of a handful of known homosexuals who served in the Lincoln brigade, distinguished himself as a guerrilla fighter behind enemy lines. He later served in the U.S. Office of Strategic Services, but was mustered out because of his sexual orientation. (Author's collection)

Right: Mildred Rackley, a painter from New Mexico, organized the first American hospital in Spain and served as hospital administrator for eighteen months. Here she points to bullet holes in an ambulance, evidence of the hazards of medical duty. Two American doctors died in combat in Spain. (Author's collection/International News Photos)

A group of American nurses and Spanish aides stands in front of an ambulance donated by the Communist party of Canada. Trained as civilian nurses, most were unprepared for the severity of the injuries they treated, the shortage of staff, and the lack of medical supplies, but they learned to improvise and developed a remarkable élan. (Author's collection)

Top: Following the tragic retreats in the spring of 1938, the Lincolns regrouped in July and launched a surprise nighttime counterattack by rowing across the Ebro River. The next morning a pontoon bridge, designed by brigade engineer Percy Ludwich, enabled reinforcements to continue the attack. (Author's collection)

Bottom: Officers' school at Tarazona, June 1937. Volunteers with previous military experience rose rapidly through the ranks, but often lacked the discipline of professional soldiers. Wallace Burton (*third from left*) was killed at Belchite while "dueling" with a Spanish sniper; Hans Amlie (*right*) was replaced for refusing orders to attack a few days later. (Milly Bennett Collection/Hoover Institution Archives)

At New York's annual May Day parade in 1938, the first veterans of the Abraham Lincoln brigade carried their banner at the head of the march. Here Paul Burns (*left*) and Walter Garland, both wounded in action, lead the contingent. (Author's collection)

Remembering the importance of American-made ambulances in Spain, veterans of the Lincoln brigade organized a fundraising campaign to send ambulances to the embattled Sandinista government in Nicaragua during the 1980's. Here a contingent from California stands in front of an ambulance dedicated to Dr. Julius Hene, who served in Spain and World War II, in Managua. Archie Brown in front, squatting. (Photo © David Wills, 1988)

Brigade veterans Herman Rosenstein, Edward Bender, and Morris Brier (*left to right*) participate in a protest against U.S. intervention in Central America and U.S. support of South Africa in the 1980's. (Author's collection)

Peter Carroll (*left*) with Morris Cohen in his hospital room in Moscow in May 1993. After being wounded at Fuentes de Ebro in 1937, Cohen (who used the alias Israel Altman in Spain) transferred to a special group, where he studied guerrilla warfare tactics, including radio transmission. "They were thinking of the future," he said of his training. With his late wife Lona (whose framed photograph rests on his bed), Cohen takes credit for transmitting atom bomb intelligence to the Russians.

In January 1991, veterans of the Lincoln brigade marched in San Francisco to protest the U.S. bombing in Iraq. "Struggle is the elixir of life," said Milton Wolff (*left, holding placard*) about the Lincolns' continuing commitment to political activity. (Photo by Richard Bermack. Used by permission.)

PART I

Causes

The Origins of a Crusade

Early one morning during the first week of November 1936, three somber men assembled in a sparsely furnished cubbyhole of an office in lower Manhattan to consider a secret communiqué that had come halfway around the world from Moscow. In the accents of immigrants from eastern Europe, the three spoke with urgency, because the message revealed an audacious shift in Communist policy toward the civil war raging in Spain. Sam Milgrom, a short, pudgy man of about 35, who styled himself "A. G. Mills," had summoned his two most reliable subordinates for this sensitive discussion. An experienced organizer for the American Communist party, Mills had helped arrange the first National Hunger March to Washington, D.C., five years earlier to demand relief for the rising number of unemployed in the Great Depression. Recently, he had been promoted to the Communist party's New York state committee and so had been entrusted with the latest developments regarding Spain. Now he was joined by two younger colleagues: William Lawrence, born with the name Lazar in Bessarabia in 1903; and Edward Bender, who had lived through the Russian revolution as a teenager in his native Ukraine. Working as full-time functionaries of the Communist party in New York City, the three appeared to be minor bureaucrats in a subterranean party beehive, and they all adhered righteously to the latest Moscow line.

Speaking in hushed, conspiratorial tones, Mills delivered the latest news: the highest authority in the Communist hierarchy—the Communist International (Comintern) in Moscow—had sanctioned the formation of a military brigade to defend the Spanish Republic against the recent fascist rebellion. The Americans were being urged to contribute to the forces. Uncertain about how to muster such an army, the party leadership had turned first to its warfare "experts," those few trusted officials who could claim some modicum of military experience. But the pickings were slender; Communist leaders who had served in World War I knew little about military recruitment.

The Communist central committee soon decided it was a job for rank and file party organizers—men experienced in judging a volunteer's previous activities and character. So the leadership passed the assignment to A. G. Mills. He, in turn, requested Lawrence and Bender to shoulder the responsibility. They were in their early thirties that fall and had been Communist disciples since the Bolshevik revolution of 1917; they had no doubts about the gravity of this latest mission. Since the outbreak of civil war the previous July, Spain's Republican government had offered, as Bender recalled many years later, "one glimmer of hope in a world rushing toward fascist domination." Through the late summer and autumn, he had watched tensely as the people of Madrid prepared for the military siege: "Here was one nation standing up against the fascist dictators," he remembered. "I felt honored to be asked. I felt that was something specific I could do in the fight against fascism in Spain."

So began the process of locating American volunteers for the Spanish civil war.

At virtually the same moment, John T. Whitaker, the Madrid correspondent of the New York *Herald Tribune*, was describing the darkened capital of Spain as "a doomed city." For nearly four months, rebellious troops led by General Francisco Franco had been fighting against the legally elected Republican government, leaving the towns and cities of Spain torn by bullets and bombs. In the march toward Madrid, the army had left a trail of blood and terror. As the capital braced for the first assault, Whitaker stated the obvious truth: "Franco is now ready for the kill." Backed by fascist dictators—

Germany's Adolf Hitler, Italy's Benito Mussolini, and Portugal's Antonio Salazar—four heavily armed columns were approaching the outskirts of Madrid. The fascist general Emilio Mola, preparing for what he believed would be the final battle, ominously predicted that a "fifth column" would join the rebellion from inside the city. "We shall know the guilty," Franco advised the nervous Madrilenos, trying to destroy their morale, "and only upon them will fall the weight of the law."

A poorly armed militia, mostly civilians led by their political leaders, grimly prepared to meet the attack. From the Communist leader Dolores Ibarruri (known because of her fiery oratory as "La Pasionaria"), these blue-clad urban workers had adopted the rallying cry: "No pasaran!" ("They shall not pass!") Despite mounting fear, they had resolved to defend the left-wing "Popular Front" government they had elected less than a year earlier, in February 1936. Since then, the Socialist party had dominated Spain's parliamentary Cortes, drawing allies among Communists, anarchists, and republicans, as well as Basque and Catalonian nationalists who opposed any centralization of power. But whatever a soldier's personal allegiances, the people's militia would fight for the Republic because of its broad unifying objective: to weaken the power of an entrenched upper class that had ruled Spain for centuries. The Popular Front's agenda of land reform, secularization of education, and weakening of the military, however, had aroused the contempt and hatred of the old elite: the aristocracy, the Church, the landowners, and the officer class. That was what had prompted Franco and the military to rebel against the government. "The Popular Front," General Mola said, summing up his objections on the eve of the battle, "cannot keep order." La Pasionaria offered an alternative social ideal when she told the Spanish people: "It is better to die on your feet than to live on your knees."

The battle for Madrid commenced on a gray, misty morning, November 7, 1936. As a cavalry column of Moorish mercenaries, bolstered by the rhythm of heavy drumbeats, rode toward the Toledo bridge, a hastily organized group of young men and women fired from behind rough barricades at the advancing troops. Their antique pistols and hunting rifles scarcely interrupted the charge. But suddenly, through the haze, a motorcyclist appeared with a machine gun and sent the horsemen into retreat. Italian tanks then forged ahead of Franco's professional legionnaires and mercenaries; and, after the fog had lifted, German Junkers rained bombs through the cloudy skies. Again and again, the unpracticed Republican militia, emboldened by individual heroics, met the attack valiantly, using small arms against the troops and sticks of dynamite against the tanks. The fascists made small progress that day.

At dawn of the next day, as Madrid girded for a second ground assault, the city's frantic residents witnessed a remarkable parade down the broad Gran Via: a neat procession of nearly 2,000 soldiers, dressed in corduroy uniforms and steel helmets. Assuming that the men were Soviet allies, the Madrilenos raised their fists in the Popular Front salute and shouted, "Long live the Russians!" Their error was understandable. Few citizens of Spain knew of the existence of the newly formed International Brigades, a contingent of foreign volunteers who had come to Spain to defend the Republic. These recruits had left their homes in Great Britain and France, Yugoslavia and Poland, Belgium and Austria; many were political refugees from fascist Italy and Germany. Despite scant military training, they exuded enthusiasm. And under the leadership of Soviet general Emil Kleber, a Hungarian Jew trained in the Soviet Union, they brought much more than a military presence to the Republican cause. These Internationals—ultimately they would number 40,000 troops from 52 countries—symbolized a political camaraderie that linked the Spanish civil war to the titanic ideological conflicts of the 1930's: the struggles of fascism, communism, and democracy. In the days and weeks and months that followed, these volunteers would join the Spanish militia to face the fascist tide.

News of the creation of the International Brigades raced through the Communist grapevines around the globe: the very existence of a multinational army promised to fulfill the Marxist prophecy that one day the "workers of the world" would unite against their common oppressors. In every country, such optimism encouraged the enlistment of volunteers eager to fight in Spain. When the American Communist party spread the word about recruitment through a network of district organizers, the response was immediate. From the waterfront docks and the fur trades, from union halls and ethnic associations, from bread lines and Communist party cells, dozens of men came forward within weeks to join the fight for Republican Spain. Viewing themselves as part of an international proletariat, American radicals welcomed this opportunity to take the struggle against fascism to another stage of history: it was possible now, in Spain at least, to fight back with arms.

That Communists responded so eagerly to that prospect reflected the growing militancy of American radicalism during the 1930's. Pushed by Depression conditions, the Communist party had tripled in size from a membership
of under 10,000 in 1929 to about 26,000 in 1934, and then increased steadily
to 41,000 in 1936 and 62,000 the next year, finally reaching 82,000 by 1938.
Even those numbers underestimated the Communist appeal, for the party's
rolls failed to measure an incurable revolving-door syndrome that dogged its
entire history: willing and able political recruits of various beliefs would join
the party, only to discover a vigorous program of activity that demanded intense, unrelenting self-discipline—constant meetings, fund-raising projects, organizing assignments, and protest demonstrations. Such obligations
inevitably drained a volunteer's time and energy; only the most dedicated
persisted. Still, the diminished numbers remained consistent with the Communist party's ideological self-importance. For the disciples of Karl Marx and
Vladimir Ilyich Lenin believed fervently that a small cadre of leaders—passionate, full-time revolutionaries—would ultimately wield a power far disproportionate to its numerical size.

American communism of the 1930's, while not considered the totalitarian
menace it seemed after World War II or the failed ideology of the 1990's,
nonetheless remained a suspect movement to most Americans. Yet precisely
for that reason, communism appealed to workers, professionals, and intellectuals who felt frustrated by the failure of traditional politics to alleviate the
misery of the Great Depression. For those concerned about mass poverty,
homelessness, and starvation, communism evoked a distinct idealism. It held
a vision of social harmony—"each according to his needs"—and demanded
an unworldly dedication from its believers. But the Communist movement always had a practical face. As joblessness spread around the land, the Communist party provided the impetus and backbone for mass unemployment
demonstrations that not only gained popularity but also won tangible benefits
for those out of work. When landlords evicted impoverished tenants, the boys
and girls of the Young Communist League defiantly carried the furniture back
inside, saving a shelter until the next sheriff's order arrived. And when rac-
ists went on a spree of lynchings or false arrests, the Communist party's International Labor Defense organized teams of lawyers to demand justice in the
courts. Such militancy was not generally appreciated, to be sure; Communists wore their credentials with arrogance and expressed a savage hostility

to dissenting opinion. But they were worthy fighters, daring, principled, and confident as saints about an ultimate victory. "History was going our way," the literary critic Alfred Kazin recalled of his conversion to the radical movement of the mid-1930's. "Everything in the outside world seemed to be moving toward some final decision, for by now the Spanish Civil War had begun, and every day felt choked with struggle."

Such were the ideological origins of the Abraham Lincoln battalion, the American volunteers who would form part of the Fifteenth International Brigade in Spain. The first Americans to respond to the call to arms in the autumn of 1936 were experienced political cadres, tried and tested in a variety of campaigns around the country. Their efforts had touched on virtually every radical cause since the beginning of the century: from the labor union organizing drives of the Industrial Workers of the World to unemployment demonstrations during the Great Depression; from protests against racial injustice to intellectual and ideological polemics. In those struggles, a generation of young Americans had become acutely politicized.

By Christmas 1936, while Madrid still resisted the fascist assault, the American Communist party had enlisted nearly 200 recruits; in another two months, nearly 1,000 men, enough to field the first battalion; and two months after that, sufficient volunteers to form a second battalion and later even a third. In the end, approximately 2,600 Americans would take up arms to defend the Spanish Republic. (Another 150 would serve as doctors, nurses, technicians, and drivers in the American Medical Bureau to Aid Spanish Democracy.) It was an army unprecedented in American history, based on ideology, motivated by principles. These were no mercenaries or soldiers of fortune; the volunteers earned nothing for their efforts, save pride and the satisfaction of knowing they had tried to stop the spread of fascism. They traveled to Europe by sea, and then by rail to southern France, and then, usually, by foot across the Pyrenees into Spain. They endured the expected hardships of war: thirst and hunger and lack of sleep, and they discovered other torments as well: an omnipresent danger and the sudden loss of friends and comrades who died on suncrisp days. They came to know the terror—pure agony—of a bullet or a shell or a raging bomb.

Who were these volunteers and why did they enlist?

To pose the question is to broach nearly 3,000 biographies, each linking a personal choice to a social background or an ideology. During the Spanish war, the leaders of the Lincoln brigade emphasized the diversity in the ranks, because that lent an all-American tone to the campaign. And there was surely a germ of truth to that image. The volunteers emerged from the bosom of America. They came from virtually every state in the Union (only Delaware and Wyoming were not represented) and seemingly from every walk of life. Some, like the first battalion commander in action, Robert Merriman, held postgraduate degrees; more, including the last commander, Milton Wolff, had failed to complete high school. A few were children of the well-born, among them David McKelvey White, the son of an Ohio governor, and Henry Eaton, the son of a Los Angeles mayor. Some earned their livings as artists and writers; more common occupations were longshoreman or sailor, schoolteacher or student, or "unemployed." Group photographs from Spain illustrate the self-conscious racial mix that included blacks and whites, several full-blooded American Indians, and Jack Shirai, the single Japanese American. These were deliberate images of the great American melting pot. Propagandists on the home front used those portraits to increase the base of political and financial support for the Republic. But they also reflected an authentic commitment to racial equality, a visible repudiation of fascist appeals to a master race.

Statistics may assist us in penetrating the propaganda. Despite the emphasis on pluralism in the ranks, a head count suggests the prevalence of certain demographic and social patterns. According to historian Robert Rosenstone, who tallied various incomplete rosters of the Lincoln brigade, at least 18 percent came from New York alone and over 80 percent came from the nation's eleven largest cities. Those geographical facts tell much about the cultural roots of the American volunteers, but they need to be matched with another set of statistics about their ages. The conventional wisdom says that the Lincoln recruits were "boys," as the *Daily Worker* called them, younger in years and experience than the contingents from other countries, which had been seasoned in World War I and the conscripted armies of the postwar era. Information from the recently opened Russian archives confirms that view, but only partially. A roster of over 1,600 names, compiled in February 1938, shows that the largest age groups of American volunteers—the statistical modes— were 23 and 25. (The youngest Americans were three 18-year-olds, Manuel Estevez, Arthur Greenspoon, and Chris Litsas; the oldest were 59-year-old Hans Gutman and 60-year-old Manuel Rosales.) Another roster, compiled in 1937, the year that 95 percent of the Americans arrived in Spain, indicates that 38 percent were 25 or younger; 26 percent were between age 26 and 30; and 36 percent were older than 30. But the median age—the midpoint age—of American soldiers in Spain was over 27, and the average age was even higher. Separate calculations for the African American volunteers are nearly identical, and a study of American Communists in Spain reached the same conclusions. Surveys of the American women nurses by historian Frances Patai places the median age at 26.5. These figures indicate that the average American volunteer, however unprepared militarily, was no impulsive youth.

Yet the volunteers did share one characteristic of the young: relatively few of them were married. The list of 1,249 Communists who served in Spain reveals that only 189 had ever been married—15.2 percent of the total. That so many men in their middle to late twenties remained single underscores the impact of the Depression on family life. Most of the volunteers were blue-collar workers—seamen, drivers, and mechanics were the most frequently listed occupations—and they simply could not afford to support families. Moreover, their occupations encouraged geographical mobility, a common phenomenon during hard times, and tended to delay the sinking of roots or the creation of lasting relationships.

These demographic statistics also illuminate the social origins of the brigade. Counting back 27 years from 1937 establishes the median birthdate of the volunteers in the year 1910. Most of the Lincolns, in other words, had been born on the eve of World War I and had matured amidst the major social upheavals associated with the emergence of the United States as a world power in the early twentieth century. In addition, most of the volunteers were born in urban centers. As observers or participants, they had witnessed massive immigration from abroad, the migration of rural people into the cities, and the transformation of the commercial capitals into vast industrial complexes. A survey of about two hundred Lincoln veterans made in the early 1980's found that about one-third were born in Europe and were brought to this country before the age of fifteen. Eighty percent had a parent who was born abroad. Furthermore, of the 60 women volunteers, according to Frances Patai, most were born in urban centers "from lower middle class, working class, or downright poor socio-economic backgrounds"; most were the offspring of recent immigrants. Such statistics help explain the internationalist orientation of this group, their sensitivity to the problems of people in other parts of the world.

One other demographic ingredient—a hint rather than a fact—must be added to this composite portrait. In studying the family backgrounds of surviving volunteers, one gets a clear impression that many came from what might be called broken homes. Because of the impossibility of coherent statistical research, the documentation remains scanty; but the pattern, nonetheless, is apparent. Because of the death of a parent, a divorce, or a temporary separation (a parent left behind in the old country, for example), a significant number of survivors have indicated that they were not raised in a conventional two-parent family. (Several volunteers lost a parent during the flu epidemic of 1918–19.) Indeed, many of the young men who went to Spain had spent a portion of their childhoods in foster homes and orphanages, such as the Brooklyn Hebrew Orphan Asylum, which produced at least ten alumni who went to Spain.

The sketchy evidence suggests two conclusions: first, that the sudden disruption of families appeared to be a common problem for American youngsters, especially in the cities and among the poor; and, second, that the children of such families may have formed psychological patterns—anger or aggression or outrage at injustice—that made them more likely candidates for a volunteer army. "I think I resented the world for having taken my mother away from me," suggested James Benét, who was raised by a wealthy aunt, the novelist Kathleen Norris. "And so part of my attitude to the world and, no doubt, part of the basis of my radicalism was that." Such resentment, of course, might have turned in other directions, but Benét later expressed satisfaction at having "chosen . . . the right target, the ills of society. . . . I feel that everybody ought to feel that way," he added, "whether they lost their mother or not." And whatever Benét's motives, we must also note that many volunteers did come from healthy two-parent households.

Even in those stable families, however, the desire of sons to join the International Brigades frequently aroused stiff parental conflict. To avoid such problems, many volunteers concocted stories to explain their sudden departure for Europe. When the truth emerged, so did other telling aspects of their political motivation. "Yes, Ma, this is a case where sons must go against their mothers' wishes for the sakes of their mothers themselves," Hyman Katz wrote from a hospital bed in Spain to justify his defiance of his mother's feelings. "Don't you realize that we Jews will be the first to suffer if fascism comes?" To his maternal aunt, Katz acknowledged that his decision to leave home had made him "a bad son, because in the conflict between my conscience and my mother's wishes my conscience won. But my mother is partly to blame because she sacrificed to give me a good Jewish education, and the whole history of our people has taught me to admire the prophets and fighters who died for liberty. . . . So I am a bad son," he stated, in what proved to be his last letter before his death in action in 1938, "because I fight against the greatest oppressors of my people."

This testimony underscores another dimension of the crusade; an inordinate proportion of the Lincoln volunteers—at least one-third—were Jews. Among the women volunteers, Patai found, Jews constituted a majority. Indeed, in the hospital wards and surgical theaters, their fluency in Yiddish would facilitate communication with colleagues and patients from other countries. The presence of so many Jews in Spain partly reflected their large numbers within the American Communist party, which coordinated the recruitment and organization of the International Brigades. It also suggests that American Jews, more than other ethnic minorities, appreciated the dangers of fascism in Europe. To them, Hitler was no abstraction. Even non-practicing Jews, who identified themselves as Communists rather than Jews, subsequently attested to a strong urge to strike at the fascist persecutors of their co-religionists.

"I had read Hitler's book, knew about the Nuremberg laws," remembered Vaughn Love, a volunteer from Harlem in New York City, "and I knew if the Jews weren't going to be allowed to live, then certainly I knew the Negroes would not escape and that we would be at the top of the list. I also knew that the Negro community throughout the United States would be doing what I was doing if they had the chance." Over 80 African Americans eventually served with the International Brigades, about 2.6 percent of the total. In this completely desegregated army, these blacks would rise to leadership positions and command white troops for the first time in American history. Most of them were members of the Communist party, but their political views remained inseparable from a racial identity. "I saw in the invaders of Spain the same people I've been fighting all my life," said Eluard Luchelle McDaniels, a native Mississippian who achieved fame in Spain for his ability to throw hand grenades ambidextrously. "I've seen lynching and starvation, and I know my people's enemies."

Describing the American volunteers in terms of cultural background—their race, religion, ethnicity, geographic origins, or dates of birth—too easily obscures the fact that most of their cultural kin, of whatever nationality, had no interest in the Spanish war. What distinguished the Lincolns from their compatriots, more than anything else, was a political consciousness, a belief in the frequently quoted words of Josef Stalin that "the cause of Republican Spain is the cause of all progressive mankind." It was no coincidence that the Communist party dominated the Lincoln brigade. Not only did the party organize the volunteers in 1936, but between two-thirds and three-quarters of all American recruits identified themselves as members of the Communist party or one of its affiliated groups. Even the non-Communist minority, however, whether Socialist or liberal or merely humanitarian, shared a fundamental political awareness; they went to Spain as political people. Very few admitted to any other interest. To understand their motives, therefore, one must move beyond questions of culture and personality to explore the political traditions they embraced.

2

A Radical Tradition

Although most American volunteers in the International Brigades came of age after 1930, the political ideas that inspired them had existed long before the economic crisis of that decade and the rise of fascism in Europe. The protest movements of the tumultuous 1930's rested firmly on a historical bedrock of earlier political causes: American populism and labor protests; the Socialist party and the Industrial Workers of the World; and opposition to racial, religious, and even sexual injustice. Those volunteers who went to Spain over the age of 30—over one-third of the Lincoln brigade—had often participated in these radical movements. Their lives provided a crucial bridge—a living tradition—between an older American dream and the political climate of the 1930's. The careers of three future Lincoln volunteers—Reuben Barr, Edwin Rolfe, and Harry Haywood—delineate the varieties of radical dissent in the first decades of the twentieth century.

It was at a peace demonstration in New York's Madison Square Garden that one of these old radicals received his political baptism in 1917. Reuben Barr had been drawn to the crowded arena to hear prominent Socialists, among them Eugene V. Debs, denounce President Woodrow Wilson's attempt to lead the United States into World War I. Just a few months earlier, the president had been reelected on a campaign promise to keep the nation out of the war, and the gathered throng was determined, as Barr recalled, "to keep his feet to the fire." So popular was the antiwar demonstration that the crowd had overflowed the sports arena, spilling onto the sidewalks outside to listen to the speeches through a loudspeaker system. Mounted police with heavy clubs had also arrived, together with specially furloughed sailors and marines, to harass the spectators. When the meeting ended, the uniformed men formed a gauntlet outside the exits. As the protesters left the auditorium, the troops attacked. "They tore the clothes off some of the women," Barr remembered, "and they beat the hell out of the men." Barr managed to avoid the blows. But what touched him directly was the behavior of a contingent of fellow protesters—members of the Industrial Workers of the World or "Wobblies"—who stuck together, fought back, and so protected other members of the crowd. "The fact that they could stand up and fight," said Barr, "got me enthusiastic." He promptly joined the IWW, paying the 50-cent initiation fee that entitled him to a "red card" and membership in America's most radical organization. He was fifteen years old.

"I agreed with their idea of socialism," the intense old man explained over 70 years later, shrugging off the notion of quixotic idealism. "Was that romance or ideological conviction?" As for his youth, he said, opening his broad palms, "I was older than my age."

Born on the Lower East Side of New York, Barr could remember only adversity during his childhood. His parents (the family name was Bacofsky) were Jews from czarist Russia, struggling to survive in a land they scarcely comprehended. His father worked as the night watchman and maintenance man of a huge steam laundry, dreaming that someday his American son would teach him to sign his name in English, enabling him to acquire citizenship papers, the first step on a ladder of ambition that might lead to work as an engineer. Meanwhile, Reuben's mother raised her three young children in a filthy, crowded tenement apartment, while running a small hand laundry that catered to equally harried immigrants. When Barr, as an old man, sat down to write a fictionalized memoir of his life on the streets of New York, he began with a fierce memory of being dragged at the age of five from the steamy, damp apartment into an ambulance by a health department worker who had been summoned because of the boy's high fever. While recuperating in the care of an American nurse, Reuben received his first store-bought toys and glimpsed the possibility of entering a mysterious world beyond the tenement streets.

Understanding the power of literacy, his parents encouraged Reuben's education as best they could. But he remembered mostly crowded rooms, the feeling of confinement, Old World customs, the arrival of immigrant relatives, and the drudgery of the laundry business. It was an environment he detested. But he showed academic promise and ambition, skipping a few grades at school; at the age of eight, he was selling newspapers and candy on the street. By age ten Reuben found himself in a class with an older boy, six or seven years his senior, who had recently arrived in America and spoke little English. This mature friend introduced Reuben to a more sophisticated society: theater, concerts, art museums. The son of Socialists in Russia who had been sentenced to Siberia for some unknown radical activities, the friend also gave Reuben selected books. Thereby, the young adolescent discovered "progressive ideas": Jack London, Maxim Gorky, Upton Sinclair. "That got me started," he remembered. Reuben and his friend joined the Young People's Socialist League, dedicated to creating a society without war or the conflicts caused by capitalism. This commitment led the fifteen-year-old boy to Madison Square Garden on that violent day in 1917.

Barr's subsequent experiences hardened his convictions. Armed with his Wobbly red card, he rode a freight train west, heading for the IWW headquarters in Chicago, where he met the legendary labor radical Big Bill Haywood—"a great big guy with one eye"—who encouraged him to organize farm workers in the wheat fields of Kansas. There, he joined the militant Agricultural Workers' Organization, which, because of wartime manpower shortages, had won better working conditions for the mobile labor force that perennially followed the harvests from Texas to North Dakota. Reuben learned to thresh and stack, but found the work difficult. When he heard that the IWW office in Wichita needed a secretary to manage the hall, he eagerly volunteered. In the autumn of 1917, when Reuben was barely sixteen years old, the federal government ordered a nationwide raid of IWW halls, using the wartime emergency as an excuse to rid the country of subversives. Charged with violation of criminal syndicalist laws, Reuben was arrested with 26 other Wobblies, smashed on the skull above his left eye by a policeman's blackjack (the old man automatically fingered the white mark near his hairline as he spoke of the incident), and then brought to the Wichita jail. Receiving constant beatings and bad food, the unindicted Wobblies lingered behind bars for months, bolstering their spirits with such radical songs as "The Red Flag" and "Dump the Bosses off Your Back." The militant words remained etched in Reuben's memory.

Convinced that they could never get a fair trial in American courts, the Wobblies adopted a strategy of passive resistance known as the "silent defense." Refusing to participate in what they deemed illegal trials, they hired no lawyers, accepted the inevitable judicial process, and went to jail defiantly, with sentences ranging from one to nine years. While awaiting his court appearance, however, Reuben received a visit from an IWW lawyer named Caroline Lowe, sent to him personally by Big Bill Haywood. Because of his youth and his verbal ability, she insisted, the IWW wanted Reuben to fight for acquittal. His victory, they believed, would establish a favorable precedent. Reuben did not like the idea of taking an independent course, but he allowed the motherly Lowe to change his mind. He had his day in court— and, to his surprise, he won. But the decision set no precedents. In December 1918, over a year after their arrests, all the remaining Wobblies were convicted and given long prison sentences.

By then Barr had followed the wheat fields west. "And the further west I went," he recalled, "the stronger the IWW was." He earned his keep as an agricultural worker, fought forest fires, and washed dishes in restaurants. "If I couldn't find work," he added, "like every other hobo, I bummed my way through the country, solicited food." The red card assured his entry into the Wobbly "jungles," virtually all-male communities not far from the railroad tracks, where members pooled their resources and cooked stews and coffee in discarded cans and old pots. Usually, Barr also carried a packet of IWW pamphlets, and he participated in the Wobblies' "free-speech" fights against government repression. To defy the Wilson administration's demand for wartime unity, they would arrive at some prearranged location, set up soapboxes on the public streets, and commence denunciations of the capitalist system and the war. Accepting arrest, the Wobblies would fill the jails beyond capacity, until local authorities would gladly release the prisoners to get them out of town. Wartime patriotism limited their influence. "I don't know how many minds we changed," Barr admitted.

With the end of World War I, the government continued the rigorous persecution of militant dissenters, part of a great "Red Scare." Given stiff prison sentences for violating the espionage and sedition laws, the Wobbly leadership languished in jail. Big Bill Haywood fled to safety in Bolshevik Russia, never to return to his native land. Forced underground, the remnants of the IWW lacked an effective organization. Reuben Barr, isolated from the movement, became more cautious. By 1920, he had turned his sights back east. Discouraged, though not disillusioned, he joined his father's laundry business in New York City, where for the next decade and a half his political involvement went no further than reading the newspapers. And then, one day, he read about Spain. "I was sort of resurrected," Barr said, "when the Spanish business began."

While Reuben Barr represented the older volunteers who fought in Spain, the precocious youth Edwin Rolfe fit a more common demographic profile. He was born into a family of Russian Jewish immigrants in Philadelphia in September 1909. Being seven years younger than Barr placed him in a slightly different historical generation as he entered adolescence and made the political choices that would eventually lead him to Spain. His may be the more typical story of a radical in the 1920's, an outsider in the age of "normalcy." Young Rolfe (his family name was Fishman until he adopted a nom de plume) had imbibed his radical ideas early. His father, a shoemaker by trade, was a loyal union man, organizing actively among other Jewish immigrants; his mother, also a union supporter and a friend of birth-control advocate Margaret Sanger, defended women's rights, including abortion, long before it became respectable to discuss that issue. One summer, Rolfe's parents rented a room to a boarder who was a Wobbly, and the older man regaled the children with stories of strikes and taught them songs from the IWW's "Little Red Book." As members of the Socialist party, the family looked sympathetically upon the Bolshevik revolution that toppled the czarist regime in 1917. Rolfe's parents eventually found their political home in the Communist Party of America, established in 1921.

This political background did not interfere with what Rolfe's family remembered as a "normal childhood." Despite his small stature and light frame, Rolfe excelled in sports, studied the violin, and attracted attention for his artistic skills. While still a high school student, he drew political cartoons for the Communist party's newspaper, the *Daily Worker*. But what Rolfe loved most was playing with words—poetry. He became fascinated with the modernist style, savoring the writings of John Reed, Hart Crane, and T. S. Eliot; the essays of Randolph Bourne and Van Wyck Brooks; and the fiction of John Dos Passos. A few years later, the young poet described the vitality of those days, his growing sense of self-consciousness and rebellion: shooting pool, smoking "forbidden pipes," listening to a "cat's-whisker radio," whispering rumors of sex. He remembered many hours of talk "that ripened to mature beginnings":

> the dockyard strike . . . ,
> cheaper meals in the lunchroom, freedom
> to write what we felt in our magazine,
> to admit harshness.

Rolfe's literary enthusiasm reinforced his radical identity; writing became a means of articulating revolutionary ends. He never retreated from that position. Nor was his feeling of alienation from the political and cultural mainstream without justification. His first signed article, a critical book review of *The Revolt of Modern Youth* by Judge Ben Lindsey, appeared in the *Daily Worker* the very month the newspaper's editor and business manager were sentenced to a month in jail for publishing a poem, "America," written by eighteen-year-old David Gordon, another future volunteer in the International Brigades:

> America is a land of censored opportunity
> Lick spit; eat dirt,
> There's your opportunity;
> Then you become a big man of business.
> And people take off their hats
> To you.

For his efforts, young Gordon received a three-year prison term, though after a month he was granted parole so he could accept a creative writing scholarship.

As a young author, Rolfe was especially susceptible to ideological zealotry. Two months after Gordon's conviction, he expressed the futility of moderation in achieving revolutionary goals. "What the Communist movement of today realizes," he wrote, "is that tolerance . . . is moral weakness of the most jelly-spined kind." Once a person chose the "correct" course, he advised, "let nothing swerve him from his path. . . . That is what Lenin . . . did in Russia. That is what the [Communist] Workers Party is trying to do here." This passion erupted later that summer of 1927 when the state of Massachusetts executed two anarchists accused of bank robbery and murder, Nicola Sacco and Bartolomeo Vanzetti, in a national cause célèbre. Having attended numerous public rallies urging clemency, Rolfe waited with a crowd of five thousand protesters at New York's Grand Central Station for the arrival of the martyr's ashes. It was his first assignment as a reporter. Struck by the "dogged sullenness" of the crowd, the brooding silence broken only by a shout of "Viva Sacco and Vanzetti!" he watched a police line smash through the spectators. The eighteen-year-old Rolfe ended his reportage with the defiant spirit of the victims: "The last moment belongs to us—that agony is our triumph!"

Committed to producing a proletarian literature, Rolfe became a regular contributor to the *Worker*. His book reviews were written in an angry, rhetorical voice, not unusual in Communist prose; seldom did he find a satisfactory social conscience in the many volumes of fiction and poetry he criticized. In his own short stories, by contrast, he cultivated an ear for the clipped talk of the city streets, an eye for urban detail, and a sensitivity to the pervasive squalor of working-class life. His first published story, "Disorderly Conduct," depicted a young, impoverished couple—the girl thrown out of her home for refusing to quit the "league," the boy frustrated by biblical platitudes ("Damn 'em! What good did the bible ever do them, or me,—or anybody"). The two were forced to spend a cold night huddled in a public park, only to be arrested in the morning for vagrancy. Anger, outrage, bitterness—these became dominant themes in Rolfe's youthful writing. One story of city life testified to his awareness of the radical tradition. His 50-year-old hero had once been a member of the IWW "when that was a fighting organization" and had enrolled in the Farmer-Labor party "when that had been militant"; he had been a Socialist, too. "When that goddam bunch went yellow," the old radical declared, "I did the only thing I could—joined the Workers Party."

In his poetry, Rolfe also attempted to merge a literary sensibility with an unyielding class consciousness. With titles like "The Ballad of the Subway Digger" or "Modern Croesus," the early poems focused on the risks and brutality of American working conditions.

> Slowly, relentlessly, the steel machine
> pounds in an endless rhythm. . . .
> And Jonah the feeder stands before it. . . .
> Which is the man and which the machine?

Eventually, the distracted worker gets caught by the gears and is ground into pulp. Even as Rolfe's voice matured, his subjects remained close to real workers and their daily grind:

> I have heard them at their work,
> bent under heavy burdens,
> wet with rivulets of sweat,
> utter two words, a beginning:
> "some day . . ."

Lamenting the "twilight sleep into which American poetry has fallen, drowsy, like an aged, spent woman," Rolfe pleaded for a language of strength, "the power to hate as well as love, the power to write the way one feels and acts." He would not trade "a line of Joe Hill's Wobbly songs, crude as they may be," he said, for most of the current verse. As a member of Michael Gold's Youth Literary Workshop, a cadre of revolutionary poets, Rolfe enjoyed the spirit of criticism and shared the podium for the annual "Red Poets' Night" public readings. These occasions featured older writers like Gold and Joseph Free-man, both important in Rolfe's literary development, as well as his contem-poraries Genevieve Taggard, Langston Hughes, and the erstwhile felon David Gordon. A decade later, all would be deeply involved in the cause of Spain.

If the facts of American urban life propelled Reuben Barr, Edwin Rolfe, and other children of immigrants into the radical movement, the pervasive-ness of race prejudice prompted the black minority to organize for sheer sur-vival. Without exception, the African Americans who served in the Lincoln brigade could testify to the double burden of economic hardship and racial injustice. But unlike most blacks, they had found in the Communist move-ment an opportunity to forge alliances with sympathetic whites against a com-mon enemy. Determined to prove the priority of class over race, the Commu-nist party welcomed disaffected blacks and strove to eliminate every vestige of discrimination. Blacks therefore enjoyed special status in the party and would often stand as showpieces of Communist interracial harmony. In Spain, that would prove both an asset and an embarrassing liability.

The problems of black radicalism emerged dramatically in the career of a remarkable young man named Harry Haywood, who became an important Communist spokesman on matters of race and, for a time, a leader of the American volunteers in Spain. Because of his prominence in radical circles, Haywood was not exactly typical of the black volunteers. But his dilemmas reflected larger questions of ideology, the difficulty of reconciling theory and practice, and the tremendous weight of failure. As a devoted party man and an ideological perfectionist, Haywood epitomized the opportunities and limits of communism for blacks. His commitments, personal and philosophical, also explain why blacks, with so many problems of their own in America, nonetheless went to Spain to fight against fascism. But what made Haywood's career especially influential was his role in defining the Communist party's racial agenda during the 1920's, a time of minimal black enrollment. His articulation of theoretical positions shaped the way in which black and white Communists interpreted the political events of the next decade.

Haywood (his family name was Hall; like the white radicals he adopted a nom de guerre) was born in 1898, the son of former slaves, and grew to maturity in the largely white community of Omaha, Nebraska. He was intelligent, assiduous, and ambitious. Despite occasional racial tensions, he did well in school, acquired a taste for history, and held the modest expectations of social advancement that befitted the son of an ardent admirer of Booker T. Washington. But Harry's life was shattered one night in 1913 when a white gang confronted his father at the gates of the meat-packing plant where he worked, beat him mercilessly, and ordered him to leave town. The family fled to Minneapolis. "Now," Haywood would recall in his autobiography, "we were just homeless 'niggers' on the run." A racial slur in his new school put an end to Harry's education when he was fifteen years old. Then followed a series of unskilled jobs, until Harry became a railroad waiter and moved to Chicago.

On the eve of World War I, Harry enlisted in a black National Guard regiment; he enjoyed a feeling of racial pride in the tightly segregated unit. The war created opportunities for blacks on the home front as well as in the military, stimulating a migration of southern blacks into northern cities. But these changes, which threatened the racial status quo, provoked a sharp increase in lynchings and race riots. Stationed in Texas, Harry witnessed considerable violence as the black troops eagerly transgressed local rules of racial conduct. In April 1918, the regiment sailed for France and, to Harry's surprise, the American command immediately attached his black unit to the French army. (General Pershing had no wish to weaken white morale!) For the next six months, Haywood served on the western front. He apparently saw minimal action (something that would subsequently affect his behavior in Spain), and he was glad to leave the service at the end of the war.

Resuming his work on the railroad, he arrived in Chicago one sweltering afternoon in 1919 to find the city under siege. A white mob had killed a black teenager for daring to swim in Lake Michigan near a white beach, inciting a bloody six-day race riot that would claim 38 lives and leave 500 injured. In the crisis, Harry joined other black veterans who set up defensive emplacements, including machine guns, in anticipation of a white invasion. "It came to me then," Haywood recalled, "that I had been fighting the wrong war."

He began exploring new political options. At a time when the Ku Klux Klan was experiencing a national revival, many frustrated blacks questioned the limited assimilationist goals of liberal reform groups such as the National Association for the Advancement of Colored People, which had been founded in 1911. Some turned to the Universal Negro Improvement Association, headed by the West Indian Marcus Garvey, which stressed the values of a distinctive black nationalism and proposed a "back to Africa" movement as an alternative to American racism. Harry appreciated the remarkable enthusiasm for Garvey in Chicago's South Side neighborhoods in the early 1920's. But while he sympathized with the summons to black pride and self-reliance, he rejected the premise of perpetual race hatred. "Garveyism," he would write a few years later, "served imperialism by drawing the Negro masses away from their struggle for their rights in the United States, and fostered separation of Negro masses from [the] white revolutionary workers."

Harry's brother had already joined the newly formed Workers (Communist) party, but when Harry approached him about membership, he was told to wait. Instead, Haywood entered a small, secret, all-black organization called the African Blood Brotherhood. After undergoing a blood-mixing initiation ritual, he took up the ABB program, which included organizing labor unions and rent strikes. In this way, Haywood continued to develop a sense of leadership within the black community. Six months later, he enrolled in the Communist party's organization for youth, the Young Workers League. "When we sang the Youth International at meetings," Haywood recalled, "we actually felt ourselves to be, as the song proclaimed, 'the youthful guardsmen of the proletariat.'" Two years later, in 1925, he graduated into the Communist party.

Throughout the 1920's, the Communist movement engaged in endless, debilitating factional strife. Its membership consequently remained fairly small— about eight thousand in 1923. Thus the hundred-odd black members assumed great importance, politically and symbolically, showing that the party could potentially appeal to a broad spectrum of American society. From the beginning, Haywood understood that his prime role involved organizing and recruiting among black workers. But the party had high hopes for his future. As a promising black leader, he was sent to the Soviet Union to acquire a political education. With secret credentials typed on silk and sewn into the lining of his coat, Haywood embarked for the Communist state in 1925. He would be gone for five years.

As a student in Moscow—first at KUTVA, the "university of toilers of the east named for Stalin," then at the prestigious Lenin School—Haywood studied Marxist theory and participated in a unique atmosphere of international solidarity. (Among the exiles he met there was another Haywood, Big Bill, who died in Moscow in 1928.) From this unique vantage, Haywood observed the intense factional debate that divided the world Communist movement: the purge of Leon Trotsky by Stalin; the subsequent elimination of the "right" deviationists Rykov, Tomsky, and Bukharin; and the decision of the Comintern to end the interminable conflict within the American Communist party by expelling certain recalcitrant leaders in favor of the militant faction led by William Z. Foster.

Haywood's public positions seldom differed from the official party line. For this reason, his proximity to critical decision making transformed the otherwise obscure student of Marxism into a major Communist spokesman. Most important, in 1928 Haywood enthusiastically embraced the decision of the Comintern's Sixth World Congress regarding blacks in the United States. In its official statement of policy, the Comintern described American blacks as an oppressed *nation*—"an historically developed community of people with a common language, territory, economic life and an historic tradition reflecting itself in a common culture." The party then endorsed the principle that such a nation should enjoy self-determination in the American South, where blacks constituted a majority of the population. In other words, the line read, American blacks were a colonized people; consequently they deserved the status of nationhood. Haywood would become the primary exponent of that theory: "To contend," he declared, "that the Negro question in the United States is a race question in contradistinction to a national question is to contend that the Negroes are oppressed because they are black." Such convoluted logic revealed the ideological limitations of theories constructed half a world away from American realities. Yet the Comintern's interest in race relations also stimulated renewed efforts to deal with such basic problems as lynching, segregation, and discrimination in employment and housing.

Having won the endorsement of the highest Communist echelon, Haywood returned to the United States in 1930, already a leader at the age of 32. His arrival coincided with the worst economic crisis in American history. Its impact on the black population provided an opportunity to expand Communist influence among racial minorities. That was Haywood's area of expertise, to which he brought a humorless passion for ideological argument and an adeptness at theoretical disputation. During the next half-decade, he would develop the intellectual rationale for challenging the oppression of his people. His personal prominence soon became an important symbol of multiracial working-class solidarity. And from this position, Haywood would volunteer in 1937 to assume a leadership role among the Americans fighting to save the Spanish Republic.

The dialectical enthusiasm of Harry Haywood, the poetic sensibility of Edwin Rolfe, even the frustrations of Reuben Barr—all illuminate the tentative foundations of American radicalism as the nation approached its greatest domestic crisis since the Civil War. For most middle-class citizens and their betters, the America of Harding and Coolidge and Hoover had proven the vitality of traditional promises: prosperity, mobility, security from the travails of the Old World. When the average citizen "looked toward the future of his country," observed the journalist Frederick Lewis Allen, "he could vision an America set free—not from graft, nor from crime, nor from war, nor from control by Wall Street, nor from irreligion, nor from lust, for the utopias of an earlier day left him for the most part skeptical and indifferent; he visioned an America set free from poverty and toil." Young radicals like Barr, Rolfe, and Haywood certainly wanted that freedom. But they were not willing to ignore some of those other problems: political corruption, the specter of war, the power of corporations over their daily lives. Nor were they willing to dream the American dream simply for the white middle classes that Allen assumed spoke for the whole population. They worried about others less free—farm workers in the West; blacks in the South and the cities; immigrants who spoke with accents; and a younger generation struggling to grasp the elusive opportunities for success. Such problems they understood from their own experiences; their radicalism, though influenced by foreign ideas, remained an indigenous American phenomenon.

As outsiders in the 1920's, however, the young radicals found only pockets of sympathy. The IWW had virtually vanished from the landscape; the Socialist party, which remained true to its principles, nonetheless abandoned the labor movement for the quadrennial election booth; the American Federation of Labor focused primarily on skilled craft workers; and the Communist party, when it ran a presidential candidate in 1928, polled less than 50,000 votes. Yet enthusiasm among would-be revolutionaries remained high—unrealistically so, as befits revolutionary visions—and inspired a willingness to sacrifice for the cause. "Today our party is small and the parties of the capitalists are large and strong," conceded Communist leader William Z. Foster in 1928, "but the day will surely come when the Communist Party will be the only party in the United States." That summer, the Comintern's Sixth World Congress endorsed the idea that the international socialist revolution was entering the so-called "Third Period": the "final conflict" with capitalism loomed directly ahead.

Such prophecies coincided with the collapse of the American dream. The crash of stock prices on Wall Street, the rise of unemployment, the undiminishing depression—these new realities would alter the framework within which Americans expressed their opinions and searched for alternatives. "The radical on the soap-box," noted Frederick Lewis Allen in 1931, "was far less terrifying than in the days of the Big Red Scare." Those who had already discovered a new vision—the young radicals of the 1920's—would find fertile fields in which to spread their own versions of the American dream.

"Youth forever stays / Fresh in the world," wrote Edwin Rolfe on the eve of the Great Depression, "eager for newer life." American youth born around 1910 were just then coming of age. They held American dreams and wanted to see them fulfilled, but the overwhelming economic crisis rapidly diminished their horizons. These young people, idealistic and hopeful in the 1920's, would swell the movements for economic and social justice when conditions worsened in the next decade. And in their protest, they would be joined by abundant kindred spirits.

3

Awakening in Hard Times

In the late summer of 1929, a spry, diminutive
eighteen-year-old named Harry Fisher, who would
later serve as a runner in the Lincoln brigade, landed
his first decent job at Sears, Roebuck department store
in Manhattan. It paid fifteen dollars for a 48-hour week,
a wage he relished. During the "boom" of the 1920's,
Harry's widowed mother had been so poor that she had
placed him in an orphanage while she worked in the
needle trades and raised her two younger children.
Soon after Harry got his job, his boss gave him a note
to deliver to the Bank of the United States.

"When I got there," Harry recalled, "I saw a long
line of anxious people outside. They were all waiting
to get into the bank to withdraw their savings. There
were many policemen there, allowing only a few people in at a time. I showed my note to the bank official
standing at the entrance. He admitted me. I then saw
the vice-president who was a friend of my boss. I gave
him the note and he immediately gave me a bank check
for $50,000. I took the check to another bank in the
neighborhood and deposited it. Later that day I felt
guilty when I remembered the worried faces of those
poor people who couldn't get into the bank to save the

few dollars they had worked so hard for, while this millionaire, my boss, had no trouble rescuing his money." The next day the Bank of the United States defaulted and closed its doors. When Harry returned home that night, he found his mother in tears. "For twenty years she had worked in a garment factory under sweat-shop conditions," he explained. Her life's savings, maybe $1,500, had been kept in the Bank of the United States. "Now it was gone."

So began a Depression saga all too familiar in its origins. While the crash on Wall Street ruined fortunes great and small, the effects spread to every corner of the country, until the term "depression" assumed both an economic and a psychological reality that hung like a gray cloud over the landscape. One Saturday afternoon, two months after the crash, Harry Fisher was collecting his weekly pay envelope at Sears when he heard loud cries from the women's locker room; "I rushed in and asked what happened. One of the women told me that about fifty of them had gotten pink slips in their envelopes. That was it. There was no two-week notice, no severance pay, just a pink slip saying they were not needed anymore. Most of these young women came from families where they were the only ones working, and it was impossible for them to get any other job now. . . . At that time there was no unemployment insurance, so if no one in the family was working, it meant hunger . . . and despair."

The crisis of capitalism assumed palpable form. At the time of the crash in October 1929, the number of unemployed Americans already approached half a million. Two months later the jobless levels touched three million. By the next winter, four to five million were out of work; the year after that eight million; by 1933 several millions more. Statistics sketch only the contours of suffering: so many idle workers remained uncounted; so many earned insufficient wages to live. And who could measure the inner turmoil? No government program could cope with the mounting crisis; corporate advice echoed against empty coffers. "With the present breakdown," wrote the critic Edmund Wilson in 1931, "we have come to the end of something." Historian Caroline Bird later named that something when she termed the collapse "The Failure of Wisdom."

It was during the ensuing hard times that most future Lincoln volunteers first cut their political teeth. Frustrated and angry at the failure of the American capitalist system, they initially entered the radical movement to participate in specific protest activities: unemployment demonstrations, hunger marches, militant labor strikes, antidiscrimination campaigns. In the forefront of such causes stood the American Communist party, prepared not only to condemn economic conditions but also to propose concrete alternatives. Therein lay the unique appeal of communism during the Great Depression.

Just six weeks after the crash, the Communist party issued formal demands for unemployment relief, including emergency assistance and insurance payments equal to full wages. To dramatize the ultimatum, Communist leaders then organized mass protest demonstrations in most major cities in December 1929. But in each case, local police dispersed the crowds, often with violence. The response intensified the crisis. Angry throngs, harassed by tear gas and police clubs, welcomed the Communist militancy. Their support, in turn, reinforced the party's sense of leadership. To the unemployed, the confrontations provided powerful leverage for demanding greater welfare assistance.

Steve Nelson, destined to become the political leader of the Lincoln brigade in Spain, began to work as a full-time party organizer that winter, helping to plan the protests in Chicago. Born in Yugoslavia and a carpenter by trade, he had entered the labor movement in the early 1920's when a coworker showed him a political leaflet and Nelson had to ask what the word "proletariat" meant. "I remember clear, like it was yesterday," he remarked in 1937, "that he said it would be much better for the workingmen if we ran everything collectively. I remember exactly how he said it, where he said it, how I felt when I heard it." Committed to a social transformation, Nelson joined the Communist party in 1925, on the first anniversary of Lenin's death. "I saw the logic of socialism," he recalled. "I knew I was going to be a worker, and if I was going to be a worker, I wanted to do what was best for workers."

Arriving in Chicago nearly five years later, Nelson had no trouble convincing anyone that unemployment was a problem. As a party functionary, he received five dollars a week, most of which he spent on carfare. He lived with a sympathetic family and bartered his carpentry skills for other assistance. "We couldn't just give speeches about the downfall of capitalism," he explained. "We had to be with the people." Nelson organized his first demonstration at Chicago's city hall in February 1930. He managed to utter a few sentences before the police dragged him into a car and knocked him unconscious. Undaunted, he brought another delegation to city hall a few days later to demand unemployment assistance as a basic right.

When the Communist party proclaimed that March 6, 1930, would be "International Unemployment Day," Nelson sparked the organizing drive in Chicago. After one meeting of six hundred local activists, however, the police surrounded the building, barred the doors, and proceeded to examine each participant. Chicago's notorious "Red Squad"—brutal and antiradical police—arrested the suspected Communists, held them incommunicado, and brutally beat fourteen of the leaders with blackjacks. (Besides Nelson, two of the victims—Joe Dallet of the Steel and Metal Workers' Union and Oliver Law, a black leader of the unemployed movement—would also volunteer to fight in Spain.) Two weeks after the beatings, thirteen of the fourteen had recovered sufficiently to march with 75,000 demonstrators to demand unemployment insurance. On that day, over one million Americans participated in similar protests around the country. Afterwards, Nelson still faced a trial for sedition and organizing an armed revolution. A jury voted for his acquittal.

Nelson's courage revealed the intensity of a Communist's commitment— the same stuff that prepared him for the sacrifices demanded on Spanish battlefields. To be a revolutionary agitator—merely to demand rights for the unemployed—entailed enormous personal risk. Beatings by unsympathetic bystanders or hired thugs occurred frequently. Nearly every protester could testify to police violence, which extended from the terror tactics of mounted officers against pedestrians to arbitrary arrests, third-degree interrogations, and jail sentences. Although fear was the natural response, communism taught its adherents the importance of discipline and self-control. "Comrades, keep your heads," one prisoner advised Nelson's cadre as the Red Squad bludgeoned a fellow prisoner. "They'll shoot the first one of us that takes a step." Communists respected such personal sacrifice. Neither the inconveniences of political participation nor the fear of prison dampened their enthusiasm.

For most Communists, the process of political awakening had begun with practical motivations. Unlike middle-class reformers of the 1930's, such as Dr. Francis Townsend, who proposed a revolving pension scheme to subsidize the elderly, or Upton Sinclair, who initiated the End Poverty in California program, or even the Socialist party, with its electoral pronouncements, the Communist party married idealistic rhetoric with action. Brazenly expedient, Communists brought the problems of the needy into the public arena, sometimes recklessly, often futilely, but always with the intention of winning some specific concessions from landlords or welfare bureaucrats. Significantly, about half the members of the Communist party in the 1930's came from the ranks of the unemployed; these were people motivated by necessity and pragmatism rather than by the theories of dialectical materialism emanating from Moscow. Although many Communist recruits who went to Spain came to appreciate the subtleties of the party line, their activism originated with the plain humanitarian compassion of a Harry Fisher or the indignation at personal injustice felt by a Steve Nelson. But when Nelson volunteered to go to Spain, the party initially rejected his application: he was still too valuable on the home front.

The willingness of young radicals to journey overseas to fight against fascism also reflected a prophetic aspect of American communism that emerged dramatically during the 1930's: its unequivocal opposition to racism. In the Spanish war, black volunteers would serve as equals and feel for the first time in their lives a freedom from racial oppression; and whites would experience a racially mixed community they seldom knew in America. The interracial nature of the Lincoln brigade had its roots in the color-blind agenda of the Communist party. No one played a more important role in developing that agenda than the young theoretician Harry Haywood, who had returned from the Soviet Union in 1930, just in time to help draft plans for the creation of a new party organization, the League of Struggle for Negro Rights, dedicated to expanding Communist influence among blacks.

A tireless advocate of the party line, Haywood remained nonetheless aloof from the rank and file—a personal trait that would affect his performance in Spain. Yet he had a rigorous technical mind, an ability to place isolated political phenomena within the broad theories of Marxism, Leninism, and Stalinism. True to Comintern principles, Haywood vociferously advocated "national self-determination" for the black majority living in the southern states, including, when necessary, the confiscation of white property. Even party stalwarts understood that such a grandiose program had little appeal among the black masses, much less any chance of implementation. Yet the burden of reconciling theory and action became Haywood's responsibility. During the next four years, the party—and Haywood as its chief spokesman on race relations—would insist that racial equality must come within the context of the class revolution. Only a "militant alliance with white workers," said Haywood, would enable blacks to end "the abominable national oppression which is part and parcel of the capitalist system."

As a member of the party's Negro Commission, Haywood soon became embroiled in the Communist effort to eliminate all aspects of "white chauvinism." In one celebrated case, Haywood served on a jury which convicted a Finnish American of racist behavior. Although the defendant publicly recanted, vowed to reform, and returned to the party's good graces, U.S. immigration officials, using the party trial as evidence, arranged to deport the avowed Communist. Haywood nonetheless considered the case a tremendous victory: "It had a cleansing effect on the Party—heightened the consciousness of the cadre and cleared the deck . . . of the most blatantly chauvinist practices." Certainly the party gained prestige among blacks for its ideological consistency. "I went to Spain because I owed it to the people who helped me get my job," black seaman Albert Chisholm recalled many years later. "No one in Seattle . . . was standing up for the rights of blacks at the time. The Communists were the only ones who did. I never would have gone to sea if not for the Young Communist League."

Other future volunteers of the Lincoln brigade first joined the Communist crusade during the party's dramatic fight to save the "Scottsboro boys," nine black youths arrested in Alabama in 1931 on charges of raping two white girls on a freight train. When the Scottsboro court found the defendants guilty and sentenced them to death, the Communist party dispatched lawyers through the International Labor Defense to appeal the verdict. Public rallies around the country drew many Scottsboro sympathizers into the party fold. For Harry Haywood, dogmatic to excess, the Scottsboro trials became an opportunity not only to attack southern racism, but also to unmask other "reformist" organizations, such as the National Association for the Advancement of Colored People, which, he said, "played the role of assistant hangman of Negro masses." When the NAACP belatedly pledged to win due process of law for the defendants, Haywood condemned the presumption that they could get any justice in a legal system dominated by "the white ruling class." Haywood's polemics promoted his consideration as the Communist vice-presidential candidate in 1932. But he was finally passed over in favor of an older and less doctrinaire black, James Ford.

As the Scottsboro case sharpened public opinion, Haywood continued to agitate against the rise of lynchings in the South, writing numerous articles and pamphlets that analyzed the atrocities from a Marxist perspective. By 1934, he stood at the pinnacle of the Communist party. Asked to deliver a report on the Negro question to the party's annual convention, the dogged intellectual presented an exhaustive address, warning that efforts to divide the working class along color lines would merely create a segregated economy, in which the black bourgeoisie would remain subservient to a white elite. The speech brought a standing ovation. Haywood was promptly promoted to the American Communist party's highest governing body, the politburo.

His triumph proved to be short-lived. Despite the severe impact of the Depression on the black population and despite the party's extraordinary recruiting efforts, the number of black Communists remained minuscule. In January 1932, a party census reported only 74 blacks in the New York district, 3.1 percent of that district's membership. While American party leaders lamented their isolation from the black masses of Harlem, moreover, a growing fear about the rise of fascism in Hitler's Germany demanded a shift in strategy to gain broader political support. From Moscow, the Comintern ordered a softening of relations with non-Communist groups. With this change in the political winds, the doctrinaire Haywood appeared expendable. Late in 1934, he left New York for a lesser position on Chicago's South Side. Haywood remained a visible figure at Communist party meetings, however, and two years later, he ran for Congress on the party slate. He polled exactly 899 votes.

While Harry Haywood continued to write abstruse papers with titles like "The Struggle for the Leninist Position on the Negro Question in the U.S.A.," less articulate blacks responded to the party's vigor in fighting against racial injustice. Within the movement they found a distinctive sense of dignity. Treated as equals, they enjoyed the self-conscious interracial camaraderie, unusual in American society in the 1930's. And their embrace of radical politics was more pragmatic than a mere espousal of the party leadership's polemical rhetoric. "I always felt, even before I had any notion about Marxism and Leninism," observed Vaughn Love, who grew up in an integrated environment in Dayton, Tennessee, "that I had a philosophical approach to life, a humanism not based upon religion . . . like the golden rule. . . . I believe this was the social philosophy in both white and black in my early childhood. . . . There was no racism and people were willing to live and let live, and to degrade somebody would mean they would be subject to getting a horsewhipping." As for the dialectics of Harry Haywood and the notion of self-determination, Love thought "that was sort of an excursion into possibilities."

After he moved to New York in search of a job in 1929, however, Love confronted a combination of hard times and job discrimination that kept him poor and hungry. In 1932, a Communist rally on behalf of the Scottsboro boys attracted his attention, and he started to work selling subscriptions for *The Liberator*, the newspaper of the League of Struggle for Negro Rights. Later, he joined the International Workers Order, a Communist-led fraternal organization that offered cultural programs. Among the IWO's activities was Harlem's "Suitcase Theater," in which Love helped form a group of interracial entertainers known as the "Convulsionaries." Their vaudevillian shows delighted left-wing audiences by blending ideology with satire. When news of the International Brigades reached the IWO, Love and his white cohorts eagerly pressed to enlist.

"If the generation after World War I was the Lost Generation," observed John Gates, who would become the highest-ranking American officer in the Spanish war, "we students in the first years of the Hoover Depression were the Aimless Generation. But our very uncertainty drove many of us to search for answers and for a cause to live by." Most of the young men and women who volunteered for Spain had entered the radical movement through the Young Communist League (YCL), if only because of their age. (There was no standard age at which a member of the YCL would "graduate" into the Communist party; some never did, and others remained YCLers into their late twenties.) Like its parent organization, the YCL grew steadily through the 1930's, from 3,000 in 1931 to 6,000 in 1934 and 8,000 in mid-1935. But like the party, the YCL attracted a transitory membership, suggesting that the total number of YCLers was statistically much higher. Because of Depression conditions, about half the YCL membership in 1933 consisted of the unemployed. Another 35 percent were students. Only a small proportion were actual "workers," but a sense of class consciousness permeated the organization. The economic crisis had thwarted this generation; Communist ideology offered, at the least, a vision of changing the unyielding reality. Often, too, the YCL provided social comforts and adolescent friendships to compensate for the frustration and despair of the marketplace.

John Gates's experience was similar to those of dozens of other college students who would find their way to Spain. Born with the name Solomon Regenstreit into a family of Polish Jews in 1913, he grew up in the streets of New York, skipped a few grades of public school, and enrolled at the tuition-free City College of New York in 1930. He claimed to have little political awareness. But CCNY had a tradition of student dissent, focusing on the Reserve Officers Training Corps (ROTC) and a college president, Frederick Robinson, who tolerated no criticism. Gates would soon enter the political controversies that boiled on the campus. Concerned about contemporary issues, he gravitated to the pro-Communist Social Problems Club, where he discovered Marx and "a new world" of ideas. During Gates's freshman term in 1930, President Robinson suspended the club's student leader after his arrest for distributing Communist leaflets. Gates joined the ensuing student protest. He also continued to read Marx and Lenin, taking three months off to analyze *Capital.* "As I became filled with the superiority of my new-found faith," he recalled, "I was sure there was nothing that college could teach me." When Robinson dismissed eleven students for publishing an unauthorized magazine, Gates decided to join the campus Young Communist League. That was the spring of the Scottsboro arrests. Taking to the soapboxes, the eighteen-year-old Gates condemned the evils of racial injustice. He also enrolled in the International Labor Defense, which was handling the case, and helped establish youth branches known as the Young Defenders.

As his world became more politicized, Gates confronted the economic issues of the Depression. When, in December 1931, the Communist party's Unemployed Councils announced a National Hunger March to Washington, D.C., to appeal for federal unemployment insurance, Gates joined the sixteen hundred delegates who claimed to represent some twelve million unemployed. "Charity drives, community chest donations, Salvation Army Santa Clauses might get the front pages," he reported, "but among the workers was growing the sense that their welfare was their own concern." Heartened by the experience, Gates decided to quit college to bring his views to the masses. Within months, the YCL assigned him to represent unemployed workers in Warren, Ohio. Leaving New York for the first time, he adopted "John Gates" as a nom de guerre "to symbolize," he recalled, "a change in a way of life." For the next five years, Gates would be part of the Communist cadre in Ohio, until he volunteered for Spain.

Higher education, to be sure, remained an exceptional course for Depression-generation youngsters. Milton Wolff, the last commander of the Lincoln brigade, experienced a more typical development. Raised in a struggling family in Brooklyn—"there was always a problem with money," he remembered—the gangly boy did well at school, but his main ambitions were to make the high school track team and to study painting. Both, however, required the outlay of cash, something his father, a self-employed handyman, absolutely refused. What little savings the family had accumulated disappeared after the crash. Eventually, they went on relief. Wolff quit school, found occasional jobs, and considered studying art; but mostly he hung around on street corners with his friends.

The creation of the federal government's Civilian Conservation Corps, part of President Franklin D. Roosevelt's "New Deal," in 1933 brightened the horizons. Designed to stimulate environmental projects and provide healthy jobs for youth, the program established military-style camps in which boys could work outdoors thinning forests and planting trees. The Communist party condemned the program as a system of "forced labor camps" designed to militarize American youth. But to boys like Wolff, the CCC offered tangible benefits. Oblivious to Communist rhetoric, he was optimistic about the Roosevelt administration's ability to end the Depression, at least at the beginning. Besides, the scheme enabled the eighteen-year-old, apolitical dropout to leave home for the first time. Though tall and sinewy, Wolff was unsure of his stamina and volunteered to become a first-aid assistant rather than a woodcutter. But he soon came to love the forest and the friendship of the boys who worked there, even if he did not like the food. One day, when a more experienced recruit mentioned that the staff was misappropriating food money and suggested that they organize a protest, Wolff agreed to support a work stoppage. Fearing intervention from federal officials, the camp leaders quickly instituted reforms. "That was the first time I realized there was an injustice and you could do something about it," Wolff recalled.

A second confrontation proved more painful. Wolff's closest friend suffered a minor injury, which quickly developed into blood poisoning. Responsible for first-aid treatment, Wolff pleaded with the camp doctor for assistance, but the physician ignored his call. Within a day, Wolff's friend was dead. And when Wolff supported the victim's family in protesting the procedures, camp officials refused to let him reenlist in the CCC. "I left bitter," he declared. "They didn't care shit for us. We were on the bottom of the heap." He was nineteen years old.

Back in New York, Wolff landed a job in the garment center, began to study drawing at night, and spent his spare time having fun with friends. One evening they led him to a room above the neighborhood bowling alley, where a YCL meeting was in progress. Wolff stayed to listen. He had already experienced unemployment. He knew personally about bank failures and the bad working conditions in the garment industry. He had participated in the successful CCC strike, and he was still feeling the pain of his friend's death. Wolff enrolled on the spot. Within a week, he was taking his place on the street-corner soapboxes, drawing crowds with his hitherto unknown speaking skills. His forte was antiwar addresses: he warned that fascist expansion threatened a recurrence of the horrors of the World War. "I was still a pacifist," he remembered.

For Wolff, the YCL provided, first, a social community of friends. There were young women to date and sleep with and young men with whom to explore the excitement of Greenwich Village and Harlem. He discovered also a sense of self-worth, a feeling that he could contribute to the betterment of the world. Above all, he found political coherence. Whatever the confusions of his home life, the incompetence of the CCC, the scramble of the garment center, Wolff had located a focus for his restless energy. "I found security in my political outlook. I found out you could fight city hall, that you could do something about it." He became aware of the wider world. From YCL discussions and the columns of the *Daily Worker*, he learned of foreign affairs. After the Spanish war began, he went into the subways with collection cans to raise money for the victims of fascist bombings. His commitment was complete. When a YCL official came to his club meeting, explained the nature of the crisis, and asked for volunteers to go to Spain, Wolff quickly raised his hand. Looking around the room, he discovered his was the only one in the air. "At least for the boat ride," he quipped.

If Communist theory emphasized the importance of working-class solidarity, the practical experiences of the labor movement in the 1930's reinforced the appeal for camaraderie. At a time when union workers routinely confronted the violence of employer "goon squads" and hostile police, labor organizers had to demonstrate extraordinary loyalty, self-sacrifice, and personal courage. The labor struggles thus prepared many trade unionists for leadership roles on the battlefields of Spain. Among them was the resourceful Archie Brown, one of the most dynamic labor organizers on the West Coast. His career epitomized the link between class-conscious Communist activism and the growth of militant trade unionism for practical gains.

Brown came to California in 1924 at the age of thirteen, riding the freight trains alone from his native Sioux City, Iowa. Along the way, the boy met an old Wobbly who attempted to give him lessons about the struggle between the classes, but the innocent eighth-grader assumed the agitator was talking about a fight between two classrooms! After listening to more soapbox oratory, however, the tousle-haired Brown joined the YCL in Oakland, California, in 1929, just as the stock market crash seemed to confirm the Communist prophecies about the demise of capitalism. For the next two years, he gained organizing experience in the unemployment protests around San Francisco. Then the YCL assigned him to the Imperial Valley to unionize the pea pickers. The recent arrival of migrants from the midwest dust bowl had accentuated the problems of unemployment, creating a volatile mix of Mexicans, Okies, and blacks competing for jobs. Amidst dreadful living conditions, Brown tried for two years to build a cohesive union. He organized several work stoppages, but all of them failed. "We never won anything," he admitted. Yet his optimism never wavered. In 1933, Brown moved to the San Joaquin Valley to prepare cotton workers for a major strike, which also failed. The farm owners and local police then contrived to run him out of town.

Beaten in his efforts, Brown entered another arena of labor militancy, the struggle to improve working conditions on the West Coast waterfronts. His troubles with the police followed him. Sent to San Pedro to speak at a union dance, Brown antagonized the local Red Squad, which, with the help of the American Legion, disrupted the meeting. The sheriff charged Brown with disorderly conduct, releasing him on bail. Back in San Francisco, Brown became so involved in organizing the longshoremen for the massive strike of 1934 that he forgot to file an appeal in the San Pedro case, for which he received a 90-day sentence. Later, when he protested conditions in the jail, he had to spend much of that term in brutal solitary confinement. His only pleasure was receiving smuggled fruit from a Mexican prisoner, who appreciated Brown's criticism of prison racism.

By the time Brown won his freedom in the summer of 1934, the great San

Francisco waterfront strike, marked by violence and bloodshed, had ended in a victory for Harry Bridges and the International Longshoreman's and Warehouseman's Union (ILWU). But the ship scalers' union remained on the picket line, and the tenacious Brown joined the strike committee to help negotiate a settlement. Despite a truce, however, labor contractors found workers who were willing to defy the agreement. One Saturday night in September 1935, a fracas in a San Francisco union hall resulted in a worker plunging from a second-story window. When the man died of his injuries, the district attorney charged Brown and three others with first-degree murder. Held without bail, they waited in jail for nearly three months, while the local newspapers, dominated by business leaders, refused to discuss the case. The trial began in a tense and bitter atmosphere. Brown, despite his limited education, served as his own attorney, cross-examining witnesses and battling against a conservative prosecutor and an unfriendly judge. A sudden revelation of fresh evidence turned the case. The jury saw through some perjured testimony and voted for acquittal.

Forced to work under an assumed name, Brown returned to the docks in 1936. To protest fascist advances in Europe, he organized a boycott of Italian shipping. Later that year, he helped plan a second waterfront strike that tied up the West Coast ports. "The nights were cold enough for picketing," he remembered, "but in the bargain there were the cops and the strikebreakers." The union victory helped stabilize the ILWU, and a third strike in 1937 proved equally successful. Soon afterward, a group of longshoremen, including Brown's brother, sailed for Spain. "They felt," Brown reported, "that . . . they were merely continuing the fight that started on the picket line—a worldwide fight for decent living conditions and human justice." Brown would have gone with them, but the passport office refused to issue his papers. After three efforts, he finally stowed away in 1938, arriving just in time to participate in the Lincoln brigade's final offensive. There, amid excruciating bombardment in the Sierra Pandols, he would rally the spirits of a company of militant unionists by chanting the old labor songs "Hold the Fort" and "The Internationale."

Such devotion to the working class spread from the strike movements of the 1930's to other sectors of society. Robert Merriman, for example, a graduate student in economics at the University of California at Berkeley, organized a campus protest to prevent recruitment of football players to work as strikebreakers across the bay. His interest in labor economics, whetted by the strike, led him to accept a Newton Booth Fellowship, which enabled him to study in the Soviet Union the next year. Meanwhile, Esther Silverstein, a student nurse at the University of California, helped raise money for the strike fund and once cooked three gallons of spaghetti sauce to feed the strikers. Two years later, she was working as a public health nurse at the Marine Hospital when the maritime workers called the second big strike. Because there was a flu epidemic, she had many strikers on her ward. One seaman had been beaten savagely by strikebreakers with brass knuckles. When he died of his wounds, Silverstein wrapped his body in a shroud, using the seaman's strike button to pin the cloth.

"I became sort of lefty in a gradual process," she would recall half a century later about her decision to join the Communist movement. "They were fighting to make things better and they had a philosophy to back them up. That made sense to me." The seamen she tended in the hospital stimulated her political conscience. After the Spanish war began, the patients taped a big map of Spain on the wall and followed the course of the war with intense discussions. Once a female patient arrived in a comatose state and seemed on the verge of death. Then, abruptly, she awakened, looked at Silverstein, and asked, "Has Madrid fallen?"

"No," the nurse replied.

"Are you sure?" she asked again. And when Silverstein assured her that Madrid was holding out, the patient instantly returned to sleep.

In that spirit of concern for the besieged Republic, Silverstein volunteered to serve as a nurse in Spain. She said her goodbyes to the seamen on her ward, traveled cross-country to New York, and embarked on the *Normandie*. Aboard ship, she found an envelope waiting for her. It contained 45 one-dollar bills and a single five: $50 given by her patients in case she had a change of heart and needed a return ticket. A few days later, Silverstein attended a rally for Spain in Paris, and when sympathizers unfurled a Republican flag to accept gifts for the cause, she gave away the entire $50. She was 25 years old.

These stories emphasize the individuality of each person's radicalization. Esther Silverstein's humanitarianism, Archie Brown's militancy, Milton Wolff's bitterness—each stemmed from a life's experience: family background, personality, and the unexpected, unpredictable circumstances that inform a mind, arouse a conscience, goad a person into action. Each career revealed its own logic, fulfilled its implictions. Yet these individual stories add up to more than the sum of their parts; placed together, they form themselves into patterns, reflecting the larger historical issues and trends that surrounded the separate biographies. Thus, unprecedented unemployment directly affected the lives of literally hundreds of men and women who joined the International Brigades. So did other Depression-era factors, such as dangerous working conditions, inadequate diet, and the lack of rights for minorities. Such social problems became deeply personal; the individual lifetime and the moment of history converged. The American volunteers, in other words, were unique people, distinctive in their commitments and the choices they made; and yet they were no more than the products of their times.

4

Forging the Popular Front

As the American Communist party launched the presidential campaign of 1936, candidate Earl Browder unveiled the latest ideological turn: "Communism is twentieth-century Americanism." The slogan epitomized the party's Popular Front, the Communist strategy that promoted political cooperation with non-Communist workers' groups (previously maligned as "social fascists") and with middle-class liberals. Although the program and its rhetoric hardly hastened Browder's entry into the White House, the Popular Front succeeded brilliantly as a scheme to unify American radicals. Communists also welcomed the opportunity to participate in the American mainstream. "We began to feel like we were really part of the American scene," recalled student leader George Watt, who would serve as an officer with the Lincoln brigade in Spain. "We were looking for some kind of legitimation of our feeling about becoming even more American." To be a Communist, a radical no longer had to feel like a pariah. Equally important, the Popular Front appealed to native-born Americans— especially the assimilated children of immigrants, that generation of 1910—who saw no contradiction between their patriotism and the party line. The effect was immediately apparent: party membership surged by the tens of thousands.

But the influence of the Popular Front reached even further. By linking a radical outlook to familiar American values, the Communist movement literally popularized awareness of the dangers of fascism to world peace. Indeed, most future Lincoln volunteers joined the Communist party or one of its affiliated groups during the era of the Popular Front. Americans who might otherwise have shunned identification with a "foreign" ideology drew closer to the anti-fascist camp. George Watt, for example, as executive secretary of the Communist National Student League, helped plan a merger with the Socialist Student League for Industrial Democracy and other youth groups, creating the Popular Front's American Student Union, from which numerous college students went to Spain. Similarly, the Communist unemployed movement now embraced Socialists and liberals to create the Workers Alliance in 1936. Over 350 of its members would fight for the Spanish Republic. Within the labor movement, moreover, Communist organizers brought their skills to the emerging Congress of Industrial Organizations (CIO) in steel, automobile manufacturing, transportation, and other basic industries. Numerous young men went directly from these organizing drives to Spain. And when Earl Browder campaigned for president, he sought less to defeat the Democratic incumbent than to push the Roosevelt administration to the left. Significantly, local Communist candidates usually drew more votes than Browder.

The Popular Front also provided a coherence to world events. By emphasizing the interrelatedness of fascist aggression in all parts of the world, the Communist party helped to forge a broad radical perspective about diverse episodes around the globe. From the vantage point of the Popular Front, Japanese expansion in Manchuria and China mirrored Mussolini's claims to Ethiopia; Hitler's ruthlessness to the Jews paralleled German militarization. Each fascist proclamation—the execution of labor leaders, the Nuremberg racial laws—appeared as a prelude for the next; each diplomatic demand— the rearmament of Germany, the reoccupation of the Rhineland—loomed not as an isolated strand but as part of an ever-widening skein: the fascist plan for world conquest. Such logic not only broadened the base of American antifascism, but prepared this growing minority for subsequent international crises. By the time Mussolini and Hitler began to send military support to Franco's armies in Spain in the summer of 1936, the Popular Front could draw upon a solid tradition of informed dissent. As in most radical activities of the 1930's, the American Communist party had led the way.

"Socialist, Communist—all anti-fascist workers and all anti-fascist intellectuals," wrote *Daily Worker* reporter Edwin Rolfe in 1934, "must band together . . . in a concerted drive against the Nazi pest—HERE AND NOW!" As the Nazis imposed death penalties on leading trade unionists and Communists, most notably Ernst Thaelmann, American radicals staged mass demonstrations outside German consulates around the country. (The protest chant usually rang: "Free Ernst Thaelmann and the Scottsboro boys!" Sometimes they added the name of Tom Mooney, a labor radical imprisoned in California.) Yet many Americans remained intolerant of such political displays, and public demonstrations entailed real risks. During one protest in Philadelphia, for example, an undercover officer singled out a Communist named Ben Gardner, a sometime organizer of the unemployed, and charged him with disorderly conduct. Gardner then faced a pro-German judge, who sentenced him to one year in the county jail at Holmesburg. His wife could visit him three times a month for fifteen minutes. Despite further mass protests urging his parole, Gardner served the full term. "Holmesburg," he wrote to his wife three years later from the Aragon front in Spain, "was my first long sentence and I certainly think it has had value in steeling me more."

The fascist menace seemed to touch closer to home during the summer of 1935, when the Nazis arrested a German-born American seaman and held him without trial in a Hamburg jail for keeping anti-Hitler literature in his locker. By then, grisly stories of Nazi terror had become a regular feature in the left-wing press. To protest the atrocities, the *Daily Worker* summoned the masses to a demonstration coinciding with the departure of the passenger ship *Bremen*, which flew the Nazi swastika in place of the German national flag. "Turn this sailing into an exposure of the pogromists of Germany! Demonstrate for the freedom of American seamen kidnapped by Hitler's Gestapo! Fight for the leader of the dockers of the German lines, Ernst Thaelmann!" Meanwhile, in secret, Communist party leaders planned a dramatic gesture to capture public attention.

Among those involved in the plot was a sailor named Bill Bailey, who would later serve in a machine-gun company in Spain. Twenty-five years old that summer, he had just returned from a voyage to the Mediterranean. Like many seamen, Bailey had a strongly antiauthoritarian temperament, hardened by the rigors of shipboard conditions and the rough lifestyle of the ports he visited. His political indoctrination had begun half a decade earlier when a shipmate in the Gulf ports enrolled him in the IWW. Harsh treatment of the crew had persuaded him to join the Marine Workers' Industrial Union, a Communist-led group in 1930. He entered the party soon afterward. Dividing his time between sailing, working as a longshoreman, and riding the freights in search of jobs, Bailey participated in a variety of labor disputes. By 1934, the party suggested he become a political leader. For a few days, he toured the docks with an experienced organizer to learn the ropes. But Bailey hated the rigmarole and abruptly signed up as a seaman for a voyage to Europe early in 1935.

His first port of call was on the west coast of Italy, where the ship berthed beside a naval vessel loading troops for Ethiopia. The Italian dictator Mussolini had expressed designs of military conquest, and Bailey observed uniformed fascist crowds cheering and shouting slogans to the young soldiers aboard ship. Another American seaman named Larry Kleidman, who would later volunteer for Spain, provided additional details of a similar experience: "There were 1300 'men' leaving for Africa. . . . Some of them, boys of sixteen, were in tears. A military band would lead them, then a company of well-drilled black shirts, then the recruits. When they got to the boat the band turned left, the black shirts turned right and the recruits marched right onto the boat. A bitter joke." Despite the regalia, Bailey noticed a memorable silence among the conscripts—"no enthusiasm at all," he recalled.

From Italy, Bailey's ship steamed to Marseilles, where he met supporters of the French Popular Front, who were worried about war. He then proceeded to Spain. "That was a world of difference," he would remember. "Everybody was happy about the Republic, and their enthusiasm ran over everybody." In the spirit of the Popular Front, Bailey decided to offer his greetings as a representative of the American working class. Treated as a comrade, he mingled with politicized workers all along the Spanish coast. "When I left Spain," he said, "I was full of enthusiasm." Back in the United States, by contrast, Bailey observed a marked indifference to the issues that had concerned Spanish workers. He thought the Communist party ought to arouse the public to the fascist menace abroad. Bailey eagerly embraced the plan to disrupt the sailing of the *Bremen*.

On the night of the scheduled departure, a dozen tough seamen, Bailey among them, put on their best clothes to mix with the well-dressed passengers and guests who crowded the ship's decks. In their pockets, they had placed rosary beads and prayer books, to make a point to those who would later search them. Powerful floodlights illuminated the elegant throng, which included many Communists wearing rented tuxedos. On the dock below, a huge crowd of demonstrators carried anti-Nazi placards and yelled obscenities at the German crew. Suddenly, the protesters saw a small group of men run toward the mast that was flying the black swastika. "Whoever planned it," Bailey remembered, "had no idea of ships or the wrath of the crew, officers, and passengers." Instead of merely sneaking toward the bow, as had been planned, stealing the swastika, and bringing it ashore, where it would be burned in an anti-Hitler ceremony, the conspirators realized they had to fight through a cordon of angry German seamen and an obstacle course of six-foot seawalls. Bailey led the way. He managed to scale the mast and seize the flag in his hands. But, to his surprise, the lines held tight. While the sailors brawled beneath him, he pulled a knife from his pocket and cut the flag loose. To the cheers of onlookers, the black banner drifted into the water.

As Bailey descended the pole, however, he faced the fury of the German crew and passengers. Knocked to the ground, he saw a waiter's black patent-leather shoe smash at his stomach and then into his eye. The arrival of the police ended the riot, and they promptly arrested Bailey and five others, including another future Lincoln volunteer named William Howe. Beaten and bloody, the six then received more lumps from the police, who were surprised and then angered to find religious objects in their pockets. The judicial proceedings proved more sympathetic. Supported by the International Labor Defense, by the radical congressman Vito Marcantonio, and by a noisy, chanting crowd that filled the courtroom, the seamen exulted when Magistrate Louis Brodsky, a Jew, abruptly dismissed all charges. Calling the *Bremen* "a pirate ship," the judge denounced "the black flag of piracy . . . as a defiant challenge to society" and proceeded to attack the Nazi principles emblematized by the swastika. Two days later, the German government formally protested the decision, forcing Secretary of State Cordell Hull to apologize for Brodsky's remarks. Soon afterward, the German government declared the swastika to be the official national flag.

In July 1935, the same month as the *Bremen* demonstration, fascist aggression escalated when Mussolini announced his determination to annex

Ethiopia to the Italian empire. The Western powers, fearing a general war, offered formal diplomatic protests. But the American Popular Front, hoping to provoke a more resolute opposition, moved to mobilize anti-fascist sentiment, particularly among non-Communist blacks who sympathized with Ethiopia. Leading these efforts was the black Communist Harry Haywood, recently appointed section organizer in Chicago. Persuading diverse black leaders to discard their political differences, he helped create Chicago's Joint Committee for the Defense of Ethiopia. The coalition immediately announced plans to hold a "Hands Off Ethiopia" parade as well as a petition drive to request Congress to place an embargo on arms sales to Italy. Dramatizing the local issue was the refusal of Mayor Edward Kelly, who had recently received a medal from Mussolini, to grant a parade permit on the grounds that it would offend a "friendly power."

Despite the police ban, over 10,000 protesters, black and white, participated in the noisy "Hands Off Ethiopia" demonstration in August 1935. And when the Chicago Red Squad began making arrests, the militant anti-fascists relied on rooftop oratory to keep the protest going. Oliver Law, destined to become commander of the Lincoln battalion, spoke first, until the police dragged him to jail; then another speaker could be heard from a different rooftop, continuing the message. Haywood had a turn for about fifteen minutes, using his time to denounce Mayor Kelly for bringing Mussolini's tactics to Chicago. Then he felt a blow to the head and took a beating from the police. On the way to the station house, the officers sytematically pummeled his legs and knees with billy clubs. Haywood had to walk on crutches for a month. But he continued to denounce the war, rallying black support for the besieged African state.

After Italian armies invaded Ethiopia in October 1935, public protests intensified. That month, hundreds of Americans, including several future Lincoln volunteers, were arrested for participating in anti-fascist demonstrations outside Italian consulates around the country. At New York's City College, Wilfred Mendelson and 21 other students were expelled for protesting the appearance of a team of Italian aviators on campus. President Robinson, in ordering the expulsion, referred to the dissenters as "guttersnipes," and for months radical students wore lapel buttons on campus proclaiming, "I am a guttersnipe." (Mendelson was later killed in Spain.) Near the CCNY campus, in Harlem, Communist leaders formed a United Aid for Ethiopia committee, which gathered food and medical supplies. Dr. Arnold Donawa, former head of the Howard University Dental School, supported that group and later volunteered to serve in the medical corps in Spain. So did Salaria Kee, a nurse at Harlem Hospital, who helped initiate a fund-raising drive that sent a 75-bed field hospital to Ethiopia. Vaughn Love, the Harlem black activist, spoke of enlisting in the Ethiopian army, but, he later explained, "the contacts weren't good and the war didn't last long."

By December 1935, the fascist threat had brought twenty thousand angry protesters to New York's Madison Square Garden to demand that the United States boycott the 1936 Olympics, which were scheduled to open in Berlin the following July. Already, half a million Americans had signed petitions urging an alternative site, and newspapers ranging from the *New York Times* to Harlem's *Amsterdam News* had registered objections to U.S. participation. Four year earlier, just prior to the ascent of Hitler's national socialism, the International Olympics Committee had awarded the honor of hosting the games to the German capital. (Barcelona had been a close second choice.) Now, as the Nazi regime launched a reign of terror against labor unionists, Communists, Jews, Catholics, and other minorities, anti-fascists vociferously challenged the propriety of permitting the German chancellor to preside over the Olympic festivities. Disturbed by Nazi discrimination against non-Aryan athletes, the Amateur Athletic Union (AAU) formally opposed American participation in the Berlin games, unless Germany promised to end racial discrimination "in fact as well as in theory." Assurances from the American Olympics Committee failed to diminish these concerns. Fearful of endorsing an obviously totalitarian regime, a coalition of church leaders, college presidents, and trade unionists formed the Committee for Fair Play in Sports and demanded a boycott of Berlin.

Despite the clamor, an executive committee of the AAU voted narrowly to field an American team in Berlin. Harsh feelings remained, however, and the Committee for Fair Play continued to express dissatisfaction with the decision. Meanwhile, the Soviet Union announced its refusal to participate in the summer competition. (Four years earlier the Soviets had not even been invited to the Los Angeles Olympics.) After the election of Spain's left-wing Popular Front coalition in February 1936, the Catalonian government in Barcelona took the opportunity to announce an alternative sports competition—

"Olympiad Populaire," the People's Olympics— to protest the Berlin spectacle. Anti-fascists in America welcomed the prospect. When a formal invitation reached New York in May 1936, the Committee for Fair Play promptly mustered its resources to select ten amateur athletes to represent the United States.

The team, including seven track and field competitors, one swimmer, and two boxers, consisted of working-class youth who had been associated with labor union athletics and intramural sports in New York. The single college student, a Cornell heavyweight boxer named Irving Jenkins, was the son of a textile union employee. Three contestants were African Americans, including the team's only woman. But although the athletes were not political innocents, neither did they identify with the radical tradition of the 1930's. Among themselves, they never had political discussions, nor did they advocate any cause. Their sole common concern was to oppose the Nazi dictatorship. That these amateurs journeyed to Spain to register an anti-fascist protest revealed the intensity of political feelings in America on the eve of the Spanish war.

Bearing salutations from New York governor Herbert Lehman, Mayor Fiorello La Guardia, and the International Ladies Garment Workers Union, which sent three athletes, the American team embarked with minimal fanfare from New York on July 3, 1936. Accompanying them were the treasurer of the Committee for Fair Play, Francis Henson, who had worked previously for anti-fascist refugee organizations, and the coach, Alfred "Chick" Chakin, described as a "husky, blond young fellow." Once an intercollegiate wrestling champion at Cornell University (class of 1926), Chakin coached wrestling and taught in the hygiene department at New York's City College. He was also a member of the Communist party, the International Workers Order, and the teachers' union. "Chick is most interested in the Barcelona People's Olympics," reported the *Daily Worker*, "because he thinks these games will be a powerful demonstration against fascism." His team remembered him more as a strict coach who put them through their paces.

The Americans arrived in Barcelona on a Thursday, three days before the opening ceremonies, and spent the next day wandering through the Catalonian capital with the hungry eyes of summer tourists. On Saturday, they visited the city's newly furbished oval stadium and began working out. Formal speeches and introductions would commence the next morning, but the Americans already sensed a tension in the air. Passing through France on

Bastille Day, they had heard warnings of a possible revolution. "I didn't worry about it," recalled Dorothy Tucker, a sprinter representing the Ladies Garment Workers Union in New York. "We had no fear." But pre-competition nerves disturbed their sleep.

At dawn on Sunday, July 19, 1936, the tumult of war suddenly drilled through the walls of the Olympic Hotel. "The rumbling of cannon, several thousand machine guns and rifles and the sound of marching feet" were what black sprinter Frank Payton remembered of his rude awakening. The amateur athletes were the first Americans to become involved in the Spanish civil war. Peeking through the hotel windows, they could see workers tearing cobblestones from the streets to build barricades, but sporadic machine-gun fire forced them to keep their heads inside. When the shooting abated, two of the Americans dashed into the streets to find something to eat. Another went outside, grabbed a crowbar, and helped the Catalonians dismantle a roadway to build a defensive emplacement. "The workers of Spain immediately responded to the call of the government," reported Payton. "Socialists, Communists and unionists united to eradicate fascism. Women held barricades. Some women even led detachments of workers against the fascists." Francis Henson saw priests "shooting out of church windows at the people in the streets." Later, he visited churches that had served as arms depots for the rebels. Chick Chakin watched the militia ferret fascist snipers from their firing positions in the holy buildings. "Each time a nest of snipers was routed," he reported, "the church would be set ablaze."

As the insurrection commenced, a train carrying tourists and athletes to the Olympics halted just north of Barcelona. Aboard were teams from Hungary and Switzerland, as well as the American poet Muriel Rukeyser, sent there to cover the games for a London magazine. While the crowded train sat through a day and a night on the tracks, she watched the tense response to the outbreak of war. American tourists, she observed, talked nervously, constantly, until the sound of an unidentified airplane drew a terrified silence. "The speed and externality of every incident is unbelievable," she reported. "The terror and habit of guns and warning and fear descend on every system and are absorbed. All but the hatred of fascists, which increases." When a group of passengers visited the local mayor to express their support, however, he abruptly silenced their speeches. "No," he said. "No foreign nationals can intrude in revolutionary situations." On the second day of the war, Rukeyser rode by truck into Barcelona and saw the first scars of battle. Among the athletes, she noted, "the feeling is international and sympathetic. . . . The teams are arriving steadily, all with stories of a successful Popular Front in Catalonia."

During a lull in the fighting, the athletes obtained permission to visit the Olympic stadium, forming a "colorful procession" that mirrored the explosive anxiety in the streets. The sound of gunfire prevented the staging of any events. The contestants managed to return to their hotel, one of the American gymnasts reported, only because both sides tacitly agreed to "stop the war so that we can pass." But a French athlete was killed and his teammates decided to leave the country. The next day, the teams marched again through the streets, this time to demonstrate their support for the people's militia. As weary civilian-soldiers passed them on their way toward fascist-held Zaragoza, each team—Norwegian, Dutch, English, Belgian, German, Italian, Hungarian, and American—sang in its own language "The Internationale." At a second demonstration, the athletes wore black, reported Rukeyser, to honor "the fighting dead." These foreigners also received explicit instructions from their hosts: "You came to see games," declared one of the organizers of the event, "and have remained to witness the triumph of our People's Front. Now your task is clear; you will go back to your countries and spread through the world the news of what you have seen in Spain."

Although many competitors wished to hold the Olympics in defiance of the fascist uprising, the Catalonian government ordered their evacuation. Five days after the war began, Muriel Rukeyser, along with the American, Belgian, and Hungarian teams, embarked on the small Spanish ship *Ciudad de Ibiza* and sailed overnight, through fear of an Italian submarine attack, to Sète, the first port in France. A week later, they were back in New York. Those Americans who had witnessed the first fighting now rallied behind the Spanish Republic. Francis Henson, treasurer of the Committee for Fair Play, helped to organize the American Medical Bureau to Aid Spanish Democracy. Frank Payton, the black runner and basketball player, addressed a crowd of twenty thousand at Madison Square Garden, which raised $5,700 to send to the Republic. Irving Jenkins returned to Cornell and enlisted in the ROTC program, thinking of acquiring military experience that might be useful in Spain (later, his father dissuaded him from such thoughts).

Coach Chick Chakin, a decade older than his team, became a frequent speaker at fund-raising events in New York. Yet collecting money seemed to him insufficient commitment. "If they weren't class conscious before coming here," he remarked of the Olympic athletes in Barcelona, "they quickly became so when they saw the workers" stand against fascism. Chakin might have been speaking for himself. Haunted by the sight of people killed in the streets, he resolved to join the fight. His wife later recalled the anguish of the decision—her fear, his sense of obligation. She wanted to tell the doctors about his trick knee, which, she thought, made him unfit for service. But she respected his choice. By the following spring, Chakin had returned to Spain, a volunteer in the Lincoln brigade; the next winter, somewhere around Belchite, he was captured by the fascists and killed.

"The Spanish people dying on the barricades are defending our liberties and the peace of the world," the *Daily Worker* advised its left-wing readers soon after the outbreak of war. "They must get all the help we can give them." But while anti-fascists throughout Europe and America urged support of the Loyalists (those who had remained loyal to the Republic), diplomats in the European capitals agonized about the risk of a general war. In Spain's major cities—Madrid, Barcelona, Bilbao—the military insurrection had initially failed. But then, three weeks after the fighting commenced, German and Italian military forces began to intervene on Franco's side. The news triggered grave concern throughout the world about the possibility of escalation. Amidst such anxieties the British government decided to overlook fascist involvement in Spain. Pursuing the politics of appeasement, the Tory leadership adopted a policy of strict neutrality. France, led by Premier Léon Blum, dared not confront Hitler and Mussolini alone and followed the British lead. To further discourage British and French intervention, Italy and Germany cynically agreed to support a "Non-Intervention Committee" to prevent arms and military supplies from reaching either side, ostensibly to keep the war within Spanish borders. It was a scheme the fascist dictators had no intention of enforcing. The effect, however, was to prevent the Spanish Republic from obtaining the arms and supplies necessary to preserve its existence.

American policy, in this time of isolationism, proved no more "neutral" than the policies of the other Western powers. Since the election of Spain's leftist government the previous February, State Department officials had perceived the Republic as a threat to American investment and trade. Indeed, many American diplomats and businessmen viewed the shaky coalition of Republicans, Socialists, and Communists as something akin to Russia's Kerensky government of 1917, which had proved to be a harbinger of the more radical Bolshevik revolution. After the Franco rebellion began, the creation of an anti-fascist people's army composed of civilian militiamen and workers further alarmed American conservatives. When revolutionary workers in Barcelona spontaneously seized power and proceeded to confiscate some American corporate property (the Ford and General Motors assembly plants), Secretary of State Cordell Hull denounced the arming of "irresponsible members of left-wing political organizations." As early as August 1936, just weeks after the war commenced, State Department officials were prepared to support Franco over the Republic. As in Britain, this decision could be masked under the policy of nonintervention. Although American neutrality laws made no provisions for insurrections and civil wars, Washington ordered a "moral embargo" against the shipment of war materiel to either side of the Spanish conflict.

By the late summer of 1936, the Spanish Republic stood alone diplomatically, while Franco's armies were marching toward Madrid. At the end of August, however, the Soviet Union, which initially had agreed to respect the nonintervention arrangement, reversed its policy and cautiously began to send aid to the Republican side. By October, the first military shipments from the Soviet Union had arrived in Spain, paid for by half of the Republic's gold reserves. At the same time, the Comintern proposed the creation of a volunteer foreign army—an International Brigade—to strengthen Republican forces.

Despite the aloofness of the U.S. government, anti-fascists in America quickly organized public support for the Spanish Republic. Ten days after the war erupted, a high-level meeting of Communists, Socialists, labor leaders, and representatives of Spanish groups in America agreed to form the United Committee in Support of the Struggle Against Fascism in Spain. Three days later, they attracted twenty thousand supporters to an open-air rally at New York's Union Square, a meeting that carefully balanced a program of Communist and Socialist orators. Meanwhile, two prominent unions, David Dubinsky's International Ladies Garment Workers Union and Sidney Hillman's Amalgamated Clothing Workers, cabled $10,000 to aid the Republic. Dubinsky, an avowed anti-Communist, served as treasurer of "Labor's Red Cross for Spain," which soon had to change its name to "Trade Union Relief for Spain" because the State Department forbade the use of the words "Red Cross." By October 1936, he had dispersed over $100,000. "There is no civil war in Spain," he asserted the following year. "It is an invasion of a democratic country by hostile forces of fascism and Nazism as part of a plan to subdue workers in every land. American labor cannot ignore this threat to itself."

By the fall of 1936, about a thousand foreigners had made their way into the Republican ranks. Among them were a handful of Americans. One was a seaman named Ed Scheddin, who jumped ship to join the Spanish militia. "I am . . . a soldier in the Workers' army," he wrote to his comrades aboard the SS *Exeter*. "I will carry on in the best proletarian manner. . . . I leave tomorrow for the front. You guys carry on the good work in the States." He was never heard from again. Another American was a mining engineer named Leo Fleischman, a resident of Madrid, who entered the Republican army the day after the insurrection and died in a munitions factory explosion in October. In the United States, the Spanish consulate in New York reported that over 200 men had volunteered to join the Republican army; all applicants were rejected, however, because military recruitment by a foreign power violated American law.

Ignoring the administration's "moral" embargo against sending assistance to Spain, private citizens continued to raise funds for supplies and medical aid. The North American Committee to Aid Spanish Democracy, another Popular Front organization that attracted Communists and Christians alike, opened a warehouse in New York to collect canned goods, clothing, and medical supplies. Young radicals thronged to the crusade. Some drove trucks around New York gathering old clothes; others rattled collection cans on the subways. And in Times Square, a young soprano named Ethel Rosenberg sang "Tango de las Rosas" and "Ay-ay-ay," while her husband Julius and some friends held the four corners of a Republican flag and collected coins and dollar bills. At a mass meeting in Madison Square Garden, twenty thousand cheering spectators donated $15,000 in cash and pledged $10,000 more. "The legality of the [Spanish] government is stressed again and again," observed James Benét, who described the rally for the *New Republic*, "and chafes the crowd, which is largely radical and not accustomed to pay much homage to a government merely because it is legal. They have known the law when it did not mean justice, and the best thing most of them would say for legality is that it is a tactical advantage." Benét, a Stanford University graduate who would become a truck driver in Spain, also reported that many in the crowd "feel (for they called out so during the collection) that the money should be going for arms instead of supplies."

Washington remained impervious to such suggestions. Although a State Department study, released after the war had ended, claimed that American neutrality did not intend to "aid one or the other factions" in the Spanish struggle, hostility to the leftist Republic certainly influenced the administration's foreign policy. Ironically, petitions from American Communists only reinforced prejudices against Spain's Popular Front government. Thus the Roosevelt administration worked aggressively in the fall of 1936 to enforce the moral embargo, blocking the transshipment of American aircraft through Mexico to Spain. In a widely publicized case involving a so-called "Jersey City junk dealer" named Robert Cuse, the State Department endeavored to thwart the sale of second-hand planes to the Republic. The transaction was "thoroughly legal," President Roosevelt admitted, "but [an] unpatriotic act."

Determined to stop this particular sale, the White House rushed to support stricter congressional legislation. The Spanish Embargo Act, passed hastily in January 1937, curtailed the president's discretionary power to permit arms sales to either belligerent; the United States would make no distinction between the legal government and the rebels. Only Congressman John T. Bernard of Minnesota's Farmer-Labor party voted against the measure; and the near unanimity of opinion in Congress was mirrored by the absence of significant debate in the American press. One last shipment to the Spanish Republic managed to leave New York harbor aboard the *Mar Cantabrico* before the statutory deadline, but Franco's navy eventually intercepted the vessel. The embargo, intended by Congress to protect the United States from being drawn further into the conflict, served in the end to reinforce the flawed nonintervention policy of the European powers. Moreover, the State Department proved less than vigorous in enforcing the "no credit" provisions of the trading laws. Despite government fines, for example, the Texas Oil Company provided long-term credit for petroleum sales to the fascist side. Other companies, such as Firestone, developed complicated credit arrangements to remain within the letter of the law. Such schemes reflected a widespread suspicion among American businessmen about the reliability of Spain's leftist government.

*

In the face of this corporate and government opposition, American anti-fascists struggled to awaken the nation's conscience about Spain. Like the ill-fated People's Olympics, the "Hands Off Ethiopia" campaign, and the *Bremen* demonstration, such efforts often proved to be sagas of courage and failure. But however much the American public resisted the warnings about fascism, the crusade illuminated an alternative consciousness in the age of isolationism. American citizens did not have to read the *Daily Worker* to know about Nazi racism or to discover the atrocities committed by Italian bombers in Ethiopia or to appreciate Franco's anti-democratic agenda; but if they desired to express their objections in a political fashion, their options remained limited. Those who came to the Communist party's Popular Front in the middle years of the 1930's perceived accurately the threat of fascist policies; that in the crisis they aligned with Communists testified less to their naiveté or malevolence than to the failure of mainstream politics to address the most important international issues of the decades.

5

The Tomb of Fascism

As word of recruitment for the International Brigades began to filter through the American Communist network in the autumn of 1936, large numbers of volunteers came forward to enlist. The party's organizing committee soon realized that its responsibility had shifted. Instead of having to locate a few trusted volunteers to send to Spain, they now had to worry about screening any undesirable elements from the diverse recruits who were offering their services. In this unique military crusade, symbolic of the unity of the international working classes, party leaders wanted to exclude mere adventurers who lacked a political understanding of the anti-fascist struggle. They also feared that government or enemy spies might attempt to subvert the project. The party insisted on secrecy, therefore, not because Communists harbored a devious conspiracy to overthrow a government—after all, they always boasted of their initiatives on behalf of the Spanish Republic—but because party leaders did not wish to be caught violating American recruitment laws. In any event, the leadership decided that each volunteer would have to be interviewed personally by a special committee.

One of the first applicants to face interrogation was Morris Maken, a lanky, dark-haired, Brooklyn-born 28-year-old printer who always looked like he needed a shave. Outspoken and gloomy, Maken possessed an acerbic wit that thrived on deflating pomposity. A recent convert from the Socialist ranks, he had joined the Communist party the previous year, anxious to participate in the class revolution. "They seemed very active," he later remarked in explanation of his motives, "very militant, very clear-headed." Upon learning of the International Brigades, Maken approached organizer William Lawrence and inquired about enlistment. Lawrence, in turn, asked Maken why he wanted to go to Spain. He replied that he "just didn't like Hitler and . . . wanted a chance to do something about it." Maken recalled that Lawrence "seemed to be satisfied with that sort of passionate attitude." Then the recruit was ordered to appear before a committee of three military "experts": Fred Brown, an Italian-born Comintern official from the American party's central committee who had served in World War I; Paul Crosbie, a war veteran from an old-stock family in Queens, New York, whose announcement of his conversion to communism in the 1920's had resulted in his expulsion from the American Legion; and Allan Johnson, formerly an officer in the U.S. Army. They asked first if Maken knew what he was getting himself into; the volunteer replied that he had served briefly in a National Guard unit in Brooklyn at the age of eighteen. At that point, Allan Johnson suddenly shouted: "Attention!" Maken snapped to attention. "Left face!" cried Johnson; Maken obeyed. "So I guess I passed with flying colors." concluded the cynical recruit. "That demonstrated I had real professional military experience."

Maken's sarcasm hardly exaggerated the case. Although the recruiters initially rejected volunteers without military training, the standards were soon lowered considerably. A survey of 1,745 American volunteers made in July 1937 shows that only 34 percent (including 45 war veterans) had formal military experience; another 23 percent had perhaps handled a gun; and 42 percent had no military experience at all. A few Lincoln volunteers went into action without ever having fired a shot. André Marty, the haughty head of the International Brigades, came to despise the American soldiers because of their lack of training and criticized the U.S. party leadership for failing to recruit better troops.

Medical examinations were equally perfunctory. One volunteer went to Spain with a metal knee brace; another was blind in one eye. Still another served in combat with a wooden leg! (It was discovered when a machine-gun bullet shattered the "limb.") A few reached Spain with chronic illnesses, such as asthma, that made them unfit for any service. But those were the exceptions. Most American volunteers were better fed and consequently healthier than their European counterparts.

Contrary to claims later made by anti-Communist critics, moreover, no official in the Communist party ever ordered *anyone* to go to Spain. There were no exceptions to that rule. "On this issue," party organizer Edward Bender explained forcefully, recruitment was "purely voluntary." Personal ambition within the party, the desire for prestige, peer pressure, ideological conviction—these, of course, might play a motivating role; so much so, in fact, that sometimes party leaders explicitly told volunteers that for political reasons they could *not* go to Spain. Indeed, as Maken conceded, Lawrence and Bender interviewed recruits with plain honesty. "Spain," Bender recalled repeating, "would be no picnic"; there would be much hardship and death.

Nonetheless, as Bender also admitted, "none of us really had any military knowledge." Standards of acceptance varied considerably. The recruiters rejected some applicants because of their youth, others because of an adventurist spirit that might compromise the mission. The best recommendation remained a good word from trusted Communist party officials. Bender later estimated the acceptance rate at 95 percent.

Secrecy remained a high priority. Fearful that government spies would attempt to block the sailing of a military brigade, party leaders gave the volunteers minimal information about their plans. Only after the recruits had passed their interviews did they receive instructions about passports. Although the State Department had not yet banned travel to Spain—that decision would follow passage of the Embargo Act in January 1937—the committee advised the recruits to provide false information about their destinations. Some claimed to be visiting relatives; others called themselves tourists, geologists, even Alpine hikers. Bill Bailey, notorious for his "dese" and "dose" speech, wrote that he was a "studen"; to his embarrassment, a friendly passport officer added the missing "t," approved his request, and then advised him "to keep your head down." Some volunteers, unable to obtain passports, used false names or borrowed papers. (Morris Maken, to his surprise, learned that his birth name was Mickenberg, and he now adopted that as his nom de guerre.) After the

Spanish war, only one person was charged with violating American passport laws—he was never formally indicted—but two decades later, during the Red Scare of the 1950's, the matter of perjured statements became a common accusation against veterans of the Lincoln brigade.

Party leaders also gave the recruits a list of necessary supplies, all army regulation, and advised the volunteers to visit army-navy surplus stores to purchase vintage World War I uniforms and boots. The men received their travel tickets from the World Tourist Travel Agency, which usually handled bookings for Communist leaders. In most cases, the party paid the fare, receiving reimbursements from the Spanish Republic. Lastly, the committee provided each recruit with an inexpensive suitcase—failing to realize that identical baggage would belie the men's claims to be traveling alone!

These details slowed the operation, but the main reason for delay was the need for final approval of the mission by Comintern officials in Europe. Meanwhile, the eighty-odd recruits convened several nights a week at various hired halls, such as the Manhattan Lyceum, the Finnish Workers' Hall, or the Spartacus Club. The party committee appointed the first military commander, the thickset James Harris, an ex–army officer who claimed to have served with the Red Army in China. With a penchant for harsh speech, he led the men through parade drills, using broomsticks to substitute for rifles. Most volunteers later viewed such charades as utterly worthless. Weeks passed. One night, the men noticed a police car parked outside and hastily hid all their money, passports, and papers. Amid mounting fear of a raid, they learned that the cops were merely visiting the hall manager. A few days later, to everyone's disappointment, Bill Lawrence announced that the mission had been cancelled; no one knew why. Mickenberg kept pestering him for information. Finally, in early December, Lawrence announced the welcome news: "This is it."

"How do you know this is it?" asked the inquisitive Mickenberg.

"The Comintern wants men now," said Lawrence.

On Christmas Day 1936, one day before sailing, the excited men gathered for a formal farewell. Party ritual prevailed; the volunteers listened to interminable speeches. George Bidarian, an abrasive World War I veteran who had served on the organizing committee, began by introducing Phil Bard, a painter and former head of the Artists' Union, and announced that he would serve as their political leader. Bard, a newcomer in their midst, hardly spoke;

the men had to wonder about his qualifications. But Fred Brown, representing the Comintern, presented an impassioned address about halting the fascist advance toward Madrid. Then Ralph Bates, the English novelist who had
witnessed the earliest fighting of the war, described the courage of the Spanish people and extolled the role of the party and the Soviet Union. He also
assured the men, as recruit William Herrick recalled, that "we were going
there to fight for the bourgeois democracy, at which point he winked, with the
understanding [that] we were going to fight for the Communist party." Finally,
Earl Browder himself came forward, exhorting the volunteers to uphold international solidarity. When he finished, the party chairman shook hands with
each man. That night, the volunteers made farewells to family and friends,
and the next afternoon, delayed four hours by unfavorable tides, the *Normandie* slipped down the cold, gray narrows, past the Statue of Liberty, and headed
toward Le Havre with 86 American volunteers aboard.

While Communist party leaders moved clandestinely to prepare the military contingent, a small group of politically concerned physicians was meeting quietly in a private home in New York to organize medical assistance for
the Republic. Inspired by the visit of a delegation from Spain, the doctors
announced the formation of another Popular Front organization, which they
called the American Medical Bureau to Aid Spanish Democracy, in October
1936. Quickly gaining endorsements from prominent physicians and medical
educators around the country, the bureau launched a fund-raising campaign
to send ambulances and medical supplies to the Republic. The public response exceeded all expectations. Within three months, the bureau had raised
several hundred thousand dollars, enough for twenty tons of supplies, which
ranged from safety pins and gauze to a battery-equipped operating room. Encouraged by such wide support, the doctors resolved to undertake a bolder
project: the establishment of a fully equipped American hospital in Spain,
along with a staff of physicians, nurses, pharmacists, technicians, and drivers.

The largest problem proved to be not money, but finding personnel who
were willing to abandon their practices for the uncertainties of the war zone.
Heading the search was Dr. Edward K. Barsky, a tall, handsome, charis-
matic graduate of Columbia University and surgeon at Beth Israel Hospital in
New York. Famous for his humanitarianism, Barsky also had strong political

leanings. "This is a battle not only against invaders," he would later state in Spain, "but also against the world onslaught of fascism of Hitler and Mussolini." Barsky had not intended to make the trip. But when no one else with suitable administrative skills appeared, he accepted what seemed an inevitable decision. "Somehow all at once I realized that I had been eager to go from the start," he later recalled. "Perhaps in some deep part of my mind I had known that I would go all along. Yet for days I could not get over my sense of surprise."

With similar muted enthusiasm, an experienced head nurse named Fredericka Martin agreed to lead the nursing team. "Someone from the nurses union asked me if I would be willing . . . to leave my pleasant rut," she recalled, "and, of course, I was." Finding sufficient recruits, however, proved difficult. A widowed nurse named Lini Fuhr, then a graduate student in public health at Columbia, tried to enlist sympathetic colleagues, but when the number remained small she volunteered herself. "I felt I *had* to go," she recalled, justifying leaving her own child behind, "to play my little part toward shaping a decent world."

A few weeks earlier, a nurse named Salaria Kee—"a slender chocolate colored girl," according to the black poet Langston Hughes—had offered her skills to the American Red Cross to help flood victims in her native Ohio. "They told me they had no place for me," she remembered, "that the color of my skin would make me more trouble than I'd be worth to them." When she repeated the story to a friend, the response was: "Why not Spain?" So she enrolled.

"What! You're going to Spain in wartime," her friends in Harlem exclaimed in amazement. "And alone?"

"Sure," Salaria answered. "I wasn't born twins. I have to go alone."

Barsky, however, was less than eager to accept another woman volunteer, a spunky, petite, delicately featured 27-year-old named Evelyn Hutchins, who offered her services as a driver. An impassioned feminist, she had dared on many occasions to challenge the men who denied her equality, and she would not hesitate to put her life in danger to prove she was as good as any man. Born in 1910 in Snohomish, Washington, a small lumbering town near Everett, she was just a child when her parents separated. Because her mother had to earn a living, Evelyn was left alone with a younger brother much of the time. Once, one of her mother's boyfriends sexually assaulted her. But the appearance of a steady stepfather when she was eight introduced Evelyn to a stable, if untypical, family life. Her new father was a militant stevedore, blacklisted for participating in a bitter West Coast maritime strike during World War I; her mother was an outspoken suffragette. Early in life, maybe too early, she said, Evelyn had learned to value her independence. "I always had to shift for myself and take care of myself and make my own decisions, and sometimes it would be tough on me," she recalled. After the family moved to New York, Evelyn quit high school and then left home at the age of eighteen to become a professional dancer. "I wanted to be independent," she said, even though her desire accentuated the difficulties she would face. "I was always told . . . that I must not do this or . . . that because girls don't do those things. I was told so many times that girls are inferior to men, that men can do things and girls can't, and I couldn't take it. I didn't care how hard it was on me."

Hutchins's dancing career ended soon after the Depression began, her troupe a casualty of cancelled bookings. She had to accept sleazy dates in burlesque clubs in order to eat. She even considered prostitution, among other dismal jobs. So she had plenty of reasons to listen when radical street orators spoke about economic exploitation. Still, her political position always reflected intense feminist priorities. "I remember when Mussolini issued a decree," she later remarked. "I was just a kid at the time—he issued a decree that women were not to wear short skirts, and that they were to keep their proper places. . . . I was convinced that anybody with that kind of attitude was absolutely no good for the people generally." For over a decade, Mussolini's edicts had stuck in her craw. "I never felt that I was an outstanding genius," she explained, "but people had to give me a chance to think and develop whatever think-abilities I had." She expressed similar revulsion at the Nazi policy of using women as breeders of racially superior stock. "That strikes at my very most innermost desire for freedom and self-expression," Hutchins explained. "Just being an ordinary human being I couldn't tolerate a thing like that." Although Hutchins had married in September 1936, she never allowed her domestic arrangements to interfere with her political commitments.

When Hutchins and her husband, Carl Rahman, volunteered to drive ambulances, however, Dr. Barsky replied disingenuously that chauffeurs also needed skill in automobile repairs, for which only Rahman was qualified. "I explained to them that unfortunately we were only in a position to take one," he remembered. "I didn't want to say outright that we wouldn't take a woman unless she were a nurse." On grounds of mechanical skills, however, even Hutchins admitted that her husband would be "more important." He joined the American Medical Bureau without her. But Hutchins continued to seek another way to get to Spain. "I thought it over very carefully," she remembered, "and decided they were wrong." Indeed, she raised such a storm against "male chauvinism"—the phrase originated in the Communist lexicon—that party leaders changed their minds and allowed her to volunteer. It was too late, however, for her to accompany Barsky's unit.

By mid-January 1937, the medical team was almost ready: five doctors, eight nurses, a druggist, a bacteriologist, two ambulance drivers, and a translator. But the night before the planned departure, the bureau was still short $3,000; so they threw one final party and reached their goal. Then they spent the remainder of the night packing and crating the supplies. Amidst the confusion, someone at the last minute handed Barsky a small box containing six grams of morphine, and as the *Ile de France* sailed through New York harbor, the doctor found himself worrying about how he would bring the drugs through customs.

"When the crisis broke," remembered the Communist volunteer Saul Wellman with pride, "we were ready." The speed with which the American Communist party assumed leadership in directing personnel and material aid to Republican Spain reflected its apocalyptic ideology: since the Bolshevik revolution, Communist dialectics had predicted an inevitable war against the forces of reaction. To Communists like Wellman, therefore, the rise of fascism was neither unexpected nor insurmountable. Communism had provoked its fascist antithesis; now the legions of the proletariat would fight to defend their class interests.

But although the Communist party continued to control the passage of most American volunteers to Spain, the flexibility of the Popular Front encouraged Socialists and other progressives to serve in the ranks. At the beginning, these non-Communists constituted a small minority, but enough eventually reached Spain to contradict the idea that the American units represented a Comintern monolith. The most detailed surviving roster of 1,745 American volunteers lists 999 members of the Communist party and 249 members of the Young Communist League, amounting to approximately 72 percent of the total. About 25 percent of the volunteers claimed no political affiliation. The Communists' numerical dominance reflected the party's organizational zeal and its distinct ideological position; unlike other radical groups, the Communist party was militantly anti-fascist and international in scope.

Other American radicals, to be sure, made their way to Spain. One, a native New Yorker named Justus Kates, departed alone in November 1936 and fought with the anarchist militia on the Huesca front; another, eighteen-year-old Douglas Stearns, served with a Trotskyist group before transferring to the anarchist "Battalion of Death." A few Italian-American anarchists also fought for the Spanish Republic. More prominent was Humberto Galleani, a 49-year-old refugee from Mussolini's regime and editor of the New York–based Socialist newspaper *Il Stampa*; he served with the Italian Garibaldi battalion outside Madrid.

In December 1936, the Socialist party also announced plans to field an American battalion in Spain. Magazine advertisements invited contributions for a 500-man Eugene V. Debs column, suggesting only the need to raise money to pay for its transportation. But such statements exaggerated the case. Although individual Socialists responded to the appeal and volunteered to fight, there were never enough to create a significant force. One recruit was Durward Clark, an experienced truck driver from New York. Having seen newsreel footage of Spanish women fighting in the trenches, he resolved to join the Debs battalion. Approaching the Socialist party's San Francisco office, he had no trouble enlisting, but then he waited for weeks without instructions; finally, he took a bus to New York on his own. Still unable to obtain information, Clark paid his own fare to Paris. But no Socialist organization existed there to help him. Finally, he followed a group of Italian recruits in a taxi to the Communist party headquarters, where he entered the International Brigades. Clark would eventually become the head of the American transport section (the Regiment de Tren).

One American Communist later claimed that of the 25 Debs volunteers in Spain, 18 were Communist sympathizers who had joined the Socialist ranks "for united front purposes"; 2 were Socialist party members; and 2 other "nonaffiliated comrades . . . state openly they are ashamed to have come with the so-called Debs Battalion." Most of the Socialists who reached Spain, like Durward Clark, simply entered the Communist-led ranks. Among them was Hans Amlie, the brother of the Wisconsin Progressive congressman Thomas Amlie. A mining engineer who had served as a sergeant in the U.S. Army during World War I, Amlie was so disgusted at the failure of the Socialists to build a fighting force that he took the occasion of an official visit to Spain by the Socialist party's Sam Baron to quit that organization and become a Communist. Other Socialist volunteers, such as Hilliard Bernstein, leader of the Workers Alliance in Virginia, reaffirmed their commitment to a common cause, the Popular Front: "I, the Socialist," he asserted, "had come to Spain to fight for the democratically-elected government against fascism."

When Communist leaders compared the Spanish struggle to the American Civil War, avowing that "Spain faces its Gettysburg," they spoke the language of the Popular Front. But even non-Communist liberals found the historical analogy compelling. "Tall as Lincoln, gaunt as Lincoln," wrote Ernest Hemingway, Major Milton Wolff was "as brave and as good a soldier as any that commanded battalions at Gettysburg." Such language enabled Americans to define the Spanish war in familiar terms: the Lincoln brigade was fighting to protect a government of the people. Equally important, the idea that the Spanish civil war involved an illegal rebellion against the standing government, like the South seceding from the Union, rather than an international war enabled anti-fascists of all political colors to criticize Roosevelt's policy of neutrality; on technical grounds, the United States should have supported the legal Republic. Significantly, Americans who supported Franco often drew alternative analogies to the conservative Founding Fathers and the war for American independence. ("Any democratic, liberty-loving American who cherishes the memory of George Washington," declared the Reverend M. D. Forrest, "must, with equal or greater reason, admire and praise General Franco.") Such patriotic appeals revealed both ignorance and ingenuity; in this isolationist decade, the public's interest in foreign affairs demanded a local touch.

The idiom of the Popular Front thus concealed—deliberately—the international forces that motivated Communist strategy in the 1930's. But at the same time Communist party leaders spoke in an authentic vernacular. Most American radicals saw in Spain not the fulfillment of the Communist Manifesto, but something akin to Lincoln's notion of an elected government. Indeed, the ideology of the Popular Front explicitly played down the revolutionary nature of the Spanish Republic, viewing the more radical Spanish anarchists and Trotskyists as threats to political stability. "The revolution that is taking place in our country," declared Dolores Ibarruri, "is the bourgeois democratic revolution . . . , and we communists are the front-line fighters in the struggle against the obscurantist forces of the past." For those reasons, the writer George Orwell would later condemn the antirevolutionary role of the Communist party, its thwarting of radical social change in the course of the military struggle to defeat Franco. But Communists feared, correctly as it turned out, that a truly revolutionary movement in Spain would so horrify the capitalist powers in Britain, France, and the United States, not to mention those inside Spain, that these conservative forces would prefer to see the fascists triumph on the battlefields. Americans went to Spain, in other words, not to accelerate social revolution but to stabilize it. That is why the language of anti-fascism appealed so readily to radicals and liberals alike.

"For the first time in history," wrote a volunteer named Gene Wolman, shortly before his death in battle, "for the first time since Fascism began systematically throttling and rending all we hold dear—we are getting the opportunity to fight back. Mussolini rode unopposed . . . to Rome. Hitler boasts that he took power without bloodshed. . . . In little Asturias the miners made a brave, but unsuccessful stand against the combined reactionaries of Spain. In Ethiopia the Fascist machine was again able to work its will without any unified opposition. Even in Democratic America the majority have had to undergo every sort of oppression without being able to fight back. . . . Here finally," Wolman exclaimed, "the oppressed of the Earth are united, here finally we have weapons, here we can fight back. Here, even if we lose, . . . in the fight itself, in the weakening of Fascism, we will have won."

Another volunteer, Wallace Burton, was a veteran of World War I and the French Foreign Legion when he went to Spain. In Albacete, the American training base, he encountered the California-born correspondent of the *Moscow News*, Millie Bennett, who had once had an affair with his identical twin brother. The two had a brief fling before Burton moved to the Aragon front. Bennett, who had a reputation for wildness, asked Burton how he could tolerate the discipline required of a good Communist soldier. "I would have been here regardless of my political affiliations," he replied from the trenches outside Belchite, "because a war is a break in the monotonous economic system, because I detest Fascism in theory, Mussolini and Hitler in particular, monarchy, clerical supremacy, landowners with feudal ideas, and the idea that Hitler and Mussolini might possibly obtain another part of the world to foster their silly [ideas] on." As for Communist theory, he said, "the party is making use of the world-wide sentiment against Fascism to fight its main enemy just as many people whose only desire is to protect Democracy [are] working with the Party. Most people here," Burton concluded, "believe the defeat of Fascism is the most important thing regardless of political future desires." Three weeks later, he too was dead.

Burton, Wolman, Amlie; even party leaders like Earl Browder, William Lawrence, or Harry Haywood—all understood that the Spanish war encapsulated a world crisis that would affect all nations, all people. If the fascist dictators could be stopped in Spain, then perhaps history could continue to unfold toward what they believed would be an inevitable conclusion: the ultimate revolution of the proletariat. That is why Soviet leader Josef Stalin and the Comintern were prepared to sacrifice the revolutionary impulse of the Spanish peasants and working classes; the Popular Front demanded a temporary truce. And to Communists everywhere the alternative appeared to be much worse: If the fascist dictators triumphed in Spain, where or when could they be stopped? As Hyman Katz wrote to his Jewish mother in New York, "If we sit by and let [the fascists] grow stronger by taking Spain, they will . . . not stop there, and it won't be long before they get to America. . . . If I permitted such a time to come . . . all I could do then would be to curse myself and say, 'Why didn't I wake up when the alarm-clock rang?'" The American volunteers thus embraced the Spanish Republic's most fervent promise: "Madrid will be the tomb of fascism."

6

The Politicization of Culture

When a Communist addresses an international conference," wrote the French novelist André Malraux in an attempt to galvanize support for the Spanish Republic, "he puts his fist down on the table. When a fascist addresses an international conference, he puts his feet on the table. A Democrat—be he American, English, or French—when he addresses an international conference, scratches his head, and asks questions." Scornful of such liberal inhibitions, Malraux had abandoned mere pen at the outbreak of the Spanish war to help organize the Republican air forces. (His military adventures would inform the novel *Man's Hope*.) During the spring of 1937, Malraux proceeded to visit the United States, seeking aid for Spain. "It is good that writers and artists have their share of responsibility here," he told a New York gathering of intellectuals who had raised funds to send an ambulance to the Republic, "so that this swelling tide of democratic voices may be the roar which comes from the other side of the ocean to muffle the dull noise of human suffering."

Spain in wartime captured the passion and the professional interest of the finest writers of the decade, most of whom were not content to scratch their heads. A survey of prominent American authors found them nearly unanimous in support of the Republic; only the Californian elitist Gertrude Atherton endorsed General Franco. Besides publicly expressing their opinions, writers from the "democracies" flocked to Spain to bear witness to the most dramatic struggle of the age. From England came the poets W. H. Auden and Stephen Spender; the youthful writers John Cornford and Julian Bell, both killed in battle; and, most famous subsequently, George Orwell, who was wounded on the Aragon front and returned home to write the bitter *Homage to Catalonia*, which depicted the suppression of a people's revolution in Barcelona by the Spanish Communist party. The French writer Antoine de Saint-Exupéry flew into Barcelona in 1936, accompanied a contingent of anarchists to the Madrid front as correspondent for *L'Intransigeant*, and reported the horror of fascist bombardment of innocent civilians. His compatriot Simone Weil volunteered to provide medical assistance, "with notions of sacrifice," but soon recoiled from the sheer waste of life.

Ernest Hemingway, foremost of his generation of American novelists, sailed to his beloved Spain in the spring of 1937, assuring inquisitive reporters that he wanted to "see what the boys are doing with the new toys they've been given since the last war." Already Hemingway had offered generous support to the Republic, paying the passage of two military volunteers, arranging for the purchase of ambulances, and working on a documentary propaganda film, *Spain in Flames*. Believing that the Spanish war would be "a dress rehearsal for the inevitable European war," he promised to write "anti-war war correspondence" to keep the United States out of the conflict "when it comes." He also collaborated with Dutch filmmaker Joris Ivens and cameraman John Ferno in preparing another documentary film, *The Spanish Earth*.

"I was in Paris in 1937, a year when 'Not Valid for Travel in Spain' was stamped across American passports," remembered the literary journalist Dorothy Parker, who wanted to assess the war firsthand. "So I went to our embassy to see what I might do to have my passport so altered that I might visit Spain." There she encountered "the most courteous young man in the world," who provided the appropriate counsel. But as she was about to leave, he inquired, "by the way," which side Parker intended to visit, and when she replied, "the Loyalist [Republican] side," he added: "But, of course, you'd have much more fun on the Franco side." Such political indifference, typical of official American attitudes during the war, intensified the frustration of intellectuals who sympathized with the Republic.

"If Fascism creeps across Spain, across Europe, and then across the world," warned the black poet Langston Hughes in a radio broadcast beamed from Madrid to the United States, "there will be no place left for intelligent young Negroes at all. In fact no decent place left for any Negroes—because Fascism preaches the creed of Nordic supremacy and a world for whites alone." Similar sentiments were voiced in the writings of numerous American observers of the war: Theodore Dreiser, Lillian Hellman, Josephine Herbst, even John Dos Passos, who later criticized the Republican effort after the Communists executed one of his friends.

In the baking heat of July 1937, the American writer Malcolm Cowley, who had disavowed the expatriate tradition in his influential memoir *Exile's Return*, now journeyed back to Europe to attend an International Writers Congress that was held in Valencia and Madrid to assert the intellectuals' sympathy for the Republic. "Spain is fighting international fascism," he wrote to the *New Republic*. "In that sense she is fighting for us all." Shocked by the wanton destruction of defenseless cities, Cowley lamented this "new kind of warfare, without reason, without honor, a blind malice." He also recorded his disgust at American consular officials who blocked his adoption of a Spanish orphan he wished to bring to the safety of the United States.

Why did so many intellectuals venture into Spain?

"Undoubtedly the famous egotism of the writer, his mental habit of writing himself into dramatic experience, partly accounts for this step," observed the novelist Ralph Bates, a tall, lean Englishman who had served as political leader of the Anglo-American Fifteenth Brigade and could speak authoritatively to the League of American Writers in 1937. "But more than this is our sense of sharing the responsibility for the war. Those writers who have spread democratic ideas are really responsible for the fact that hundreds of thousands are now dead because they refused to live under fascism."

The literary observers thus struggled to translate the ordeal of war to an American audience; their battlefield was the American mind on the home front. When Hemingway described his visit with an American casualty named Robert Raven, a former student at the University of Pittsburgh who had been blinded in a grenade attack, the novelist stressed the relevance of the struggle to American readers. "It still isn't you that gets hit," advised Hemingway, "but it is your countryman now. Your countryman from Pennsylvania, where once we fought at Gettysburg." Returning to the United States, Hemingway addressed the Writers' Congress at Carnegie Hall in 1937 and spoke about the moral stakes of the war: "A writer who will not lie cannot live and work under fascism," he said. He also arranged for a White House screening of *The Spanish Earth*, which was received appreciatively by both Franklin and Eleanor Roosevelt, though it did not lead to a change in the administration's noninterventionist policies. Hemingway then embarked on a fund-raising tour of Hollywood, collecting donations to buy and equip twenty ambulances. Three more times he would return to Spain under siege, gathering on each occasion the facts and insight that would inform what many consider his greatest novel, *For Whom the Bell Tolls*.

Even before Ernest Hemingway had journeyed to Spain and André Malraux had crossed the Atlantic in the opposite direction to address artists and writers in New York, numerous American intellectuals had responded more literally to the Spanish battle cry. Among the volunteers of the Lincoln brigade, a surprisingly large number were creative people—writers, artists, musicians, or young men and women who showed artistic promise and ambition. Thirty-five members of New York's Artists' Union, including their first president, fought for the Spanish Republic (half of them died in the war). Their commitment to Spain expressed an important dimension of their generation's politicization, the blending of aesthetic energy with radical beliefs. Like other hard-pressed workers, these writers and artists had learned their trade in the struggles of the Great Depression.

Radical intellectuals of the 1930's first discovered a collective identity in the Communist party's John Reed Clubs, which had been founded in 1929. Inviting "writers, artists, sculptors, musicians, and dancers of revolutionary tendencies," the organization planned, so the party stated, "to assist in the development of a proletarian culture . . . to inspirit the workers, to interpret and publicize the events of the class struggle, to take active part in the assault upon capitalism." In classes, exhibitions, and readings, the John Reed Clubs reaffirmed the basic Marxist assumption that all creative work inevitably reflected the material conditions of its production. Typical of this attitude was the work of Phil Bard, a slender, soft-spoken New York painter who became the political leader of the first American volunteers in Spain. A founding member of the John Reed Club while still in his early twenties, Bard had also won a competition to design murals for the offices of the *Daily Worker*. His paintings, which covered over 500 square feet, illustrated the prevailing aesthetic subjects: "Capitalism in the USA"; "Hunger, War, and Fascism"; "Building Socialism in the Soviet Union"; and "Revolt of the Farmers." During the three months he labored on his murals, Bard proved his commitment to proletarian values by altering his paintings to comply with the spontaneous criticism of the workers in the newsroom.

For such artists, politics and aesthetics remained inextricably interwoven. But with surging unemployment, creative workers needed more than artistic sympathy. In 1933, the Reed Clubs formally appealed for government patronage of public art to provide jobs for starving artists. That year, Bard helped create an Unemployed Artists' Group, which obtained federal and state money for needy painters, sculptors, and graphic artists. In 1934, when the group became the Artists' Union, membership grew to 700 and doubled again the next year. Phil Bard served as the first president.

Heading the union's unemployed section was a dark-haired New Mexico–born painter named Mildred Rackley, who had already seen fascism on the loose in Europe. Raised in the isolated drylands of the American Southwest, she was a veritable Daughter of the American Revolution who scarcely understood the subtleties of political strife as an adolescent during the 1920's. But Mildred quickly appreciated the implications of modern painting when she encountered the artist's colony in nearby Taos. Hers, she later explained, was "the revolt of youth against parents and nonsense." Traveling to Europe in 1930 to study painting and visit museums, she landed in Hamburg, Germany, where the economic depression had begun to undermine the shaky Weimar Republic. From her apartment balcony, she could watch the noisy parades of uniformed Nazis, accompanied by loud chanting, singing, and the vicious beating of unsympathetic bystanders. Mildred was glad to leave for southern Europe, where she took up residence on the Spanish island of Mallorca. Just months after Spaniards had overthrown an inept monarchy in 1931, she witnessed their jubilation at the political future: "so beautiful," she would remember, "to see the Spanish people enjoying making their own decisions about their schools and their religion." She supplemented her meager savings with translation work, particularly after the rising number of German refugees required such assistance.

By the summer of 1935, Mildred had moved to New York and was thrilled by the vitality of the artists' community she discovered. Supported by various New Deal agencies, especially the Works Progress Administration (WPA), unemployed artists had found opportunities to develop their talents while experimenting with new techniques. But despite the intellectual ferment, Mildred remained acutely sensitive to the poverty that permeated the landscape. "It was a time," she said, "when you couldn't see things happening and say la-de-dah." One day, out of sheer frustration, she marched into the headquarters of the Communist party, introduced herself to the startled Earl Browder, and offered to organize the farm workers in her native New Mexico. "Thank you," he replied; "we'll consider it." In the fall of 1936, Mildred was painting a mural for the Treasury Department when Dr. Edward Barsky telephoned to ask if she would like to accompany him to Spain as secretary-translator for the newly formed American Medical Bureau. "Yes, I would," she answered, and soon she was sailing back to Europe with the first unit of American doctors and nurses.

Government support of the arts, meanwhile, remained precarious. Rumors of a rollback of WPA funds brought over 200 angry artists to a protest demonstration at the Arts Project offices in New York in December 1936. Bushy-haired Paul Block, a talented sculptor and impassioned speaker, reminded the artists to remain nonviolent, whereupon the throng staged a sit-down strike to stop the budget cuts and layoffs. WPA officials promptly summoned the police, who pounced on the demonstrators. Block, according to one eyewitness, was "slammed across the head with a club, dragged across the floor, stepped on, and thrown bleeding into an elevator." In the end, the police made 219 arrests; 15 artists required emergency medical treatment. Found guilty of disorderly conduct, all those arrested received suspended sentences. Within days, Block was again organizing the artists to build thirty floats for a Workers Alliance protest parade. Within weeks, he was planning a Public Use of Art Program to bring government-sponsored exhibitions to a wider audience; and within months, he was on his way to Spain. He would never return. Meanwhile, the same budgetary problems provoked a sit-down strike in the WPA's Federal Writers Project. Barricading themselves in the government offices, the protesting writers nervously sang "America" and "Solidarity Forever" for fifteen tense minutes before the police agreed to depart peacefully. "We won," exulted a young Indiana-born writer named Walter Grant. But he lost his job anyway. "The front line trenches of the world class struggle right now are in Spain," Grant concluded a few weeks later, "so cheerio. I'm off to the wars!"

With a similar intellectual fervor, the poet Edwin Rolfe had struggled throughout the Depression to integrate his political outlook with an aesthetic sensibility. His first collection of poetry, *We Gather Strength*, appeared in 1933, when he was 23. Many of the poems had the hard edge of self-conscious ideology, but he showed moments of lyrical brilliance, and his work continued to mature. To the left-wing magazine *New Masses* Rolfe frequently contributed topical poetry—about the problem of lynching, for example, or the anniversary of Marx's death. He also supported the John Reed Clubs' new literary magazine, *Partisan Review*, launched in 1934. This journal reflected a significant change in Communist attitudes toward cultural activity. As party leaders recognized the importance of building coalitions with non-Communist groups against fascism, the literati encouraged a liberalization of what passed for proletarian writing. Indeed, the editors of *Partisan Review* promised to resist "every attempt to cripple our literature by narrow-minded, sectarian theories and practices"; art and literature, while based ultimately on political values, would be judged by aesthetic standards. Rolfe served on the journal's first editorial boards, helped screen the poetry, and contributed his own work to the early issues.

That Rolfe remained a party man testified to the softening of Communist orthodoxy. In a major essay on the state of radical poetry that appeared in *Partisan Review* in 1935, Rolfe traced his personal journey from the writers' workshops of the 1920's to the more tolerant climate a decade later. Communist poets "put into verse form the speeches that we made or would have made at street-corner meetings," he confessed in explaining his first work. "Every poem was a call to action: an exhortation to the reader to awake from his lethargy and join the class-conscious forces of the working class." Such "journalistic verse," he admitted, "was not literature." In 1935, however, Rolfe could express optimism about a new generation of radical poets who accepted a more liberal definition of their art. "I suggest to the revolutionary poet the possibility of writing didactic verse as *one* of the means by which he can solve his present difficulties," Rolfe proposed. "There are others, to be sure: each dependent upon the individual predilections and abilities of each poet." Nor was this mere ideological posturing. Privately, Rolfe also denied that "a play, or a poem, or a piece of music, should ever be merely and exclusively a political effort!" Such attitudes would later inspire his defense of Ernest Hemingway when veterans of the Abraham Lincoln brigade denounced the novelist's views of the Spanish war.

But toleration had its limits. In the spring of 1935, Rolfe's essay on poetry served as a point of discussion at the first American Writers Congress, a gathering of left-wing authors summoned as part of the Communist effort to build coalitions with writers outside the party. The congress proceeded to establish the League of American Writers, which supplanted the party's John Reed Clubs. Soon afterward, *Partisan Review* became a casualty of shifting concerns and suspended publication in 1936. But the next year, two former members of the editorial board, William Phillips and Philip Rahv, together with Dwight McDonald, Mary McCarthy, and Fred Dupee, announced they were resuming publication. Communist writers now raised a storm of protest, for the new editors appeared to be avowed supporters of the heretical Trotsky. By then, Edwin Rolfe had different literary preoccupations; he was living in Madrid and editing the battlefield newspaper *Volunteer for Liberty* for the International Brigades. The prospect of Trotskyists adopting the title *Partisan Review* enraged him. "If you were here," he wrote to his wife, "you would understand why it isn't enough to be passively bitter or politically opposed to these bastards. . . . Their stinking pro-fascist actions here should convince anyone who really is for the workers that they're fit only to be spat on, crushed."

Amidst such partisan quarrels, Rolfe's poetic voice had nonetheless attained a rich maturity. His second collection of poetry, *To My Contemporaries*, appeared in 1936. The central theme remained the class struggle; he depicted victims of oppression and misery, ending always with assertions of revolutionary transcendence. Occasionally, as critic Joseph Freeman pointed out in the *New Masses*, Rolfe lapsed into clichés. But there was also a lyrical passion, a mastery of language that translated individual suffering into a feeling of love for humanity. Consider the title poem, for example:

> The Indians are dying on their reservations,
> black men are lynched, the jobless legions creep
> from day to hungry day, driven from railway stations.
> We have no place to sleep.
> But in the subway on a winter morning . . .

> The girl across the aisle—her eyes are blue—
> reading the *Mirror*. Open your eyes, it's you
> she's smiling at. Don't close your eyes again.
> Don't surrender to the ache in your limbs,
> the heaviness in your head. Look at her!

In the face of constant oppression, Rolfe wrote, such gestures required courage, acts of will to overcome the stifling inertia:

> Return with me to cities where the wind
> finds chasms between skyscrapers, where men
> reveal their thoughts in action, where mills
> and factories are continual testament
> to the war that only villages can hide.

But even the villages of the 1930's could not escape the depredations of failed capitalism, as Rolfe's literary comrade in Spain, Alvah Bessie, could well affirm. (Like Rolfe, Bessie would write a classic account of the Spanish war, *Men in Battle*.) Through the depths of the economic crisis, Bessie had tried to support his writing by working the submarginal soil of rural Vermont. Tending vegetable gardens with his wife, raising chickens, chopping wood, hiring out as a day laborer to the local potato farmers, he scarcely survived. "We'll watch you eat," he informed a friend who was coming for a visit. "With long practice of under-eating, the stomach becomes shrunk." The ordeal of poverty and malnutrition made an indelible impression on Bessie's life and his writing; in the fullest sense, he never recovered from the hard times.

The fair-haired, blue-eyed boy had been born into pampered affluence in 1904. His parents, American-born Jews, provided all the material comforts as well as a good education and summer camps, where he developed a life-long interest in natural history. Their politics were utterly conservative: years later, Bessie would remember how angry his father had become when the fourteen-year-old boy applauded a movie that showed the Russian peasants overthrowing the czar. They sent him to Columbia College—"a gift," he recalled, "and therefore not completely appreciated"—where he received a fine liberal arts education that in no way prepared him for the rest of his life. Soon after graduation in 1924, a classmate advised Bessie that the Provincetown

Players were casting Eugene O'Neill's *Desire Under the Elms* and needed some extras. Thus commenced a variety of bit roles and understudy assignments that put him on the edges of New York's theatrical scene, a world awash with much creative talent (many of Bessie's colleagues later made their fortunes on stage and screen) and a bohemian outlook. Little of it rubbed off. After four years, he had composed two novels, both of which he disliked and destroyed, and had translated Pierre Louÿs's exotic *Songs of Bilitis* from French. ("If you want to see a . . . piece of asshole display," he wrote half a century later, "see the 'notes' to my translation . . . and shame on me for that.") He had reached a moment of decision. The year was 1928; he was 24.

For reasons Bessie himself never understood, he saw his future leading in one of two directions. The first choice was to become a pilot in the U.S. Army Air Corps. He volunteered, underwent a physical examination, and was told he had not passed because one eye was different from the other. Bessie learned later that the diagnosis was phony; the physician had rejected him because he was a Jew. That left him with his second option, to go to Paris and become a writer. He gathered his savings, sold his library, and followed in the wake of the "lost generation." Aboard ship, he wrote his first short story, about a boy who commits suicide after killing a bird; and he saw it published in Paris in 1929. Yet Bessie expressed considerable ambivalence about his literary interests: he was still immature and homesick for a woman he had met on the eve of his departure. After only two months in Paris, he returned home. He had no trouble finding a job, at first: bookstore manager, clerk in a newspaper morgue, proofreader and fact checker for *The New Yorker*. All eventually ended as the Depression spread through the publishing industry.

Then, in 1930, Bessie married Mary Burnett, a painter, puppet maker, and writer; and the economic strings started to tighten. They decided to move to rural New England, working first as servants for a wealthy architect, then as tenants on some luckless land. They had one son and then another. Bessie tasted the ashes of poverty. Ironically, these proved to be productive years. He continued to write good short stories and saw them published in such magazines as *Scribner's* and *Story* as well as in annual anthologies of the "best" short fiction. But their themes showed the terrors of sheer survival—people, usually couples, living on the verge of desperation. His most important work was his first novel, *Dwell in the Wilderness*, a beautifully written depiction of a single family over fifty years of social change. It revealed a large measure of literary control, and on its merits, Bessie won a prestigious Guggenheim Fellowship in 1935, the year the novel appeared. He saw it as an "opportunity to continue with his major work." But then his career did not follow that direction. By the end of the decade, he would inscribe a copy of the novel to Edwin Rolfe, calling it "this memoir of my dead life."

"For the first five years of my life as a writer I wrote short stories," he would later explain. "I was chiefly interested in . . . examining my own emotions, my own reactions to the world and my surroundings, my personal relationships with my wife and other people. To understand how a grown man could be so narrow . . . has something to do with the fact that I was brought up in a well-to-do family, sheltered from the hard facts of life, protected from the necessity to earn my own living and given somehow to understand that other people who had less money than my parents were in some way . . . inferior to me." Then came the Depression. "Like millions of others," Bessie continued, "I learned a bitter lesson . . . and it was a lesson that literally saved my life and made me, I believe, a useful human being instead of a man who juggled with words. . . . For I learned that my problems as a writer were exactly the same as the problems of the farmer who lived down the road from me . . . when he could not get a living for his children out of the potatoes he grew (and I helped to pick) at such expense of labor."

Bessie's development during the mid-1930s involved a major personal catharsis; but it also illuminated a larger transformation of consciousness that affected many other intellectuals of his generation. The metamorphosis from a writer "interested primarily in the beauty of words," as he put it, to one with a social conscience emerged clearly in a long series of reviews, essays, and articles Bessie wrote during the years in Vermont. He began as a literary critic, complaining about "inverted sentimentality" or the lack of "valid emotion" (both in Hemingway). But as the writers of the 1930's increasingly turned to contemporary social problems, Bessie's critical pieces confronted a new terrain. He sided, in the beginning, with literary tradition. "When art departs from its sole function," he wrote about a Marxist-influenced novel in 1934, "when it seeks to dignify a cause, no matter how worthy, it does lose its status as art, it does become propaganda, it dilutes the elements that make it timeless, enters the realm of the purely temporal and contingent." Artistic propaganda, he warned, diverted literature from its only aim: "the reflection of life, as it is lived, in the round, without . . . making of its materials evangelical props for . . . [a] set of ideas."

After the publication of his novel in 1935, Bessie returned to the city, becoming assistant editor and critic for the *Brooklyn Eagle*. To his surprise, he found himself drawn into parlor-room quarrels about "communism, fascism, and the need for social change . . . by people who, only a few years ago, considered politics beneath the attention of an adult intellect." He began to meet literary radicals and Communist writers, whom he defined as "liberals who have felt the necessity for action." A bitter East Coast seamen's strike in 1936 impelled his own involvement. When the *Eagle* attacked the strikers, Bessie drafted a rebuttal and brought it to the headquarters of the National Maritime Union. He then retyped the piece on union letterhead and brought it back to his newspaper, which not only printed the letter but also reversed its editorial stand. Bessie's home became the headquarters of the Brooklyn Citizens' Committee, which supported the strikers. Conversations with the maritime workers solidified his radical beliefs; soon thereafter, Bessie joined the Communist party. (His wife, meanwhile, had an affair with one of the seamen, precipitating their separation.)

Bessie's writing now became overtly political, dealing with such subjects as student antiwar movements, lynching, Soviet films, the League Against War and Fascism. And, inevitably, his attitude toward art and propaganda also changed. In a piece about the Communist novelist Louis Aragon, he praised all writers "who have . . . seen the impossibility of remaining aloof from the more immediate problems of the day." When the French novelist Malraux toured the United States in 1937 to gain support for the Spanish Republic, Bessie arranged to interview him in a mid-Manhattan hotel. (Edwin Rolfe, too, made a pilgrimage to Malraux for the *New Masses*.) "He is that rare being," wrote Bessie, "an artist and a man of action, the one inseparable from the other." But when Bessie added that Malraux was "a perfect refutation of the charge of 'propaganda' raised against socially conscious writers," the publisher of the *Eagle* disagreed. In the ensuing argument, the writer resigned. Bessie found what he considered more useful employment with the public relations office of the Spanish Information Bureau in New York.

Malraux remained his ideal. Following the Frenchman's example, Bessie began taking flying lessons in order to bring some practical skills to aid the

Spanish Republic. On July 4, 1936, according to a framed photograph that hangs in Bessie's former study in California, he flew solo for the first time. Six months later, with his marriage on the rocks, Bessie sailed for Spain. He was 33, older than most of the American volunteers, and they dubbed him "Papa." Still a literary man, he carried along a pocket notebook (eventually there would be four) in which he recorded the experiences of war. "I came to know other people for the first time in my life," he later explained of his political awakening. "And I have been concerned, since that time, more with the problems of other people than with my own problems. . . . For the people and the words have become one."

That so many American intellectuals supported the Spanish Republic underscored the ideological imperatives of the 1930's. Not only did left-wing artists and writers envision a society that would respect and encourage their artistic production; they also realized that inimical fascist doctrines threatened the essence of independent creativity. They were therefore simultaneously idealists, looking for a better world, and realists, who well understood their enemies. In seeking integration with the larger society, moreover, these committed creative workers rejected the aesthetic isolation that had characterized the "lost generation" of the 1920's. Rather than fleeing America and its discontents, Depression-era intellectuals affirmed their identity with the masses; when they went to Spain, it was to fulfill this ideal of camaraderie with the people. Yet theirs was no romantic crusade. To Bessie and Rolfe; to Phil Bard, Paul Block, and Mildred Rackley; even to noncombatants like Hemingway and Hellman and Hughes—Spain constituted an Armageddon, after which creative minds would either be redeemed or plunged into darkness.

PART II

Spain

Into the Valley

War," wrote Edwin Rolfe, "is your comrade struck dead beside you, his shared cigarette still alive in your lips." Whatever the political loyalties of the American volunteers—Communist, Socialist, anarchist, or adventurous anti-fascist—the war in Spain soon brought an ineluctable common denominator: death and its avoidance. The slaughter of the unprepared American soldiers began in the Jarama Valley near Madrid in February 1937, leaving long lists of maimed and dead; the toll leaped at Brunete on the Madrid front the following July and rose again that summer at Quinto, Belchite, and Fuentes de Ebro in the Aragon region. In the winter of 1938, Americans fell at Teruel, the "North Pole" of Spain. And then in March commenced the frantic retreats across the Spanish plains, burdened with tremendous losses. A surprise recrossing of the Ebro River during the second summer, in July 1938, brought brief moments of victory, but these, too, were soon dulled in an agony of bullets and bombs. These military epics inspired numerous cases of individual courage, for which the Lincolns became justly famous. But even their heroism could not mask the grim backdrop of staggering human loss. The pervasive sense of catastrophe inevitably produced other casualties, psychological and political. But in the primary sense, the ends of battle remained entirely visceral.

When Millie Bennett, correspondent for the *Moscow News*, entered Brentano's bookshop on the rue Opéra in Paris in early January 1937 in search of a Spanish dictionary, she was surprised to see her old Moscow drinking buddy, Robert Merriman, snatching books about Spain by the fistful. Why, she wanted to know, wasn't he in the Soviet Union pursuing his agricultural studies? Merriman replied that he intended to find work on the new collective farms of Spain; but, Bennett reported, "he didn't look me in the eye when he said it." Soon the two Californians were charging around Paris to buy a revolver, cartridges, and (with memories of the World War) gas masks to fit over their horn-rimmed glasses. These gadgets would never be used in Spain. But the two laden Americans, in Merriman's words, made an "unusual united front" on the train from Paris to Barcelona the next day. En route they experienced no special delays. The international border remained open; American passports did not yet prohibit travel to Spain. Barcelona, Merriman noted, was "aflame with posters of all parties and all causes," a colorful form of communication made necessary by the high rate of illiteracy. The Americans proceeded to Valencia, headquarters of the International Brigades.

No American battalion then existed, and Merriman tried to figure out a way of joining the anti-fascist ranks. He visited the headquarters of the Spanish Communist party, the Soviet consulate, and the Ministry of War. When finally steered to the brigade offices, he lacked documentation to validate his reliability and qualifications. Eventually he managed to obtain permission to visit Albacete, the brigade training base, but to his annoyance he was given a round-trip ticket. Merriman's previous military experience amounted to two years in the Reserve Officers' Training Corps at the University of Nevada (at a pay rate of $8.50 a month) and a summer course worth a second lieutenancy. But he was intelligent and healthy—six foot two, according to Millie Bennett, "and as broad as the side of a house"—and he was passionate for the cause. A conversation with the base commander, Augusto Vidal, apparently proved sufficient. Merriman scrawled a note to Bennett explaining that he would be staying at Albacete to train the newly arrived American contingent.

Merriman's unusual enlistment has raised questions about his motives and background. Some have seen him as a Comintern agent sent from the Soviet Union to command the American legions; others, citing his wholesome, all-American demeanor, insist he was a non-Communist idealist, determined only to halt the spread of fascism. The distinction is more than academic, for it underscores the political nature of the International Brigades. In a confidential report to the State Department, the American consul in Moscow expressed doubts that Merriman had joined the Communist party "since he is the type of person who values too much his own freedom of speech and action to subordinate himself to any organization which maintains rigorous discipline." But according to the consul, another knowledgeable observer asserted that the longer Merriman remained in the Soviet Union, "the more violent pro-Soviet he became in language and action and the more critical he was of the American Government." During the tourist season, the consul alleged, Merriman would agitate among visiting Americans, trying to persuade them to support a change in American foreign policy. When Merriman sought information about joining the International Brigades, however, he used personal rather than political connections, soliciting information from his Moscow tennis partner, the journalist Louis Fisher, who had already visited wartime Spain and had helped purchase arms for the Republic.

Merriman's private diary, hitherto read selectively, reveals the complexity of his motivations. His difficulty in finding a way to enlist in the brigade—chasing around Valencia from office to office in search of a pass, for example—and his lack of credentials suggest strongly that he was not sent by the Comintern on a party mission to Spain. Yet his personal idealism contained an explicitly political component. "The actual fighting with weapons," he scribbled on the eve of his first combat, "is the highest stage a real communist can ask for. . . . Long live Communism! Long live the Soviet Union! Men may die but let them die in a working class cause. Men die and mean to die (if necessary) so that the revolution may live on. They may stop us today but tomorrow we still take up the march." Such confessions, intended for no one's eyes but his own, tell much about the courage and convictions of this American volunteer. Eventually, the camaraderie of war would clarify Merriman's commitments, and he would formally apply for membership in the Spanish Communist party. But it was not the party card that was important; rather, men like Merriman sought a sense of participating in—indeed, accelerating—the flow of history. That consciousness would have important military consequences.

By the time the 27-year-old economist took charge of training the American volunteers, they numbered about one hundred, but groups of various sizes continued to arrive. One of the first recruits, Julius Toab, kept a diary of his early experiences in Spain. "We received a royal welcome. We got laid," he noted on January 15. "Men began to arrive that night. Stories of escaping from fascist Germany by swimming rivers[,] climbing mountains, hiking for hundreds of miles. . . . [From] all parts of the world they came. Always coming. Anti-fascists. The international Brigades."

By the third week of February 1937 the American battalion totaled nearly four hundred men. Soon after Merriman's arrival, the volunteers held a meeting to choose their name. Alfred Tanz, a New York lawyer who would become battalion quartermaster, remembered a long discussion in which the men proposed various designations. Although the machine-gun company insisted on honoring imprisoned labor leader Tom Mooney (and thereafter called themselves the "Tom Mooney company"), a larger consensus preferred the American symbols of the Popular Front. Merriman registered the result in his diary: "Long Live the Lincoln Battalion."

The *battalion*, as he noted correctly, formed part of the Fifteenth *Brigade* (which included three other battalions—British, French-Belgian, and Spanish). The American volunteers always scoffed at the confusion of "brigade" and "battalion," some viewing the use of the term "Lincoln brigade" as a form of Communist propaganda designed to inflate the size of the American group. Ignorance is a more likely explanation. (Among the critics of *Daily Worker* headlines, which used the terms interchangeably, were such loyal Communists as Edwin Rolfe, who expressed embarrassment at the confusion.) The idea of a Lincoln brigade also proved a convenient, if inaccurate, way of including those American volunteers who served in other branches of the military, such as the Washington battalion, the MacKenzie-Papineau battalion, the Regiment de Tren (transport section), and the John Brown artillery battery, as well as various individuals and small groups that worked with other units. (One American anti-aircraft battery could not choose a name: half of the men voted to honor the Chinese revolutionary Sun Yat-sen; the other half picked Hollywood actress Joan Crawford, claiming that she would respond by sending them cigarettes. The stalemate proved insurmountable.) The American Medical Bureau, comprised of doctors, nurses, technicians, and drivers, was also attached to the International Brigades, but the personnel provided services for volunteers of all countries, and a few doctors served directly with the Spanish Republican army. Ignorance aside, however, the notion of a Lincoln brigade did conceal the extent of American casualties, particularly when Spanish recruits filled the empty positions. By the last battles, able-bodied Americans would constitute far less than even a single battalion.

Merriman's dubious qualifications for leadership typified the inadequacies of the first Lincoln commanders. When he entered the base at Albacete, the highest military officer was James Harris, a former U.S. Army sergeant who had been appointed by the New York Communist party. Although Harris had tried to organize a training program, teaching the men the diamond-shaped advances used during World War I, his military knowledge appeared limited. More seriously, Harris's lack of self-discipline—he was frequently drunk—undermined his authority with the rank and file. Initially, Merriman became Harris's adjutant. He was assisted by another volunteer with scant experience, Stephen Daduk, a pilot who had fought with the Republican air forces in the battles over Madrid in the autumn of 1936. Wounded in combat, Daduk arrived at the American base and began offering military instruction. His expertise proved to be exaggerated, however, and after a confrontation with Harris, Daduk was suspended.

Without challenging the lines of command, Merriman assumed greater responsibility for the lecture program on military tactics—scouting, fortifications, and signaling—as well as the drafting of daily orders. He taught the men how to fieldstrip the few rifles and machine guns that were available; but without ammunition to waste, they received no firing practice. Not until the Lincoln battalion actually moved toward the front lines would Merriman obtain permission to stop the advance long enough for the men to fire five shots each into the nearby hills. For some, that was the extent of their shooting experience. As the Lincolns prepared for battle, moreover, Harris became more unstable; one day he was too drunk to work.

The problems of military leadership mirrored the deficiencies of the political command. Within the Spanish Republican Army—as in the Soviet Red Army upon which it was modeled—there existed a political structure known as the commissariat, which exactly paralleled the military organization. At each level of command—division, brigade, battalion, company, section—a political commissar shared authority with a military officer. The dual system underscored the political nature of the Spanish war; civilian leaders, facing Franco's military rebellion, did not fully trust the officer corps. Consequently, the political commissars could even take command from their military counterparts.

The commissars, however, served primarily as morale officers. They were responsible for explaining the political rationale of military decisions—providing, for example, reasons for particular strategies and tactics. The commissars also dealt with such everyday problems as food, clothing, cigarettes, and mail. "Most officers from the old style armies are unsatisfactory," Merriman explained to the visiting journalist Anna Louise Strong. "They are accustomed to command by iron discipline." But a people's army, "made up of strong individuals with strong beliefs," he said, required a different kind of control. "We must depend on voluntary discipline from the men." And that demanded a continuing process of political education, in which the soldiers could acquire an understanding of military problems and decisions.

Saul Wellman, who would serve as a battalion commissar near the end of the war, emphasized the personal obligations inherent in Communist ideology. Far more important than the sheer power of the commissars, he suggested, was the ability of party leaders to touch a volunteer's political convictions: "Comrade, you are here for a greater motive. . . . You are advancing the cause of socialism." Such appeals would inspire men to draw upon their own reserves of strength. "The main role of the commissars was indeed political," agreed John Gates, the last American commissar of the Fifteenth Brigade. "Indeed, it would be difficult to explain how poorly armed men could fight a much more powerful army for so long and so well, if it were not for their political convictions." Good commissars also led by example. They were "the ones who gave the guys the strength to carry on," remembered the black volunteer Vaughn Love, "and that [became] contagious."

Given the importance of the commissars, the first American leaders appeared woefully inadequate. Phil Bard, appointed by the American Communist party in New York, lacked any military skills. When the Lincolns moved to the town of Villanueva de la Jara for exercises, Bard remained at Albacete to handle battalion affairs; chronic asthma soon forced his return to the United States. As his replacement, Bard appointed another volunteer named Marvin Stern, a New York seaman, who soon offended the local mayor by demanding to know why he had not yet collectivized the land. Argumentative and arrogant, Stern nearly came to blows with several of the men. Angry with his leadership, the Lincolns elected a political committee to bring their grievances to the brigade command. Commander Vidal's response was to call them "naughty children." Morale quickly drooped. Some of the men began to talk about deserting the International Brigades for the Spanish infantry. Rumors of anti-Semitism among the seamen created additional problems. "Drunkenness increases," observed one volunteer, "and we start a jail." At last, the volunteers mustered enough organization to force Stern's resignation.

As their first elected commissar, the Lincolns chose Sam Stember, a World War I veteran and a participant in the Bonus March protests of 1932. He had gone to Europe in 1917 "to save the world for democracy," he said, and it still needed to be saved. Despite his political orthodoxy, however, Stember was a weak man, low on the Communist party totem pole in Albacete. He proved incapable of challenging the French officers, led by the formidable André Marty. Under Marty's authoritarian hand, the French controlled the distribution of food, uniforms, and equipment—the elemental supplies of which the Lincolns never seemed to have enough. Stember's inability to negotiate with Marty and his staff soon undermined his influence among the soldiers. The commissar nonetheless recognized Captain Harris's imbalances and backed Merriman's suggestion that he be replaced. But before they could act, the battalion received orders on February 13 to move toward the front lines.

As the Lincolns headed into the Jarama Valley, their primary strategic goal was to defend the vital Madrid-Valencia road from fascist penetration. If the Republican lines fell, Franco could isolate Spain's capital city and bring the war to a rapid conclusion. The Americans well understood the importance of their mission; but the inadequacies of their preparation quickly began to cause problems. Summoned into the bullring at Villanueva de la Jara, the Lincolns stood in formation to listen to speeches by brigade commanders, including Marty, who explained the urgency of halting the fascist advance. As the officers spoke, a small convoy of unmatched trucks lumbered into the ring. They carried boxes of greased rifles—vintage 1914—and steel helmets, which were distributed among the volunteers. Then Merriman ordered his men into the trucks, and in a somber mood the raw Lincoln battalion drove into the night. Harris, drunk again that day, had disappeared. The hum of a light plane overhead accompanied the ride. But the arrival of enemy bombers caught the Lincolns by surprise. The bombs, fortunately, missed their mark. In the nearby town of Morata, the men climbed out to eat a hot meal, but before it was digested they were ordered back aboard for the last leg of the trip.

Riding in the first truck was a 25-year-old graduate of Indiana University named Walter Grant. The son of a Congregationalist minister from Marion, Indiana, Grant had been raised in an intense midwestern religious environment. He had acquired some military skills as an ROTC cadet and had also developed a religious sensibility against social injustice. In 1930 a Ku Klux Klan lynch mob killed three black prisoners in his hometown. Grant had fallen to his knees in prayer, helpless against the terror, and he emerged from the experience with his faith deeply shaken. He proceeded to earn a master's degree at Indiana and taught in the English department. But the Depression forced staff cuts and Grant moved to New York, where he found work on a WPA Writers' Project. His faith took a secular turn. "The world is there to be saved," he wrote, "and the minister's son feels it is his duty to contribute to the rescuing process. . . . He cannot accept the world as it is because he has learned to believe it can be made better." For Grant, it was a short step from evangelical Christianity to the Communist party. "While it is true there is a Communist International," he wrote to his family from Paris on his way to Spain, "there is also a Fascist International, which at the present time is a far more serious menace to world peace."

So Grant rode in the darkness in the back of the lead truck toward the Jarama front. Unfamiliar with the landscape, he probably did not realize that the driver had missed a left turn. The driver of the second truck blindly followed the mistake. Inside the third vehicle, an ambulance, rode Dr. William Pike, a volunteer with the American Medical Bureau, who noticed the road to the left. He ordered the driver to stop, then directed the convoy on the proper course. The Lincolns never again saw the missing trucks. But fascist documents indicate that the two trucks continued in the wrong direction until they came under enemy fire. The first truck was shot off the road; the second crashed into it. The survivors took refuge in a small gully, but they were easily overpowered. Walter Grant and about twenty other Americans thus became the first of the Lincoln casualties. Also lost were all the battalion records.

The logistical errors had just begun. Ordered to dig trenches, the bewil-

dered Lincolns asked, "With what?" Helmets, bayonets, and bare hands had
to substitute for the missing shovels. In their ignorance, they dug against the
skyline. At dawn artillery shells and machine-gun bullets smashed into their
positions. Sniper fire and shrapnel claimed the first casualties. Then a row of
Italian bombers appeared overhead. Seeing a metallic glint, the black volunteer Oliver Law, a six-year veteran of the U.S. Army, shouted in his southern accent to Merriman, "Lookee, boss, they're dropping propaganda leaflets." Instead, a cluster of bombs landed so near, said Merriman, that the explosions scorched the earth. After the raid, and a long, long silence, the un-
abashed Law exclaimed, "Boss Merriman, them sure was powerful leaflets."
By the end of the first day, Harris had to be sent to a hospital; Daduk "cracked
up" and went to a rest home; and the brigade command bawled out Merriman
for not keeping his men down. Two days later, Harris returned, reclaimed his
rank, and led the men on a bright, moonlit night across the Republican trenches
into no-man's-land for night maneuvers. Whatever the commander's intentions, the march soon deteriorated into a rambling procession, interspersed
with desultory fire from enemy lines and a raging quarrel between Harris and
Merriman. The latter apparently prevailed and brought the men back to their
lines. Harris, "still abnormal," according to Merriman's diary, went by ambulance the next day to a hospital, never to return to the battalion.

The Lincolns moved into new trenches on February 23 and then received
orders to go over the top for the first time. They numbered exactly 373, officers and troops. Backed by a pair of Soviet tanks that distracted enemy fire,
they advanced through thickets of olive trees, firing sporadically at the fascist
lines. They drew a light return fire—until one of the tanks billowed in flames
and the other clambered away in retreat. Left exposed to rifles and machine
guns, the Lincolns clawed for cover. Of the battalion's eight machine guns,
Merriman reported "none working." Screams of "first aid" pierced the air. But
the slightest movements drew a hail of bullets and efforts to rescue the injured
invariably multiplied the number of casualties. Stranded in the open field at
nightfall, the Americans stumbled back to their lines. After a hellish night
trying to organize the rescue of a wounded officer, Joe Gordon walked behind
the lines, "feeling punch-drunk, too tired even to see," and bumped into a
comrade who had spent the night hiding under his blanket. Merriman blamed
the debacle on the failure of the battalions on the flanks. "We could have bro-

ken through that night," he wrote, "if we had been given support." The day's toll: 20 killed, nearly 60 wounded. The battalion now numbered fewer than 300.

The Lincolns scarcely had time to absorb their losses. Stuck in shallow trenches, easy prey to enemy marksmen, they struggled to dig deeper. Joe Gordon, yesterday's hero, caught a bullet in the head that left him blinded in one eye. "Boys had little to eat and drink," Merriman noted, "and it meant death to carry food across the road." When a hugh urn of coffee finally arrived, a volunteer named Bob Norwood took a moment too long to swallow his drink. A sniper's bullet smashed his brains into the remaining brew. Amidst such pressure, a fresh contingent of seventy Americans arrived in the lines. Some of them, including an actor from Boston named John Lenthier, still wore civilian clothing. None had more than a few days' training; some had even less. Barely able to dismantle their weapons or follow battlefield instructions about infiltration and self-preservation, they would soon join their slightly more experienced comrades in a major assault on the enemy positions. "Some kind of attack was an absolute necessity at this time for the sake of the whole front," Merriman later explained. "Deserters from the fascist lines had told us that the enemy had no reinforcements."

Heavy artillery was supposed to launch the Lincolns' first major attack at dawn of February 27, 1937—a wet and dreary morning. But the guns did not fire on schedule, and when the barrage commenced three hours late, the shells landed well wide of the objectives. "We waited without promised machine gun support," Merriman reported, "without telephone, artillery going to the left and not helping us. . . . The armored cars were behind the hill, no tanks in evidence, no horses. . . . Ceiling low. No planes." He telephoned brigade headquarters for explanation. Colonel Vladimir Copic, the Yugoslav commander of the Fifteenth Brigade, ordered Merriman to advance. The American protested the futility of the operation, emphasizing that the flanking 24th Battalion had not moved either. Copic insisted that the flanks were seven hundred yards ahead of the Lincolns and that Merriman was looking not at enemy entrenchments but at the second lines of the 24th Battalion. He gave the Lincolns fifteen minutes to cover the distance. Merriman continued to protest, but Copic screamed that the Americans must move into the hills "at all costs." When three Republican planes, instead of the promised twenty, appeared overhead, Merriman felt obliged to order the attack.

Thus commenced the slaughter. Having approached mutiny to protect his men, Merriman determined to lead the attack. Raising his left arm, he climbed from the trenches into a blistering fire. Almost immediately, a bullet slashed into his shoulder, cracking the bone in five places. Someone grabbed his legs and dragged him back to safety. But the attack proceeded, with the Americans leaping from the wet earth into the scorching cross fire of machine-gun bullets. In loosely organized waves they ran through an olive grove and toppled onto the soil, some few rising to move forward again, some killed instantly, some merely grazed, some forced by the continuing barrage into unconsciousness and death. One American, with experience in the New York National Guard, advanced about 25 yards and found "nobody there." He took refuge behind a skinny olive tree, using a penknife to scrape the dirt into a protective mound. He dared not move to fire at the enemy. But, to his astonishment, he saw a figure ahead of him so untrained as to be bearing a full pack on his back. This was John Lenthier, the young actor from Boston, who had once been arrested for protesting the banning of Clifford Odets's play *Waiting For Lefty*. Just minutes before the attack, he had confided to a friend that there were only three things in the world he cared about: the theater, the labor movement, and his wife. Shot while running, he sprawled like a turtle on the ground, unable to turn because of the weight on his shoulders. There he died a slow and painful death. From the trenches, a patched and bleeding Merriman watched the attack disintegrate. "Our men advanced under impossible conditions and did it without murmur," wrote Merriman three days later. "Our boys plenty brave . . . great boys and it grieved me to see them go."

A wash of afternoon rain turned the battlefield to muck. It had no effect on the pace of the enemy fire. Worse, by then the Lincolns had lost virtually their entire command. The leadership passed to David Jones, who upon realizing his position blurted out, "I don't know about military things a fuck." He would have to rely for advice on the British lieutenant George Wattis. In the confusion, the men left in the trenches raged at new orders to carry ammunition to their comrades already gnawing the sodden terrain in front of them. Efforts to advance the attack continued to fail—partly because of withering enemy fire, partly because of the impossibility of coordinating the command. Wattis compounded the problem by ordering the outstretched troops to retreat to the trenches before dark, providing the fascists with excellent targets. Not until nightfall could the Lincolns return to the lines, wounded helping wounded, dragging each other and crawling to safety. The battalion had been ripped to pieces. Bodies littered the stark terrain; three days later a soldier was found breathing among the corpses. On the morning of February 27, Merriman had reported 263 men in the lines; the next day, the battalion counted about 150. One veteran recalled that before the battle the trenches were so crowded it was impossible to avoid bumping shoulders and elbows; by nightfall the survivors had to patrol the line just to maintain contact with their nearest comrade.

What had been accomplished? Ernest Hemingway, who interviewed many of the survivors, labeled the attack "idiotic" and averred that future historians would regard the orders as "an act of monumental stupidity." Yet however incompetent their leaders, the Lincolns acquired a reputation for courage and valor, the heroism of shock troops, that became part of their mythology. "The Americans had health, zeal and courage," wrote *New York Times* correspondent Herbert Matthews as an epitaph, even if "they knew nothing of soldiering and had precious little time to learn it in." They were, he added, "still raw as soldiers, but they were ripe in spirit." As part of the legend, moreover, some observers suggested that the terrible massacre constituted an important victory. In the aftermath of battle, to be sure, Merriman bitterly criticized brigade leaders for ordering the offensive and denied vehemently that the Americans were responsible for its failure. Yet "from a military standpoint," he insisted, the "attack was a good thing. It showed the fascists that we were strong; it convinced them, in fact, that we were stronger than we really were. It discouraged them from further drives on this front." Edwin Rolfe, in his history of the war, confirmed Merriman's view, describing Jarama as "a complete success, in a way which none of the Americans who took part in it could then foresee. For the attack of February 27th," Rolfe explained, impressed "the insurgents with one inescapable fact: that the Jarama front was too heavily, too perfectly defended. From that day until the very end of the war, the rebels never succeeded in advancing another meter along the line which, they had hoped, would cut the Madrid-Valencia highway, effect the encirclement and the capture of Madrid." Less passionate historians observe that the fascist advance had already been blunted ten days before; the failure of the Republican offensive simply confirmed the stabilization of that front.

*

Suffering no illusions on the battlefield, the wounded Merriman demanded "to have it out with Copic," the commander who had ordered the attack. Instead, he was taken to a frontline medical unit, where the horror was etched still deeper. "It was a butcher shop," he declared. "People died on stretchers in the yard. . . . Went to the operating room. Pulling bullets out of man who had become an animal. Several doctors operating on stomach exploring for bullets while others died." A doctor taped Merriman's arm to a board, and sent him to the new American hospital at Romeral del Toledo. "Nightmare of a ride," he remembered. "Lost our way. Three and a half hours going but had to give up while I lay on the floor of the ambulance." The sound of English-speaking voices cheered him, and Merriman began a long and painful convalescence that would prepare him for more battles and more frustration.

Just two days earlier there had been no American hospital to receive the casualties of Jarama. Dr. Edward Barsky had led the first American medical units into Spain at the end of January, expecting to find an International Brigades hospital service to assist. "In Spain," he wrote later, "we found that this hospital was a pure fantasy. . . . For myself, I know that I clung to this dream until I was actually walking on the streets of Madrid." With head nurse Fredericka Martin and his assistant, the painter Mildred Rackley, Barsky toured the frontline first-aid stations around Madrid, bullets singing past their ears, and visited the hospitals behind the lines. Spanish officials finally advised them to find a suitable hospital location nearer the American soldiers at Jarama. Two weeks later they were still looking when Barsky received military orders by telegram: "In forty hours be ready to receive wounded." Touring the nearby countryside, Barsky spotted a new schoolhouse, still unfinished inside, at Romeral. The place had no running water, no sanitary facilities, no telephone, and, in Rackley's words, "a very feeble electricity line"; the bumpy roadway outside seemed perilous even to ordinary traffic.

Facing a deadline, the fifteen-member medical contingent began to create a hospital. With the support of the local mayor, Barsky supervised the transformation of the empty building into a modern, 75-bed facility, complete with operating theater, kitchens, and wards. Masons ripped through the walls, electricians wired the building, carpenters built tables and bedsteads, agricultural workers cleared the roads. "I can't tell you the feeling it gave me when we took the first bus over the road," reported Rackley, "and all along the way, *Salud! Salud!* from every one of them." Meanwhile, the nurses and technicians unpacked crates of beds and medical supplies, while others scoured the building's interior. When Martin discovered that the unit's two sterilizers had not arrived, she dispatched Rackley to Madrid to find replacements—and food for the staff and the expected patients. The work proceeded without pause, through the day and night and into the next day. While the men at Jarama hugged the trench walls and threw themselves into battle, no one at Romeral slept.

No sooner had they finished unpacking the trucks than the first ambulance arrived; by day's end, six more had come. "It was an ordinary truck with a canvas top," reported pharmacist Harry Wilkes. "Inside the truck on the floor were mattresses upon which about 25 wounded lay. Two were already dead. Several others were very low. The rest suffered excruciating pain due to fractures and the ride over the torturing road." Barsky, an established surgeon; Martin, head nurse at New York's Bellevue, Fordham, and Lying-In hospitals; Lini Fuhr, nurse and social worker—none had ever seen such injuries before. "I cut through clothing of boys I had danced with on our way to Spain," remembered Fuhr. "I have seen the results of dum-dum bullets"—deep wounds caused by bullets that exploded on impact, bones shattered and splintered to produce secondary wounds. Shrapnel left immense gashes and holes, and there was inordinate skull and brain damage because the head made a perfect target. Within hours, bleeding men filled all the beds in the hospital; soon, they occupied all the borrowed mattresses that lined the floor. Stretchers lay in the courtyard outside while the doctors sorted the patients and improvised relief. To keep the shock patients warm in the unheated building, Barsky placed small cooking stoves beneath the stretchers. Nurses opened their own veins to transfuse blood into dying men. (It was in the Spanish war that the Canadian physician Norman Bethune would perfect a means to preserve blood plasma for later use.)

This first shift lasted forty hours. Barsky never stopped operating, debriding wounds, sewing torn intestines, amputating shredded limbs, setting bones. One night, in the middle of an operation, a battery went dead, forcing the crew to rush for flashlights; Barsky managed to remove a shattered kidney. His motions became mechanical. "None of us could afford to stop," he said; "I tried to exclude emotional feeling." But one nurse acknowledged the special strain involved in the work: "There's nothing impersonal about it. These patients are our comrades, are a part of us. When they suffer, we suffer and learn to hate more. There's a terrific drain always." Freddy Martin took special pride in her nurses, some of whom worked until they dropped, literally. Suffering from swollen feet, many had to walk in patients' floppy slippers. "We are going to need iron-lined guts for this job," Martin concluded. Celia Seborer, who had gone to Spain as a lab technician, "was appalled at the sight of so much blood and such bloodless faces. Their cries and groans haunted me for days," she said. Two months later, she had become skilled at dressing even horrendous wounds "and quite hardened to all sorts of groans, grunts, shrieks, and moans." Such adjustments, begun in the aftermath of Jarama, would continue over the next eighteen months. The war would become increasingly dangerous, the scars of battle permanent.

On the Jarama front, meanwhile, the survivors of the Lincoln battalion suffered through a cold and rainy season. With the original leadership gone, the Belgian captain Van den Berghe assumed command of the American volunteers. But one day in early March, to the surprise of the battle-weary survivors, there appeared the familiar face of Allan Johnson. He was dressed in the same suit of civilian clothes he had worn in New York when he interviewed the volunteers. "We hugged him literally," recalled one veteran, grateful that the Americans would no longer be isolated from the brigade command. When Johnson became liaison officer with headquarters, the battalion command passed to Martin Hourihan, a tough Irish Catholic seaman and former Wobbly, who had taught school in rural Alabama. Hourihan could boast of six years' service in the U.S. Army. More important, as a squad leader he had kept his men alive on February 27. Although the major offensives and counterattacks had stalled, the front remained tense and uncertain.

In mid-March, a surprise attack by Franco's Moors on nearby trenches galvanized the men into action. When panicky Spanish Republican troops fled their positions, a heroic stand by British and American soldiers beat back the assault, though the fascists seized some of the outlying ground. That day, while rushing to stop the Moors, Robert Raven, sometime student at the University of Pittsburgh, felt a grenade burn his eyes, causing him to drop his own grenade, which exploded at his feet. His agony, described in a dispatch by Hemingway, symbolized the blind, unyielding courage of the inexperienced volunteers.

In early April, Hourihan led the Americans in retaking the trenches lost in March. A few weeks later, he endeavored to mount another offensive, but the prudent Lincolns balked, refusing orders to expose themselves to enemy fire. None was punished for disobedience. Thereafter, the Americans held the stabilized lines, waiting for replacements. They maintained their anxious vigil until June 17, 120 days after they first entered the lines. Only once was the battalion relieved. But no sooner had the men taken showers, caught a night's sleep in an abandoned church, and paraded in a May Day demonstration than Allan Johnson announced that a new fascist threat required their return to the trenches. The expected attack never came.

A British volunteer named Alex McDade immortalized the ordeal in a poem he placed on the trench wall "newspaper." The Americans sang it to the tune of "The Red River Valley," and it became the standard song of the Lincoln battalion:

> There's a valley in Spain called Jarama,
> It's a place that we all know so well,
> For 'tis there that we wasted our manhood,
> And most of our old age as well.

> From this valley they tell us we're leaving,
> But don't hasten to bid us adieu,
> For e'en though we make our departure,
> We'll be back in an hour or two.

> Oh, we're proud of our Lincoln Battalion,
> And the marathon record it's made,
> Please do us this little favor,
> And take this last word to brigade:

> "You will never be happy with strangers
> They would not understand you as we,
> So remember the Jarama Valley
> And the old men who wait patiently."

8

The Ideology of Commitment

M ore clearly than any combat of the past," wrote
an American volunteer in 1937, "the war in
Spain is a fight to the finish between all that is new
and generous and hopeful in the world, and all that is
old, cruel and fetid. It is the thing that moralists had
almost given up hoping for—a clear-cut struggle between the powers of light and the powers of darkness,
and very little twilight zone to confuse us. How," he
wanted to know, "can one . . . stay out of this struggle?" The decision of the political Left in Spain—and
the Comintern elsewhere—to confront the Franco insurrection with military force defined the conflict as
an ideological struggle between world socialism and
fascism. "It was a highly political war," explained the
rank and filer Morris Mickenberg. "The first and primary meaning of everything was the political meaning. That is how we lived, that is how we thought, that
is how we talked to each other." Indeed, the men engaged in endless political dialogue and debate, av-
idly followed world events, and viewed their commitments in ideological terms. "The level of political
consciousness is amazingly high," Edwin Rolfe wrote

in his first letter from Spain, "and willingness—eagerness for the most difficult work—is the rule."

Dominating all political passions was an overwhelming commitment to
communism and to the leadership of the Communist party. Although defenders of the Lincolns often played down the role of the party in Spain, preferring
to emphasize the Popular Front coalition, it is clear that its influence remained preeminent. Certainly a large majority of the volunteers were party
members, and most of the others had been screened by party committees in
America. "The cause enveloped us all," explained Saul Wellman many years
later. "It was powerful. It was accepted. There was no policeman forcing you
to go along. The loyalty to that cause was the paramount thing. And what gave
us the mortar that held it together was the Communist ideology." Even Socialist volunteers, who went to Spain in hopes of joining the Debs column, acknowledged the efficacy of the Communist organization and its distinctive
militancy.

Throughout the war, the Communist leadership kept close tabs on the performance of party and nonparty members, expecting higher achievements from
those who identified with the revolutionary vanguard. In nominating soldiers
for officers' training or promotion, for example, a volunteer's standing in the
party carried additional clout. A few non-Communists became military leaders of the brigade; they were the exceptions that proved the rule. Yet the politics of the Popular Front muted some of the party's sectarian tendencies. When
Mildred Rackley reported that one of the non-Communist doctors ought not
to be trusted, Comintern representative Robert Minor called the hospital administrator and her friend Dr. Barsky on the carpet for two days because, as
Rackley explained, "as a Communist I had not carried forth to the utmost degree our united front policy with a person with whom we were obliged to work."
Minor's tolerance, however, aroused the wrath of the more militant André Marty,
who condemned him in a letter to Earl Browder for following "a fake path: the
path of . . . 'Americanism.'" Such private infighting belied the tentative truce
of the Popular Front.

The omnipresence of Communist ideology also introduces questions about
the possible abuse of authority within the ranks. When one of the first American volunteers, the Socialist Hilliard Bernstein, arrived in Spain in January
1937, his outspoken criticism of Stalin infuriated a British officer, who called
him a "Trotskyite" and ordered his transfer to another battalion. Another

American maverick, the anarchist Pat Reade, made the mistake of vocalizing his anti-Communist "wobbly outlook" while serving in a French company, provoking his comrades to question his anti-fascist loyalties. Such allegations, in this period of Stalin's anti-Trotsky purge trials, could jeopardize a man's life; indeed, Spanish political rivals—Stalinists, Trotskyists, and anarchists alike—would execute many a foe. Significantly, however, both Bernstein and Reade were returned to the American battalion, where they enjoyed greater political tolerance. There is no surviving evidence that any other Lincoln volunteers were persecuted or punished in Spain for their political beliefs.

During the war—and since—anti-Communists also accused the Communist party of ruthlessly sending men to Spain to fight against superior military forces, without regard for the human toll. Such charges now appear unfounded. In the course of hundreds of conversations and interviews with Lincoln veterans by numerous scholars, not one person claimed to have been sent to Spain on a party assignment against his will. Nor was any coercion necessary; there was simply no lack of eligible volunteers to join the ranks. Indeed, in many cases it was the party that rejected certain Communist functionaries deemed more important for the continuing class struggle on the home front. "They twice refused me permission to go," Joe Dallet assured his worried mother, "and only gave in finally after I had pestered hell out of them and repeatedly insisted." And when, in the middle of the war, party leaders in Spain decided to save some of the cadres from the slaughter by ordering the repatriation of certain wounded veterans, many American volunteers, including the recalcitrant Mickenberg, resisted the chance to go home. "We felt terrible," remembered Bill Wheeler, who was sent on a speaking tour of the United States; "we felt like quitters." Other veterans would congregate in a café near the offices of the Friends of the Abraham Lincoln Brigade in New York, "order one drink after another and read the newspapers about Spain, Spain, Spain." One group of seven eventually managed to reenlist and crossed the Pyrenees for a second tour of duty.

Such enthusiasm reflected passions inherent in Communist ideology. "We all ought to be thankful," wrote nineteen-year-old George Kaye, who rebuffed an opportunity to go to college in order to participate in the political struggles. "We're living in the most important period in the history of civilization. We are actively engaged in helping humanity pass to a higher state of society, to a life of happy and united mankind fighting to conquer nature, instead of a mankind divided into classes, fighting among themselves." For party stalwarts, the opportunity to fight against fascism brought immense satisfaction. When the volunteers who climbed the Pyrenees with Edwin Rolfe reached the summit, they spontaneously began to sing "The Internationale"; those with Joe Dallet wept for joy.

These personal feelings expressed the Communists' vision of their vanguard status in the process of historical development. But although Communists believed fervently in the inevitable triumph of the working classes, they also acknowledged the temporary historical constraints imposed by the fascist counterrevolution. Devout Communists they may have been, but the logic of the Popular Front, formulated by the Comintern, put distinct limitations on their revolutionary zeal. As Edwin Rolfe remarked, "nothing is more important to us here . . . than winning the war." Victory, in other words, would supersede any revolutionary intentions; there was no secret agenda.

Communist ideology also stressed the importance of a militant proletariat. At a time when the American public opposed intervention in any European wars (even when expressing sympathy for Republican Spain), the volunteers could claim to be waging war, paradoxically, to create a lasting peace. "The fight for a democratic Spain is a step toward socialism and only with World Socialism can we secure World Peace," Gene Wolman told his family. "We are . . . fighting for . . . a future society which will produce that type of individual who will know better than to fight against his fellow men." One Berkeley undergraduate insisted that "the sooner fascism is defeated . . . the sooner 'good will toward men' can be put into practice. . . . If this presupposes the extermination of aggressors who refuse to abandon their aggression . . . , then that is not the fault of the 'reds.'" Less doctrinaire volunteers reached similar conclusions. For Don MacLeod, another Berkeley undergraduate, previous political involvement had been limited to attendance at a student pacifist conference. But when his college roommate, Hamilton Tyler, suggested they could work for peace by fighting fascism in Spain, MacLeod reconsidered his opinions and joined the campus branch of the Young Communist League, because that was the only way he knew to get to Spain. His ideological position had hardly changed. "I am more of a pacifist than ever," he wrote after a year in Spain. "Peace is too great a thing to ever attain without paying a great price and it is impossible to wish peace into the world while fascism is from day to day assaulting a greater and greater part of the earth's people."

These rationalizations indicated a genuine ideological devotion, the linking of political convictions with a sense of personal pride. Ben Gardner, for example, who had served a year in prison for picketing the German consulate in Philadelphia, acknowledged "the honor to be on guard duty" at the Lincolns' training base behind the lines, "the wonderful feeling of holding a rifle with bayonet, guarding Democracy. For the first time in my life I felt that it is not capitalist property I'm guarding, as I did in the National Guard, but the property of the workers, the people of Spain." Similar letters appeared frequently in the left-wing press in the United States; occasionally, sympathetic groups such as the Friends of the Abraham Lincoln Brigade or the Workers Alliance published them in pamphlet form to gain wider support for the Republican cause. Edwin Rolfe, who had a good ear for nuance, realized that this correspondence sounded like propaganda and pronunciamentos. "They do it because they feel the necessity for help terribly keenly. . . . Their earnestness and intensity takes the form of sloganish writing," he conceded, "but it's all truthful and deeply felt."

The Lincoln volunteers who went into action at Jarama had no doubts about their ideological motivations. Chosen by party leaders in New York, they viewed their assignment as part of the struggle against fascist reaction. "We shared common views, common ideology, and a common belief and a common faith," recalled William Herrick, who later had second thoughts about his party affiliations, "and that is why we were all on that ship going to Spain to fight against fascism." Even the cynical Mickenberg suspended his disbelief. "A lot of it was romantic talk," he recalled of the conversations aboard the SS *Paris* on the way to Spain. "One of the things we were quite sure of was that we were about to enter an army that was something new under the sun, a proletarian army, the first in the history of mankind. That . . . was a most exhilarating thought." The trip by rail from Paris to Barcelona reinforced his enthusiasm. "It was just about the most wonderful experience a man could have in a lifetime," he remembered, "to see these many, many hundreds of men from all parts of the world, . . . men who looked haggard, sick and frail. They had gone through hell to get to Paris. They were wonderful. So we had a very joyous time of it . . . pioneers of the proletarian army."

Mickenberg soon noticed that party discipline sometimes exceeded common sense. Despite "the much vaunted efficiency" of the party leaders, for example, he realized "that every single man Jack [was] carrying precisely the same baggage and the same kind of imitation leather suitcase." He was irked, moreover, when his military credentials identified his political affiliation as "anti-fascist." "I was very proud of being a Communist," he explained. "I had no reason for concealing it, certainly not in Spain." Mickenberg made no protest, but he did avoid surrendering his passport to brigade authorities, even though it later meant he had to wear his old lice-ridden pants, the only ones with pockets large enough to hold the document. Mickenberg bristled at other constraints. From the first weeks in Spain, he remembered a continual barrage of speeches. Some dealt with military matters, but many examined political subjects. Robert Merriman, he recalled, spoke intelligently about agricultural problems and collectivization, while Sterling Rochester, a black volunteer who had come to the brigade from the Lenin School in Moscow, addressed the problems of minorities "in all places, ages, and climates." Mickenberg also observed the endless problems of establishing authority—disputes between Merriman, Harris, and Commissar Stember.

All the shortcomings of the leadership—inexperience, lack of discipline, a pathetic shortage of good judgment—climaxed in the slaughter of February 27, when the Lincolns went over the top into a shower of machine-gun fire. Mickenberg lay in the exposed no-man's-land for nine hours, until darkness permitted him to crawl back to the trenches. "Nobody could say to himself why he had survived and somebody else had not," he recalled. In the light of day, fear and the wonder of survival were replaced by anger. Mickenberg, ever adept at wordplay, referred to Merriman as "Murderman"—a name that stuck. ("In the battalion he was a strong rank and filer," a knowledgeable observer said of Mickenberg, "but so strong in his rank and file sentiment that he felt himself superior to most of the officers." That attitude would cost Mickenberg opportunities for promotion.) But with Merriman hospitalized with a shoulder wound, the men sought other targets. Some spoke openly of shooting the officers. An enraged Arthur Madden, a volunteer whose request for truck driver duty had earlier been rejected by no less an authority than André Marty, angrily accused the British officer George Wattis of causing needless casualties by ordering a second attack at the point of a gun. Most vulnerable was Commissar Stember, who during the heat of battle had gone to the cook house safely behind the lines to find food and drink for the men. His absence from the trenches destroyed whatever credibility he might have claimed.

"Here we were," Mickenberg remembered, describing the prevailing sentiment. "We were Communists, trade union Communists, members of mass organizations. We were skilled in the arts of protest. It had been our whole life in the United States. What were we going to do about this outrage?" Unwilling to resume their posts—only a torrential downpour kept the enemy from walking through their trenches—the stunned Lincolns talked indignantly among themselves, discussed alternatives, until finally they demanded to have a mass meeting to express their grievances. Brigade officers, including Stember, tried to stop the meeting, warning the men of the consequences of violating military discipline, abandoning the front, and exposing themselves to the fascists. "They tried every trick in the book to stop the meeting," said Mickenberg. But finally the demands of the men prevailed.

On the afternoon of March 1, the Lincolns placed a handful of men on sentry duty in the trenches and marched half a mile behind the lines for a meeting with the commissar of the Fifteenth Brigade, the Frenchman Jean Barthol. "Everybody who wanted to talk talked," remembered Mickenberg. "It was a wonderful thing to happen. You got all that off your chest." But the purpose was more than therapeutic. After a bitter litany of organizational failure and military idiocy, the men agreed to four formal demands. First, they requested immediate removal from the front lines—some because they needed rest, others because they wanted to be sent home. Second, the Lincolns demanded a minimum of two weeks' training under the guidance of experienced officers—"not," in Mickenberg's words, "our own self-selected amateurs." Third, they asked for a formal court-martial of those responsible for sending the soldiers over the top "without preparation, without fulfilling the battle order that had been outlined to us earlier." These complaints revealed a people's army standing up for its rights. Yet except for a handful of deserters who did not stay for the meeting, there was no attempt at mutiny or breach of military discipline, as some anti-Communists have subsequently charged. The appeals, however emotional, remained within the limits of command. And the Lincolns' final demand, which Mickenberg dubbed "pitiful," demonstrated a continuing allegiance to the Communist movement: The Americans requested permission to contact the central committee of the Communist party of the United States, which might help them confront the power of party leaders from other countries who controlled the International Brigades. "It sounded like nothing so much as a child crying for its mother," Mickenberg later complained. "We felt if Earl Browder knew about this he would never have wanted it to happen."

A unanimous voice vote approved the list of grievances and elected a committee of five to carry them to brigade headquarters. Then the meeting adjourned and the Lincolns returned to the front lines. Meanwhile, the five delegates presented their demands to brigade leaders, including Colonel Vladimir Copic, who had overridden Merriman's objections and ordered the ill-fated attack. Copic had no intention, of course, of permitting a court-martial of himself. And a French commissar made no apology for the attack, stating that in war mistakes were often made. But the brigade agreed to examine the conduct of Lieutenant Wattis, who had been accused of drawing a pistol to order men out of the trenches and erroneously repositioning a machine gun. "He was an accomplished actor in the role of British officer from his military mustache to polished boots," recalled one American volunteer. "He had enough skill to judge exactly how far to expose himself while sending men out to die." The ensuing session constituted a Communist party trial, with brigade officers serving as judges and Commissar Oscar Hunter representing the Americans. The panel heard several witnesses, including three Lincolns, and permitted Wattis to cross-examine their testimony. In the end, the evidence showed that the machine guns had been placed properly and that Wattis had not threatened anyone with a revolver. The tribunal found him innocent.

As for the request for removal from the lines and retraining, the leadership agreed to one day's rest, but insisted that an expected attack by Italian fascists made any alternative impossible. The road had to be held. Brigade commissars promised to inform the American Communist party about the perilous state of affairs. Then, having made these concessions, brigade leaders offered the five delegates better assignments. Some became company commanders. Barthol appointed Arthur Madden battalion commissar to share responsibilities with Stember, whom he hated; the two would fight constantly until Madden was sent to officers' school. The Russian-speaking Robert Gladnick, who had helped translate the battalion's complaints to Copic, received, in Mickenberg's words, "his heart's desire"—a transfer out of the infantry into a Russian-led tank corps. "So every single one of the five members of the committee got bribed into something," observed Mickenberg, "and the protest evaporated."

The underlying anger did not easily abate. Meeting a correspondent from the *Daily Worker* near the front lines, Mickenberg replied to a question about the latest news by suggesting, "You can say that the battalion was named after Abraham Lincoln because he, too, was assassinated." Mickenberg's friends hustled him away before the journalist could get his name, perhaps to report him to the commissars. Discontent remained close to the surface. Martin Hourihan, appointed to replace Merriman as battalion commander, found the men surly and reluctant to follow orders. As often as not, he admitted, they would reply: "Go fuck yourself." He arranged the transfer of his most disgruntled critics to other brigades.

To rebuild morale, party leaders also established an unofficial core of "the best elements" to muffle complaints and restore confidence in the leadership. "Working almost like a party group in a mass organization," Hourihan reported, "these men became instrumental in building up the morale of the men and establishing military discipline." Yet two months later, the Lincolns ignored Hourihan's command to launch another dangerous offensive, a defiance for which they suffered no reprisals. And the men never forgave Stember for remaining in safety far from the front. Twelve days after the protest meeting, their anger exploded when Stember published an article, "Single Command," in the brigade newspaper *Our Fight*. "Those who challenge the military or political authority of . . . commanders," he wrote, "are self-seekers who are no less guilty than the deserters who have been sentenced to hard labor in the labor battalion." He warned that a recurrence by these "disruptive elements" would result in "severe measures." Outraged by this threat, the men voted no confidence in their commissar, forcing him from his post. "The [political] commander," the *Daily Worker* would announce a few months later, "was sent back" to the United States "on the vote of the battalion to tell of their needs and to make the American people understand what they are fighting for." Such gross distortions rankled the men in Spain, but none would threaten the Republican cause by exposing Stember's weakness.

"When the battle terminates, we count the dead," wrote William Herrick, one of the first Lincoln casualties at Jarama, who went on to live for more than fifty years with a fascist bullet encased in his neck and to write several novels about the psychology of revolutionaries. "The more dead the better we feel. We have survived the many. We, the survivors, are the chosen." After their baptism of fire at Jarama, the Lincolns' commitment to Republican Spain assumed more than an ideological dimension; the cause became deeply personal, part of their lifelong identity. And it introduced obligations to those comrades who had been less fortunate. "When we were pulled out of the lines," wrote Edwin Rolfe later in the war, "I felt very tired and lonely and guilty. Lonely because half of the battalion had been badly shot up. . . . And guilty because I felt I didn't deserve to be alive now, with Arnold and Nick and Paul dead." Such "survivor guilt," as psychologists define that reaction, reinforced a sense of responsibility for continuing the anti-fascist crusade.

Their political conscience also made the Lincolns better soldiers. In an exhaustive postwar study of battlefield psychology, conducted by Yale University sociologist John Dollard in 1942, the Lincoln veterans acknowledged an intimate connection between political convictions and their personal feelings during military action. Foremost among their emotions, Dollard found, was a sense of terror. "Fear is normal," he concluded. "Experienced men admit it and are not ashamed." Indeed, nearly two-thirds of Dollard's respondents confessed that they had suffered moments of panic when they "lost their heads . . . , couldn't control themselves and were useless as soldiers for a little while." On the positive side, this fear enhanced an instinct for self-preservation, making the men "cautious under fire."

The Lincoln veterans described a hierarchy of wound fears: first came abdominal injuries, then wounds to the eyes, brain, genitals, legs and feet, hands and arms, face, and torso. They acknowledged a range of "most-feared weapons," with bomb shrapnel deemed the most frightening, bullets the least. The survivors reported a much greater fear of the sounds of war—the noise of exploding bombs—than of any visual experience. Such fears produced palpable physical reactions, which could also be arranged hierarchically: most common were pounding of the heart and rapid pulse; then came muscular tenseness, a sinking feeling in the stomach, dryness of the mouth and throat, trembling, sweating, loss of appetite, prickling sensations, ringing in the ears, and involuntary urination and defecation; very few people vomited or fainted. "Fear begins with strong bodily responses," Dollard concluded, "and is then registered on the mind."

Despite the prevalence of fear, Dollard found that the Lincolns had learned to control their visceral responses in order to function effectively in battle. To alleviate their concerns, for example, men spoke openly about personal fear, thus sharing the knowledge of their common dilemma. But according to Dollard, such candor was best expressed prior to going into action. Once in combat, panic could become dangerously contagious, jeopardizing everyone. Yet the veterans observed that courage, too, became contagious. Nearly all the respondents said they fought better after observing others behaving calmly and coolly in a dangerous situation. The best remedy for fear, the men suggested, was to focus on the work at hand, moving one's mind from the abstract to the physical. "When a man stops reacting to danger signals," Dollard explained, "he is no longer afraid."

The most important of Dollard's findings, however, revealed the power of political ideology. In a rare display of unanimity, the Lincoln veterans asserted that knowledge of war aims and a personal identification with the Republican cause improved their battlefield reliability. "If a man knows what he is fighting for," Dollard reported, "and has an intense personal need to win, his zeal in battle will tend to triumph over his fear." Hatred and anger also solidified morale. Although the death of a close friend produced flashes of rage and a desire for revenge, Dollard found that a more impersonal antipathy to the enemy created "a sustained, steady anger which lasts until the final battle is won." These motives—the result of intelligent learning and political beliefs—lay at the basis of the Lincolns' celebrated esprit de corps. That is why they accepted the discipline of their officers, fought against overwhelming military superiority, and maintained their commitment to defeating the fascist enemy.

The sole female respondent in the postwar study, truck driver Evelyn Hutchins, also stressed the value of political consciousness. During the war, she had experienced several close calls when fascist aviation bombed and strafed the vehicle she was driving. She had also suffered exhaustion from working eighteen-hour shifts, double-clutching her truck over twisting mountain roads. "I had bad dreams all night," she told a magazine interviewer in 1937. "I'd always be driving a car and something would go wrong with it"— she would awaken in a cold sweat. But in daylight, she boasted, "I've never lost my nerves yet." To Dollard, Hutchins reaffirmed her unwavering self-discipline: "I just wouldn't give in to letting them frighten me. I would not permit it to happen to me." The fascists, she explained, "wanted to break our morale, and I wanted to show them that they were not going to do it. When anybody did crack, I just got mad at him for giving in." She insisted, moreover, that these victims were "not too clear on the issues. . . . They were there for personal reasons. Some of them were maladjusted at home. With some it may have been adventure. With some a number of their friends went, and they were ashamed not to go along—something like that." But the point Hutchins made—an idea repeated by many other Communist observers—was that intellectual understanding, correct ideology, could triumph over physical fear. "A soldier who is politically conscious that he is right," concluded guerrilla fighter William Aalto, "and who has a feeling of community with his society . . . will do his job well." Significantly, both Aalto and Hutchins received the highest political ratings from Communist leaders at the end of the war.

"Dear," wrote Al Hawkins to his wife, in a statement reiterated by many of the Lincoln survivors, "I didn't turn chicken under fire the other day—and was I surprised." Committed to a political cause that celebrated collective behavior, each soldier nonetheless had to validate his personal integrity in battle. Equally important, the Communist volunteer had to show his courage to the other men. "It is not bravery that keeps men from breaking," explained Ben Iceland about the ordeal of fire; "rather it is shame—shame at the thought of acting like a coward in front of your comrades—shame at being the first to give way—shame at the thought that you, who had come thousands of miles to fight, could not take it. So men act nonchalantly, when inwardly they are consumed by fear." From such testimony it is perhaps no wonder that the legend of the Lincoln brigade revealed countless stories of individual bravery. In the numerous oral histories taken during the preparation of this book, the most frequently recounted battle memory (usually told with modest requests of anonymity) involved an individual who exposed himself to enemy fire in order to rescue a fallen comrade. Ironically, such heroes often joined the casualty lists themselves, requiring yet another mission of mercy.

The bravery of the Lincoln volunteers had ideological roots. To many young Communists, joining the party had involved a genuine psychological conversion, similar to the experience of religious rebirth. The seaman Bill Bailey, famous from the *Bremen* affair, described his politicization as a process of self-awakening that brought him a new sense of dignity. Like many young Communists, he not only viewed himself as a "new man" but felt and acted with a new sense of responsibility. "Comradeship" entered his vocabulary. He developed a "respect for people," stopped hustling and cheating, and sought difficult political assignments, of which Spain was one. Edwin Rolfe, who left the relatively safe offices of the *Volunteer for Liberty* to serve in the front lines, captured the intensity of the Communist commitment. "The war has ripped all illusions from even the youngest of the volunteers, leaving only the reality," he wrote from the combat zone. "That reality is harder than anyone who has never been under machine-gun fire and bombs and artillery fire can ever know. Yet the men of the [Lincoln brigade], knowing it well, chose and continue to choose to fight for Spain's free existence . . . to be true to themselves and their innermost convictions."

Beneath that bravado, nonetheless, lay great agonies of self-doubt. Just two weeks before Rolfe filed his story about American courage, the Oklahoma-born Barney Baley nestled in a rocky shell hole and scrawled in his diary: "There's my self-respect to consider. If I failed to do my bit at a time like this I'd never feel right afterward. . . . I was born a rebel, a champion of the underdog. . . . May I die that way when my time comes." Scrutinizing his comrades, Baley observed a common commitment—"a clearer, more sensitive approach and conception to life, a refusal to tolerate and accept cheapness, tawdriness. So we came to Spain." Two days later, Baley went "another round in my fight of Bolshevik determination vs. instinct of self-preservation. Again, my better angel, my Dr. Jekyll, won out. But how long, O God! how long. Standby for expected attack." To his eternal gratification, Baley held fast.

Alvah Bessie, the novelist, was 34 years old when he prepared for his first battle. Despite his political sophistication, he too admitted the primacy of psychological considerations in explaining his decision to enlist. "I wanted . . . to work (for the first time) in a large body of men," he wrote in the notebook that became the basis for his classic book, *Men in Battle*, "to submerge myself in the mass, seeking neither distinction nor preferment—the obverse of my activities the past several years—and in this way to achieve: self-discipline, patience and resignation, unselfishness. In fine, to complete the destruction of my early training in order to build again a life that would be geared to other men and the world-events that circumscribed their lives."

But if the true Communist had to surrender all sense of self to fulfill the psychological imperatives, anti-Communists among the Lincoln veterans would later condemn those totalitarian tendencies. "To change the world totally was to change man totally," wrote veteran William Herrick about one of his fictional volunteers in the Spanish war. "He was expunging the individual ego, overthrowing its dominance . . . and in so doing destroying . . . the tradition of personal freedom which had helped form him as a man." More orthodox Lincolns emphasized the beneficent results of their transformation. That is why so many veterans expressed—and still express—the honor of dying, as Barney Baley put it, "in the company of such comrades." Communist ideology, in other words, reinforced a psychological predilection for self-sacrifice. The two were inseparable.

The proximity of death, however, created endless risks of self-deception. Sidney Kurtz, assigned to broadcast radio programs from Madrid back to the United States, confessed that he had come to Spain not only to fight against fascism, "but primarily . . . to fight against my own indolence, uncertainty and indecision." For Kurtz, the Communist movement provided coherence and direction. "Never in all my life have I felt the strength and quiet confidence course through me as I do now," he wrote. Yet Kurtz also suffered incapacitating anxieties that may well have saved his life. Facing his first battle on the Jarama front, he wondered "whether the coming test would bring out in me the potentialities I always thought I had, or whether under fire I would break." But before the test could be met, Kurtz collapsed with sunstroke and diarrhea and found himself in a hospital. Then he developed appendicitis and had to undergo surgery. "If ever sickness was the result of wish-fulfillment," he admitted, "then this was it." Kurtz subsequently requested repatriation, but he agreed to accept the radio job instead. There he could safely contribute to the war effort, while boasting about how his political conversion had "changed my life so completely, redirected me into channels where there is little danger of grounding on a reef."

Kurtz's ambivalence—the tension between self-discipline and fear—permeated the brigade. Whatever inner commitments motivated people to volunteer in Spain, the conditions of war swiftly destroyed their psychological defenses. Even before the first Lincolns entered the front lines at Jarama, an air attack caused panic among the inexperienced soldiers. "Men ran and showed early weakness," noted a worried Merriman. A few days later, Robert Gladnick saw the man next to him killed. "I lost my nerve completely," he later admitted; Gladnick could not function for several hours. The battalion's first commander, James Harris, exhibited similar incapacitating symptoms. As he drew nearer to battle, Harris began acting erratically. Sent for treatment to Dr. William Pike, head of the brigade medical corps, Harris rambled in a hallucinatory way and defecated into his underpants. Nonetheless, he returned to the battalion, in Merriman's words, "still abnormal and talked loudly and accused me of having him confined in Albacete. Confused man." After Harris led the men on a midnight march through no-man's-land, brigade leaders evacuated him to a hospital behind the lines. Nearly two decades later, some anti-Communist Lincolns would claim that Harris had been the victim of a party purge; the contemporary record shows more clearly a pattern of mental breakdown.

The Jarama debacle of February 27 accentuated the problems of morale. "The men had all physical breakdowns," remembered Gladnick, "and they suffered the very same way I had suffered a few days earlier." Fortunately, Dr. Pike could help many of them recover. Born in New York City in 1904, he had studied at the Rush Medical School in Chicago (thanks to the angliciza-tion of his family's name, which enabled him to evade the quota against Jews). A small, intense man, he had launched a private practice in the depths of the Depression, but soon found he could not earn a living. He located a more secure position as a psychiatrist in a New York state hospital. The experience would prove extremely valuable in Spain. Describing himself as "absolutely apolitical," he nonetheless had published a few articles on the advantages of socialized medicine, warned of the dangers of tobacco, and campaigned against the distribution of laxatives to children. He identified, as he put it, "with those who had been badly treated, pushed around."

Even before embarking for Spain, Pike helped interview other volunteers to screen the medically or psychologically unfit. As he observed the recruits, the doctor began to apply the psychiatric insights he had gained in his work. Many of the volunteers, Pike observed, harbored expectations of becoming heroes, a common notion among young soldiers, which may have been accen-tuated by their Communist beliefs. Viewing the war in Spain as an apocalyp-tic battleground between the revolutionary working classes and the forces of fascist reaction, these civilian-soldiers saw themselves as the vanguard of history. However much they might attempt to stifle their private egos, they perceived themselves to be daring, audacious fighters, and their honor within the Communist movement confirmed that self-image. "They were going to be heroes, and therefore be recognized," Pike explained many years later. "This was seeking gratification through recognition."

Such grandiose expectations soon collided with the stark realities of war: inadequate food, poor shelter, tremendous danger. Most of the Lincolns, to their credit and pride, managed to function effectively. But Pike found that for some the confrontation with "the harsh reality knocked their fantasies sky high." Soon after reaching the Jarama front in February 1937, Pike discovered that a group of about a dozen brigadiers, most of them British but some who were American, were suffering severe shell shock. Having retreated far from the line of fire, they lived in fear in the dark shelter of a cave. They would appear at its entrance only for their food. As Pike reported, "they came down one by one, hands, lips trembling, faces twitching, eyes downcast, ashamed." The physician determined to bring them back to the land of the living by rebuilding their self-esteem. "They would recover little by little," he predicted; "work would serve to gradually readjust them, work would take their minds from those bursting shells, remove the feeling of futility and failure."

He began by assigning these men to specific tasks in safe areas. To get from the front lines to the medical base, stretcher bearers had to climb over hills and rough terrain, an hour-long journey that imperiled the lives of the wounded. Pike instructed the shell-shocked soldiers to construct a roadway, protected from enemy fire, that would reduce the trip to twenty minutes. "It was surprising how quickly it restored their morale," he recalled. "They became cleaner, neater in appearance, and they worked like beavers." Within days, the opening of "Pike's Turnpike," as the men dubbed the road, testified to the value of work therapy. Pike then assigned these men to stretcher bearing in safe areas. "This work of helping their physically wounded buddies, decreasing their minutes of pain, restored the confidence of these mentally wounded. Gradually they were brought closer to the battle lines, into the second stations, then the first, and finally into the front lines—far removed from their trembling fear. They were," Pike concluded, "men again."

While Pike improvised programs of work therapy for the most traumatized volunteers, other worried men simply deserted from the Jarama front and headed toward Valencia. Three or four did not get very far before they were intercepted by more stalwart volunteers. Touched by appeals to their pride and their political commitments, this handful turned around and resumed their positions in the trenches. They suffered no punishment for their temporary departure. Within two weeks of the Jarama slaughter, however, six other deserters had arrived at the American consulate and requested assistance in obtaining repatriation to the United States. Although the local consul claimed these deserters were "in great danger" if they were arrested by Spanish authorities, the State Department in Washington refused to assist American citizens who had entered Spain illegally. To the immense satisfaction of the consul, five of the six soon disappeared from Valencia, heading for the French border dressed as civilians. At least one of them appeared subsequently before federal investigators in the United States, and it appears likely that all managed to return home safely. The sixth, an unnamed "American negro," remained at the consulate (perhaps because his visibility would hasten his arrest) until he could be evacuated with the permission of the Spanish government. Despite other instances of near mutiny, the International Brigades relied primarily on political persuasion to strengthen morale. The only reported case of a military execution at Jarama involved an unnamed first-aid officer, probably a Canadian, who had been caught stealing cash and other valuables from the bodies of wounded comrades.

The psychological patterns that emerged during the first battles at Jarama would reappear in subsequent military encounters. As the Dollard study indicated, fear remained a pervasive factor; but so did the Lincolns' ability to control it. "Here at the frontier of death," wrote the ambulance driver James Neugass as the brigade headed toward its next battle at Brunete, "the last backward step has been taken / the final decision made the last doubt thrown away."

9

The Discipline of Command

While the Lincoln battalion lived in the trenches at Jarama through the wet spring of 1937, new recruits from America continued to swell the ranks. They would never be as innocent as the first volunteers. By March 1937, the French government had finally succumbed to British pressure and closed the Franco-Spanish border to military assistance. With U.S. passports stamped "Not Valid for Travel to Spain," Americans had to find alternative routes to enter the Republic. The choices were limited, the risks grave. Indeed, getting into Spain sometimes proved as dangerous as fighting the war. For individual volunteers, the journey became part of a ritual experience, a test of stamina and courage that cemented bonds of loyalty among the Lincolns and forever after separated them from those who had stayed at home, who had quit in Paris, who had not made the crossing. "It was so dark," recalled Alvah Bessie of his passage across the Spanish border, "we stayed close enough together to be able to put out our hands and touch the dark and reassuring back ahead. The meaning of the word 'comrade,' so often heard in Spain, began to become clear."

The most frequently traveled avenue to Spain crossed the steep Pyrenees; to negotiate it the volunteers required the assistance of professional Basque smugglers, who were unusually strong, sure-footed, and intimately familiar with every mountain trail. Here the risk of capture by French border patrols accentuated the physical torments, because the journey had to be undertaken in pitch darkness in a single night. "Most of the guys were like me, just city slickers," reported Milton Wolff, who was among the first Americans to make the ascent. "We were dressed in fancy shoes, in fancy clothes, and looked like anything but a mountain-climbing expedition." As a recent CCC worker, Wolff considered himself in excellent physical condition. But the climb demanded all his energy and concentration. "It was very, very grueling, going up and up, and always thinking we were reaching the top and never getting there." At each crest, the Americans asked their guides if the next hill would be Spain. "Paciencia, paciencia," they would reply. Weaker men collapsed and had to be carried by relays of comrades, or even left behind, hopefully to be rescued on a subsequent night. Members of the international nonintervention inspection committee later claimed to have found the remains of two hundred men who fell from precipices or dropped from exhaustion. Nonetheless, to most Americans, the ordeal of passage confirmed the value of their objective. "Weary as we were," said Wolff, "we cheered and yelled at the top of our lungs."

The easiest way to travel from France to Spain—embarking from a Mediterranean port—was hardly the safest. At midnight of May 30, 1937, for example, 250 Internationals set sail from Marseilles aboard the *Ciudad de Barcelona*, a pleasure ship destined for Barcelona. As the ship hugged the Spanish coast, a Republican seaplane flew overhead, and passengers could see the pilot gesticulating frantically. Before the crew could decipher his signals, they heard a dull, loud thud and felt the ship begin to tilt. An Italian submarine had fired a torpedo broadside. Seven minutes later, the entire vessel sank beneath the waves. "I remember the screaming faces of men trapped at the portholes," recalled the Brooklyn-born Abe Osheroff. Diving into the sea, he began to swim for safety; but almost immediately, he stopped, pulled back by an urge to help the non-swimmers. That apparently proved to be a typical response. "What I'll never forget," reported another survivor, "is the absolute lack of hysteria. There was no jostling, no pushing, no mad scramble for life preservers and boats." Some fifty men died, including at least twelve Americans. Others swam to the nearby shore or boarded rescue boats sent from a coastal village. What the survivors remembered, besides their terror, was the spontaneous spirit of self-sacrifice.

The arrival of fresh recruits provided enough manpower not only to replenish the decimated Lincolns, but also to form additional American battalions. The first new contingent, headed by the Yugoslav-American Mirko Markovicz, voted to name themselves after Tom Mooney, the imprisoned California labor leader, who had already lent his name to a machine-gun company. But Communist party leaders in New York telegrammed their disapproval, considering the Mooney case too inflammatory. In the spirit of the Popular Front, party leader Robert Minor proposed Jefferson or Washington, and the more conservative of the two prevailed in the George Washington battalion. The naming of a third battalion stirred greater controversy, as the men deadlocked between Patrick Henry and Tom Paine. Robert Merriman, still recuperating from his wounds but in charge of training the new outfit, recommended a Canadian name to create an international flavor and acknowledge the role of the many Canadian volunteers. The result was the MacKenzie-Papineau battalion, known as the Mac-Paps, which commemorated two anti–British imperialists of the nineteenth century.

Each battalion consisted of nearly 500 Americans (fewer in the Mac-Paps). Each was divided into three infantry companies and a machine-gun company equipped with heavy, water-cooled weapons. Every company, in turn, split into three sections; and these reduced to groups or squads. At each level of the organizational structure, the military commander shared responsibility with a political commissar. The Washingtons and Mac-Paps, led largely by American officers, managed during the stillness at Jarama to receive substantially more training than the first volunteers. Milton Wolff, who had originally intended to become a first-aid man, found himself in the Washington battalion's machine-gun company, receiving instructions from Walter Garland, a black veteran of Jarama. "He sure knew his stuff, and he had been in action," Wolff would recall. "This gave us more confidence in ourselves. . . . The only thing to warp our joy in life," he added, "was that we had four old machine guns, rather worthless . . . ; they were bastard machine guns, with different locks and different springs." As ever, the Spanish Republican Army, strangled by nonintervention policies, lacked sufficient materiel to arm and train its soldiers thoroughly. But by the early summer of 1937, the Washingtons were prepared to join the Lincolns in the next battles. Meanwhile, the Mac-Paps would be kept in training.

After the fiasco at Jarama, the American Communist party moved quickly to appoint veteran organizers to assume political leadership of the Lincolns in Spain. Foremost among these was Steve Nelson, then working among the anthracite coal miners in western Pennsylvania. When the first call for volunteers had spread through the Communist ranks, Nelson had recruited a group of eight from the Wilkes-Barre area, including himself. "I felt that I couldn't ask anyone to do things that I wasn't prepared to do myself," he later said. But at age 34, Nelson appeared too old for combat, and the party used that excuse to send him back to the mining district, where he was considered too valuable an asset for the home front. A few weeks later, however, the near mutiny after Jarama demanded a reversal of that decision.

Nelson hastened to Spain in the company of Joe Dallet, another organizer who was expected to provide political leadership. "Conspicuously trying to be inconspicuous," they led a group of 25 volunteers from Paris to southern France, where they expected to board a waiting ship. But the boat was late; it would be daylight before they could reach a safe harbor. So at dawn the men disappeared below deck. Peeking through the cracks in the planking, they celebrated their first sight of the Spanish coast, only to be brought to an abrupt silence by the sound of a rapidly closing diesel engine. As the men cringed quietly, a French inspector climbed aboard, peered into the hold, and promptly arrested the entire group. Hoping to muster support among the French populace, Nelson proposed that they drop their tourist alibi and admit their intention to help the Spanish Republic. French authorities nonetheless treated them like common criminals, though public pressure may have aided their defense. After a stormy trial in the town of Céret, the Americans received three-week jail terms, most of which they had already served. Then they were ordered out of France. But no one watched which direction they took.

Nelson's delayed arrival in Spain complicated his responsibilities. Appointed commissar of the Lincoln battalion by base officials in Albacete, he reached the men just before May Day of 1937. By then, the Americans had been in the front lines continuously since February. They had seen little fighting in recent weeks, and their morale had deteriorated from inaction. Now they craved good food, a bath, a chance to relax. On April 30, the weary battalion was moved to the town of Alcalá de Henares, and the men began to unwind. They spent the night sleeping in the bombed-out church where Cervantes had been christened. The next day they marched in the local May Day parade, posed for pictures, and tried to find something to drink. That afternoon, Nelson addressed them for the first time. Appealing to their pride as fighting anti-fascists, he stressed their support on the home front. Recent gains by CIO labor unions in the United States, he said, presaged an increasingly sympathetic political climate. Nelson's warm sincerity proved "a tremendous success," according to one volunteer; "the men felt like a million dollars." But that night, to their amazement, the brigade command ordered the Lincolns to return to the trenches. Nelson's talk, however, had fired their spirits; they would handle the adversity. And, as Paul Burns remembered, "the lice were glad to see us back on the hill."

What had caused the abrupt reversal of orders? According to Nelson, the brigade had received a report of an imminent fascist attack; fortunately, it never came. But some of the Lincolns have offered an alternative explanation that, even if inaccurate, illuminates the political climate in the brigade. Stated simply, many Americans later blamed their predicament on the anarchist insurrection that commenced in Barcelona in May 1937. At a time when the Lincoln battalion was helping to defend Madrid from encirclement, the political crisis forced the withdrawal of Spanish troops from the front lines to suppress the dissidents in Barcelona. Most Lincolns therefore regarded the uprising as an act of treachery and subversion.

That view of the anarchist upheaval underscored the ideological limits of the Popular Front. In its effort to build alliances with all anti-fascist groups, the Spanish Communist party had insisted that more radical elements, particularly the anarchists, soften their revolutionary demands. Such a posture would appeal to the so-called democracies—France, Britain, and the United States— and perhaps, as the Soviet Union cabled the Spanish premier in December 1936, "prevent the enemies of Spain from regarding her as a Communist republic." The Spanish Communist party, therefore, opposed the social revolution that occurred spontaneously in Catalonia during the first days and weeks of the civil war. This stance represented an extension of the Comintern position, dovetailed with Stalin's foreign policy, and so protected Soviet military assistance to the Republic. The Spanish Communist party thereby increased its size and influence dramatically. From a prewar total of forty thousand, party membership leaped sixfold by March 1937. Yet many left-wing Socialists and anarchists bitterly resented the Communist position, arguing that a revolutionary society could never be conquered by fascist armies.

The controversy exploded in gunfire on the streets of Barcelona just as the Lincolns returned to the trenches. As Republican soldiers seized the anarchist-held telephone exchange, the anarchists and other dissidents erected defensive barricades in the streets. "A strange and wonderful sight," George Orwell called it. "With the kind of passionate energy that Spaniards display when they have definitely decided to begin upon any job of work, long lines of men, women, and quite small children were tearing up cobble-stones, hauling them along in a hand-cart . . . and staggering to and fro under heavy sacks of sand." Meanwhile, the Republican government ordered assault troops to crush the rebellion by force of arms. The crisis, described vividly in Orwell's *Homage to Catalonia*, epitomized the radical dilemma in Spain: whether to harness the revolution in order to wage the war against Franco more effectively or to encourage the revolution and its defense of autonomy at the risk of weakening the unity of the Republic. For Communist propagandists, moreover, the Barcelona uprising served to repudiate the so-called counterrevolutionary activities of Stalin's nemesis, Leon Trotsky, who allegedly had formed a conspiracy with fascist fifth columnists to incite the rebellion.

That several officers of the Lincoln battalion believed they had been returned to the lines in May 1937 because Spanish troops had to be withdrawn to suppress the Barcelona insurrection revealed much about their political beliefs. For one thing, it reinforced their antipathy to the anarchists and Trotskyists who seemed to imperil the Republican cause. "Soldiers giving their lives at the front and those 100 percent revolutionaries, our trotskyite friends organize a revolt in the rear," complained Jerry Warren (Weinberg) to a friend in Brooklyn. "If I ever see a Trotskyite at the front I'll sure as hell shoot him." Such statements echoed the opinion of non-Communists within the brigade. The Socialist Hilliard Bernstein, despite his own troubles with Communist zealots, expressed an immediate hostility to the "damn fools" who had fomented the uprising in the rear. Jack Fahey, another Socialist who had gone to Spain with the "mythical Debs Column," publicly resigned from the party because it had challenged the crushing of the Barcelona rebellion. Similarly, Hans Amlie dismissed the "contemptible few pigmies" among the Socialists who had failed to back the Communist position. Edwin Rolfe, who later covered the trial of the dissident leaders for the *Daily Worker*, described the affair as "Trotskyist treason" against the Republic.

This denunciation of Trotskyists, anarchists, and left-wing Socialists, besides serving sectarian purposes, reflected a larger commitment to the Popular Front strategy. To be sure, many of the Lincoln volunteers did define their mission in revolutionary terms. "The American working class and the antifascist movement as a whole [have] made a good investment," declared Ben Gardner. "A large core of young comrades who will be invaluable to our work in the States. Who can and will be in the forefront in the developing Peoples Front against reaction." Another soldier saw the war as a learning experience, "a school for the training of Communists, who will go back to their own countries to rid them of poverty, hunger, exploitation, and all that goes with that." Indeed, the American Communist party would later place a large number of Lincoln veterans in positions of responsibility.

During the Spanish war, however, the Communists usually submerged their revolutionary impulses in the name of discipline. "Our purpose throughout three years of civil war was not to set up some sort of workers' republic, be it socialist, anarchist, or what have you," Steve Nelson later stated. "There was clearly a progressive content to the political program of the Popular Front that would have extended civil liberties, strengthened the bargaining power of workers and spurred land reform. And there were openly revolutionary currents within it. Yet the goal of the Popular Front was not a socialist republic." Party spokesmen in Spain constantly reiterated that line.

In the wake of the May insurrection, the highest-ranking American Communist in Spain, Robert Minor, addressed the battalion for two hours on that point, asserting that the Trotskyist revolutionaries were really in fascist pay. The irreverent, lecture-weary Morris Mickenberg would later observe that "this was a man who raised major questions and delivered Robert Minor answers." But most of the Lincolns saw no contradictions in the party position. "If we have a well organized discipline while we are preparing for the revolution," wrote one soldier to the home front, "we will have it during the revolution." The curtailment of revolutionary expectations showed the power of the party line in Spain. But, paradoxically, it also suggested a pragmatic, nonideological current within the ranks. Volunteers who had come to fight fascism saw military victory as the primary objective. Facing constant shortages of supplies, they could only look with dismay at a weakening of the effort because of political disputes behind the lines. Decades later, most Lincoln veterans clung to that view. "You can't stick a Joe Bianca up on a rock to have his guts torn out on the one hand," said Milton Wolff, referring to the death of a seaman considered "the best soldier" in the ranks, "and on the other practice the fine art of humaneness toward a faction sitting in the rear giving aid and comfort to the enemy."

While the leadership of the battalion closed ranks around the Barcelona crisis, Steve Nelson endeavored to resolve more mundane problems of morale. To his tasks, he brought an understated confidence and a genuine respect for the men. He understood their needs and their fears; he treated them as members of the same political vanguard. "I have been in the working class movement for fifteen years," he told a reporter. "I know what it means to lose even one class-conscious fellow strong enough to come here. It means five, ten years of work to develop these men—the wealth of the progressive movement in America." Nelson would not waste their talent. He assumed his responsibilities with a simple tour through the lines, learning quickly that the men wanted better food. Investigating further, he discovered that the battalion's best cook, the Japanese American Jack Shirai, had vociferously rejected the kitchen for a rifle in the lines. Nelson saw the importance of appealing to Shirai's pride—not just emphasizing the necessity of providing good food for the soldiers, but establishing the value of his work. "We're making a complete cleanup in the kitchen," he announced. "It won't be a punishment place anymore. . . . It'll be an honor to work there." Shirai agreed to take charge, provided he could keep his rifle nearby. "In such instances," Nelson explained, "the job was to suggest, to stimulate, to cut through red tape and release the men's own initiative."

Nelson encouraged the Lincolns to improve their trenches, establish a library, and handle matters of discipline; but his brilliance as a commissar emerged most dramatically during the crises of military action. "He knew every man in his command, his strength and his weakness," said one volunteer. "He was all over the field when we needed him. Took a look to see that munitions were coming up; got the water headed to the boys; dropped in to see if the kitchen was doing all right. . . . Nothing too big or too little for him to pay attention to." Even Mickenberg acknowledged Nelson's competence, calling him "a very good human being; a strong man, a clear-headed man." Nelson's popularity was no accident of character; he cultivated the love of his men.

"They must learn the basis of the whole struggle—the fundamentals of the whole war," he said about his ability to influence the men. "You must be one of the boys, concern yourself directly with their problems. . . . I trusted the men and they trusted me." Indeed, when the Lincolns next went into action, the men began to spread the word: "Don't let 'em get Steve."

Steve Nelson's success at restoring battalion morale contrasted with the experiences of other commissars who had been catapulted into positions of authority. Consider, for example, the case of Bill Sennett, a lower-level party organizer in Chicago. Upon volunteering for the brigade, he received instructions to visit Earl Browder while passing through New York on his way to Spain. The top Communist leader gave him a two-inch square of silk with which to identify himself and a message for party organizers in Paris (one of whom was the Yugoslav Tito, then working with the International Brigades). As one of the *responsables*, Sennett carried currency for members of his group and helped enforce discipline aboard ship; when volunteer Irving Goff, a professional acrobat, attracted the attention of other passengers, Sennett ordered him to stop performing and remain inconspicuous. After the group reached Albacete, brigade leaders appointed Sennett commissar of one of the companies of truck drivers in the Regiment de Tren.

True to his Communist ideals, Sennett treated the assignment with utmost seriousness. Upon receiving instructions from the commissariat to curtail social activities, Sennett demanded strict enforcement. "I took things too literally and carried out commands without question," he later admitted. Frustrated by his rigor, the men called a political meeting, voiced their complaints about his authority, and voted for his dismissal. "I felt terrible," Sennett recalled. "It was quite a blow to my ego. How could I not get along with the men?" To save face, Sennett promptly volunteered for combat duty. A few months later, however, he returned to the Regiment de Tren and was re-elected commissar. "It was a case of the men making the decision," he explained. Interestingly, the Regiment de Tren also elected its regular officers, choosing the Socialist Durward Clark as commander. "He imposed discipline by personal example only," recalled Sennett. "But nothing could have been more rigorous. Our regiment was always haunted by the fact that our most valuable man was the least political."

*

Ideology and idealism transformed the brigade leadership, for better and for worse, following the arrival of another preeminent American commissar, the black leader Harry Haywood, in May 1937. A veteran of World War I and a member of the Communist party's highest political committee, the 39-year-old theoretician had volunteered eagerly to go to Spain, despite Browder's attempts to dissuade him. Yet Haywood's problems began almost immediately, when he had difficulty climbing the Pyrenees and had to spend a night alone with a special guide. "I felt ashamed and somewhat humiliated," he said. Appointed adjutant commissar of the Fifteenth Brigade, Haywood lacked Nelson's enthusiasm for mixing with the men. Lincoln veterans remembered his presence by the formal military outfits he wore: tailored clothes, knee boots, Sam Brown belt, binocular case strapped to the hip. Few could recall any conversations or personal interaction with him. "Harry's downfall," said Nelson, "was that he was not part of the men."

The appointment of Harry Haywood nonetheless illuminates the role played by American blacks in the Lincoln brigade. Committed self-consciously to an ideology of racial equality, party leaders took pains to recruit capable blacks and encouraged their advancement through the ranks. Such promotions represented a deliberate challenge to traditional stereotypes about black leadership. And because Communist ideology demanded the elimination of racial chauvinism, blacks in the brigade suffered no negative discrimination. Even the celebrated Ernest Hemingway received what he called "a package . . . in the teeth" from an American doctor "because I used the wrong word for negro (in describing my financial condition)." When boxer Joe Louis knocked out the German Max Schmeling for the heavyweight title in 1938, Lincoln volunteers sent the champion a telegram from Spain applauding him for "KAYOING MYTH OF ARYAN RACIAL SUPERIORITY."

This spirit of racial justice drew many blacks to Spain. Some saw it as a chance to avenge Mussolini's conquests in Africa: "I wouldn't be in Ethiopia," explained the black seaman Albert Chisholm, "but I'd be fighting the Italians in Spain, striking a blow against fascism." The poet Langston Hughes, who interviewed numerous black volunteers, reported that many "had come to Spain to fight against the people who oppress Negroes in the American South." Eluard Luchelle McDaniels, a talented story writer and watercolorist who abandoned the ambulance corps for the front lines, put it succinctly: "I would rather die here than be slaved any more." For black flyer James Peck, "what we were fighting in Spain was a species of that thing which at home had kept me, a trained pilot, grounded, while keeping hundreds of thousands of other Negro youths from being what they wanted to be." In the Lincoln brigade, these men could find respect and dignity.

"I felt like a human being, like a man," recalled Crawford Morgan, in a reminiscence typical of the black veterans. "People didn't look at me with hatred in their eyes because I was black, and I wasn't refused this or refused that because I was black. I was treated like all the rest of the people were treated, and when you have been in the world for quite a long time and have been treated worse than people treat their dogs, it is quite a nice feeling." Such experiences underscored the appeal of communism as an alternative to the racist status quo. "Folks over here don't treat me / Like white folks used to do," Hughes wrote in a poem to Alabama that appeared in the brigade newspaper *Volunteer for Liberty*:

> I done met up with folks
> who'll fight for me
> Like I'm fightin' now for Spain.

In the face of such antiracist passions, the performance of Commissar Harry Haywood shocked and dismayed most Communists. Whatever his military experience in World War I, the more mature Haywood obviously felt tremendous stress about going into battle. He avoided the front lines and lingered around brigade headquarters. (The men erroneously interpreted his absence as an indication of aloofness.) And to calm his nerves, Haywood kept a canteen full of brandy nearby. Yet his drunkenness aggravated his fear. At the beginning of the battle of Brunete in July 1937, he literally trembled at the sound of artillery. "As we approached closer to the line, shells were bursting in our area," reported one officer. "Haywood seemed a bit shaken and as we continued his condition became worse—he was 'cracking up.'"

Nelson, observing Haywood's alcoholic condition, ordered him to the rear. But his afflictions pursued him. Edwin Rolfe, who had to write a radio broadcast for the incapacitated Haywood, dismissed him as a "coward and shit." Years later, in his memoir of the ordeal, Haywood described himself as a victim of brigade politics—his criticism of Colonel Copic, he said, had precipitated a conspiratorial purge against him. But party leaders in Albacete, including Robert Minor, William Lawrence, and Ed Bender, recognized his inadequacy and urged him to go home. Writing of the episode, Langston Hughes depicted a particular embarrassment among the black volunteers. "When I suggested that perhaps the man was shell-shocked," he wrote, "they said, 'Shell shocked nothing! If it just hadn't been a *mixed* unit—white boys and all—waiting to obey his orders! Imagine!. . . . A disgrace to the race, that's what he is!'" Hughes, himself a noncombatant, drew a more sympathetic conclusion. "At least, *he was there* at the front," he said. "At least, he went to Spain."

Haywood's travails followed him home. To the press, he touted the role of "the brave Negroes who are . . . battling against the despoilers of Ethiopia, the lynch-loving Hitlers, and against their worst enemy—international fascism." But within party circles, his reputation had been destroyed, the result, said Haywood, of "malicious rumors." Browder, citing "mistakes made in Spain," dismissed Haywood from both the politburo and the national committee of the Communist party. After twelve years on the party payroll, Haywood needed a job. But when he found work at the Soviet pavilion at the New York World's Fair, party leaders thought he was too visible and had him fired. Haywood then accepted a low-level organizing job among blacks in the Chesapeake area, but problems of money forced him to quit. The tension may have contributed to the massive heart attack he suffered in the fall of 1939. Temporarily disabled, Haywood retired to California.

Before leaving Spain, however, Haywood had participated in one of the most critical decisions affecting the Lincoln brigade in Spain: the appointment of Oliver Law as battalion commander, the first black officer to command white troops in any American army. Oliver Law's notoriety—the *Daily Worker* proclaimed him, with no small exaggeration, "Hero of the Jarama Front"—has raised numerous questions about his military experience, about his capabilities as an officer and, most disconcertingly, about the circumstances of his death. Because of an enduring bitterness among some survivors of the battalion, oral testimony remains controversial, often partisan, while the documentary evidence is skimpy at best. Nonetheless, some facts are indisputable, and the weight of memory appears strong enough to resolve most of the riddles surrounding Law's career.

Sturdy, muscular, dark-complexioned, he was born in 1899 and raised on a ranch in west Texas. As a teenager, he served in the U.S. Army during World

War I, and he reenlisted after the war, eventually attaining six years' experience. His highest rank in this segregated army was private first class, which he held only briefly. After leaving the military, he worked in a cement factory and then moved to Chicago, where he drove a Yellow Cab, loaded cargo as a stevedore, and operated a small restaurant that failed. During the Depression, Law became active in the unemployed movement, joined the Communist party, and worked with Harry Haywood to organize mass protests against Mussolini's invasion of Ethiopia. He sailed for Spain in January 1937. Despite his military experience, he remained innocent of the perils of aerial bombardment, as Merriman had discovered to his amusement. In any case, Law held little responsibility at Jarama. Assigned to the machine-gun company, he was appointed group leader, of which there were three, all of whom ranked below the two section leaders as well as the company officers. During the fighting on February 27, however, Law performed admirably. Belated allegations of cowardice and drunkenness, made by anti-Communists to condemn the brigade leadership, have no historical foundation. Mel Anderson, a volunteer from Michigan, vividly remembered spending most of that day in the trenches next to the sober, courageous Law. "We came to wipe out the fascists," Law told a reporter soon afterward; "some of us must die doing that job. But we'll do it here in Spain, maybe stopping fascism in the United States, too, without a great battle there."

The annihilation of the battalion leadership at Jarama accelerated Law's advancement. Appointed section leader soon after February 27, he rose to commander of the machine-gun company two weeks later when a skirmish took the life of his superior officer. The promotion may have reflected the deliberate antiracist policies of the Communist leadership. Other black comrades, such as machine gunner Walter Garland, also received preferential advancement. But unlike most of the other American recruits, both Law and Garland had military experience and had earned their promotions on merit. "Good record as officer at [the] front. Showed good morale and discipline under fire," noted the experienced battalion commander Martin Hourihan in recommending Law for officers' training school. And when Hourihan became ill two months later, Colonel Copic selected Law to replace him temporarily. Significantly, American officers who questioned some of Copic's appointments at this time raised no objections about Law's assignment.

Brigade politics continued to affect his career. When Hourihan transferred permanently to the regimental staff in the late spring of 1937, the choice of a battalion commander fell between Law and Garland. "The idea was that we do something about advancing a black," admitted Steve Nelson, one of the three Americans involved in making the decision. Since Garland was still recovering from his wounds, recalled Nelson, Law seemed the "natural" choice. "But the thing that mattered most," he insisted fifty years later, "was that the two had military experience." In fact, neither Law nor Garland had much of a military background, and there was never sufficient time to train them as officers. But given the scarcity of any qualified men, Law's background appeared, in Nelson's words, "a great asset, even though we may have exaggerated it in our own minds." To Nelson, Law "was the guy who had the most experience . . . [and was] the most acquainted with military procedures on the staff at the moment." Allan Johnson, the highest-ranking U.S. Army officer to serve in the International Brigades and a stalwart party man, also participated in the discussions; he too supported Law's promotion. The third man involved in the selection was the newly arrived commissar Harry Haywood, who had respected Oliver Law as a Communist in Chicago and whose commitment to black advancement represented a lifetime's passion.

But if Oliver Law emerged as the best-qualified battalion leader at that time, some of the volunteers questioned his rapid promotion. Ray Steele, a particularly effective machine gunner at Jarama, bitterly resented having been passed over for commander of the machine-gun company and spoke aloud of his dislike of Law. Other dissenters became abusive. One night in May 1937, a volunteer named Virgil Morris, already assigned to building fortifications on a punishment detail, told Law he preferred the labor company to the regular battalion. Reminding the soldier that it was "not an honor being in the labor company," Law declared that "men came thousands of miles to be an honor to the people who sent them and not a disgrace." Morris then retorted that "at least in the labor company you are treated like [a] white man." When Law rejected another volunteer's request for a leave, he was told, "Fuck off, Law, you are no fucking good to anybody and you never have been." Morris Mickenberg later claimed that some of the men adopted the protest slogan "Restore the whites to equality with the Negro." Such racially charged sentiments, however, were not widely approved. When Steele objected to Law's appointment, recalled David Smith, "he did not receive much support from the men."

Doubts about Law nonetheless surfaced during the Brunete offensive. Although Hourihan assigned the Lincolns to a specific tactical position, Law apparently failed to place his men properly. "The commander of the Lincoln battalion disappeared" is the way Hourihan described his inability to locate the troops. And when he did find the battalion, he denounced Law loudly in front of the men and assumed command, leading the Lincolns into formation against the fascist-held Villanueva de la Canada. For his troubles, Hourihan was soon cut down by enemy machine guns. Mickenberg, who witnessed the fiasco, concluded that Law was an "incompetent commander." Still another Lincoln battalion officer, who even today insists on anonymity, remembered Law crouching on the ground in fear. "Law was cowardly at Brunete," he said; "he was completely inexperienced."

These criticisms, however valid, nonetheless obscure other truths about Law's leadership. As with many other men in the Spanish war, his caution—and his courage—varied according to battlefield circumstances. Numerous soldiers who appeared brave one day might become fearful and inept the next—and vice versa. Whatever Law's problems outside Villanueva de la Canada (the word most often repeated is "inexperienced"), he showed no lack of confidence in leading the Lincolns in the attack against Mosquito Ridge on the morning of July 9. Harry Fisher, the battalion runner, watched Law advance ahead of his men, waving a pistol and urging them forward. "He was the first man over the top . . . he was in the furthest position." Fisher also saw Law drop with a fascist bullet in the chest. "There is absolutely no doubt of the courage of Oliver Law," he insisted. Other eyewitnesses have confirmed Fisher's account.

In recent years, however, rumors have appeared claiming that one of the disgruntled Lincolns, angry and frightened by Law's incompetence, fired the bullet that killed him. These accounts also suggest that the men subsequently urinated on his corpse and left it to rot in the sun. But the prime source of this story is the vigorous anti-Communist William Herrick, who described such a scene in his novel *Hermanos!* Herrick acknowledges that he learned of such an atrocity secondhand, from three or four of the perpetrators. Two of them are dead. The other two, when confronted with Herrick's tale, vociferously denied it. Even more convincing, David Smith, the first medic to reach Oliver Law, also saw him shot in a furious burst of enemy machine-gun fire and attempted to staunch the bleeding with a coagulant, finally dragging the wounded man to a first-aid base, where he expired. To these rebuttals, Herrick responds: How do they know where the bullets came from? The answer, from Fisher, Smith, and Mel Anderson, is simple: unlike Herrick, they were there. Oliver Law, good military leader or not, died with the respect of his men.

The Fires of Brunete

Marching orders came on the night of July 2. As Franco's armies pressed into the Basque provinces in the north of Spain and fascist artillery continued to rain on Madrid, the Republic launched a major offensive to relieve both sectors. An advance toward the village of Brunete, just west of Madrid, promised to end the siege against the capital, while simultaneously diverting fascist forces from the drive into the north. According to the plan, the Fifteenth Brigade would march into the Guadarrama Valley, then seize the dominating heights, known as Mosquito Ridge. After weeks of inactivity, the Americans were eager to enter the war, and the rejuvenated Lincoln and Washington battalions commenced a tense three-night hike that brought them around the outskirts of Madrid.

"All of a sudden real comradeship burst into being," reported Philip Detro, a non-Communist volunteer from Conroe, Texas, who hoped to become a writer after the war. "Comrades who before hardly spoke to each other now became very friendly. Everybody opened up." The excitement was palpable. "We were tickled pink," recalled Wolff, still an untested private. "And it was July

4th and we were really hepped up." Beneath the excitement, however, throbbed an intense anxiety. "The boys were confident and kidding," reported Samuel Levinger, the twenty-year-old Socialist son of an Ohio rabbi, as the Lincolns moved into action. "But there was a solemn, deep undertone to all the kidding, for we realized fully that . . . many would not come out of it alive. 'I wonder if I'll stop any lead,' said a particular friend of mine. 'Well if I do, I'll be in good company. The greatest fighters for freedom died in battle.'" No one knows what happened to that particular friend, but Levinger's war journal was published posthumously in 1937.

By the end of the long march, the men were weary and drawn, agonizingly thirsty even before the battle had begun. "Everybody suddenly became subdued," Detro remembered. "The men were getting ready to meet the test and were steadying themselves." Told that the attack would be preceded by planes and artillery and warned specifically not to be alarmed by the tumult, many of the volunteers nonetheless jumped in fright when the big guns spoke at dawn on the sixth. "Don't be alarmed," Wolff remembered yelling, "they are our guns"; but, he admitted, "I was convincing myself at the same time."

Almost immediately the plan of attack went awry. The Washingtons, diverted to capture the town of Villanueva de la Canada, found themselves pinned down by machine-gun fire in stifling hundred-degree heat. Six of the eight men in Wolff's squad collapsed of sunstroke. On the other side of town, the Lincolns also came under heavy fire and struggled to dig into the bone-dry dirt. By nightfall, the Americans were exhausted. But brigade headquarters ordered that the attack continue. Together with five other battalions, they charged into the enemy emplacements, overpowering the sparse defenders. Villanueva fell before midnight. The battalions then paused for a day of rest and reorganization, during which they buried their thirty dead. Already, from the crest of Mosquito Ridge, the fascists were bombarding their positions.

For the next five days, the Americans lived in a crucible of fire, confronting bullets, artillery, aviation, and a boiling Spanish sun. Attempts to wrest the enemy from the surrounding heights produced terrific casualties. There was no way to reach the top. The brigade leadership finally ordered the battalions to hold the gains they had won. But now the Americans became targets for aerial bombardment. "All night there was speculation [about] what was to be next," reported Morris Mickenberg, ever the critic. "Some of the guys said it was a new military trick borrowed from the Red Army; we were to creep up behind the enemy and catch 'em in the rear." Mostly the men waited in the heat for the next assault and killed time arguing: Did intellectuals make good comrades? Was Al Capone really tough? Then came the aviation; the fascists dominated the air. "I was hugging the earth, pressing into it with my hands, with my feet, with my face," said Mickenberg, "but the roar set the whole ground shaking and the ground was pushing you up, pushing you up higher and higher, shoving you over to them; here he is, don't let 'im get away from you." Such vulnerability touched every soldier. "And where," Mickenberg wanted to know, "was our anti-aircraft, where were our planes, where were our guns to help us, to drive 'em away? They were all killed," he concluded with small irony. "The fascists had everything and we had nothing. . . . We never had a chance, we lost this war long ago."

It was here, in a desperate charge up Mosquito Ridge, that Captain Oliver Law was killed. Battalion commissar Steve Nelson immediately took command. "I grit my teeth and acted as though nothing happened even though my insides were turning over," Nelson recalled. "You couldn't let it show. There wasn't even time to let it show." Relying on common sense and military discipline, Nelson emerged as a capable leader. But the American officer corps had been decimated. Among the wounded were Martin Hourihan, Walter Garland, Hans Amlie, Paul Burns, and Philip Detro. The battalions had been chopped in half, losing over 300 men, including the cook, Jack Shirai, who died at his gun. Hereafter, the Lincolns and the Washingtons would be merged into a single command, officially called the Lincoln-Washington, but usually known just as the Lincolns. The Yugoslav-American Mirko Markovicz, who had gained military experience in World War I, was appointed battalion commander; Nelson remained his commissar.

Once again the casualties overwhelmed first-aid stations and hospitals. Dr. Irving Busch, chief surgeon of the American medical corps in the Brunete campaign, reported that American physicians treated over 2,500 wounded and performed over 1,000 operations. Esther Silverstein, the San Francisco nurse who arrived in Spain just before the offensive, remembered endless hours of duty and physical exhaustion. "Constant threat of sudden death from the skies kept us under such nervous tension," she wrote, "that our physical discomfort seemed intensified." Two American doctors, Randall Sollenberger of Baltimore and Harold Robbins of Hollywood, died in separate bombings.

*

After seven days of action, the Americans withdrew from the front lines, bled white and exhausted. But before they could rest, word of a new fascist attack led to a hasty redeployment. Under intense pressure, the Lincolns moved in an all-night forced march, the men often dropping from exhaustion, being kicked awake by their officers. But at dawn they still had not reached the objective, making them easy targets for enemy aviation. "We dug our faces into the earth, our bodies prone," wrote Henry Eaton to his family. "No thunder could be so deafening; the stench of high, sulphurous explosives choked in our mouths. Then crash, and a weight is forcing me into the soil." The comrade next to him was blown onto his back, chopped apart "as if a giant biscuit cutter had been plunged into his back, his skull, his buttocks, and left gaping holes." As the battalion writhed under fire, a Spanish runner arrived, demanding instant relief for the soldiers in a nearby line. Again the Lincolns reformed into sections and went into battle. Their presence enabled the lines to hold. Over the next few days, they entered a series of engagements, shifting from one hot sector to another, testing their strength and draining their resources. "The men and things about you become curious, new and desirable—you don't want to die," remarked William Titus, a 25-year-old poet from Grand Rapids, Michigan. "You become afraid to die, hope you won't and go on to do it if you must."

At one point, the new officers of the Lincoln-Washington battalion—Markovicz, Nelson, and Garland (before he was wounded)—were ordered to a meeting with brigade Colonel Klaus, a Prussian officer who had replaced the wounded Copic. Bringing out a contour map, he directed the Americans to move their men to an exposed position in order to protect a company of Spanish marines. "A deep silence fell on the group as the Colonel's words were translated," remembered Nelson; "we all seemed to get the gist of the urgency of his words *before* they were translated." Markovicz, speaking to Nelson in their native Serbo-Croatian, said "This can't be done. I am against it." Klaus, sensing the response, eyed Markovicz and responded, "That's an order."

Still speaking their own language, Nelson asked Markovicz how they could disobey the colonel. "If you accept this order," said the experienced Markovicz, "I will hold you responsible before the Americans back home for whatever happens." Unable to understand this conversation, Klaus demanded that they speak in English, with which his translator was familiar. "We have no time to waste," he said, demanding that Markovicz give him a clear answer.

"Commander Klaus," the Yugoslav replied, "this is a disastrous order. I will not order the American battalion to carry out this order because it will result in a disaster, like the one in Jarama." As he spoke, Markovicz kept his eye on Nelson, looking for support. "He should have known," the commissar later reported, "that I had no choice . . . we could not disobey an order."

"Markovicz, I gave you an order which I received from division," Klaus declared. "You and I are under military orders. This is not a debating discussion here. We must act, especially since we are International Brigades, whose role is to develop discipline."

"Then," Nelson reported, "Klaus stood up and with unmistakable military bearing said, 'I order you to carry out the order.' Markovicz also stood up and said, 'Colonel Klaus, I cannot carry out this order.'

"Then Klaus stepped closer to Markovicz and extended his hand and said, 'Markovicz, I order you to surrender your weapon.'

"Markovicz reached for his pistol and with an expression of obedience and surrender he handed the gun to Klaus." Taking the pistol, the colonel turned and passed it to Nelson, along with responsibility for carrying out the order. "Tell the men that Markovicz has been ordered to report to the division. You are in command until we get a replacement."

Nelson and Garland proceeded to the battalion and moved the companies as instructed. "That was one more sleepless and frightful night for me," recalled Nelson, "and especially Garland, who could not stop shaking his head at what we went through and what was to come." In the morning, however, Nelson learned that the expected danger had not materialized and the orders, so offensive to Markovicz, had been cancelled. Aside from losing his command, Markovicz would suffer no consequences for defying Klaus.

By July 25, three weeks after entering the battle lines, the Lincolns had earned a reprieve. A six-hour march brought them to a rest area, and the men immediately collapsed. But at nightfall word reached the brigade that the Republican lines, nine miles away, desperately needed reinforcements. The battalion commanders and commissars doubted that the soldiers could be mustered in time. Among the rank and file, some spoke openly of desertion, of refusing to return to battle without some rest. "The men felt that they had reached the point of utter physical exhaustion, could do no more," recalled a volunteer named Paul Wendorf, "that if the government had to count on them to stop the fascists . . . it was about time to call it quits." But Nelson again insisted that the men would move, if they understood the reason for the order. He began to address his weary comrades. Standing on a large flat rock, he summoned the exhausted troops and told them what they had to do. "There were murmurs from the back of the crowd," he recalled, "and someone shouted, 'For God's sake, Steve, you're not going to tell us to go back!'" But Nelson proceeded to explain the military threat, both to the Spanish troops in the line and to themselves in the rear. Through the silence, he heard a single voice, the sculptor Paul Block, saying, "You're right." And so the Lincolns moved into formation and marched back to war. Just five hundred yards out, another messenger arrived, reversing the order. "Everyone," Nelson remember, "felt not just good, but proud."

In the face of Brunete's horrors, the sheer difficulty of soldierly activity ironically had a beneficent face: for many, the ordeal of war created a psychological shelter—a numbness—that enabled the Lincolns to transcend their fear and anxiety. "All along the road to the burning, ruined town," wrote Henry Eaton, shortly before his death in battle, "we had the human qualities drained from our vitals. We became dumb automatons, unable to feel because horror had surpassed our ability to meet it. . . . I have no emotions left to drive me crazy."

Milton Wolff, who first saw action at Brunete, recalled vividly his ability to deflect the suffering around him. He remembered seeing his first wounded comrade: "There he was, laying there holding his chest, very quiet and pale. Here was a man I knew very well. I was impressed, but I don't think I was scared. I was not mad or angry. I was not sad. I had an empty feeling." Soon afterward, Wolff came upon a group of enemy dead: "We looked at them for a long time, wondering whether we killed any of them. And that was all." Wolff's entire machine-gun company virtually vanished before his eyes, victims of sunstroke and wounds. He watched the man directly in front of him receive a bullet through the head, killing him instantly. "It didn't disturb me at all," he stated. "I coldly said, 'he's dead, we can't do anything, we might as well bury him.' That thing kept happening to me like a dream. I felt then, that this had happened to me before." Another time, Wolff stood beside a battalion commissar, who was killed inches away from him. On still another occasion, four battalion commanders had huddled together when "suddenly we heard 'plunk' and the fellow beside me lay dead." Even more remarkable was Wolff's response to another long battle in which he participated: he had no memory of it at all! Despite months of frontline combat, Wolff returned from the war without a wound; he was one of the very few Lincoln veterans to do so. Yet he took no refuge in the doctrine of fatalism; to the contrary, he felt deep anger at those casualties—such as Captain Detro, wounded while carelessly urinating—who had not protected themselves. And for the rest of his life, Wolff suffered nightmares as he relived the toll of the Spanish war.

Such belated symptoms haunted many other veterans, especially after they left the dangers of the front for safer quarters. During one rest period, Dr. Pike observed a sudden increase in what he called psychopathology. "Men became hysterical," he recalled, "some with convulsions, weeping, mourning, reacting to the stress of war. They did not do this at the front, but once released from the burden of fighting, their emotions erupted." Pike treated the worst cases with sedatives such as phenobarbital. With psychic defenses down, moreover, the dread of bombing assumed nightmarish forms, awakening men with cold sweats. One volunteer described a vivid dream of capture by the enemy. "The fascists beat up the prisoners one at a time," he fantasized. "It was soon to be my turn. How would I take it? My brain began to work. After all, I thought, I'm just a microbe in this world—almost nothing. Supposing they torture me—so what? I began to feel happy. I don't remember being tortured in my dream, but those thoughts are still dear to me." Even in this man's unconscious, the ideology of the larger cause offered solace. And, as truck driver Evelyn Hutchins said of her nightmares, "there are a lot of things worse than dreams."

Some symptoms did not disappear so easily. One volunteer recalled meeting an older black veteran in Paris who was still shell-shocked from his ordeal. "'At's a real war down there,' he said, rolling his eyes. 'Don't let anybody fool you, 'at's war, 'at's REAL war down there.'" The veteran was promptly led away, lest his fears infect the new recruits. One of the early beneficiaries of Dr. Pike's work therapy, Jason Patrick Gurney, suffered a relapse at Brunete; he "went off the deep end," as nurse Fredericka Martin put it, "seeing his friends—on three occasions—reduced to meat fragments." He would suffer to the end of his life from "invisible wounds earned in Spain." Another hapless volunteer was nineteen-year-old Sol Davis, who narrowly escaped the sinking of the *Ciudad de Barcelona*. Once in training camp, he complained of physical distress, including chest pains, and confessed his self-doubts about continuing in the war. Although the doctors found no clear evidence of illness, they permitted him to stay behind the lines. But that proved no haven for Davis. Caught in a bombing raid, he emerged with severe shell shock and had to be shipped home. "My ears keep ringing," he explained four months later. "I can't sleep. I haven't slept hardly at all. I just rest." Plagued by such symptoms, Davis died just a few years later. Other shell-shock cases, including temporary blindness, severe headaches, or "nerves," seem to have occurred infrequently, with few lasting problems. One such victim, embarrassed by his temporary breakdown, actually paid his own fare to return to Spain in order to redeem himself, only to be sent home again by skeptical authorities.

The ordeal of battle also produced a steady stream of deserters who fled from the ranks. For many reasons it is difficult to provide the exact number of such unofficial departures from the war: because most of the volunteers entered Spain illegally; because many used false names on their passports; because the fascist side routinely killed captured soldiers; because many deserters were caught by government officials and returned, willing or not, to their battalions; because most deserters took pains to conceal their routes of escape; because some of them probably had no desire to associate with former comrades after the war—all these factors tend to lower the number of known deserters. But because most of the volunteers complied with the request of the International Brigades to surrender their U.S. passports at the training base in Albacete, those who attempted to return home without permission of military authorities usually had to reapply for appropriate documentation from the nearest American consulate.

Following the State Department policy of nonintervention, consular officials generally refused to help disaffected volunteers leave the country. Nor would the American government provide funds for destitute soldiers to pay for their transportation home, even outside Spain. (In an exceptional case, the consul at Gibraltar, William Chapman, dipped into his own pocket to provide food and shelter for three deserters.) Usually, the State Department attempted to contact relatives or benefactors in the United States to finance the return trip; occasionally, too, the consuls helped Americans find work aboard a ship heading home. But whatever their opinions of the Lincolns, diplomatic officials always endeavored to verify citizenship and so recorded the names of those deserters who sought formal repatriation.

From these State Department archives, supplemented by interviews with surviving veterans and by the newly opened Communist party records in Russia, the number of deserters from the Lincoln brigade can be placed at about one hundred, conceivably several dozen more. That statistic comprised about four percent of all military volunteers. According to consular documents, the stream of men seeking repatriation continued throughout the war, though the numbers increased significantly during and just after major battles. Some of the deserters, exhausted by sleeplessness or separated from their comrades, simply fled in terror for safety. But the consular records suggest that the decision to abandon the war often was a deliberate act, rather than the result of spontaneous impulse. Indeed, several volunteers made the effort more than once. The documents also show how these deserters managed to leave the country: the most common route of escape was through one of the major Spanish ports, usually Barcelona or Valencia; then a deserter could stow away on a merchant ship with the help and sometimes the encouragement of sympathetic seamen. In this way, Americans would arrive in such foreign ports as Marseilles, Algiers, Gibraltar, Bordeaux, even Hull in England. A few deserters managed to travel over land, evading Republican authorities until they could cross the French border. On several occasions, groups of deserters fled together, suggesting that demoralization could spread through a unit. Such a pattern enabled individuals to leave the ranks without confronting the issue of betraying their comrades.

Consider the following case of four Americans from the Washington battalion. On July 24, 1937, during the fighting around Brunete, they arrived together at the U.S. embassy in Valencia and requested assistance in returning home. Following official policy, the consul refused to provide help. The four then hastened toward the French border, but they were arrested by Spanish officials near Barcelona and put in jail. Upon inquiry from the local consul, however, Republican authorities offered to release the men to hasten their evacuation. All received special travel certificates that took them to Marseilles and from there to Paris and New York. Before the four departed the embassy in Valencia, the American military attaché to Spain, Colonel Stephen Fuqua, took the opportunity to interview two of the men about their backgrounds. Fuqua had a professional interest in the war. His loyalty to U.S. policy prevented him from openly violating nonintervention, but he had visited the American training base at Tarazona and spoken briefly to the soldiers, apologizing for his inability to express his personal sympathy for the Loyalist cause. Moreover, Fuqua surreptitiously provided the brigade with U.S. military manuals, and inside the box of books he hid two pistols. His reports to the State Department about the American deserters help to illuminate their motives and the credibility of their testimony.

One of the runaways was 27-year-old James Doyle, whom Fuqua described as "a blue eyed southerner with fine features . . . and a pleasing voice." In explaining his desertion, Doyle complained about "poor food, poor [sanitary] conditions," "casualties and physical hardships," "and because I didn't get along well with the man in charge of me." Fuqua concluded: "Unquestionably not actuated by any political ideals in his coming to Spain." The second deserter was 22-year-old Vachel Lindsay Blair, whose name alone suggested populist roots in his native Ohio. Lacking just six credits for graduation from Western Reserve University in Cleveland, the tall, rawboned Blair said he went to Spain "because I don't think a great deal of Mussolini and Hitler." He told Fuqua the war had reached a stalemate stage and he had decided to leave because it would drag on too long. "Both of these men," Fuqua reported, "saw battle conditions they had not realized, the realities of which have completely cured them from any further desire to engage in warfare."

Their fellow deserters offered more complex stories. Robert G. Bready, a 28-year-old accountant and the son of a Methodist minister from Bainbridge, Ohio, said later that he had "mixed motives" for going to Spain: "We were anti-Fascist, we wanted to see first hand what was going on and undoubtedly . . . wanted a thrill." But danger was another matter. Assigned with one other American to guard an ammunition dump, Bready grumbled for four days about the situation, simultaneously urging and threatening desertion. He abruptly disappeared before seeing any action. At the Valencia consulate, Bready admitted "confidentially" that he was on parole from the Ohio State Hospital at Toledo. A newspaper reporter who interviewed him later noticed that his voice had "a fearless rapid monotony." He mentioned nothing about his unusual departure from Spain and insisted that the Spanish people were merely fighting for middle-class goals against the army and feudalism. "To call the loyalists 'Reds' is crazy," he said.

One year later, however, Bready expressed different opinions. Indeed, he had sold what one Lincoln veteran called "a very vicious" article to the Hearst press attacking the Spanish government. He also absconded with money collected in Ohio to aid Chinese resistance against the Japanese invasion. He boasted that he had "made a career of drinking." Bready now began carrying a gun, partly out of "a childish kick," as he put it, and partly because he felt "a little nervous about possible retaliation from the Communists" for his magazine work. He even spoke about returning to Spain to join Franco's army. But one morning in December 1938 he got into a drunken argument with his father and shot him to death. Bready, one of the very few Lincoln veterans ever convicted of a violent crime, was sentenced to a term of one to twenty years in the Ohio penitentiary for manslaughter.

Hamilton Alden Tyler, the fourth of the group of deserters, was the least violent of men. He had been raised in California, had joined the Young Communist League at Fresno State College, and was known as a political activist on the Berkeley campus of the University of California. "Naturally I went to college," he wrote in an unpublished, partially autobiographical novel, "but I never could get around the feeling that I was missing the real thing." Determined to fight in Spain, Tyler recruited other students from Berkeley, who already had the example of Robert Merriman as the local scholar-soldier. But the realities of war proved insurmountable for someone of his temperament. "Politics don't last as long out here as men," he wrote. "You just listen to those commissars because you have to." Under the stress of Brunete, Tyler broke completely: "It was as though everyone knew the end to be naked animal fear, the rabbit fleeing before the coyote."

By the time Tyler reached Barcelona his mental stress mirrored a serious physical collapse. In Marseilles, he was diagnosed with jaundice and nearly died. After being released from the hospital there, he nearly died again on the boat trip home. But Tyler well understood the underlying nature of his ailment: he "spent his days recovering more from the spiritual than the physical part of his exhaustion," he wrote, finding "it strange . . . to accustom himself to the lack of pressure, of fear, of feeling the possible finality of each moment." During World War II, Tyler became a conscientious objector. Later, he turned to nature studies, became an active lepidopterist, wrote books about Pueblo myths and organic gardening, swallowtail butterflies and owls. Spain, said this self-styled intellectual in retrospect, was "a negative experience, but educational."

When the literary tourist Malcolm Cowley hitched a ride from Madrid to brigade headquarters at Albacete during the battle of Brunete, he found himself accompanying three American deserters. They were, he reported, "not so much ashamed as crestfallen. They had been forced to change their picture of themselves, to admit that they weren't heroes after all." The next day, Cowley encountered the three again:

"'Well what did they do to you?' I asked.

"One of them answered, 'They're going to make us stand guard duty tonight, the bastards.' Then he grinned. He was a nice kid; later I heard that he had been sent to the front again at his own request."

After withdrawing from the heat of the Guadarrama Valley, the Lincolns moved to a rest camp at Albares, near enough to Madrid to permit the men to explore the capital. One of their favorite haunts was the Hotel Florida on the Gran Via, where Ernest Hemingway had established an unofficial headquarters for Americans on leave from the front. There he wrote his only theatrical script, *The Fifth Column*, while living with the journalist Martha Gellhorn, who would become his third wife. She always thought it odd that they could walk just a few city blocks into the war zone. Across the street from the Florida, the Capital Cinema featured the Marx Brothers in *A Night at the Opera*, while the Paramount showed Charlie Chaplin's *Modern Times*. The fascists, Edwin Rolfe reported, often timed their artillery fire to coincide with the end of shows to catch more civilians in the streets. "All this was very strange, like movie music," wrote Gellhorn of the sounds of war; "and you had to keep telling yourself that men were making this, and men were out there half a mile away where the shells hit."

Despite the hardships of wartime and the random explosions that devastated Madrid, the Florida struggled to maintain some of its prewar glamour with finely polished silverware, table linens, and sophisticated service. But the menu seldom varied: one slice of bread, garbanzos cooked with onions in olive oil, a single orange for dessert, cheap wine, and rough brandy. "There was never enough food," the scrawny Rolfe would later write, "but always poetry." Most American volunteers, unaccustomed to the diet, suffered from dysentery; several developed symptoms of vitamin deficiency. But in Hemingway's rooms, the Lincolns could enjoy rare luxury. Here they indulged in hot baths, drank his whiskey, and shared the delicacies—hams, cheeses, even caviar—that he always managed to appropriate; they threw craps on his floor, listened to phonograph records, and mingled with beautiful women. The Lincolns long remembered Hemingway's magical fifth of Scotch that seemed never to diminish in quantity or quality, "and no visiting American Brigadier was denied the pleasure of his company, or cigarettes, or a long pull at this bottomless bottle," as long as they asked him first.

Hemingway's other watering hole was the Café Chicote, which he remembered from prewar days as the place where "the good guys went" to find conversation and the most beautiful women in Madrid. "It was the best bar in Spain, certainly," he wrote, "and I think one of the best bars in the world, and all of us that used to hang out there had a great affection for it." After the war started, the proprietor, Pedro Chicote, fled to the fascist side, and the waiters managed the club, maintaining its standards in all respects, except with regard to the availability of good liquor. Now the bar and tables were always crowded with soldiers in uniform and civilians frazzled by the bombardments; the café was smoky and awash in the rhythmic music the Spaniards made by clicking spoons.

Hemingway sat drinking at a crowded table at Chicote one warm afternoon shortly after the fighting had ended at Brunete in the summer of 1937. His companions included Evan Shipman, who had driven one of Hemingway's ambulances from Paris into Spain and then enlisted in the Washington battalion, and Herbert Matthews, the *New York Times*'s Republican war correspondent (the *Times* had dispatched the pro-fascist William Carney to cover the other side), as well as some Lincoln soldiers on leave and some Spanish women. The 21-year-old Milton Wolff, steered there by Captain Detro, entered the bar to say hello; he had just been appointed commander of a machine-gun company. Although fairly interested in fiction, he had barely heard of Hemingway's literary reputation and remained unimpressed with the intellectual chitchat. "Ernest is quite childish in many respects," Wolff wrote to a friend in Brooklyn. "He wants very much to be a martyr. . . . So much for writers," he concluded. "I'd much rather read their works than be with them." Wolff nonetheless stayed for the drinks that Hemingway bought and left with one of the women. Because of his incompetence with the language, Wolff learned very little about the small, dark-eyed woman, but he spent the next week in her company at the Hotel Gran Via. Only later did Edwin Rolfe explain that Hemingway had arranged the affair. "I just wanted to cheer you up," a Hemingway-type character remarked in a similarly situated story, "Night Before Battle." "Grow up," the soldier replied; "what's one more?" The Hemingway answer: "One more."

Just three weeks after leaving the Brunete front, the brigade abruptly received orders to move. Many of the Lincolns were still ensconced in Madrid hotel rooms. Two New Yorkers, Edwin Rolfe and Paul White, spent a frantic night pounding on doors to get the men ready; a few would not let themselves be found. But by morning, the reconstituted Lincoln brigade was heading for action on the Aragon front.

11

A Disciplined Army

Beneath a dry, dazzling summer sun, the Lincoln brigade rode by truck through the hills and deep valleys of the Aragon region in the third week of August 1937 to face another test of commitment and courage. Their ultimate objective, so the strategists planned, would be the capture of Zaragoza, believed to be a pro-Republican area in fascist hands. Such an offensive would also divert Franco's troops from the Basque provinces of the north. But first, the Lincolns would have to pass through a line of fascist-held towns: Quinto, Belchite, and Fuentes de Ebro. Among the men, the mood was grim, lacking the banter that had masked their feelings before Brunete.

As the battalion prepared for action, the commissars explained that the seeming tranquility of the area reflected the dilatory spirit of the Catalonian anarchists who had held the Aragon front since the beginning of the war. As fervent supporters of Spain's Popular Front government, most Lincolns despised the anarchists and had considered them virtual enemies of the Republic since their political insurrection in Barcelona the previous May. When Steve Nelson arrived at the new position, he noticed that the baggage of the departing soldiers included Ping-Pong tables, balls, and a windup phonograph. He expressed the hope that the International Brigades would prove more aggressive at fighting the war. Meanwhile, command of the Lincolns had passed to the experienced Hans Amlie, the maverick Socialist who had once hoped to enlist in the Debs column and who had recently recovered from wounds suffered at Brunete. A new recruit to the Communist party in Spain, Amlie lacked the ideological discipline and tenacity of his superior officers. These included Steve Nelson, who had been promoted from battalion to brigade commissar, and Robert Merriman, also recovered from his wounds, who served as brigade chief of staff. Though genuinely passionate about the Republican cause, Amlie dared to question military orders to protect his men. Fortunately, both Nelson and Merriman demonstrated a remarkable flexibility in their confrontations with the new battalion commander.

The Aragon offensive began with an attack on the town of Quinto, nestled on the road to Zaragoza, in the last week of August 1937. In coordination with other battalions, the Americans helped encircle the town and then followed their roaring tanks into the sunbaked streets. Advancing slowly, they withdrew at nightfall to safer trenches, but returned the next day to engage in dangerous street fighting against snipers and a fascist rear guard that held positions within the thick walls of the local church. By tossing bottles of nitroglycerine, igniting bundles of hay, and cutting off the enemy's water supplies, the Lincolns managed to clear the town after two brutal days. Unlike Jarama and Brunete, Quinto inaugurated a personal kind of fighting, demanding individual initiative and bravery. American losses were relatively light, the fascist toll much higher.

The Lincolns also captured nearly a thousand prisoners. "Haggard bad looking lot," Merriman noted in his diary. Guarded by Spanish soldiers, some of the fascist officers were shot spontaneously, purportedly for insulting their captors. Few Americans questioned these actions; indeed, Merriman seems to have disapproved only of the needless taunting of a brave fascist officer before his execution. Such indifference mirrored the fascist treatment of Republican prisoners of war, especially the Internationals, whom Franco considered a satanic red menace to Spain. With very few exceptions, fascist policy was to take no prisoners. At Jarama, Franco's Moorish troops had butchered some of the wounded in no-man's-land. Yet the Republican side viewed enemy officers with the same intolerance, deeming them beyond rehabilitation. "Selected officers," Merriman noted after the victory at Quinto, "questioned them, and finally shot them." He also admitted that "our men," which included Spanish and other nationals, "started to loot the town—bad but a fact"; and he considered punishing the looters "by shooting if necessary." The Americans exercised greater discipline, in one case leaving their loose change on a countertop to pay for some purloined groceries.

As the Aragon offensive continued, the Lincolns headed next toward the fortified town of Belchite, famous for having repulsed the Napoleonic armies of the nineteenth century. Entrenched in shallow positions several hundred yards outside the town, the Americans fell under sniper fire from the hovering church tower and immediately began to count heavy casualties. By the end of the first day, all the company commanders and many of the adjutants had been killed. "We had to go forward," Steve Nelson later explained, "yet that seemed like suicide. On the other hand, if we stayed in the trench, we'd be picked off like sitting ducks. And a retreat over bare ground would cost more lives than an attack. Therefore we had to go forward."

Merriman, chief of staff at brigade headquarters, ordered the Lincolns to take the church. Amlie passed the word to his men. But enemy cross fire proved insurmountable. In one assault 22 men started toward the town. None made it; only two survived. Merriman ordered another assault. Amlie told him it was not possible. Merriman reiterated the importance of the military orders. Still Amlie refused. A furious Merriman then handed the phone to Nelson, who tried to reason with Amlie. Facing intense machine-gun fire, Amlie was beyond reason. Then Merriman grabbed the phone and warned Amlie that he might face a court-martial. "What am I going to do?" Amlie asked one of his adjutants. "Court martial at the front means shot." A few of Amlie's men now offered to refuse *his* orders. While the battalion commander contemplated that alternative, Nelson decided to approach the front lines himself. Heading toward Amlie's position, he discovered a culvert that ran directly into Belchite, making a frontal assault unnecessary. Summoning his soldiers, Nelson led a diversionary attack, which spared Amlie additional problems.

The conflict, however, hinged on the question of military discipline, the same issue that had confronted Merriman at Jarama and Markovicz at Brunete. Merriman, as his diary attests, castigated Amlie's judgment. And yet he was now responsible for the very kind of unreasonable order that had undermined his own position the previous February 27. As he later explained, Colonel Copic had sent him to Belchite "with orders I couldn't repeat to Americans and, even though softened over, put me in a tough position." Copic's superior, General Walter, he added, "ordered me to take the church and clear the way to the town. *Gave me a party order to do it.* In addition and against my protest promised me a major rating as soon as the church fell." Merriman's confession underscores both his personal compassion and his commitment to military duty. Whatever his private doubts, he conceded that higher authorities better understood the point of any single attack; the capture of Belchite was imperative to maintaining the Republican advance toward Zaragoza. Merriman could not be bribed by promotion to take that difficult position. And yet it is clear that a "party order" held greater power in the chain of command. Amlie, the nouveau Communist, lacked that essential commitment to discipline. (Later, to Merriman's annoyance, Amlie would support rank and file objections to saluting officers and would plead for more furloughs from the front.)

Once Nelson's diversionary attack commenced, the Lincolns moved directly into Belchite and began house-to-house fighting. Again casualties climbed rapidly. The seaman Wallace Burton, who liked to engage in duels with fascist snipers, caught a bullet between the eyes. "It doesn't yet seem possible," wrote his lover Millie Bennett, ten days later, "that my stout, vital, life-loving darling is part of that barren Aragon mesa." The six-day siege also claimed Henry Eaton, who thought it ironic that the fascists always seemed to make their last stand inside churches, and Samuel Levinger, son of a rabbi and a student leader from Ohio State University, who had a premonition that he "would not come out . . . alive." Among the wounded were Steve Nelson, who caught bullets in the face and groin; Hans Amlie, who was shot in the head, not seriously, but hurt sufficiently to justify his replacement as battalion commander; and Robert Merriman, who, perhaps to assuage his guilt, recklessly led a grenade assault that left his face torn by splinters.

Nelson's replacement at Belchite, his adjutant commissar, David Doran, now showed the same improvisational ingenuity as his mentor. The 27-year-old Doran (born Dransky in Albany, New York) had been active in tough organizing campaigns for the Communist party since 1930. He had worked among the unemployed in the South, building interracial alliances to win relief benefits; he had organized textile workers in North Carolina and once was dragged from the steps of city hall in Charlotte with instructions never to return—he came right back with an even larger demonstration. Then the party sent him to Pennsylvania to organize coal miners and steelworkers. His success prompted the YCL to promote Doran to national director of trade union activities. In the spring of 1937, he took the occasion of an international youth congress in Paris to pay a visit to his comrades in Spain and, once there, persuaded the leadership to let him stay.

"This war they are fighting now is so deep-going and thorough that one just feels its momentum sweeping far past the defeat of fascism here," Doran wrote soon afterward, suggesting his disapproval of the limited goals of the Popular Front. "The war may end with the defeat of Franco, but its effects will plant the people firmly toward a complete liberation." This faith in the power of ideology would bring satisfying results at Belchite. While the Lincolns were bombarding the impregnable church tower, a fascist prisoner indicated that his group might be persuaded to surrender. Doran promptly commandeered a sound truck, which began to blare the Spanish national anthem, "Himno de Riego," drowning out the sounds of battle. When the song ended, the voice of a Spaniard could be heard on the loudspeaker, reading a hastily written appeal by Doran. Urging the insurgents to respect the brotherhood of all Spaniards, the speech warned that otherwise they faced an inevitable slaughter. Through the silence that followed, some of the enemy came forward to surrender. That alone appeared to be a great moral triumph for the anti-fascist cause, suggesting that ideological warfare might yet defeat a superior military force.

Doran had much to gloat about: "Always did want to test myself and am not entirely disappointed." But it would take another three days before the Republic could claim the conquest of Belchite. Furious at the delay caused by the snipers in the church tower and at the shooting of a brigade doctor, Colonel Copic promptly ordered the execution of fascist prisoners by a firing squad. Merriman also succumbed to personal temptation. While again complaining of looting at Belchite—he had recently threatened execution for such offenses—the chief of staff acquired two red bedspreads for his wife, Marion, who was working as a clerk at brigade headquarters at Albacete. (She was the only American woman besides Evelyn Hutchins who served in the Fifteenth Brigade.) At Belchite, Bill Bailey, who had torn the swastika from the *Bremen*, captured another red and yellow fascist banner and sent it to the Maritime Federation of the Pacific in San Francisco.

Meanwhile, as Steve Nelson recuperated from his wounds in Valencia, he was assigned to escort the prominent Americans who visited Spain to offer moral support. Among them were Congressman John Bernard of Minnesota, the only representative to vote against the U.S. neutrality law, and the writers Lillian Hellman and Dorothy Parker. Nelson's reputation impressed Comintern leaders in the International Brigades, and they decided not to risk his return to the front. Instead, the party chose him as a delegate to the twentieth anniversary celebrations of the Russian revolution, which would be held in Moscow that fall. Nelson departed for Paris to await a visa. There, however, he received a cable from Earl Browder, instructing him to report to Communist party headquarters in New York. Nelson arrived to learn that he had been promoted to the party's highest committee and assigned a national speaking tour on behalf of Spain.

Nelson would remain an important party functionary. Much later, he would come to question the contradictions between Communist ideology and its Stalinist implementation. But he expressed no regrets about the party's role in the Spanish war: "What other American organization," he asked, "mobilized so many men and women to fight for Spanish democracy?" Yet he also acknowledged that the party's sectarian history had unfortunately isolated Communists from other sources of support. By 1937, he later said, "we had no more resources to contribute and could not persuade those outside the immediate belt around the Left to see Spain as their struggle. If we had gained more popular support, perhaps we could have pressured Congress to change its disastrous policy of 'neutrality.'" For Nelson, then, the political lesson of Spain—belated, to be sure—was "that Communists couldn't go it alone and ignore other democratic forces."

The Republican victory at Belchite had failed to produce a sustained drive toward Zaragoza, forcing division leaders to reexamine their strategy. Withdrawn from the lines, the Lincolns nursed their losses. When Ernest Hemingway visited the battalion in September 1937, he was impressed with their esprit de corps. "Since I have seen them last spring they have become soldiers," he cabled in a report to America. "Those that were left were tough with blackened matter-of-fact faces and after seven months they knew their trade." Meanwhile, the third American battalion, the Mac-Paps, had completed an intense three-month training program, which included classroom lessons in tactics and extended maneuvers. In mid-September, the Mac-Paps formally joined the Fifteenth Brigade. Three weeks later, the two American battalions climbed aboard trucks and headed toward their next action near the town of Fuentes de Ebro. They would go into combat at dawn, October 13, 1937.

On the eve of battle, however, the peculiarly political character of this volunteer army assumed preeminent importance. Word had reached brigade commissar David Doran that the Mac-Paps were experiencing serious morale problems, and he promptly summoned a remarkable meeting of the half-dozen leading Communists in the battalion, as well as the local American representative to the Comintern, Robert Minor. The discussion commenced with vague complaints about the abuse of authority; but it soon switched to open denunciations of the battalion's political leader, Commissar Joe Dallet.

Like his colleague in the commissariat, Steve Nelson, the 30-year-old Dallet had been sent to Spain because of his political maturity and his zeal. During their imprisonment in southern France on the way to Spain, Dallet had startled Nelson with a long narrative about his pampered childhood. In his youth, he had enjoyed all the advantages of affluence—a college education at Dartmouth, foreign travel, piano lessons—but, he confessed, his wealth had given him no pleasure. "It was like living inside a soap bubble," he said. When he experienced a conversion to communism in the late 1920's, Dallet rejected all the sophistication of his past. He cultivated a tough, proletarian style. "His way of speaking was deliberately profane and deliberately ungrammatical," observed Nelson. Perhaps his elegant background explained Dallet's dogged—and dogmatic—militancy. In 1930, he worked with the Unemployed Councils in Chicago. Then he moved to Ohio, where he defied the large steel corporations by organizing workers, faced police clubs while speaking in public, and ran for local office on the Communist party ticket in Youngstown. A fervent ideologue, he could not bear to miss the fighting in Spain. Believing that there was no other way to defeat fascism "than to beat it on the battlefield," Dallet resented his appointment to commissariat duties. "I haven't even had a smell of the front so far," he complained. "My work is mainly . . . responsible for the 'spiritual force,' i.e., morale and all that goes with it, including health, educational work, cultural work, discipline, recreation."

Determined to prove his tough proletarian credentials, Dallet adopted an authoritarian style that often antagonized the men. He seemed impervious to their individual problems, stood aloof from their friendship. He ignored their needs and opinions, and when they questioned his judgment, he scathingly called them "anti-leadership." The problem crystallized when a member of the battalion staff, Abe Osheroff, approached Dallet about a personal predicament. One of the volunteers Osheroff had recruited in Brooklyn had been complaining of heart palpitations and chest pains and showing other signs of fear. Feeling somewhat guilty for bringing this man into the war, Osheroff asked Dallet if it would be possible to give him a job behind the lines. The commissar responded in fury, attacking Osheroff for encouraging his friend's malingering, and he threatened unnamed reprisals. Worried about his own well-being, Osheroff brooded for days before confiding in some of his hometown friends. They immediately took his side, confronted Dallet, and warned him that any accidents would be repaid in blood. The episode demonstrated the depth of hostility between Dallet and his men. Others resented his hoarding of scarce tobacco, which he smoked from a large, Stalinesque pipe. He would break up card games and deliver punishments and fines for minor violations of brigade rules. "He was trying to do the right thing," Nelson later said of Dallet, "but the right thing was wrong. Discipline has to come from political conviction, not from military books."

The situation climaxed at the dramatic all-night party meeting just outside Fuentes de Ebro. When Dallet responded to his critics that, although hated, he had prepared the men for battle, his arrogant self-defense further inflamed their anger. Doran, perhaps deflecting criticism from his own leadership, castigated Dallet for needless discipline, neglect of the younger men, and contempt for human problems. To be sure, Dallet's adjutant commissar, Saul Wellman, defended the commissar's regime. But after eight long hours of intense criticism, Dallet at last acknowledged his shortcomings. He then expressed apologies—Merriman called it "a last confession"—and offered to resign as commissar. But with only hours left before the attack, a change in command seemed militarily inadvisable; and politically, the point of the meeting had not been to condemn an individual but to stimulate his personal transformation. The party leaders told Dallet to demonstrate his sincerity the next day on the battlefield. Robert Minor concluded the meeting with a windy, irrelevant peroration, extolling the volunteers as "the cadres of the international revolution."

For the Communist leaders of the Fifteenth Brigade, the confrontation with Dallet reaffirmed the validity of Marxist dialectics and the party apparatus.

Osheroff, for one, enjoyed the immediate satisfaction of vindication and personal safety. But on a deeper level, the volunteers understood the ideological force of the encounter. "It demonstrated that the party was a self-correcting organism," recalled Irving Weissman, one of Dallet's critics. "That was my immediate feeling. . . . I felt it as a cleansing, perhaps even a purification." And Dallet apparently felt the same way. He was particularly friendly to his staff as they walked back through the dark to the front lines. Hours later, he would prove his commitment irrevocably. Leading the Mac-Paps over the fortifications, he was shot almost immediately in the skull and shot again before he could crawl back to the trenches. "Earlier discussion might have saved his life," Osheroff speculated many years later. "Given the opportunity to strengthen his act, he might not have needed to demonstrate his worthiness." Later, in America, the party would commemorate Dallet's service with the publication of his letters from Spain.

The morning after Dallet's rebuke, the American volunteers learned once again that raw courage could not overcome inexperience, poor coordination, and superior military force. An innovative attempt to use tanks to penetrate enemy lines failed when some of the Russian-trained drivers misread the contour maps and drove the heavy vehicles into deep ditches. Those who managed to keep moving then accelerated too quickly ahead of the infantry, trapping the men aboard behind enemy lines and leaving the others in open terrain. Not until darkness could the Americans retreat from their exposed positions. (Shocked by the fiasco, Soviet military officials requested a personal report from the Lincoln battalion commissar, John Robinson, who journeyed to Moscow to explain the series of logistical errors to Red Army officers. According to one Soviet veteran, the disaster led to the recall—and execution—of Colonel Copic.) For the Americans, the human toll was again heavy: nearly 80 dead; 150 wounded.

The advance to Zaragoza promptly stalled. It was a failure both military and political, for brigade officers soon learned that the Spanish battalion of the Fifteenth Brigade had committed the same outrage as the former anarchist defenders of the Aragon front. Calling a truce with the enemy, the political commissar had led a small party of Spanish and Cuban soldiers into no-man's-land, where they exchanged newspapers and presents with the fascists on the other side. "One of their men and one of ours left their trench, walked over the parapet, and approached each other in that bleak grim piece of ground between us," reported an American eyewitness. "Pretty soon the parapets on both sides were lined with men. Now the battlefield was full of unarmed peaceful men." The spontaneous cease-fire troubled the officers on both sides, and a single fascist sniper, from far away, tried to disrupt the truce. "It seems," observed the discouraged Merriman, "now that the Italians [have] left their side and the Internationals our side—the front will settle down for the winter— they will make up and football will start again." Most of the Americans nonetheless were grateful when a Spanish brigade moved forward to relieve them.

Problems of morale had been lurking beneath the surface for weeks. When the Lincolns first moved to the Aragon front in August, the number of deserters arriving at the American embassy in Valencia abruptly increased. The consul elaborated on two Americans who had come together. "Both professed to be thoroughly tired of the war." Asked why they had chosen Valencia, rather than the more proximate Barcelona, the deserters cited the successful evacuation of earlier refugees at the time of Jarama. When told that the consulate would not help them, they headed toward brigade headquarters in Albacete, saying that a detention camp, "the usual treatment accorded would-be deserters," appeared preferable to an attempt to reach France without passports. Four days later, however, they returned to Valencia, telling the consul that their reception at Albacete had been "cool and firm, but that they had not been threatened with punishment for having left the front." Instead, base commissar William Lawrence had given them a pep talk and persuaded them that the "wise thing" was to return to their units. Although they were "volunteers," in other words, "they were not free to return to the United States." Both men proceeded back to the battalion on the Aragon front. Neither was punished, nor did they make any other effort to desert again.

Equally illuminating was the case of William Howe, who had joined Bill Bailey in the *Bremen* affair in 1935. The circumstances of war had quickly killed the bloom of his radical ardor. When Bailey met him in Spain, Howe complained bitterly of the military discipline. Already he had visited the American consulate in Barcelona seeking repatriation; a U.S. official had walked him to the front door, pointed to the mountains north of the city, and advised him that he would have to escape the same way he had entered Spain. Howe returned to the lines. But after the battle at Belchite, he again disappeared. "He is a man of more than [the] ordinary intelligence of a seaman," the American consul at Gibraltar remarked, in reporting Howe's arrival as a deserter. "He is now fully disillusioned and through with the whole communist matter . . . saying that his experience of about eleven months fighting with the Reds in Spain had brought about the disillusionment finally and permanently with him." Perhaps Howe had simply told the consul what he thought he wanted to hear. But in any case, after Spain, Howe vanished from the radical movement.

The indecisiveness of some volunteers reflected the enormous complexity of human responses to the hazards and opportunities of war. Heroes of one day might appear irresolute the next, in a curious cycle of emotional intensity. After several weeks of military training, for example, a twenty-year-old, Brooklyn-born soldier named William "Red" Cantor began to feel that he had made a mistake in enlisting, and he applied for permission to go home, pleading that he was still a minor. Merriman rejected the claim, noting that Cantor was "off on [the] wrong foot again." The next month, when the brigade passed through Valencia on the way to the Aragon front, Cantor deliberately missed the train and visited the American embassy, appealing for assistance in obtaining repatriation. Told he would have to escape alone, Cantor said he would try. But the same afternoon, he returned to the office, army pack on his back, and announced he would rejoin his comrades. Then, just five days later, during the second day at Quinto, Cantor heroically dashed through sniper fire to drag a wounded soldier from an exposed rooftop. Yet despite his valor, Cantor still wanted to go home. Once again, he arrived at the embassy in Valencia, inquiring if the United States had altered its policy toward deserters. Again denied assistance, Cantor and another comrade found a sympathetic British seaman, who helped them stow away on a ship bound for Gibraltar and Galveston, Texas. Cantor later married the sister of another Lincoln veteran, Maury Colow, who for years remained unaware of his relative's odyssey. "He was a totally anarchistic individual," said Colow, in an effort at explanation.

The rash of desertions during the Aragon offensive led to a toughening of brigade policy. "Sad bunch in general," observed Merriman of thirteen deserters who had been arrested for leaving the front. Four of them had fled in a stolen ambulance. "Decided to have a tough trial and hard sentence," Merriman noted. The commissars presented the problem to the men, who voted for resolutions "demanding tough sentence even death. General reaction," Merriman noted, "in favor of tight policy in this regard." The ensuing trials lasted two days, with the commissars serving as prosecutors. "This court is not only military," stated Commissar Doran, "but also [a] workingclass anti-fascist tribunal." Some of the deserters quickly confessed their crimes; others lied blatantly to save their skins. The final verdict: two sentenced to death, the others to live in the lines without leave for varying periods of time, the least being one month for a twenty-year-old. But the harsh penalties disturbed the brigade leadership. Some commissars worried about the effect on world public opinion. In the end, the brigade remanded the sentences. None of the deserters faced a firing squad.

Commissar Doran's authoritarian streak, however, antagonized the volunteers. It was his duty, for example, to implement the Spanish Republican Army's new policy of military discipline—expecting the men to salute their officers, ordering the wearing of stripes and proper uniforms, and allowing a "two-pot" table to separate military officers from the rank and file. Good Communists hated the implicit arrogance. "They're trying to make an army out of us . . . marching, saluting, etc.," complained one volunteer. "But most of us here now, have been through Quinto, Belchite, and Fuentes and, gee, it's hard to go for that sort of stuff." In these new circumstances, some Lincolns began to question their private commitment to the Communist leadership; subsequently, a few dissidents would trace their rejection of the party to its "arbitrary and dictatorial attitude . . . toward the ranks." But those were exceptions. Most volunteers accepted military authority—respect for officers, the censorship of mail—as an essential ingredient of the war.

Two personal imbroglios nonetheless illustrate the problems of Doran's regime. The first involved the sprightly five-foot four-inch Pat Reade, veteran of World War I, the Irish Republican Army, and the Wobblies. Brave to the point of recklessness—he would pause while laying communications lines under fire to roll and smoke his cigarettes—Reade was a die-hard anarchist and an outspoken anti-Communist. Initially assigned to a French transmission company, Reade quickly got into trouble because of his argumentative disposition; but Commissar Steve Nelson accepted his grumblings, matched his arguments, and valued his courage. Doran lacked that tolerance. One day, he simply dismissed Reade from the brigade for "always attacking the party." Reade, broken-hearted and near tears, could only say goodbye to the men he had come to love. Yet—and this is also important—the removal of Pat Reade represented one of the only documented instances of an American who was persecuted in Spain for his political beliefs.

The second conflict involved Benjamin "Butch" Goldstein, a loud former professional boxer and onetime butcher, who had left the officers' training program, saying "my own father and mother couldn't make me go to school—dey tink dey can make me!" As his battle-weary battalion waited for proper quarters near Teruel, Goldstein complained to Doran about the delay. The commissar advised him to mind his own business, after which Goldstein told Doran to "go fuck himself." Doran promptly ordered his arrest for insubordination. Other officers quickly intervened, urging Doran to drop the matter, and Goldstein returned to his group. But hours later, when arrangements still had not been made, Goldstein returned to headquarters to demand accommodations. Another exchange occurred; Doran again ordered his arrest. "He did that because he thought he was a big shot," explained Goldstein, "and no one should talk like that to a big shot." He stayed under guard all night. The next day, Merriman discussed the matter with Goldstein and asked him to apologize. Goldstein refused. Other commissars and officers arrived by turns, asking him to make a concession. "I believe in conscious discipline, not imposed discipline," he stated, "and . . . I wouldn't apologize." Finally, a party meeting was held in Goldstein's cell and at last, for the sake of the party, he agreed to say the two words that brought his freedom: "I'm sorry." "In no other army in the world," concluded veteran historian Art Landis, "could this have happened." And while his fellow officers were obviously reluctant to undermine Doran's authority, party leaders in New York were preparing to withdraw the unpopular commissar. Before they could act, however, Doran's fearlessness cost him his life.

After the bloodletting of the Aragon, the Americans returned to the Madrid area, where the soldiers obtained passes to visit the capital. Heavy snowfalls and cold virtually ended their fighting. Three days before Christmas, they exulted at the news that Republican armies, without any assistance from the Internationals, had captured the frozen mountain town of Teruel. Most considered it an omen of imminent victory: the Spanish people's army would quickly rid the country of Franco and his fascist allies. Christmas proved a happy season; morale was high. Two fun-loving men, recently promoted through the ranks, now commanded the Lincolns: Philip Detro, the tall Texan who bragged of his family's lineage in the Confederate army; and his commissar, Fred Keller, an Irish Catholic from New York, who had been politicized while organizing a union in the building services. Both became close to Ernest Hemingway, who admired their guileless enthusiasm. Neither was a party man. "Where I come from," Detro liked to remind Keller, "we shoot Communists."

Although American battalions had not participated in the capture of Teruel, three tough, athletic volunteers—Alex Kunslich, William Aalto, and Irving Goff—had been working secretly behind enemy lines with a detachment of Spanish guerrillas to prepare for the Republican offensive. Before Spain, Kunslich had been a college student, but he had quit to help organize the longshoremen in New York; Aalto was a Finnish-American truck driver from the Bronx, one of a half-dozen known homosexuals among the American volunteers; and Goff, a premier body builder (famous as the "Adonis" of Coney Island's Muscle Beach), had worked as an adagio dancer and professional acrobat before becoming an organizer for the Communist party in New York.

At Albacete, the three had volunteered for the difficult, dangerous guerrilla assignment. With Soviet instructors they had studied infiltration techniques, bivouacking, and the use of pressure-sensitive explosives that could destroy railroad tracks, bridges, and power lines. Such operations demanded the utmost care. They worked only at night, with small groups of six or seven, relying on Spanish guides to bring them into fascist-held areas, where they might stay for weeks at a time. Goff well remembered his initiation into fascist territory: "I froze up; my mind went blank. A second or two at most, but it felt like two hours. . . . Your mind tells you . . . you're in a dangerous position; you're encircled by the enemy, and that was an overwhelming impact on your nervous system." His uncontrollable fear soon passed. In their first operation, the Americans reached within two hundred yards of fascist-held Córdoba, planted a single artillery shell filled with dynamite and a detonator called a *cuña* (a "wedge," but also a "cunt"), and blew up a train, killing over one hundred Italian troops.

Before Teruel, their objective was to destroy the main supply bridge that spanned the Albarracin River. The operation, possibly the model for Hemingway's novel *For Whom the Bell Tolls*, differed somewhat from its fictional re-creation, which, according to Lincoln veterans, contained numerous errors of fact. Most important, unlike Hemingway's heroes, the Spanish guerrillas never intended to confront enemy troops. "These were not suicide missions," Goff stressed; they were planned carefully to allow for safe entry and safe exit. Though armed with light machine guns and rifles, the guerrillas endeavored to plant the explosives and leave before the weight of a passing tank or truck triggered the *cuña*. Despite cold temperatures and thigh-deep snow, they climbed the mountainous terrain at night and found the target unguarded. But as a precaution the small group crawled quietly on hands and knees toward the little bridge. They experienced no trouble in setting the explosive and immediately left the area. Later, from a distance, they heard an explosion and watched the small structure crumble into a ravine. Then they destroyed nearby telephone communications. But their noise attracted a fascist cavalry patrol, which started to pursue them. As the guerrillas fled on foot, the deep snow stymied the fascists' horses, enabling the band to escape. The bridge remained down for a couple of days, preventing reinforcements from reaching the fascist defenders at Teruel.

The American guerrillas would stage equally dramatic raids behind enemy lines later in the war. The most impressive involved the liberation of over 300 prisoners from a fascist fortress at Motril the following spring. Infiltrating enemy lines, Goff and Aalto led a team of 25 guerrillas, which cut communications lines, killed the prison guards, and then armed the prisoners with hand grenades. "We weren't a raiding party," Goff boasted; "we were a battalion." But the sudden arrival of an enemy force changed the plan. While the freed prisoners raced toward Republican lines, the rear guard, consisting of Goff, Aalto, and two Spaniards, leaped from the rocky cliff into the Mediterranean Sea and swam frantically to escape rifle range. The Spaniards drowned, but the two Americans used the cover of darkness to return to shore at the edge of the cliff, just beneath the enemy camp. Trapped by the presence of enemy scouts, the naked men huddled in the shallow waters for 48 hours, starving, thirsty, cold, and increasingly exhausted. Finally, in desperation, they dared to swim through enemy fire to a cave, where they rested for another day. Then, moving across sharp, slippery rocks, they reached a farmhouse, where Spanish peasants fed them. Eventually, they returned to their base. The extraordinary experience of these American guerrillas, as we will see, would help the United States form underground groups in Europe during World War II.

*

Exultation about the capture of Teruel ended abruptly on the last day of 1937, when heavy fascist counterattacks threatened the recent gains. Fearing a breakthrough, the Internationals rushed back to the front. Snow, bitter winds, and freezing temperatures added to the peril. Trucks and ambulances skidded off the mountain roadways or stalled against heavy drifts. In desperation, the drivers pushed some vehicles over the precipices to keep the roads clear. Digging trenches in the frozen terrain proved extremely difficult, though the activity generated a comforting body heat. Food—canned or fresh—froze solid. The men subsisted on soup, which had to be consumed quickly before it refroze. Frostbite and chill added to the casualties. Working in unheated stone buildings, the American medical staff struggled to keep their hands warm enough to operate. (Frozen limbs, however, did facilitate certain amputations.) Edwin Rolfe later referred to the campaign as "Spain's Valley Forge."

While the weather attacked the brigade's strength, the ensuing military confrontation revealed the superiority of Franco's mechanized weapons and supplies. From the heights of Celadas, the so-called "North Pole," the Lincolns could only watch, too far away to become directly involved, as waves of fascist troops backed by artillery and bombers attacked Republican lines on another hill. "With a few pieces of artillery we could have done some good work," lamented an American sergeant. "But they must have been confident that we had none, judging from the way they were coming." As the fascist assaults continued, the Lincolns were hit with enormous artillery bombardments and air raids, which spread fear but claimed relatively few casualties. Captain Detro, refusing to stoop before the fascists, eschewed the communications trench at Teruel and caught a bullet in his thigh. He was an exception. "When I first arrived in Spain," explained Dr. Irving Busch, "most of the casualties were bullet wounds. Today most are caused by shrapnel from bombs and artillery shells." Still, within weeks, Detro was dead from complications. ("Take it standing," he had written to his mother from his deathbed.) Meanwhile, the Mac-Paps, defending positions below the enemy, sustained heavy losses.

During January and the early part of February 1938, the Americans remained in action, constantly facing superior firepower. As in previous engagements, they demonstrated remarkable courage and stamina: they held difficult positions against overwhelming forces; they led a bold diversionary attack against enemy lines at Segura de los Baños. Each success, however, proved to be a prelude to yet another fascist offensive. Experience in trench warfare enabled the Americans to minimize their losses, but they lacked the materiel and the supporting fire to halt the enemy advance. By the third week of February, Franco had reconquered Teruel. The commissars tried to take solace from the length of the struggle: what the Republic had won in a few days in December had taken two arduous months for the fascists to repossess. "We stayed there in the snow while the fascists bombed and shelled us incessantly," Milton Wolff later wrote, "until we were on the verge of cracking under the strain. We didn't crack—and we repulsed their furious counter-attacks. We had still to meet that pressure under which no man could stand up."

12

The Great Retreats

In the first week of March 1938, the Lincolns were back in the Belchite area for rest and reorganization when word reached brigade headquarters that the fascists were launching a heavy offensive against Republican forces in the Aragon. Facing a combination of air attack, artillery, tanks, and infantry—the mechanism of what would later be called "blitzkrieg" in World War II—the Republican lines were collapsing. Merriman belatedly ordered the Americans into the breach. "There's machine gun fire on all sides and ahead," reported Frank Rogers in his diary. "We are outnumbered five to one." Scattering for cover, the Lincolns attempted to form defensive lines five times, firing all night into the dark. But with exposed flanks they could hardly withstand the tremendous assault.

Thus commenced what became known as the "Great Retreats." At battalion headquarters, Rogers could see his men running from the fascist advance toward the base, many falling before artillery and strafing planes. At that moment, a single shell crashed directly on the battalion command post, wounding Rogers and killing the rest of the leadership. With tanks approaching, Rogers used his rifle as a crutch and hobbled back through Belchite. Each time the men attempted to regroup, however, fascist forces had already pressed beyond them, threatening encirclement. Tanks, artillery, planes—all tore at an army unable to defend itself. Individual heroism by men like machine gunner Joe Bianca stalled particular drives, but many Lincolns fled in terror. Merriman and Commissar John Gates divided the battalion into two groups and retreated hastily to form new lines. Enemy forces bit at their heels.

After a desperate all-night march, the Americans discovered to their horror that the fascists had passed their flanks, thwarting a holding action. And again they marched, exhausted beyond measure. Many threw away their equipment and weapons. Hunger and thirst added to the desperation. Another effort at regrouping lasted but a day and a half. Milton Wolff noticed that the men were digging peculiarly shaped foxholes, so that "they would be able to take up positions in them facing not only the front and the flanks but the rear as well. They were so tired that they were determined to dig in there and stay put. But it wasn't meant to be." Realizing that the fascists had again flanked their positions, the Lincolns endured an agonizing 50-mile retreat toward Caspe. By March 15, six days and 75 torturous miles after the attack began, the Lincolns and the Mac-Paps had shriveled from five hundred men each to about one hundred weary, aching survivors.

At Caspe, brigade commissar David Doran rallied the remnants. "Whatever the cost," he told one of his staff, "we've got to stop them here. If help comes good. If not, we will at least have given the rest of the army a chance to dig in behind us." He repeated that order to the assembled men, appealing to their idealism and their pride and their hatred of fascism. The Americans responded in character. Poorly armed, underfed, dead on their feet, the brigade stood to meet the enemy—and not merely in defense of Caspe but in a direct attack on the road into town. They fought there for a few hours, until superior firepower drove them back into town and out the other side. But then they rallied again, forcing their way back into Caspe and toward the enemy positions in the hills. The Fifteenth Brigade could not hold these gains. After three days of constant fighting, the surviving 250 men, who now constituted the entire brigade, were forced to retreat. Their defense had stabilized the lines, at least temporarily. Sixty miles beyond the point of their initial breakthrough, the fascists had to reestablish their plan of attack.

Alvah Bessie, the novelist, critic, and would-be aviator, had crossed the

Pyrenees just a month before. Militarily ignorant, he had been training in Tarazona and lamenting the loss of his "precious individualism" when news of the retreats hastened his initiation into the war. "You haven't had as much training as you might have had," Major Allan Johnson advised the newest Lincoln recruits, "but what you lack in training you make up in enthusiasm and anti-fascist conviction." Someone asked Bessie the question, "Are you fit to go to the front?" Answering in the affirmative, he soon found himself among the last survivors of the battalion. "They had week-old beards," he wrote; "they were filthy and lousy; they stank; their clothes were in rags; they had no rifles, no blankets, no ammunition, no mess kits, no pack-sacks. They had nothing but the rags in which they were dressed and the filth with which they were covered." Nor did the veterans appreciate the scrubbed, clean-shaven rookies: "They did not answer our questions except in grunts or with expletives." Indicative of the battalion's desperation, the inexperienced Bessie was immediately made a corporal—"a curious position for such as me," he noted in his diary, "with my background of idiosyncratic isolation."

Milton Wolff, veteran of every action since Brunete, assumed command of the battalion; John Gates became battalion commissar. (Brigade officers Merriman and Doran remained their immediate superiors.) Wolff and Gates had risen through the ranks in Spain and had not only proven their courage in battle but also shown an instinct for survival. On several occasions, Wolff had emerged from perilous encounters unscathed, while men inches away had died. Gates had led dangerous missions on the Córdoba front before joining the brigade commissariat. He had been the last to leave Caspe. Both were intelligent and resourceful, willing to take chances, but neither was impulsive or reckless. They gave the veterans plenty of latitude during this lull. But they also inspired them, so the men would fight with their new weapons. It was only a matter of days before the fascist attack would resume.

When the enemy approached, however, the brigade could do little more than offer a rear-guard defense against immensely superior forces. Even this resistance proved futile when the fascists overran the Republican lines. Within two days, the Lincolns had commenced yet another anxious retreat. But the enemy had already passed beyond them, infiltrating the roads and surrounding countryside in a rush toward the town of Gandesa. Doran, who had boldly rallied the Americans at Caspe, now called for a fight to the last man. Merriman overruled him. Instead the exhausted battalion would try to catch the enemy from behind, perhaps to lift the siege at Gandesa. By this time, the Lincolns were sleeping on their feet, as Bessie put it, "aching in every muscle." One company actually walked into a fascist encampment, stumbling over the sleeping enemy. Those in the lead managed to run right through; the rest were never heard from again. At one point—no one remembered exactly where—the Americans were forced to leave behind the wounded. "That was a painful occasion," recalled Clement Markert, who had abandoned his studies at the University of Colorado to come to Spain just a few weeks before. "We walked by the wounded. The doctor volunteered to stay with them, and . . . I suppose he was killed there too. The wounded didn't make it easy for us to walk off and leave them. Some of them were cursing us for deserting them, and yet," he added, "what could you do? You could only barely manage yourself if you were not wounded."

The remaining companies, commanded by Merriman, took refuge in the heights above the Gandesa road and determined to attack the fascists from the rear. But heavy fire forced them to retreat to higher ground. Surrounded and vastly outnumbered, they waited for nightfall to attempt an escape. After an anxious day's stay, the Americans quietly moved off the hill in single file and began to march, in Wolff's words, "through the dark in hostile, unknown territory. . . . There wasn't a man who made that trip who didn't feel death walking by his side." Around midnight, the leaders of the column marched directly into an enemy camp. "Rojos! Rojos!" shouted the guard. Some of the Americans leaped down the nearest embankment and ran desperately for the hills. Merriman and Doran charged ahead; at that moment, both disappeared forever. Fascist officers later reported finding Merriman's last diary: "We shall fight until the end," it read; "even if every one of us must die."

The luckier Americans scattered around the countryside, living by their wits, trying to reach Republican lines on the far side of the Ebro River. Bessie found himself among a conglomerate of Internationals, speaking a half-dozen languages, and crossed the bridge into Mora la Nueva. "We looked back . . . across the broad, swift and shallow stream, swollen and muddy now in the spring freshets," he recalled. "As we watched, the great iron bridge rose slowly and majestically into the air and slumped into the river." The remaining Lincolns were trapped on the other side. Hiding in the hills, beseeching the aid of friendly peasants who offered them food or blankets, they steered in small groups and singly toward the Ebro. Some managed to reach the river's edge only to attract enemy fire when they entered the cold, rushing waters; many drowned in the effort to cross. A fascist patrol captured Fred Keller, who had been wounded in the hip. But the former Golden Gloves boxer overpowered his guard, then led a group of Americans to the Ebro. When some hesitated to enter the swollen river, Keller swam across to show them it could be done, then returned and swam back a third time, assisting the injured. "He is young and strong as a bull and he has all the courage in the world," wrote Herbert Matthews of the exploit. Meanwhile, other Americans, like Wolff and Leonard Lamb, wandered alone for days, reading the North Star, as Lamb put it, "as conscientiously as I had ever read a shirt for lice," until they managed to cross the river.

Most never succeeded. Those who were captured could expect no mercy. As in any war, there is no count of the men who may have been shot while attempting to surrender or of those wounded who received a coup de grace to hasten their deaths. But an exhaustive study made by a former American prisoner of war, Carl Geiser, found that of the 287 known American captives, the fascists killed 173. That statistic accounted for one-fifth of the total American dead in Spain. Such summary treatment represented Franco's official policy toward the International volunteers. Only one American prisoner captured during 1937 (at Brunete) survived, only three taken at Teruel in January 1938. Among these was the former Wobbly organizer Reuben Barr, who at age 35 had sailed for Spain under an assumed name. Sentenced to death, Barr dared to write letters not only to his family, but also to President Roosevelt. "I am suffering from the same disease Nathan Hale succumbed to," he wrote. Perhaps this audacious correspondence to the White House convinced his captors that Barr was too important to execute. In any case, his sentence was not carried out, though his guards punished him for "spreading anti-Franco propaganda among the prisoners." Barr would be among the last Americans to leave Spain.

During the period of the Great Retreats, when the advancing fascists seized numerous Internationals, Franco altered his policy about prisoners—temporarily—so that he would have live bodies to exchange for his own captured soldiers. At this time, Geiser found, the enemy snared 87 Americans. These prisoners, most of them incarcerated in a concentration camp at San Pedro de Cárdenas, received rough treatment—bad food, inadequate clothing, poor medical care, and brutal beatings. Because of the political sophistication of the inmates, however, morale remained high. Indeed, the prisoners viewed the ordeal as the embodiment of fascist totalitarianism, the very evil they had come to fight. Their own government, however, offered no assistance. Even when U.S. officials learned of their fate, the State Department did little to ameliorate the suffering; the government claimed that its policy of nonrecognition toward Franco obviated any intervention. Not until after the fall of Madrid in 1939 would Franco feel obliged to release these American prisoners (together with a handful of those captured later).

As the fascists poured across the Spanish plains, the problem of individual discipline assumed tremendous importance. Amidst the confusion and terror, an instinct for survival, matched by physical strength and plain luck, determined who lived and who did not. "Each man was for himself," Milton Wolff later stated, "and the way he acted demonstrated clearly how important he thought the war in Spain was to him as an individual." Those who remained in groups usually attempted to form a rear guard to slow the fascist advance. Others, cut off from comrades, wandered desperately across the landscape, trying to avoid capture. Some, like David Sachs, panicked. A YCLer from New Jersey who had paid his way to Spain because his comrades thought him untrustworthy, he had recently served a jail term for desertion and had been assigned to dig fortifications. When fascist aviation appeared, he became markedly "jittery," refused to take cover, and instead bolted across a field. He became, as one eyewitness reported, "a perfect target" for a strafing plane.

Some, thoroughly exhausted, lost the will to fight. Among these were two close friends, the painters Douglas Taylor and Edward Deyo Jacobs, both members of the Artists' Union in New York. The Utah-born Taylor painted in oils; Jacobs, scion of an old New York family that traced its lineage to the early Dutch colonists, had achieved a reputation as a cartoonist. Together, they had haunted the art scene in Greenwich Village, and in Spain they served as mapmakers in the headquarters company of the Mac-Paps. "Bullets, shells, bombs—hugging the earth, hungry, thirsty in turn—war," Taylor wrote to his mother, "there is nothing worse than war—yet I must go on fighting." When he was not making maps, Jacobs produced illustrations for the brigade newspaper *Volunteer for Liberty*, as well as for the official brigade history. "For the first time in my life I am doing art that really has some real social significance," he wrote of his labors. "The idea of revolutionary art seemed rather pompous in the states." Somewhere in Spain Taylor and Jacobs had acquired a large and heavy volume of Goya etchings, which they carried in and out of combat and which provided them with a constant source of discussion. But a sprained ankle slowed Jacobs's movements during the retreats. And when he became too fatigued to take another step, Taylor refused to leave his side. Together, they disappeared.

"There's nothing more horrible than to be running all the time," remembered Saul Wellman, commissar of the Mac-Paps. "We were under fire, surrounded, being bombed by planes, cut up, being caught and fighting every day in a new position." Running for their lives, some men retreated all the way to France; for them the war was over. "It was considered a disgrace to quit that way," conceded one war-weary volunteer, "but it was foolish to continue." Others fled that far only to experience second thoughts about their behavior and voluntarily returned to their units. Still others, arrested by Spanish authorities for lacking proper documents, eventually requested permission to rejoin the battalion. And some accepted a bleak, Spanish cell as a preferable alternative to facing fascist armies.

"The circumstances around which they deserted were important to know," explained one veteran who interviewed and reassigned deserters after the Great Retreats. He remembered one man who had run away after eavesdropping on a conversation between two officers. Speaking sarcastically, these officers had joked that the battalion would have to go over the mountains into France. "This man heard this and took it as gospel truth." Subsequent investigation found this improbable story to be true! Others responded to what they saw with their own eyes. "A man might be scared from seeing very heavy casualties. . . . He would think everything was lost and would pick himself up and run because he was influenced by what he saw immediately around him." This officer also detected an important political pattern among the deserters: they were "men who didn't understand fully what they were fighting for." Whereas most of the volunteers had come for idealistic political reasons, some went to Spain to get away from problems at home. "It was amongst the men who were trying to escape reality at home, and who came for adventure that we found most of the deserters."

Brigade policy, with a few exceptions, permitted the return of deserters. Typical punishment was assignment to a labor battalion, which required work on fortifications and trenches. Then, after interviews, men who had completed their sentences were attached to appropriate units. "In 99 percent of the cases," stated the examining officer, "they became very good soldiers." Some asked to return to the front, where they served well. According to the officer, "there were a few cases where a man kept on deserting continually." Significantly, all these cases involved violations of *military* discipline; within the Lincoln brigade, there was no punishment for political dissidence.

The problem of morale also affected the men and women of the American Medical Bureau. "It is hard to be sick away from home, among strangers," observed Dr. Frances Vanzant, the only woman doctor from the United States, "and we can't allow them to become demoralized, homesick, discouraged." The medical staff tried to keep patients busy and, given the shortage of help, welcomed the participation of convalescents in sharing the work. But during the retreats, the clearly marked hospitals and medical stations offered no sanctuary from artillery and bombardment. "We had the feeling of being in a dream—a crazy dream of a special kind of hell," remembered nurse Sonya Merims. "The only reality was the work we had to do, and we went on." One bombing demolished her hospital; a flying rock smashed her ribs; her nerves shook. Nurse Helen Freeman nearly lost an arm. "I began to realize that our army was not going to be able to stop the fascist advance," Ruth Davidow recalled. "And I was not ready to die. For the first time in my life I felt I had to decide whether I wanted to live or die. Either—or. And I decided that I wanted to live." But although she obtained formal permission to leave the Spanish army, Davidow's commitment had rooted too deeply. About to depart on a train, she abruptly wheeled around and returned to her base. The joyous Spaniards embraced her.

Such transformations reflected the terrific ordeal by fire—and its transcendence. But the nurses and doctors who saw the struggle through sometimes succumbed to severe depression. "It was a hellish experience," recalled Dr. Pike. "The hopelessness of the position, fascists everywhere." Their planes seemed to pinpoint every supply dump. "Every time you put up a little hospital tent it was bombed." Several of the medical personnel, he reported, "developed neurosis because of extreme depression, and had to be evacuated to the rear." Even the seemingly inexhaustible Edward Barsky finally had to be ordered to rest.

The tension between psychology and ideology would haunt some volunteers for years. One was Bill McCarthy, a fatherless altar boy raised by the Christian Brothers in New York. A strong class consciousness brought him into the maritime labor movement and then to Spain. Fighting in the seaman's machine-gun section, McCarthy experienced several brushes with death on the Aragon front, but showed no particular problems. He also witnessed the ugly execution of fascist prisoners of war at Belchite. He offered no complaints, but the memory disturbed him. Half a year later, during the retreats, a bomb explosion lifted McCarthy into the air and dropped him with a crash of shrapnel and rubble. He emerged in a daze, not knowing who or where he was.

"I was trembling and shaking," he recalled. "And I trembled and shook for quite a while." As the battalion cracked apart, McCarthy headed toward the rear. Stopped for lacking a *salvo conducto* (a safe conduct pass), he was brought before the brigade commissar, who ordered him to a hospital and then, as McCarthy put it, to the "laughing academy" or "cracker factory." Eventually the brigade approved his evacuation from Spain. But McCarthy suffered intense guilt. "I would get a kaleidoscope of faces," he said of the ensuing nightmares. "First eye sockets pouring out. . . . Empty eye sockets. And they would come up real close and then fade away. . . . And I figured, these are the guys that I let down."

To assuage his guilt, McCarthy felt obliged to take extraordinary measures to demonstrate his anti-fascist convictions. One year after returning from Spain, while serving as a seaman in Genoa, he drunkenly launched a tirade against Mussolini. Arrested and given the notorious castor-oil treatment, McCarthy served a two-week jail sentence for insulting Il Duce. A dozen years later, while protesting the Korean War, McCarthy climbed a lamppost in New York City to shout antiwar oratory. When he refused to come down, firemen and police beat him savagely, damaging the sight of an eye. As he got older, McCarthy began to express remorse for his participation in the war; he even wrote a public letter to the bishop of Barcelona lamenting the execution of the fascist prisoners. He drew closer to his early Catholicism. He became an alcoholic. He gave away his meager savings to help other veterans. "So," he wrote, shortly before his death in 1988, "forty five years later, lamppost, jail, loss of eye, I'm still trying to make up for my crack-up in Spain." McCarthy's last request, fulfilled by his friend Bill Bailey, was to have his ashes buried amid the ruins of Belchite, his point of crisis.

The perilous condition of the Lincoln brigade following the retreats introduced a new political dimension to the question of desertion. At a time when Franco claimed to have destroyed the International Brigades and prepared to launch another offensive to split the Republic in half, many Americans recognized at last that the only hope for victory depended on outside assistance from France, Britain, or the United States. Yet just at this time a few American deserters began to trumpet accusations against the Communist leadership in Spain. For John Honeycombe, a 37-year-old Communist organizer from Los Angeles, it took five days of running, walking, and hitchhiking to cross the French border. Exhausted and beaten, "extremely nervous," in the words of a *New York Times* reporter, he depicted the total collapse of the Republican armies—claiming that 8,500 Americans had been killed! He also stated that "the Communist International is the only thing that keeps the war going."

Honeycombe's story, disseminated throughout the United States by the Associated Press, proved a severe political blow, imperiling efforts on the home front to build a mass movement against the American embargo. Lincoln veteran David McKelvey White, a Brooklyn College instructor who had returned from Spain to become secretary of the Friends of the Abraham Lincoln Brigade in New York, promptly denounced Honeycombe's charges, accusing the deserter of self-justifying lies. Milton Wolff, now commander of the Lincolns, charged "Crummycombe" with drunkenness and multiple prior desertions. But Honeycombe had touched a sympathetic nerve in the United States. "My experience in Spain," he told a reporter, "has taught me that before we can make Communism work, we must change the human element in the leaders." Such statements, repeated by other American deserters during the spring of 1938, suggested that beneath the Lincolns' celebrated esprit de corps lay a caldron of dissatisfaction and broken morale. More seriously, these charges aroused concern that American volunteers were suffering under the totalitarian discipline of the Communist party.

Allegations of harsh treatment within the brigade drew national attention when two deserters from New England, Abraham Sobel and Alvin Halpern, appeared before the House Committee on Un-American Activities, headed by Representative Martin Dies of Texas, in 1938:

THE CHAIRMAN: If those boys were allowed to return to the United States today, would they come back?

MR. SOBEL: Every one of them.

THE CHAIRMAN: They are sick and tired and fed up with it?

MR. SOBEL: Yes.

THE CHAIRMAN: Disillusioned?

MR. SOBEL: They certainly are.

THE CHAIRMAN: They are prisoners over there today, is that not a fact?

MR. SOBEL: Virtually prisoners.

From Spain, a group of wounded Americans denounced those remarks as "an unmitigated lie." Sobel, according to one of his officers in the transport regiment, had been jailed for drunk driving and put in a labor battalion for looting and stealing. Halpern, said the veterans, was known as "Hot Air Al." More damning, former commissar Carl Bradley, head of the first group of Lincoln veterans in New York, produced a letter from one of these deserters, which stated that "comradeship was something I really found, for every man I met there in Spain would lay down his life for the preservation of ideals and the lives of his comrades." Amidst the controversy, another veteran offered a more sympathetic analysis: "Sobel did very good work in Spain. He was a very good anti-Fascist. . . . The false statements he made to the Dies committee were made to cover up his desertion." But the political impact remained unchanged. "Spain was Red! Red! Red!" observed Bradley. "This is the line of Sobel, Halpern, and Dies."

In the aftermath of the retreats, the brigade leadership resolved to tighten discipline in the ranks—with some tragic results. A seaman named Paul White was the first victim. Long before Spain, he had been active in the Communist movement on the East Coast waterfront. He had helped plan the *Bremen* protest, and he had recruited numerous volunteers for Spain. During the summer of 1937, Merriman had praised White's work in organizing trucks and supplies to transport the Lincolns to the Aragon front. When the fascists broke through the lines the following March, the brigade leaders sent White to get additional ammunition. Instead, he grabbed an empty ambulance and headed for the French border. He had deserted under fire. For weeks the Lincolns heard nothing of his whereabouts and assumed that White had made his way home. Then, during the period of rebuilding the battalion in the spring of 1938, an old friend of White's, Bill Bailey, went on an errand to gather supplies from a town near Barcelona.

Taking advantage of his freedom, Bailey stopped at a local whorehouse and took a Spanish woman upstairs to bed. Just as they undressed, however, an air-raid siren announced a fascist attack. Despite Bailey's pleas to wait, the woman leaped from the bed, took her clothes, and ran down to the nearest *refugio*, the air-raid shelter. Bailey felt too frustrated to move. All through the attack he lay in the bed, listening to the planes and the anti-aircraft artillery. Only when the firing ceased did he decide to seek shelter. Dressing quickly, Bailey ran downstairs, opened the door, and peered along the street. Looking back at him from another doorway was Paul White. Bailey asked him what he was doing. White replied that after he had reached the French border, he had begun to feel remorse. His wife had recently given birth to a son and he wanted the boy to be proud of his father. He had decided to rejoin the brigade. So when the all-clear siren sounded, Bailey and White found a truck to take them to a nearby camp. But when Spanish authorities inspected their papers, White lacked a *salvo conducto*, and was promptly arrested.

Brought to brigade headquarters, a somber Paul White offered a complete confession. "After Belchite," he admitted, "I knew I was afraid to go into action again." But the fascist breakthrough had forced his return to combat. "I tried all this time to overcome my feeling of fear," he said. "I felt we were doomed and fighting futilely." When the Lincoln battalion moved into action near Battea, "I could not make it," White explained, "and dropped out of line and made up my mind to desert and try and reach France. As I ran towards the Ebro and met more deserters and routed troops, my fear grew. . . . If I succeeded in getting to France, I still would have to face everyone at home but I had lost all control.

"I kept going and debating whether or not to turn back. I spoke to the [mayor] at the border town in which I was arrested and asked where the commandancia [command post] was located. He told me and I decided to eat and make a final decision. I was arrested before I had done this.

"Once I was in custody I decided that I had been saved from wrecking my life completely."

These details, slightly different from the recollections of Bill Bailey, were leading White to a moment of truth. "I realize that 'safety' of the kind I was seeking would never compensate me for the loss of everything and everyone I value," White said in a plea for compassion. "I ask for one chance and that is to serve in the lines and wipe out this stain on my military and Party record.

"I am 29 years old and am certain that I can serve in the ranks for many years as a class conscious worker. I have had plenty of time to think before making this statement and sincerely believe I will be stronger in my work and devotion if given the opportunity to redeem myself. I regard my position now as the most serious crisis in my life and am ready to meet it."

As Paul White pleaded for his life, Bill Bailey returned to the machine-gun company with news of his imminent return. What he did not know was that military policy had changed. According to brigade commissar John Gates, on the very day of White's arrest the Fifteenth Brigade had received orders from the division headquarters to punish all deserters as an example to others. Three men—a Spanish anarchist, a Republican Moor, and Paul White—would face a formal military tribunal. Appearing before a court-martial composed of members of his own company, White was too terrified to speak. He presented no defense of his actions. And by a unanimous vote, the court sentenced him to death. The next morning six volunteers from his company formed a firing squad and executed Paul White. "I couldn't bear to look at it," remembered one officer; "it was a human horror." News of the execution, received as a one-page leaflet, shocked and outraged the Lincolns. According to Bailey, Joe Bianca, hero to the seamen, expressed the prevailing mood as he walked around shouting at the top of his voice, "Those sons of bitches!" That day, the division command reversed its orders, discontinuing the policy of executions.

Official orders did not necessarily prevent other forms of execution. Evidence about these matters remains extremely sketchy and usually derives from deserters of dubious reliability or from anti-Communists who express bitter hatred for the battalion leadership. Such allegations usually depend on rumor and hearsay; seldom are they told by eyewitnesses. In all these cases, moreover, the alleged executioners were not Americans but the French, German, or Russian leaders of the International Brigades. But one potential exception appears in the record. According to historian Robert Rosenstone, who interviewed Lincoln veterans during the 1960's, a company commissar acknowledged that he had been advised to "wipe out" an alleged Trotskyist troublemaker, lest his ideas contaminate the morale of the battalion. During action at Teruel, this commissar accompanied the dissident on patrol, intending to kill him. But a nighttime blizzard separated the two men; the commissar could only hope that the brutal weather would settle the matter. The next morning the soldier was brought back suffering from severe frostbite. He was immediately sent to a hospital and subsequently evacuated home, never learning how narrowly he had escaped death.

Two other criminal cases survive. The first involved Harry Wilkes, a pharmacist attached to the American Medical Bureau. Involved in a variety of black-market schemes, including drugs, currency, and fine art, he was executed in 1938. Another case concerned three Finns, including a Finnish American, who got drunk and wrecked a town near Barcelona. Arrested by Spanish authorities, they escaped from jail, were rearrested, and escaped again. Caught for a third time, they were brought to a court-martial and sentenced to death. When members of the International Brigades refused to carry out the order, Spanish soldiers performed the execution.

Although these are the only recorded cases of official executions, the possibility of assassination remained a genuine risk for soldiers who blatantly violated military discipline, as at least one volunteer would discover. His story entered the official records in mid-November 1937 when the U.S. consul in Valencia reported that three disaffected Americans had appealed for his assistance to return home. The triumvirate—Jacob Rotter (real name Philip Conway), Albert Wallach, and Bernard Abramofsky (real name Leonard Aibel)—stated that they had enlisted in "a purely American unit" and so did not accept the jurisdiction of the Spanish Republican Army, which prevented them from leaving the country. They also assured consular officials that they were willing to cooperate with the American government "in their hope that they could stop other American boys from coming over here to be slaughtered." And when the consul reiterated his inability to help them escape, the three concocted a story about the mass arrest of a group of dissident Americans who had been given a fake court-martial and then taken back to the front to be executed. "No doubt," conceded the American diplomat who interviewed them, "the statements of these boys may be exaggerated." Without further assistance forthcoming, the three departed Valencia; two weeks later, they appeared before the Barcelona consul to request repatriation. The U.S. military attaché, Stephen Fuqua, who interviewed the three at Barcelona, said that "they gave the . . . impression of being typical cowards fleeing from danger."

American diplomats provided virtually no assistance to these men, but as part of its bureaucratic thoroughness, the State Department did initiate an inquiry into their backgrounds. About Rotter, they could find no verifiable evidence; his statement to Valencia officials, in which he claimed to be the son of a New York newspaper editor, could not be confirmed. Further details about him do not exist in the records. But the cases of his two accomplices illuminate all too clearly the consequences of cowardice and chronic dishonesty.

The problems of Albert Wallach, described as "a tall handsome chap . . . with ingratiating manners," began en route to Spain, when he suffered a hernia aboard ship and required emergency surgery in Paris. To avoid paying the hospital bill, Wallach's comrades kidnapped him from bed and hid him at their hotel. The caper seriously endangered the transportation of other volunteers to Spain, especially when French officials issued a warrant for Wallach's arrest. But his character aggravated the perilous situation; he was an obvious liar. According to brigade historian Sandor Voros, Wallach told "tall stories about himself—about having been a captain in the national guard, about having been the secretary of Governor Lehman, about having been a newspaperman—but his tales did not jibe." Later, at the Valencia embassy, he would claim to have served as a reserve officer in the U.S. Army and to have come to Spain "primarily to do investigative work regarding the Communist party." Similar fabrications weakened his credibility in Paris. For although he claimed to need further medical attention, the Americans in charge of volunteers concluded that he was malingering and ordered him into Spain.

It proved an unfortunate decision. During training, Merriman noted, Wallach was criticized for spreading rumors; he responded by requesting a safe job. Denied that escape, Wallach avoided battle anyway. Captain Hans Amlie, calling Wallach "my smart Jew deserter," told Fuqua that he had deserted at Brunete and then, after being brought back, deserted again at Quinto. Returned to the Lincolns a third time after Teruel, Wallach was next seen working at the front in a labor battalion during the retreats. Voros concluded that Wallach had been killed in the ensuing action, but instead Wallach apparently took advantage of the military collapse to desert again. He was rearrested in civilian clothes around Barcelona and confined in the brigade prison at Castillo de Fells. A fellow prisoner named Edward Horan (a.k.a. Palega) remembered Wallach's claim to be working both for the anarchist party and for the American consul in Barcelona. He also recalled that around May 1, a month after the retreats, Wallach was led from his cell.

When Wallach did not return to the United States at the end of the war, his father conducted a personal investigation into his disappearance. Dressed as a seaman, he mingled with some of the Lincoln veterans in New York. He learned from Horan that his son, "after being brutally beaten and starved over quite a period was taken in an unconscious condition out to the court yard and without court martial . . . deliberately murdered" by an American attached to the Spanish military intelligence (SIM). Confronted with this story, Commissar Gates would only confirm his knowledge of Wallach's death in Spain. In testimony to the Dies committee, the elder Wallach accused Lincoln volunteer Anthony DeMaio of the crime. Fifty years later, DeMaio steadfastly denied knowledge of any murders at Castillo de Fells. In any event, the prime informant in the case was Horan, himself a deserter and an anti-Communist undercover agent for the Chicago police. He later reiterated the charges before the U.S. government's Subversive Activities Control Board. Horan's veracity can be neither corroborated nor disproved.

Of Wallach's accomplice, Bernard Abramofsky, however, there is much clearer evidence. As a member of the youth section of the International Workers Order, Abramofsky had formed part of an amateur vaudeville troupe known as the "Convulsionaries." Along with his cousin Harold Melofsky (Meloff), a flabby man with a melodious voice, and friends like Ernie Arion and Vaughn Love, Abramofsky sang original songs, both in Yiddish and in English, and created skits that satirized the political situation. The group proved popular in Spain, fashioning pantomimes that amused the Spanish villagers and verse that tickled the soldiers. ("The general, the banker and the priest in pink / It won't take long for their boat to sink"). And they remained militantly political. "A communist for years," wrote Melofsky shortly after landing in Spain, "I now find myself fighting to make the world safe for democracy." Assigned with his cousin to a machine-gun company, he wrote of their impatience to move to the front.

The war came soon enough. At Brunete, Ernie Arion, "the gay, lovable, singing fellow," died during the first charge at Mosquito Ridge. "When I first came here," Melofsky wrote a few weeks later, "I didn't give a damn about

death . . . and when Ernie keeled over, he did so firing at the Moorish mercenaries. . . . Now we do care. At least I do. I want to live very much, because
I want to bring that lesson of unity I learned in this Spanish University to the
states." But while the death of Arion steeled Melofsky's resolve, Abramofsky
drew different lessons. Terrified by the firing at Brunete, he had feigned collapse in a wheat field and allowed himself to be carried behind the lines in a
stretcher. "He groaned and moaned on the stretcher as we sweated up the
scorching hills," Milton Wolff recalled, "and all the time the son of a bitch
was faking it . . . he hadn't been hit at all." Shortly afterward, Melofsky reported to friends in New York that "Cousin Bernie disappeared someplace,
and I don't know where the hell he is. . . . I hope he doesn't get into any
trouble." A few weeks later, Melofsky served courageously at Quinto. ("The
stupid fascists," he remarked, "certainly were surprised when we only shot
their leaders.") But at Belchite, just days later, his talented career suddenly
came to an end.

Abramofsky needed no other push. With Rotter and Wallach, he fled to the
embassy in Valencia and then to Barcelona, accepting an ignominious incarceration over the terrors of war. Returned to the lines after Teruel, he deserted again during the retreats and was arrested in Barcelona. Spanish authorities brought him back to brigade headquarters. Commissar Gates, disgusted at Abramofsky's behavior, returned him to the battalion. But the Lincoln commanders did not want Abramofsky around. Having deserted three
times, he was viewed as a threat to the already shaky morale of the troops.
Gates, muttering that Abramofsky ought to be shot, insisted he stay with the
battalion. On the night before May Day, one of the officers took Gates at his
word. Leading Abramofsky for a walk alone, he fired a single bullet into the
deserter's head. Word of the death spread through the battalion, disturbing
both the rank and file and the leadership. When Gates asked Wolff what had
happened, Wolff told him not to worry. To party leaders, he "claimed total
ignorance." With no other evidence available, the brigade dropped the matter; the killer could not be brought to trial. Although Gates later said he was
furious at the outcome, battalion leaders saw the shooting more simply: Abramofsky had threatened the battalion's unity.

The murder of Bernard Abramofsky, the execution of Paul White, the allegations about Albert Wallach, the criminal proceedings—terrible as they
appear, emerge as exceptional cases. Even if *all* the other charges of assas-

sination proved true, the number of Americans killed outside combat would total less than ten. (Today, most Lincoln veterans express remorse that anyone was executed for violating military orders.) The rarity of these killings undermines the notion, made popular by George Orwell's *Homage to Catalonia*, that the International Brigades enforced discipline by terror. No one, it should be emphasized, was punished for political dissent. And numerous military deserters were permitted to return to the ranks without penalty or stigma. (Significantly, many veterans remain unaware of most cases of desertion.) Recognizing that any soldier might lose his resolve, Commissar Steve Nelson informally authorized the issuance of passes for some deserters to allow frazzled volunteers to recuperate safely behind the lines. But most of the Lincolns did not require such special privileges. Indeed, the historical record vindicates the findings made by Yale sociologist John Dollard in 1942: Although fear among the Lincolns appeared to be nearly universal, an overwhelming sense of responsibility prevailed.

"You Are Legend"

As the numbed survivors of the Lincoln brigade gathered on the northern bank of the Ebro River on the seventh of April 1938, the men suddenly heard a Spanish voice shout, "El Lobo!" The figure loping up the hill toward the hastily constructed headquarters shack was a welcome, if disheveled, sight: the battalion's missing commander, Milton Wolff, who had been wandering behind fascist lines alone for four days and nights. "You built this thing plenty low," he growled, bending his six-foot two-inch frame into the shelter. "I guess you guys didn't think I was coming back." Then he grabbed a plate of freshly cooked garbanzo beans, clutched some long-delayed letters from his girlfriend in New York, and disappeared into a deep silence. "Now he sat doubled up over his beans and his letters," observed journalist Vincent Sheean, "his gaunt young face frowning with concentration. I think he knew how glad they all were to see him, and wanted to ignore it as much as possible."

Wolff's unexpected return brought one of the few moments of joy for the battalion. Now, only a little more than a hundred Americans remained in the ranks; their empty places would be filled by Spanish recruits. "But for the benefit of the folks at home," Alvah Bessie noted in his diary, "the [Lincoln-Washington] remains the [Lincoln-Washington] and is 100 percent American and numbers about one thousand or two thousand." Such deceptions could not fool the veterans. Bessie found "demoralization great. Many men talk openly of fucking off across the French border." With jangled nerves, some soldiers drowned themselves in red wine; one man walked around with a stick in his mouth "to prevent his teeth from chattering and equalize pressure" in case of an air attack. "Home and repatriation," Bessie observed, were the main subjects of conversation, an "unmistakable wish-fulfillment." Members of the transport division, lacking the distractions of retraining, used their leisure to write parodies, such as the following (sung to the tune of "The Internationale"):

> Arise, and seek repatriation
> Arise, you would-be transferees,
> The P.C. [Communist party] thunders condemnation
> But we'll get across the sea.
> No more chick peas, no more refugios
> Arise ye braves, and head for home.
> The Earth shall rise on new foundations
> But we'll stand pat, no more to roam
> Tis the final journey, each one back to his house
> The International Brigadeer
> Is a man and not a mouse.

Commissar John Gates, appointed to replace the missing David Doran, assumed responsibility for rebuilding the battalion. Gates had already gained a reputation for strictness. "Today we accept the discipline and forms of the regular army as a matter of course," he said in a eulogy to his predecessor. At Albacete, it had been Gates's task, if not his decision, to reverse the policy of offering some men the possibility of repatriation after six months' military service. That plan had been introduced after the battles on the Aragon front in 1937, in an endeavor to spare the lives of valuable cadres. The idea had not worked as planned. Transferred to a "veterans company," over 100 Americans awaited repatriation, but the diplomatic situation complicated their removal; few actually departed Spain. Besides, many of these volunteers did not wish to leave in the middle of the war. Even Morris Mickenberg, already hostile to the party leadership, declined an opportunity to go home. "I felt very sure we were going to win the war within a few more months," he recalled. "We still had that spirit of great optimism." He was prudent enough, however, to welcome a desk job in Madrid working for the *Volunteer for Liberty*, Radio Madrid, and the brigade censorship.

For the Regiment de Tren, however, Gates's shift in brigade policy had brought catastrophic consequences. Among the transport workers, the possibility of an early departure had sparked great enthusiasm. One officer even invited the men to sign a list requesting immediate repatriation. When Gates cancelled that policy, those who had admitted a desire to leave found themselves transferred to the infantry, a far more dangerous assignment. And whatever the original intentions, the policy of early repatriation had conflicted with the exigencies of the war. "It was politically wrong in every respect," Gates insisted. "What kind of fighters could you be? We had taken an oath for the duration." So the commissar had spent several months visiting every unit in the brigade, explaining the reversal of policy. His speech boiled down to three sentences: "It was wrong. It was reversed. You're not going home."

After the retreats, Gates continued to fight the rumors of repatriation. At one point, he interrupted a training session to call a battalion meeting, angrily attacking rumors of an early homecoming. Insisting that the Spanish Republic needed the Lincolns, he not only dismissed the fantasies of withdrawal, but refused to retract an epithet he had hurled at one of his critics: "If you can't call a cocksucker a cocksucker," he said, "then we've got into a fine state of affairs." He was not, in short, an endearing man; he did not try to be. "I became intolerant of criticism," he later admitted. "I increasingly used vile language against subordinates, and disciplined people for minor questioning of my authority."

Bessie, who listened to Gates's diatribe, doubted whether such polemics served any good. Indeed, while none of the men dared to challenge Gates directly, Mickenberg waited for the commissar to leave and then took the stump. In a sonorous voice laden with sarcasm, he described a vivid scene he had recently dreamed: the Lincolns were returning to New York by special airplane; the men had been ordered to parachute directly into Central Park. But as they landed, he said wryly, they discovered they were surrounded by Johnny Gates giving speeches. According to Bessie, Mickenberg probably articulated the frustrations of many men. But Bessie, a disciplined soldier and Communist, worried more that the "reactionary press" in the United States would learn that the Americans were dissatisfied—that they were no longer volunteers!—and were being held against their will. "What vile use (and dangerous use)," he said, "could be made of that information."

If the Lincoln volunteers did not love John Gates, they respected his judgment, and he knew they would remain in the fight. Fresh volunteers reinforced their continuing commitment. Edwin Rolfe, who had come to Spain the previous spring, had been removed from combat assignments, over his protests, to become the editor of the brigade newspaper *Volunteer for Liberty*. While posted in Barcelona in March 1938, he bore witness to the saturation bombardment of the city, a three-day ordeal that terrorized the population and heralded a form of warfare that would soon become familiar around the world. "The sound of an explosion close by, or the sight of a man lying on the street covered with a blanket, blood slowly oozing away from him, or the whistle of a bomb descending," he wrote, "is horrible. And between times every sound sets your heart beating furiously and violently, and it continues to beat even when the sound is gone." Soldiers considered such attacks more dangerous than bombs on the battlefields; and they felt more helpless. Two weeks later, when Rolfe received news of the disastrous retreats, he volunteered to rejoin the battalion. Bessie described him as frail, bird-like; and after some conversation, he concluded that Rolfe was the gentlest man he had ever met. "But he had the iron of conviction in him just the same." Also joining the ranks was Arnold Reid, Rolfe's college friend from the University of Wisconsin, who had written for the *New Masses* in New York and then run the International Brigades operation in Paris. Having worked with revolutionaries in Cuba and Mexico, Reid served as company commissar of the Spanish battalion.

More remarkable, seven veterans who had been sent home the previous year now returned to the fight. Most had been wounded at Jarama or Brunete, including Joe Gordon, who had lost the sight of an eye. News reports of the retreats had aroused their concern for old comrades; they could no longer watch the war from the sidelines. Among other new volunteers was Archie Brown, the San Francisco waterfront organizer, who had stowed away on a German ship after the State Department refused to give him a passport. Within weeks he was giving stirring speeches on the theme "You can't kill the working class."

Telling the story of Lenin's brother, whose premature death had nourished a revolutionary zeal, Brown assured the remnants of the brigade that even if they were "completely wiped out, the working class would lose some of its best sons, true, but new and better cadres would take our places. The movement on the whole would be strengthened not weakened." That Barney Baley, who had earlier heard Brown's oratory in Oakland, copied the speech into his diary testified to the power of ideology.

The last of the legendary recruits was James Lardner, son of the writer Ring Lardner. He had come to Spain as a correspondent for the New York *Herald Tribune* but felt frustrated by his inability to contribute directly to the antifascist cause. Contemplating enlistment in the Lincoln battalion, he carefully drafted a list of reasons for volunteering for military service and showed it to his colleagues Ernest Hemingway and Vincent Sheean. Both discouraged his enthusiasm. But Lardner persisted, enlisted, and found pleasure in his acceptance by the rank and file. "If it is any comfort to you," he wrote to his mother in New York, "I still hate violence and cruelty and suffering and if I survive this war do not expect to take any dangerous part in the next."

While the commissars collaborated with military officers to build discipline and morale, leaders of the American Communist party were also operating unofficially to motivate the volunteers. Just as party members had rebuilt the fighting spirit after Jarama, so selected cadres formed a small Communist organization within the brigade. Since so many of the Lincolns belonged to the party, there appeared no conflict of purpose in the creation of such cells. But few men participated consciously in these political activities. Commissar George Watt described them as "steel rods" that braced the men for adversity. At the level of company, battalion, and brigade, these cadres chose Communist party secretaries, distinct from the commissars, whose authority derived from the moral force of Communist ideology.

Although party leaders like Robert Minor or William Lawrence might wield great influence in the selection of commissars and military officers, the party secretaries exercised slight power. Rather, they endeavored to keep their fingers on the pulse of opinion and assisted the commissars from below. After Teruel, for example, Commissar Wellman discovered that many men were breaking out in scabs. The American doctor Julius Hene diagnosed the problem as the result of insufficient fat and recommended adding nuts to the diet.

Wellman commissioned party secretary Joe Gibbons to find the nuts. Gibbons, in turn, stole a truck from the anarchists, drove to Andorra, and returned with the requested supplies.

Party leaders seldom held meetings. (The Joe Dallet session was exceptional.) But party decisions possessed great authority because individual Communists respected the leadership and valued their membership in the group. For true Communists, indeed, expulsion from the party remained a serious punishment. And party members gave one-third of their pay to the Communist party (they gave another third to the Spanish Red Cross and kept one-third for themselves).

The power of the party nonetheless could easily be used in ways that deviated from its idealistic purposes, as John Gates soon discovered. Shortly after becoming brigade commissar, he received an order to report to André Marty, the much-feared head commissar of the International Brigades. Gates had met Marty only once before—"a big imposing giant of a man," he remembered—and they had not gotten along. Responding to some insignificant remark, the French leader had launched a tirade against the Americans in Spain, calling them cowards and "cowboys." As a matter of honor, Gates had defended his men and criticized the French soldiers for chronic drunkenness. Marty had then invoked the revolutionary traditions of 1789 and the Paris Commune. They had parted, as Gates recalled, "on very bad terms."

Half a year later, the abrupt summons to see Marty in Barcelona aroused Gates's fear of disgrace and dismissal. Before seeing Marty, therefore, Gates visited Comintern representative Robert Minor and showed him his orders. Minor instantly blanched. At a time when Gates and the other Americans knew nothing of the Stalinist purges inside the Soviet Union, the more knowledgeable Minor apparently saw something dangerous. "Have faith in the Spanish Communist party!" he exhorted Gates, and he began making telephone calls in Gates's behalf. Backed by the American party, the commissar did not have to meet with Marty. Instead, a female political leader authorized his return to the brigade, warning him, "Don't talk like that to your superiors."

When the shoe was on the other foot, however, Gates could be equally imperious. He and Mickenberg had crossed swords on numerous occasions and the battalion comic had invented a ditty about Gates that he admitted was "bitterly satirical, vicious." Mickenberg also defied Gates's efforts to quell rumors about repatriation; relying on his wit, he invented an "organization" known as "FONICS" (Friends of the Non-Intervention Committee) and regaled the men with impending "news." As the Lincolns prepared for battle in 1938, he deliberately infected a minor hand injury to avoid combat. His behavior aroused the wrath of party leaders. "Bad. Trotskyist. . . . Very bad," the commissars wrote in assessing Mickenberg's record in Spain. "He is a very slick and smooth character. Because of his ability to discuss politics he has been able to influence a number of comrades." As a sign of his irreverence for authority, Mickenberg had the audacity to ask Gates how his profile would look. "Vile. Contemptible," Gates replied. The commissar proceeded to cite various snide remarks Mickenberg had made during his service in Spain. "I marveled at . . . these little wonders," Mickenberg later claimed: "first, that this thing had been remembered; second, that it had been reported; third, at Gates' marvelous memory to bear in mind a little piece of information . . . [that was] so tenuous, irrelevant, unimportant." Mickenberg would pay a price for his caustic wit. On the ship returning from Spain, a special party meeting heard charges against him and voted to suspend Mickenberg from the membership. "I was rather shocked and upset," he remembered. Later, he would feel only bitterness and take revenge in his own way.

Many rank and file Communists, while loyal to the party, shared Mickenberg's distrust of the leadership. Party secretary Joe Brandt, who worked assiduously with Gates to mold political discipline, was a frequent target of the men's venom. Browder had sent Brandt to Spain with a personal letter of introduction to represent the party. Gates glanced at the newcomer's military outfit and told him to get rid of his fancy boots and jacket, before assigning him to the brigade staff. Brandt saw his job as parallel to that of the commissars: providing political explanations for the military situation and reiterating the principles of the Popular Front. Veteran soldiers wanted no such lessons. Instead, they sang a piece written by Mickenberg:

> My name is Joe Brandt
> And I run a herring stand
> On Delancey Street
> Right over Grant
> I'm battalion party organizer
> Chief activist activizer
> I'll be a soldado

When the masses get wiser
Workers of the world, goodnight!

The good-natured Brandt, ever willing to win the men's approval, would sing his own parody.

Besides the commissariat and the unofficial party structure, the volunteers also heeded the authority of the Spanish military intelligence (SIM). As an independent branch of the Republican army, SIM, in the words of one former intelligence officer, "was responsible only to SIM." Within the International Brigades, a Serbian émigré named Fein headed SIM; he reported directly to André Marty. An authority on agricultural collectivization, Fein had taught in the Soviet Union's Communist University of Western Minorities (KUNZ), and he chose as his subordinate a former American student there. This officer, in turn, selected a staff from the available volunteers. All were probably party members. At the highest levels, SIM remained subservient to the Soviet secret police, the NKVD, which enabled the Communists to eliminate political dissidents. Steve Nelson had no doubts that the NKVD "must have operated" in Spain; but of the Americans, he added, "we had nothing to do about it."

Among the Lincolns, about half a dozen men served at different times with the military intelligence. Their task was to investigate cases of sabotage or treason within the ranks. The importance of the assignment, however, has apparently been exaggerated by critics of the Communist party. "I had power," acknowledged one SIM officer. "But I never caught a spy," he added. "I never arrested anyone." One common charge (repeated several times in the interviews for this book) was that fascist or Trotskyist health workers subverted the care of Republican patients by needlessly amputating the limbs of wounded soldiers or by contaminating the food and milk in the hospitals. "Plain bullshit," was the response of another informed SIM official. "There was never a substantiated case of such sabotage. Not one name. Not one incident." This officer insisted that within the Lincoln battalion they "could *never* verify any charges." At most, they would find cases of drunkenness or irresponsibility that might have caused problems. But there was "never a single case of finding an enemy agent."

Some evidence survives, however, to show that American volunteers worked indirectly with Soviet intelligence during the Spanish war. These activities began after the fighting on the Aragon front, when a group of about a dozen Lincolns received orders for "detached service." Without a clear sense of their mission, they left their units and entered a special training program outside Barcelona. A trusted member of the American Communist party screened the names and eliminated a few men. Then, using aliases and false identification, dressed in civilian clothes, they commenced intensive training in guerrilla tactics, sabotage, and espionage under the tutelage of two Spanish instructors. They worked with explosive devices, studied cryptography, and learned radio transmission. But unlike the Spanish guerrilla team that included Kunslich, Goff, and Aalto and worked behind fascist lines, this unit never went into action in Spain. (One team was apparently preparing to attack an Italian naval base on the island of Mallorca, but the mission was cancelled.) Indeed, these activities were so secret that a militia unit once mistakenly arrested the entire group, requiring the direct intervention of André Marty to obtain its release.

There remain only tantalizing clues about the purpose of this unit. Midway through their training, one of the volunteers secretly departed Spain to assume special duties in Paris. He described his assignment as "Jimmy Higgins work for the Russians." Serving as an errand boy for party functionaries, he purchased expensive goods at department stores, including feather pillows, blankets, and a truck ("it seemed so odd to me," he said). "You continue like this," a party leader told him; "you may get to Russia and see Stalin." At one point, his superior gave him permission to visit his sister living in Scotland; party officials provided him with the altered passport of an American soldier killed earlier in the war. Yet despite such perquisites and the safety of his assignment, this volunteer disliked political work. When the retreats began, he asked to return to the battlefront, where he rejoined the brigade. Another member of the special detachment completed his training and received orders at the end of the war to suspend all party work and "lay low" for further instructions. A few years later, Steve Nelson saw the man and his wife in a San Francisco restaurant. When he approached them, the man tried to avoid contact. Nelson had the pleasure of telling him that he could emerge from the underground. Other members of the special unit, as we will see, did have an opportunity to put their espionage training into practice; after Spain, they went to work for Soviet intelligence.

*

Through the warm months of April, May, and June 1938, the Lincolns re-built their army and resumed training for a new offensive. Across dry riv-erbeds, they practiced "rowing" boatloads of men under cover of darkness. Although Bessie continued to chronicle the low morale—griping, homesick-ness, intoxication, insubordination—in his diary, his own commitment was sturdy and he came to appreciate the ambivalence of his comrades. They, too, remained devoted to the cause of Spain; they, too, dreaded the thought of de-sertion. "But they were human," he realized. "They were tired; they were homesick; they were a bit afraid." Whatever the Lincolns might hope or de-sire, however, they knew their war was not yet over.

On the evening of July 24, 1938, Captain Wolff assembled the retrained Lincoln battalion for an important meeting. Moments before, a letter had ar-rived, enclosing a clipping from the *New York Times* that listed the names of Americans held in Franco's prisons; most of them had been presumed dead. The Lincolns listened raptly while someone read the names aloud. In the si-lence that followed, Wolff raised his hand and began to speak. "Before an-other day is over we'll be in action again," he announced in his booming Brooklyn accent. He explained the larger objective of their offensive: to di-vert fascist pressure from Valencia. Then he described the tactical difficulties of crossing the Ebro without air support or artillery. Mickenberg drew a quick laugh by asking Wolff how, after they had crossed the river, they would find their way back. But the commander ignored the quip. He pleaded with the men to maintain their discipline, assuring them of the thorough preparations and the likelihood of success. Then, with his right fist high, Wolff cried: "Viva el ejército popular! Viva las Brigadas Internacionales! Viva la victoria final!"

As the battalion moved into action, their fighting spirit rebounded. True, a few of the volunteers deserted from the lines; some, like Mickenberg, de-parted with self-inflicted injuries. "But the remarkable thing," declared Wolff many years later, "was that though fully conscious of the odds against us and though suffering staggering losses in long, drawn out grueling campaigns, we all went back to the front time after time . . . always with a belief in the pos-sibility of victory. Maybe we were naive, maybe we believed in miracles, maybe we were stupid but there is one thing for sure: for us there was no other way."

Shortly after midnight, the Lincolns crept silently into small, flat boats and proceeded to row themselves across the slowly streaming Ebro River. The op-eration succeeded by surprise. Overcoming scant enemy resistance, the Lincolns captured numerous prisoners on the far shore and soon were outpacing their communications lines. Brigade officer Howard Goddard, sent to make contact with the advancing Lincolns, drove into an enemy ambush, but he managed to persuade his two hundred captors that their cause was hopeless. To the amazement of the brigade staff, Goddard marched his prisoners back to camp, though his failure to reach the battalion slowed the attack. Still, the advance proceeded well for about two days. But as Franco shifted his troops from the Valencia front, the Lincolns began to meet stronger opposition. Outside Villalba de los Arcos, they met a terrific firestorm of aviation, artillery, and machine guns that ended the advance. After five days of action, the exhausted Lincolns earned a spell of rest. Already the battalion could tally fifty killed and five times as many wounded or missing. Arnold Reid was dead; so was Joe Cuban, one of the seven veterans who had returned to Spain. The Americans now numbered fewer than 100.

After sporadic fighting during the next two weeks, the beleaguered battalion climbed a craggy slope of nearly solid rock, known only as Hill 666, in the Sierra Pandols. Ordered to hold this position against a counterattack, the Lincolns clung to the rock for ten days, while fascist bombs and artillery smashed their ranks. Unable to dig into the granite surface, or even to fill sandbags sent up by mules, the men built stone parapets that fragmented into deadly splinters at a direct hit. One shelling killed seaman Joe Bianca, considered by his comrades a perfect soldier and therefore invulnerable. "All day, hour after hour they kept it up," wrote Bessie of the siege; "and the body was utterly exhausted and indifferent to conscious fear, but straining to the snapping point. . . . It was impersonal; it had nothing to do with men or with machines; the steel and the noise that filled the air—they came from nowhere, but you knew they were directed at you by some agency with more than human guile." So terrible was the onslaught that some Americans feared to fire at the enemy, lest their audacity bring even worse revenge. Amidst such hell, the Lincolns held their places. At one point, Archie Brown helped beat back a fascist charge with hand grenades and even had the men singing "The Internationale" (though Bessie, for public consumption, said it was "The Star-Spangled Banner").

Withdrawn at last from the peaks, the Lincolns remained in the combat zone for another month, filling various breaches in the Republican lines. The month was September 1938, the time of the Munich crisis, when Hitler threatened to invade Czechoslovakia, and Britain and Frence scrambled for a negotiated settlement. For two years, the nonintervention agreement had starved the Spanish Republic of foreign assistance; even the courageous Internationals represented more moral support than military. Now, as the Republican armies faced another major defeat, Prime Minister Juan Negrín appealed desperately for an end to German and Italian aid to Franco. In a dramatic speech to the League of Nations in Geneva, he announced on September 21 that all International volunteers would be withdrawn from Spanish territory and he pleaded for a similar removal of Franco's foreign allies. Thus would end the military history of the Abraham Lincoln brigade.

But even as Negrín spoke, the Fifteenth Brigade had been committed to battle. It was too late to change their orders. Commissar John Gates halted all mail and newspapers, lest the news leak out. But rumors ran thick; no one wanted to be the last to die. And the final battle proved devastating. "Their planes came over in waves all day long, some bombing, some strafing," wrote Edwin Rolfe. "Their rapid-fire batteries never ceased for long, transforming the hills and valleys into a landscape of flying metal and huge, low-hanging clouds of smoke and dust." At night, Wolff ordered a reconnaissance patrol into the nearby hills; James Lardner never returned. The battalion, Gates told Wolff, had to hold one more day. Many of the Spanish troops seized opportunities to abandon their positions and fled to the rear. But the Americans under Wolff held fast and waited. They were still there when a relief column came to replace them; only then did they withdraw from the lines.

While Great Britain and France pursued a policy of appeasement toward Hitler and Mussolini and the U.S. government increasingly sympathized with the Franco side, the Lincolns hoped, in Edwin Rolfe's words, for "the slightest sort of fair play at Geneva." The idea that the Western democracies would soon awaken to the fascist menace helped sustain morale, even in the face of military defeat. "The non-intervention farce can't last forever," Rolfe wrote optimistically, "and the big democratic powers will have to aid Spain if they know what's good for them." Rolfe took heart at President Roosevelt's dramatic "quarantine speech" in October 1937, which warned of the danger of the spreading fascist contagion; but the administration's subsequent failure to alter its policies depressed him. "The one thing needed now in the U.S. is a movement strong enough to force Congress to end the neutrality business," he wrote the following spring.

As small groups of Lincoln veterans returned from Spain, they joined the protests against the American embargo. "We didn't go to war to involve America in war but . . . to keep us out of war," explained Edward Flaherty, one of three brothers who fought together at Jarama and then went on a speaking tour of the United States. "The men of the Lincoln Battalion feel that the American nation cannot sit quietly in its own room and close the door on a fire that is raging in the building." The signing of the Munich Pact by England's Prime Minister Neville Chamberlain and France's Premier Edouard Daladier, which doomed Czechoslovakia, took place just after the Lincolns were withdrawn from the lines in September 1938. The agreement confirmed their predictions about the spread of fascism. "Not only must we get Hitler and Mussolini out of Spain," a bitter Edward Barsky advised a rally at Madison Square Garden, "but we must see to it that Chamberlain and Daladier do not get into Spain." His despair was echoed across the ocean. "We had hoped that the Nazi on-slaught on Czechoslovakia would start the world war, and then we in Spain would become part of it," remembered Clement Markert, who served as a scout at brigade headquarters. "One regiment of French troops would have changed the whole battle in Spain. That was what I was hoping for. But when it didn't happen, I knew the war was lost."

The inability to alter U.S. foreign policy, to end nonintervention, to save the Spanish Republic—the failure, in short, to awaken the American con-science about Spain left a profound, enduring impression in the minds of the Lincoln veterans. Many simply could not believe that a democratic govern-ment would allow another republic to fall, "felt the shame of the infamous embargo," as the Regiment de Tren declared upon leaving the war, and pledged solemnly to "give unsparingly of our efforts for the cause of Republican Spain." In a formal farewell to the Spanish people, the Lincolns summed up their ex-perience: "We have learned to rip off the demagogic mask of fascism to ex-pose its full savage barbarity. . . . We have learned that fascism can never conquer a country whose people are united. We are departing full of confi-dence in the ability of the heroic Spanish People's Army to bring this war to victory. And we are leaving with a promise—a pledge solemn and grave—. . . that we will dedicate our lives to help to smash fascism forever so that freedom, peace, and democracy prevail." Beyond rhetoric, the Lincolns were making an enduring commitment to Republican Spain. "I felt that I was going to continue the war, but on another front," explained Milton Wolff. "That was the only way I could justify leaving."

Wolff remembered a feeling of overwhelming sorrow at hearing the news of withdrawal. For despite all the morale boosting and the pride of individual heroics, the Lincolns had tasted a full measure of defeat. "That feeling of loss never quite leaves you," recalled veteran Abe Osheroff. "It was the good fight— and we lost." Archie Brown, who helped establish a base at Ripoll for the weary veterans prior to their departure from Spain, depicted them as "mentally, psychologically, physically exhausted." Half a century later, he would speak of the experience in haunted, hushed tones: "To be defeated—to have your ass whipped! Do you know what that means?" Now the horror seeped into consciousness, stoking deep anxieties and guilt at survival. "Men dying in battle speak after speech has failed," wrote Edwin Rolfe, "are alive only in other men, and die when they die." So, too, the poet William P. Smith lamented the loss of fallen comrades:

> I hear you sobbing in the night,
> But in the day remember this:
> That we are they.

Alvah Bessie, ever after, would dream of his dead company commander beckoning from the grave: "Alvah, come, come."

Spain, for most volunteers, proved to be a moment of truth, a time of testing political beliefs and personal ideals against a bedrock of human suffering, endless fear, and omnipresent death. In such situations, opinions hardened into ideology, vague feelings and nuances ripened into passion. Fred Keller, a battalion commissar sent home early because of injuries, regretted the loss of "clarity and understanding" at home—"that fine healthy feeling that comes with fighting for what you think is correct." Some of the politically innocent—there were many in the medical corps—emerged from the war with stronger commitments. "I was politicized my whole life," recalled Ruth Davidow, a nurse who had gone to Spain impulsively to protest Roosevelt's policy of nonintervention, "but when I got to Spain it jelled. So much I learned in

Spain. I learned what international solidarity meant." For the young American volunteers, Spain destroyed romantic abstractions, offering instead a harsh unyielding reality. "I had never realized before coming to Spain what the real truth of democracy could mean and with what furious proportions one could hate," wrote Walter Schuetrum, an ambulance driver from Wisconsin State University. The war, he said, had "rapidly transformed [him] into a nut the fascists will never crack. . . . Our minds become different from what they were, impressions are seared into our memories, we become conscious fighting anti-fascists in a cause that eclipses everything!"

While most of the Lincoln veterans shared such sentiments, indeed strengthened their attachment to Communist anti-fascism, a few came to reject the ideological rigidities that had brought them to Spain. "I hate fascism as much as I ever did and I realize that something drastic must be done to make democracy work," a veteran named Edgar Lehmann told the City Club in Milwaukee, "but I have concluded that communism isn't the way out. . . . I came to hate the methods of the communist leaders." Another ex-Communist named William G. Ryan wrote numerous articles denouncing the party's incompetence and murderous intolerance in Spain. "It was only when we began to doubt that our equivalent of the four freedoms would emerge from the struggle," he later claimed, "that morale sagged and defeat followed." Such dissidents could be dismissed by the Left because they were deserters from the battalion; they could be seen as masking their fear and shame under the guise of ideological disagreement. But a few needed no rationalizations to justify their dissent.

Robert Gladnick, transferred to a Russian tank corps after the debacle at Jarama, became a beneficiary of the perquisites afforded to Soviet officers—luxurious housing, lavish food, and liquor—and claimed to have witnessed arbitrary political repression. "I had already broken with the Communist movement mentally in Spain," he later said, "and I knew I had no intentions of getting back into it." Another of the original Lincolns, William Herrick, hospitalized with a neck wound, personally suffered from petty Communist tyranny. After his nurse (and lover) reported him for making an "opportunist" antiparty remark, a German commissar made him stand at attention in his office until Herrick urinated in his pants. He was also forced to witness the execution of Spanish dissidents by a firing squad. Herrick understandably grew suspicious of the Communist leadership. Some of his rank and file friends, loyal Communist themselves, reinforced his fears. "The great majority of the Party leaders," the gritty Joe Gordon informed him, "are mostly petit-bourgeois intellectuals, opportunists bootlicking bastards." Furloughed home in 1937, Herrick contemplated renouncing the party, but he needed financial assistance from the Friends of the Abraham Lincoln Brigade for rehabilitation; he still felt an emotional attachment to his comrades in Spain. He decided to bury his doubts, at least publicly.

Herrick's hesitation to betray his friends underscored the war's most powerful legacy. "That was the sense of comradeship—both in the Brigade and with the Spanish people," wrote Alvah Bessie. "In Spain these men experienced the interdependent love of human beings for each other, unrestrained by considerations of expediency or polite behavior. It was felt everywhere you went." And the Lincolns returned from Spain with a feeling of responsibility to remain loyal to each other and to the cause that brought them together. As in all armies, this commitment touched first one's fellow veterans, but it extended to the Spanish people and to other comrades in the fight against fascism. For communism focused on an international scale, the solidarity of the working classes throughout the world.

Soon after arriving in Spain, Edwin Rolfe composed an elegy for the dead that captured this spirit of internationalism. He saw the poem as an alternative to the narrow patriotism of World War I—Rupert Brooke's "corner . . . that is forever England." Instead, said Rolfe:

> Honor for them in this lies: that theirs is no special
> strange plot of alien earth. Men of all lands here
> lie side by side, at peace now after the crucial
> torture of combat.

In a solemn ceremony on the football field in the town of Marsa, while a treacherous dogfight between fascist and Republican fighter planes raged overhead, Milton Wolff relinquished his command to a Spanish successor. Counting officers and noncombatants, there were barely 200 Americans left in the country. Out of 2,800 volunteers, nearly one-third were dead; virtually every military survivor had been wounded at least once. Now, in a series of formal gatherings, the Spaniards would pay homage to the American volunteers.

The farewell ceremonies climaxed in Barcelona at the end of October as the Lincolns formed ranks in a plaza far from the center of the city. "After a time the bugle sounded," Archie Brown wrote to his wife; "we fell into ranks nine abreast and proceeded to march. Overhead zoomed the air fleet. The little Moscas [flies] . . . came down almost to the tree tops. The chatos and bombers performed higher up. . . . The people cheered. The bands were playing but you could hardly hear them." As spectators raised their fists in the Popular Front salute, Brown could read the ubiquitous placards: "International brothers—we will never forget you"; "We will fight to the last man—so that all of us will be free from fascism"; "Our adopted sons—Spain loves you." While the police tried to keep back the throngs, "girls broke through the lines and showered us with kisses," reported Brown. "One would run out with tears on her cheeks—she would grab the first man and pull him down. Then several others broke through." Amidst kisses and a rainstorm of flowers, the men could barely march. "After each attack we would bravely reform our ranks and plunge onward only to find that the 'enemy' had pulled a . . . surprise attack on us. This kept on for several kilometers."

As the remnants of the Lincoln brigade reached the reviewing stand, they saluted Dolores Ibarruri, "La Pasionaria" of the Republic. She bade them farewell. "They gave up everything," she said of the International volunteers, "their loves, their countries, home and fortune; fathers, mothers, wives, brothers, sisters and children, and they came and told us: 'We are here. Your cause, Spain's cause, is ours—it is the cause of all advanced and progressive mankind.'" Hardened veterans wept as she spoke. "You can go proudly," she told them. "You are history. You are legend."

PART III

Veterans

Coming Home

Driving a battered, bullet-shattered ambulance, a remnant of the Spanish War, two young women sped east through the Gulf Plains toward Florida during the last week of March 1939. Behind the wheel sat veteran truck driver Evelyn Hutchins; at 29, she was lean, outspoken, and vivacious. Next to her, wearing the nurses' patch of the American Medical Bureau, was 27-year-old Ruth Davidow, who had worked to exhaustion in Spain's frontline hospitals. The vehicle served as a dramatic prop for their speaking tour through the southern states. Two weeks earlier, Hutchins and Davidow had launched their journey at a "Lift the Embargo" rally in Washington, D.C., and they had already spoken to audiences in Virginia, Tennessee, Louisiana, and Texas. Now the weary travelers were heading for Tampa, where they were scheduled to address a group of pro-Republican, Spanish-born cigar workers and their families.

During the tour, the two veterans had struggled to arouse the American conscience about Spain. By then, Franco had nearly conquered the country. Madrid and Valencia alone stood in stubborn defiance. But for as long as the capital resisted the fascist armies, Franco could claim no victory. So the women were pleading for assistance—for money to buy food and medical supplies and for vocal support to persuade the White House and Congress to end the policy of nonintervention. Usually on this trip, Hutchins and Davidow had reached receptive ears. They had collected dimes and dollars, gathered signed petitions to send to Washington, seen their winsome pictures in the local newspapers, and sometimes provoked supportive editorials.

As they drove into Tampa on the last day of March, however, the radio was broadcasting the feared news from Spain: Franco had entered Madrid. That evening, a sympathetic priest opened his church for a pro-Republican meeting. "The church was full and the people were standing outside in the street," remembered Davidow. "And they all wept, because Spain was being defeated." Invited to speak from the pulpit, neither woman could overcome her grief. Asked, at last, to sing the spirited war song "La Quince Brigada" ("The Fifteenth Brigade") Davidow started boldly, but midway through she began to weep and soon the whole congregation wept with her. "And when Spain then actually fell," she recalled, "I cried my eyes out. I don't like to talk about it really," she added some fifty years later. "I don't want to remember. Because when I think back to it, I am still quite crushed."

That sense of tragedy never left the veterans of the Lincoln brigade. Having gone to war with a militant ardor, the confidence of participating in an epic that would turn the course of history, few could accept the somber reality of defeat. "So much blood had been spilled, so much suffering endured, so much heroism displayed, so much sacrifice cheerfully accepted," wrote Alvah Bessie, "that final defeat was totally unacceptable to the mind." Like Davidow, many simply could not speak about Spain. But the triumph of the Franco dictatorship deepened even that grief. For the news from Spain was endlessly bad. Starvation, disease, inadequate shelter—all afflicted a civilian population that the Lincolns had come to love. Two million Spaniards, so the veterans would learn, had been incarcerated in Franco's prisons, and the fascists were executing their Republican comrades by the thousands and tens of thousands. For the veterans, the sadness of Spain turned easily to anger and bitterness. Too well they understood that the United States, for reasons of politics, had participated in the death of the Spanish Republic.

*

When the largest contingent of returning soldiers landed in New York in December 1938, cheering well-wishers crowded the West Side docks. Families and friends embraced, even as other anxious parents and sweethearts searched the veterans' faces and made tense, usually futile inquiries about missing relatives. But what Milton Wolff remembered most about that day revealed a more ominous reality: there were "more cops than people." Already U.S. customs officials had seized the volunteers' passports for violations of the neutrality laws. Then, as the Friends of the Abraham Lincoln Brigade (FALB) organized a parade through midtown Manhattan, intending to place a memorial wreath for "those who died for democracy" at the eternal light in the park at Madison Square, police refused to permit the ceremony. The angry veterans had to place their flowers at the iron gates outside the monument.

For the Lincolns, the imbroglio came as a mild shock. It epitomized the government's attitude toward their sacrifice—not one of indifference, in the spirit of nonintervention, but rather one of active opposition. And so the incident illuminated another, deeper truth: their continuing powerlessness. Radicalized before they had embarked for Spain, the veterans remained outsiders, unwelcome and shunned by respectable politicians. As the Spanish war continued toward an agonizing defeat, the Lincolns confronted another struggle on the home front to obtain recognition for the cause that had so completely enveloped their lives. "For me it had never ended," said Wolff of this commitment. "I was young. I was anxious to continue." For his comrades—a defeated, frustrated army—the Spanish war was not over.

"You can be afraid to come home," admitted James Benét, a driver in the Regiment de Tren, who resumed his editorial job at the *New Republic*, "and we were afraid, that the folks wouldn't understand, that we had changed too much or they had, that Hitler and Mussolini had fooled them, that Chamberlain had fooled them, that maybe they just wouldn't get it, wouldn't be fighting the way the Spanish do." Those fears proved to be prophetic; the American people, the Lincolns would discover, had not yet absorbed the lessons of Spain. "The war of bullets and steel would be left behind," wrote Edwin Rolfe seven months after his return from Spain, "and the war of nerves and incessant threats would begin." Although public-opinion polls during the Spanish war had showed that a majority of Americans favored the Loyalist cause, an influential segment of the population endorsed Franco; for them, communism seemed far worse than fascism. Those sympathies prevailed in the State Department and other branches of government. And even when Americans did support the Republic, they did not generally consider the Spanish war important to U.S. interests. To the contrary, even as late as 1941 most Americans preferred to halt the spread of fascism without direct U.S. military participation.

The Lincolns, therefore, did not receive the joyful welcome that has usually greeted veterans of other American wars—with the exception of those who, three decades later, returned from another unpopular battlefront in Vietnam. Ironically, the Spanish war would later come to symbolize the last gasp of American isolationism, just as the Vietnam war constituted a retreat from post-Munich global interventionism. There were other analogies with Vietnam veterans. In both cases, the returning soldiers obtained minimal assistance and support from the larger society. For Spanish war veterans, moreover, the U.S. government scrupulously refused to provide funds to bring wounded volunteers back from Spain, though the financier Bernard Baruch wrote a check for $10,000 for that purpose. "They were willing to fight for something they believed in," he explained, "and I had the money to bring them home when they got hurt." His generosity was exceptional.

But if the Lincoln veterans, like Vietnam soldiers, faced a troubled homecoming, the volunteers of the 1930's enjoyed important psychological and ideological advantages. For while Vietnam veterans would suffer from what became known as post-traumatic stress syndrome, which reflected the agonies of combat and defeat and popular rejection, the Lincolns found solace in the righteousness of their sacrifice. To be sure, many Lincolns did suffer from the traumas of the war. But, unlike most Vietnam veterans, they held political values that justified their suffering. That proved the strength of the radical tradition. For the Lincolns, the postwar problems reinforced their convictions, forged their identity as radicals, and so minimized the self-destructive frustrations that afflicted the survivors of Vietnam. And unlike the isolated veterans of that later war, the Lincolns always knew they had each other.

According to the FALB, over 1,500 Americans had returned from Spain at various times, 600 of whom lived in the New York area. After interviews with social workers and medical examinations, they received clothing and other essentials and three weeks' maintenance support from the FALB at ten dollars a week. Those from outside New York also obtained bus fare home. At least three-quarters of the veterans needed medical care, ranging from minor dental treatment to multiple operations for shattered bones or rehabilitation for missing limbs. Over 200 men required hospitalization; at least 15 remained in hospitals as late as December 1939. None could expect public assistance. On Thanksgiving Day 1938, Barney Baley visited the patients at the Joint Disease Hospital in New York; "the place depressed and unnerved me," he wrote laconically.

Sympathetic doctors and dentists, some of them veterans of the American Medical Bureau, provided pro bono care. Even so, the cost of medical treatment exceeded $100,000. Dependent on private donations, the veterans joined with the FALB in numerous fund-raising events—dances, house parties, memorial meetings. Among the more visible speakers at these functions was Robert Raven, the maimed, blinded soldier Ernest Hemingway had interviewed in a Spanish hospital. Touring cross-country on behalf of Spain and the veterans, Raven seemed to embody the tragic toll of the anti-fascist war. Less obvious were the emotional strains that kept him depressed, frustrated, and volatile. Requiring constant attention, he married his nurse, but could not suppress the rage he felt for this dependence. One night, he threatened to blind her and then slashed his wrist in a suicide attempt. A court eventually ordered him confined to a mental institution for a year. Thereafter, he exhibited no obvious signs of mental distress. At least two other veterans—a nurse named Hannah Hershkowitz, "who returned in bad health [and] was extremely depressed by her ill health"; and John Brannan, a commercial artist wounded at Jarama—committed suicide soon after coming home.

Such cases of postwar stress, even if underreported, appear to have been exceptional. As sociologist John Dollard found in his 1942 survey, the Lincoln veterans, despite experiencing a crushing military defeat, suffered relatively little psychological damage. Their intense commitment to the Spanish Republic and their ideological convictions provided a coherent explanation of the failure. They identified the problems of defeat as political, not personal, and they continued to seek a victory in that political context. Equally important in explaining the rarity of mental collapse was the fact that the Lincolns helped their own. For example, they donated direct financial assistance to Raven for years and eventually joined with the Communist party in subsidizing his flower business.

Besides health problems, the veterans worried primarily about jobs. Ten years after the stock-market crash on Wall Street, nine million Americans remained unemployed; finding work was not easy. Among the New York veterans, the unemployment rate in December 1939, one year after their return, ran between 40 and 50 percent. "The veterans are not only victims of the general economic crisis," explained the FALB, "but they are especially discriminated against by employers because they cannot show continuous residence and [a] consistent employment record and experience." The FALB also suggested that the high unemployment percentage reflected the large number of unskilled workers among the veterans. Perhaps, too, like returning soldiers from other American wars, the Lincolns simply had trouble readjusting to the expectations of civilian work. One factor certainly distinguished Lincoln veterans from other ex-soldiers: they also faced political discrimination in the workplace. Fred Keller, for example, lost his job at Radio City Music Hall after union pickets charged he had killed nuns for five dollars each! "Now I know the sensation of political persecution," he told his friend Ernest Hemingway.

Veterans with special skills tried to resume their careers. Both Alvah Bessie and Edwin Rolfe landed book contracts from New York publishers and with puny advances began to write about their experiences in Spain. Dr. Mark Strauss returned to his profession two days after coming home. He also became a medical consultant to the furriers' union, providing virtually free services for Spanish war veterans. In several cities, veterans attempted to organize cooperative enterprises (dry cleaning, for example, or egg distribution), but these usually failed for lack of capital or mismanagement. Meanwhile, the FALB and the Communist party persuaded left-wing trade unions, such as the furriers and the electrical workers, to find positions for needy veterans. Lini Fuhr became an organizer for the CIO's Association of Hospital and Medical Professionals and served as the first president of the nurses' union. Bill Bailey settled his unpaid maritime dues and returned to sea. Archie Brown went back to the San Francisco waterfront. The Communist party also absorbed its former organizers: John Gates became head of the Young Communist League in New York; Steve Nelson assumed leadership on the West Coast; others found places in various state and district organizations. The Soviet Union recruited a number of veterans, including Milton Wolff, to serve as security guards for the Russian pavilion at the New York World's Fair.

To add to the Lincolns' difficulties, government agencies viewed partici-

pation in the Spanish war as evidence of Communist leanings (usually a correct judgment) and so discriminated against the returning veterans. When Wolff
volunteered for a reserve commission in the U.S. Army in March 1939, stating that he had gone to Spain "sincerely believing that in fighting for Spanish
Democracy I was helping preserve American Democracy," the War Department rejected the offer on the grounds that he had fought in Spain. Similarly,
the U.S. Public Health Service rebuffed Dr. Strauss's application. Resident
aliens who had served in Spain also encountered an unfriendly reception by
immigration officials and faced deportation. The Yugoslav American George
Delitch, who had lived in the United States for thirty years, fought with the
Allies in World War I, and been repatriated to America by the War Department in 1920, languished on Ellis Island while the State Department proposed returning him to his native land. The FALB paid the maintenance costs
of such people at $1.75 per day per person. "These men are heroes," pro-
tested Ernest Hemingway about seventeen members of the International Brigades held at the immigration center for lack of documentation. "Their heroism and their value to American society are being disregarded and cast into
disrepute . . . by an avalanche of legal technicalities." Eventually, the FALB
found havens for some of these veterans in other countries such as Chile and
Mexico; others, like Delitch, managed to establish their residence rights. But
for foreign-born veterans of Spain, the threat of deportation would remain a
serious problem for four decades.

Although friends of the Left glorified the Lincolns, most veterans did not
appreciate such postures. "Wish I could kid myself into the returning hero
pose," Barney Baley wrote in his diary, "say that the Party, et. al owe me a
living and a good one, but I can't." Instead, he rode a bus cross-country to his
home in southern California and got a job taking care of an old man. "Otherwise," he recalled ruefully, "I was a gentleman of leisure." Baley used his time
to write poetry, some of it published under the title *Hand Grenades* in 1942:
"learned the hard way," he wrote, "that

> Only those battered most by Capital,
> Welcomed sincerely back the boys from Spain.
> Others had blighted me like April frosts;
> I lived embittered.

"I didn't feel like a hero," explained Milton Wolff, whose military rank thrust him into the limelight. Some political comrades who had not gone to Spain "distanced" themselves, perhaps, he speculated, because of envy; others "overlionized" him. When he attended a YCL meeting of his local branch, they "treated me with such reverence I didn't go back again. I never joined the party for that reason, though I always felt friendly to them." Wolff also maintained a friendship with the prominent journalists he had met in Spain, particularly Vincent Sheean and his wife Dinah. Wolff had impressed the writer soon after the Great Retreats when, in response to Sheean's offer to bring him something from Paris, he had requested a copy of Thomas Mann's *Joseph in Egypt*. Now, in New York, Sheean introduced Wolff to a wealthy investor who offered to underwrite his college education and family expenses. Wolff, not yet ready to abandon his class consciousness, turned him down. For similar reasons, and with the encouragement of the Communist party, other veterans would choose trade union careers rather than return to school, where they might have acquired the background to enter the professions. Relatively few Lincolns made that choice.

Wolff assumed a prominent role in the veterans' affairs; his activities on behalf of Spain and the Lincolns substituted for a traditional occupation. Other veterans stuck close to their wartime comrades because those were the best friends they had. But many Lincolns, for personal and political reasons, had no interest in identifying themselves with the Spanish war. Of the 600 former soldiers in the New York area, 500 initially joined the veterans' organization. At one meeting, at which the Spanish Republican premier Juan Negrín appeared, 400 veterans attended; but usually the participants numbered less than 150. In other cities, attendance was much smaller. "We have maintained the interest of only about one-third of our membership," the veterans admitted at the end of 1939. "This is very bad, and . . . is the Number One problem." But no solutions emerged; the proportion of active veterans steadily declined during the next two decades.

Those who had deserted the ranks in Spain were generally unwelcome among the Left. Hamilton Tyler's girlfriend was told explicitly to drop either him or the YCL. (She chose marriage.) Another deserter, Alfred Amery, received a warm reception from Communist party leaders, but not from the veterans, who refused to allow him to march with them in the May Day parade of 1938. But most others were forgiven their failures in battle, provided that they did not publicly attack the brigade, the Republic, or the Communist party. All a deserter had to show, as Wolff put it, was "a conviction that past weaknesses have been recognized honestly." Besides, given the chaos of the Spanish war, desertions were seldom a matter of common knowledge. "Ray buggered off—was sick and left," wrote Robert Merriman's widow of one deserter, "but everyone is keeping very mum about it. . . . It most certainly will not be made public, especially since he seems all okay otherwise. . . . You might throw this letter in the fire . . . nobody likes to be called a buggerer-off whether it's true or not."

Another category of disaffiliated veterans included the ex-Communists and anti-Communists, who usually wanted nothing to do with the veterans' organization. In January 1939, one veteran compiled a list of sixteen hundred names—"American Communists and Sympathizers Who Fought for Loyalist Spain"—because, he noted, "a great many of them are party to a scheme of helping Soviet Russia secure passports to use at a later date." What he did with this list remains unclear. A few veterans subsequently admitted they had cooperated with the FBI in identifying Communists soon after they returned from Spain. By contrast, another handful of dissenters quit the Communist party because it was not sufficiently revolutionary. They would criticize the brigade leadership for following the party line too closely, but as radicals they refused to aid government inquisitors. Still, relatively few Lincoln veterans—no more than a dozen—publicly challenged the purposes of the brigade. Dissidents, to the extent that they existed, apparently withdrew from the political scene.

More typical were the dedicated Communists who simply had no time or inclination to participate in a veterans' group. For them, it was a question of the tail wagging the dog: Although as veterans they enjoyed a certain status in the party, they deemed political work more important than veterans' activities. Having survived Spain, they wanted to address other political issues, such as trade union organizing. "My basic philosophy is you've got to work from below," explained David Smith, who had virtually no contact with other veterans. Instead, "as a conscious decision," he accepted a series of organizing assignments in various industries. Only much later in life did he become active in veterans' affairs.

Clement Markert, a 21-year-old undergraduate at the University of Colorado, took no interest in the veterans either, because he "didn't want to become an old soldier before my time . . . , didn't want to be chained to the past." Instead, he returned to Boulder, where he was graduated summa cum laude, first in his class. When the American Legion attacked his presence on campus, however, Markert had to defend himself before the university's board of regents. "I pointed out I was in favor of the communist system, that I wanted to completely socialize the country, that I wanted to take all their wealth away," he remembered. He admitted, further, that he was an atheist. "I could just see them shaking in rage." But he also cited his academic achievements and suggested that his expulsion would constitute an act of self-criticism of the university's standards. The board voted unanimously to keep him. Markert finished college and went on to study zoology at the University of California at Los Angeles.

Another reluctant veteran was Reuben Barr, once a teenaged Wobbly. Because he could not find his birth certificate, he had gone to Spain in 1937 with a false passport and an assumed name. "I had no idea that I would ever return," he explained. "I was certain that I would die there; or we would be successful and my future would be in Spain." Instead, Barr was captured by fascist troops and placed in prisoner-of-war camps; he was the last Lincoln to return home, arriving in March 1940. Two weeks later, he appeared at a conference in New York to publicize the plight of other prisoners in Spain. "Guerrilla warfare still goes on," he reported; and an underground press continued to operate. "Many anti-fascists," he said, "still expect to carry on because they are fighting and will continue to fight until they win a victory." But Barr's use of a false passport—his nom de guerre was Conrad Stojewa—raised questions about his citizenship, and the government threatened deportation. Sympathetic lawyers advised Barr to avoid contact with the political Left. He found a job as a traveling salesman, got married, bought a house, and stayed away from political activities for the next forty years. He had not altered his opinions or abandoned his ideology. But as he had done in the Red Scare of 1919, he sought safety through inaction.

It is impossible to estimate how many other veterans, for similarly idiosyncratic reasons, chose political isolation. An unknown number apparently wanted nothing but a "normal" life. "I call myself an independent thinker," said one, who demanded anonymity fifty years later. "I have the same principles as when I was a young man; I'm not ashamed of having gone to Spain." But this veteran had no contact with other Lincolns; never, after 1938, did he participate in a single political movement. Eighteen months' service in Spain at the age of 25 proved to be the exception to an utterly apolitical life.

Many Lincolns felt no such diffidence. Like Wolff, they embraced Spain as their special cause. Under the auspices of the FALB, the first returnees had been agitating on behalf of the Republic since 1937. Veterans, some still recovering from wounds, traversed the country, collected funds, and attempted to sway public opinion to change the nation's isolationist neutrality. Often, they succeeded primarily in arousing counterattacks from local conservatives. In Massachusetts, where Catholic sympathy for Franco remained high, a legislative committee investigated the FALB, reflecting a political climate that encouraged government harassment. At Boston's Symphony Hall, the police arrived to arrest speaker Edward Flaherty, wounded at Jarama, for violating parole on a four-year-old suspended sentence for auto theft; he went to prison for three months. "I was entertained and I was heckled," recalled Lini Fuhr of her tour; "tomatoes or roses were thrown at me." On Armistice Day 1937, a handful of veterans, including David McKelvey White and Phil Bard, placed a commemorative wreath at the eternal light in Madison Square; the American Legion formally protested the ceremony.

In December 1937, just before the battle of Teruel, three prominent veterans in New York—Steve Nelson; William Lawrence, base commissar at Albacete; and David McKelvey White—summoned the Lincolns in the area to an organizational meeting of what would become a permanent veterans' group, the Veterans of the Abraham Lincoln Brigade (VALB). About fifty men attended the first session. Like most Communist-led meetings of that era, the agenda created no serious objections. The veterans proceeded to adopt a constitution, pledging to maintain friendly relations between their members, to assist in the rehabilitation of wounded men, to rally public support for Republican Spain, and to aid "the peace and anti-fascist movement." Then they drew up a list of nominees for executive officers and arranged to mail out ballots. Paul Burns, survivor of Jarama and Brunete, was elected the first commander.

Four days later, on Christmas Eve, this first veterans' organization staged two public events. The evening began with a social gathering to mark the anniversary of the sailing of the first shipload of Lincolns, a dime-a-dance affair to raise money for the FALB. Afterwards, some of the veterans went to Times

Square to form a picket line outside Woolworth's to protest the sale of products made in Japan. The police promptly arrested nineteen veterans, including the blind Robert Raven, for disturbing the peace. "It is hard to imagine the surprise and bitterness I feel," Raven told the city magistrate who heard the case the following month; "I am arrested for exercising the very rights that I went to Spain to fight for, the right to tell people about the menace of fascism, the right of free speech, the right to defend democracy." The result: a dismissal of all charges.

The creation of the VALB coincided with an increasingly rancorous debate on the home front about U.S. policy toward the Spanish war. Two months earlier, President Roosevelt had spoken forthrightly in Chicago about the dangers of fascist expansion, even suggesting that the democracies of the world "quarantine" the aggressor nations. Roosevelt's speech, widely touted in the American press, had presented no concrete proposals; indeed, the president had none to offer the nation. But several congressional representatives, including Jerry O'Connell of Montana and John Bernard of Minnesota, took the opportunity to introduce a so-called "peace" resolution, calling for a revision of the neutrality laws so that Republican Spain could purchase arms and military supplies.

On Lincoln's birthday in 1938, the VALB organized its first lobbying contingent to visit Washington, D.C., to urge passage of the measure. After placing a wreath at the Lincoln Memorial, 75 veterans marched three abreast to the Tomb of the Unknown Soldier at Arlington National Cemetery. Then they listened to speeches from a Popular Front assemblage—Communists, Socialists, liberals—all of whom condemned fascist intervention in Spain. Black veteran Doug Roach read a letter of support from the National Negro Congress. One delegation proceeded to the White House bearing a message that endorsed the president's quarantine speech and denounced a "neutrality" policy that denied "a friendly democratic country her international rights." Another group visited the German ambassador to protest the presence of Nazi troops in Spain, and a third picketed outside the Italian embassy while an airplane circled overhead with a banner that read "Quarantine the Aggressor." In the end, however, the veterans returned to New York without having altered the government's position even slightly.

So began a pattern of public opposition that embroiled the Lincolns for the next year and a half. Wherever they lived, whether in rural Wisconsin or downtown Manhattan, as individuals or in alliance with other sympathetic groups, the veterans attempted to publicize the dangers of fascism and to encourage a more interventionist foreign policy. Already they held a place of honor in the protest movements. In Brooklyn, they marched at the head of an anti-silk parade to support a boycott of Japanese products; on May Day 1938 the veterans walked down Broadway at the front of the vast Communist pageant. They paraded with the American League for Peace and Democracy; they rallied at the tenth national convention of the Communist party. They formed processions to honor the dead of Spain; and they led delegations to stop the government from deporting alien residents who had fought with the International Brigades.

As larger numbers of veterans came home in the autumn of 1938 and the cause of Republican Spain seemed imperiled, these campaigns became more vitriolic and militant. To protest the concessions made to Hitler at the Munich conference in September 1938, 25 Lincolns led a noisy demonstration outside a pro-German Bund meeting in Chicago; only police intervention prevented a violent confrontation. Similar protests blanketed the country. "The Spanish people . . . are defending the whole world against the aggression of Hitler and Mussolini," argued Milton Wolff at a "Lift the Embargo" rally in New York. Three hundred veterans then journeyed to Washington, D.C., to meet with officials of the State Department, the White House, and Congress in an effort to muster American aid for the dying Republic. In New York, the VALB joined with the veterans of the American Medical Bureau to Aid Spanish Democracy (a separate veterans' group organized during the summer of 1938) and established a permanent picket line outside the Italian consulate to protest Mussolini's intervention. On the West Coast, a dozen pickets, led by veteran David Thompson, were arrested for "carrying banners without permit" at the German consulate to protest the Nazi seizure of Czechoslovakia and the invasion of Spain. (All charges were subsequently dismissed.) "It is hard for us who have come back from Spain," explained Thompson's cousin, James Benét, "to talk or write calmly about the need for helping our friends and comrades."

Anger, frustration, sorrow—such sentiments solidified the Lincolns' identity as political outsiders, but these feelings also reflected the hostile climate that surrounded them. Numerous business and government leaders, as well as the Roman Catholic church, had supported the Franco side and showed no sympathy for Lincoln veterans. In Cleveland, Ohio, for example, the city council responded to pressure from conservative Catholics by revoking permission for the veterans and the FALB to hold a "tag day" in December 1938 to raise funds for rehabilitation. Despite stormy council meetings and a public rally, the conservatives carried the vote. The next month, the central labor council of the American Federation of Labor in New York suspended two teachers' unions for Communist influence; both groups, so the charges read, had participated in the parade of returning Lincoln veterans to Madison Square. On Lincoln's birthday in 1939, the War Department reversed the precedent set the previous year and refused to allow the veterans to place flowers at the Tomb of the Unknown Soldier.

Such harassment, reminiscent of the organizing struggles during the Depression, became an integral part of the veterans' lives. In the summer of 1938, Detroit-based veteran Robert Taylor was entertaining some friends from Spain when the local police Red Squad raided the house, ransacked his possessions, and held him incommunicado at the police station for two days. The arresting officers had recently testified to the House Committee on Un-American Activities, accusing Taylor of illegally recruiting volunteers for Spain. Inquiries by Taylor's attorney won his release. Taylor promptly sued the mayor and police commissioner, but dropped the case when the police chief resigned. With this arrest, however, the police opened a political file on Taylor and followed his activities closely for the next forty years. They also kept his private letters and documents, seized illegally, until 1990.

"Veterans of the A.L.B. are seldom attacked as such," observed the VALB newsletter, *Volunteer for Liberty,* "but instead are slandered on other counts in an attempt to weaken the esteem the American people hold for them." Because Lincoln veterans became involved in a multitude of political causes, government attacks on radicals and Communists inevitably affected them. In one extraordinary legal case, a California sheriff arrested two veterans—Luke Hinman, an ex-Wobbly, and Bill Wheeler, who had served two tours with the Lincolns—after they went directly from the Spanish battlefields to organizing farm workers in Marysville. The charge: violating the state's anti-picketing laws. Hinman left the jail after one week, but Wheeler spent 39 days behind bars without a trial. After his release, he sued the sheriff for false imprisonment and managed to collect $300. With that nest egg, Wheeler proceeded to organize the deliverers of telephone books. In another California labor case, veterans Ramon Durem and Steve Daduk faced one-year prison terms for contempt of court. Other Lincolns went to trial in Pennsylvania and Maryland. Such pressure created another common experience to keep the veterans together.

The willingness of Lincoln veterans to undertake dangerous and unpopular political work testified to their enduring militancy, their personal courage, and, usually, their Communist commitments. But after the Spanish war finally ended in 1939, the level of enthusiasm and participation visibly dwindled. "Most of the men were anxious to return to some type of normal life," remembered Milton Wolff. Preoccupied with marriage—"it was almost epidemic"—jobs, and family obligations, most veterans ignored the calls for meetings and demonstrations. Former commissar Saul Wellman later estimated that less than ten percent of the veterans became activists after Spain. "Our work here has bogged down," complained one veteran in Los Angeles. "Partly due to incompetence, partly to apathy." What the veterans needed was an issue that could arouse their political instincts, awaken their partisan attachments. The cause was not long in coming.

15

Between the Wars

O minous was the mood during the summer of 1939 as Europe braced for a general war. Having used the Munich agreement to occupy Czechoslovakia, Hitler now threatened to invade Poland. Great Britain and France, realizing at last the futility of appeasement, promised to oppose further Nazi expansion. But for veterans of the Lincoln brigade, the battle lines between fascism and its enemies were not so clearly drawn. Thanks to the aid of Hitler and Mussolini, Franco presided over a dictatorial peace in Spain, and the so-called bastions of democracy— Britain, France, and the United States—had conspired in the fall of the Republic. No Lincoln veteran of any political persuasion argued with those facts. As Communists, moreover, most Lincolns accepted a rapprochement with the capitalist West—the Popular Front—only as a temporary expedient.

The Lincolns had special reasons to distrust the Western Allies. Since the fall of Barcelona in 1938, those countries had imposed harsh conditions on the Spanish refugees, civilian and soldier alike, who had fled for safety from Franco's troops. The United States and Britain had closed their doors to the displaced populations. France, forced to accept thousands of starving, terrified Spaniards, made no effort to ameliorate the incredibly bad conditions inside the refugee concentration camps. They were "unfit for human habitation," declared U.S. ambassador Claude Bowers. "Everyone slept on the ground," affirmed the *New York Times* correspondent Herbert Matthews about one camp; "there was not a single latrine for those 25,000 people." But such reports never reached the American public. Protests by French diplomats in Washington, D.C., persuaded Matthews's editors to kill his stories. "Like all neutral observers there at the time," the journalist recalled, "I was hot with rage and helplessness." Several Lincoln volunteers, caught in the camps before they could be repatriated, witnessed the brutal treatment. "Spanish comrades are so incensed," noted Sid Kaufman in his diary, "they say the next war has to be against France even if it has to be on the side of Franco!" The Lincoln veterans had no illusions about the Western democracies.

Toward Stalin and the Soviet Union, by contrast, the loyalty of most Lincoln veterans remained uncritical and unexamined. But it was a relationship plagued with difficulty. Problems first surfaced in July 1939 when the right-wing radio priest Father Charles Coughlin used his weekly broadcast to denounce the spread of atheistic radicalism in America and vowed that his Christian Front movement "will fight you in Franco's way." This threat of a fascist-like repression provoked widespread anger, particularly in its apparent blessing of the atrocities in Spain. But when the pro-Trotsky Socialist Workers party appealed to American Communists to form a united front and join in protest demonstrations against a Coughlinite mass rally in New York, the Communist party refused to participate.

The VALB docilely followed the line. At a veterans' membership meeting in mid-August, passions ran high. In one order of business, the local post formally expelled Lou (Levine) Kupperman. His exact transgressions remain unclear, but the veterans charged him with "undermining . . . confidence in the anti-fascist struggle," "slandering the . . . leadership of the International Brigade," and "spreading false statements about the number of casualties in Spain." Another veteran named Henry Thomas then arrived at the meeting carrying an armload of leaflets that urged the Lincolns to protest against Coughlin at Union Square. As Thomas handed out his papers, the veterans noticed the signature at the bottom: "Independent Veterans Committee for Anti-Fascist Action." When someone objected to the label, Thomas fled from the meeting, dropping his leaflets as he ran. "There is no doubt that the veterans oppose Coughlin and everything he stands for," the VALB newspaper *Volunteer for Liberty* rationalized. "But . . . the Coughlinites have been trying to cook up a riot to get some publicity for a long time. To go out and demonstrate against them . . . would be just exactly what they wanted." Thomas's independent committee clearly defied the VALB's claim to speak for all Spanish war veterans. But whatever the Lincolns' motives for attacking him, their position on Coughlin mirrored that of the Communist party; there would be no alliance with Trotsky supporters. Similar problems occurred in the Milwaukee post, where the veterans expelled three men—one on charges of theft, the others on grounds of "slander and provocation."

Such quibbles exploded abruptly with the news of the signing of a Nazi-Soviet Non-Aggression Pact in August 1939. Shocked by an agreement between archenemies, the Western capitals now awaited a formal declaration of war. The Pact served two purposes: for Hitler, it guaranteed that an invasion of Poland would not lead to a two-front war; and for Stalin, the agreement offered assurances that Germany would move into western Poland and no further. In America, anti-fascists cringed at Stalin's willingness to negotiate with the German dictator. But whatever their private doubts, most Lincoln veterans stood with the Communist party. "I was staggered," remembered Saul Wellman. "But you can be staggered and not go into the opposition." Indeed, most veterans described the pact as an example of Soviet diplomatic finesse. "The USSR is a socialist state, protecting herself from highly antagonistic surrounding states," explained James Benét in the *New Republic*. "This does not appear to a socialist as an act of alliance with fascism." Rather, as Clement Markert would explain, "the pact was simply a tactic to compel the bourgeois democracies to at last take up the battle against Nazi Germany."

Whatever their claims to be "fighting anti-fascists," the Lincolns now retreated from their anti-Nazi position and accepted the Communist party line that the Western democracies were no worse and no better than the fascist axis. The veterans had abundant personal experience to rationalize that argument. "I justified it," recalled Milton Wolff. "Everything I said was based on the Spanish experience—who had helped us; who had not helped us; who had been part of the sellout [of Spain]." In short, Spain had demonstrated the failure of the Western Allies to stand forthrightly against fascism. Former brigade commissar John Gates perceived another dimension of the Spanish precedent. "Hitler's plans against the Soviet Union . . . were real ones. What made him change his mind? The war in Spain taught him a great deal as to the value and effectiveness of Soviet arms."

Five days later, the Nazi invasion of Poland—which included the Condor Legion that had bombed the Basque town of Guernica in 1937—compelled additional rationalizations. "This is not our war," declared the VALB, echoing the Communist party position; "the present European war is not an antifascist war but an imperialist war. . . . We not only will not take part in it, but we will emphatically oppose our country's . . . giving assistance to either side." Renouncing efforts to draw the United States into World War II, the veterans specifically endorsed the neutralist policies of the Soviet Union, "which has consistently led and aided the cause of peace and of truly democratic peoples throughout the world." The ensuing period, known as the "phony war"—when Britain, France, and Germany prepared for their first major battles—seemed to justify the Communist view that the Allies lacked the desire to wage war against fascism.

The Soviet invasion of Finland in November 1939 again placed the party—and its advocates in the VALB—on the defensive. But, as before, the veterans exhibited no reluctance in supporting the Soviet position. "We learned our lessons well," explained David McKelvey White. "We will not forget, we of all people will not forget, the friends and the enemies of a free Spain." By such reckoning, Germany and Italy could be lumped with France and Britain, even with the United States, because all had been "branded with the blood of the Spanish people and of the brave men of the International Brigades." At the VALB's third annual convention in December 1939, the veterans reaffirmed the view that the present war "was not for freedom, but for profits." Instead of U.S. intervention on behalf of the Allies, the Lincolns demanded the rescue of thousands of International Brigadiers still held in French concentration camps, and they flaunted the Communist party slogan: "The Yanks are *not* coming!"

Even as the VALB parroted the party line, the Lincolns claimed a certain authority about the issues of the war. At a meeting of the National Negro Congress in Washington, D.C., in April 1940, black veteran Pat Roosevelt contrasted his Spanish war experience with the segregationist policies of the U.S. Army. "If Milton Herndon, Doug Roach, and Oliver Law were alive today they would tell us how the people of Spain were betrayed," he told the conference. "Yes, we should have a war—a war on the economic and civil liberties front, a war against jim-crowism, a war which will unite Negro and white to wipe out inequality in the United States. In this war," he vowed, "the Veterans will be in the front lines—Negro and white—just as we fought together in Spain." The Lincolns, denying any contradictions in their anti-fascist commitments, had no trouble condemning the hypocrisy of a segregated democracy.

The refusal to support the Allies nonetheless accentuated tensions in the ranks. For an anti-Communist like Robert Gladnick, the pact confirmed all his bad experiences with the Stalinist system, both in the Soviet Union and in Spain. Other veterans questioned their leftist attachments and severed relations with the Communist party. Esther Silverstein, who identified as a Jew and had "sat shivah," mourning for ten days when the Spanish Republic fell, objected to any agreement with Hitler; she immediately quit the party. Still others, deeply disillusioned but unwilling to jeopardize their friendships with fellow veterans, simply made excuses to avoid further party work; as long as they kept silent, they would remain welcome members of the VALB.

More vitriolic protests came from militant radicals, who published a series of dissenting statements in the Trotskyist newspaper, *Socialist Appeal.* "I am no longer a member of the Stalinist party," announced Henry Thomas, who dated his protest August 16, the day he fled the VALB meeting and a week before the announcement of the pact. Questioning "the sincerity of the Communist leadership" in Spain—he had been accused of desertion—he also challenged the lack of revolutionary militancy on the home front. "The Communist Party had thrown the hammer and sickle out the window," he declared, "while I was fighting fascists in Spain." Three weeks later, another veteran named Peter Sturgeon announced his resignation from the party, complaining, like Thomas, of the Communists' loss of revolutionary zeal. The idea of a Popular Front and collective security with non-Communist nations, he said, blatantly violated the principles of Marx and Lenin. "Break with the party of sellout, betrayals, and lies," advised a third veteran, John Kendzierski of Toledo, Ohio, announcing his shift to the Socialist Workers party. To these objections, the New York VALB responded by expelling Thomas and Sturgeon. Both had gone beyond criticism of the Communist party. They had not only maligned the International Brigades but had proposed the formation of an alternative veterans' group. The VALB took no notice of Kendzierski, perhaps because there was no veterans' group in Toledo.

One dissident who would not be ignored, however, was Morris Maken (who upon his return from Spain dropped the nom de guerre Mickenberg). The brigade comic had never made peace with the Communist leadership. After the war, Maken had accepted a probationary status in the party and tried to reconcile his antiauthoritarian impulses with the dictates of the leadership. He made no protest when the VALB voted to denounce all sides in World War II, though he was surprised to realize that the veterans had already published leaflets explaining their position before the vote had been taken. Under the eye of the leaders, Maken left the meeting with a batch of handouts and promptly deposited them in the nearest wastebasket. A few others, he said, did the same. One of these dissidents was Robert Gladnick, who felt no shyness in taking an anti-Communist position. Another was William Herrick, who had muffled his antiparty feelings because of personal friendships and his dependence on the veterans for rehabilitation. With the help of the FALB, he had obtained a job with the furriers' union in New York. Angered by the Communist position on the war, however, Herrick began to look for alternative socialist groups. He attended several meetings of the Independent Labor League, where he heard speeches by such anti-Communists as Norman Thomas, Sidney Hook, and Bertram Wolfe. Another veteran observed him there, however, and party leaders warned him of the consequences. When Herrick persisted in his heretic ways, he lost his job with the furriers.

"Hero in Spain; Victim of the Pact": Beneath the picket sign, Herrick and Gladnick paraded through the garment district in mid-Manhattan. Threats of violence did not intimidate them. Maken, already treated with suspicion, now suggested that the three attempt to mobilize a counter-organization to build an anti-Communist, anti-fascist movement. They would call themselves the Veterans of the International Brigades, Anti-Totalitarian. For his troubles, the VALB promptly expelled Maken from the ranks; it apparently did not bother with the others. But the dissidents found a sympathetic audience in another disaffected Spanish war veteran, Humberto Galleani, an Italian-born volunteer who had served with the Garibaldi battalion and who had wide political connections in New York. His anti-Communist opinions had alienated him from the VALB leadership. He had refused to attend meetings and was eventually expelled, allegedly for absconding with money and documents relating to the repatriation of Italian-American veterans.

Soon after the outbreak of World War II, Galleani brought the dissident Lincoln veterans to meet the celebrated Italian anarchist Carlo Tresca, who published the newspaper *Il Martello* in New York. The sympathetic Tresca offered them office space. With a mailing address, the renegades attempted to build a membership. Maken even proposed that they form another international brigade to fight in defense of Finland. But only about six or eight Lincoln veterans made contact with the group, and the organizers began to suspect they were being infiltrated by party members. Frustrated by the politicking, Gladnick decided to enlist in the Canadian army. Maken, never a good organizer, accepted defeat. The counter-organization died unborn. But even its aborted existence indicated significant discontent with the party line. "The majority of us anti-fascists," wrote a disgruntled veteran, who called himself "John Brown," "have nothing to do with the Veterans' organization, the only purpose of which seems to be to parallel the Communist party line."

"Soldados," Milton Wolff told the veterans at the end of 1939, "we are under fire and the enemy is out to destroy us." Antagonism to the Communist position on the war was encouraging renewed attacks from government agencies. Earlier that year, President Roosevelt had authorized Attorney General Frank Murphy to commence investigations of various subversive activities—fascist, Nazi, and Communist—and within that broad mandate the Justice Department had conducted inquiries about the recruitment of volunteers for the Abraham Lincoln brigade. More than a year later, on February 6, 1940, at five in the morning, veteran Robert Taylor, once before a victim of the Detroit Red Squad, crossed the Canadian border on his way to work in Michigan and was seized by FBI agents. At the same time, the FBI arrested ten other people in Milwaukee and Detroit; they included one other Lincoln veteran and two doctors active in the American Medical Bureau to Aid Spanish Democracy. The charge: violation of an 1818 statute that prohibited recruitment for foreign armies.

Interrogated for hours by FBI agents, denied consultation with an attorney, the shackled prisoners entered a plea of not guilty and were quickly transported to the federal penitentiary at Milan, Michigan. They stayed there for eleven days, despite nationwide protests, until Roosevelt's new attorney general, Robert Jackson, abruptly ordered the dismissal of all charges. The Justice Department would later exonerate the FBI of illegal activity in the case. But a subsequent study by defense attorney Ernest Goodman suggested that the raids had been politically motivated. The arrests served not only to discredit supporters of Spain, but also to enhance the law-enforcement record of Frank Murphy, whom Roosevelt had just nominated to the U.S. Supreme Court.

While the FBI seized veterans in the Midwest, agents arrived at the VALB's national office in New York with a warrant for a veteran named Manny Cohen. With that excuse, they proceeded to search desks and file cabinets, empty wastebaskets, and take notes. When Wolff refused to give his name, one of the agents assured him: "It doesn't matter anyway; you'll soon have a number." The raid served primarily as harassment. "We have committed no crime," Wolff insisted. "If we had, then Roosevelt would be guilty of the same charge, because he has publicly announced that it is fine and dandy to recruit here for the Finnish white guards." But the veterans were already feeling government pressure. A grand jury had subpoenaed Wolff and other VALB officers to testify about recruitment. After the lawmen departed, the Lincolns removed their mailing lists from the office, took their records to a veteran's apartment, and burned them in the fireplace.

In this atmosphere of intense controversy, bitterness, and suspicion, the Lincoln veterans received a warning from Europe during the winter of 1940 that the French government had decided to terminate the problem of Spanish refugees by ordering their return to Spain. The news was horrifying: terror and death awaited the enemies of Franco's regime. While participating in an Emergency Conference to Save Spanish Refugees, protesting the shift in French policy, the VALB leadership resolved to move beyond bureaucratic formalities. It was March 1940.

Despite a municipal ban on protests outside the foreign consulates in New York, several dozen Lincoln veterans waited until the evening rush hour outside the French consulate. Then they moved off the crowded sidewalks with their picket signs to obstruct the dense mid-Manhattan traffic. Club-wielding police arrived in force. In the ensuing brawl, several veterans were arrested; as hoped, the story reached the press. Ten days later, the Lincolns returned to continue the protest, and again the police made arrests. But the publicity campaign proved effective. Faced with international protests, the French government reversed its policy and permitted the Spanish exiles to remain in the camps. Citing the harsh conditions there, however, the VALB continued to appeal for the abolition of punishment cages, pleaded for permission to transfer the prisoners to friendly countries in Latin America, and urged the Franco regime to free International volunteers still imprisoned in Spain. These issues would absorb the VALB's attention for years.

A few days after his arrest outside the French consulate, Milton Wolff attended a social party at the home of Vincent and Dinah Sheean. During the cocktail hour, they introduced him to their friend, William "Wild Bill" Donovan, a prominent Republican lawyer and already a troubleshooter for Roosevelt in Europe. During the Spanish war, Donovan, with the president's personal permission, had accompanied Franco's fourth army as an observer in the attacks on the Ebro front. "I believed Spain to be, ideology aside, a laboratory for the weapons of the next war," he explained. "I met no other American observer." After the outbreak of World War II, Donovan worked on behalf of Polish and Finnish relief programs. But in his brief conversations with Wolff, he made no references to his international experience. Instead, he listened to Wolff's story about the refugees and the subsequent harassment and arrest of the veterans. "I will give you a lawyer," he offered, and he told Wolff to visit his offices on Wall Street the next day.

Donovan's corporation lawyer proved of minimal assistance; nor did noisy spectators help the Lincolns in court. For violating the city's anti-picketing ordinances, Wolff, Fred Keller, and Gerald Cook received fifteen-day sentences at Riker's Island prison. Donovan's lawyer visited Wolff in jail. He "tried to tell me I was a 'great' guy—but on the wrong side," Wolff reported. "We had a long discussion and I think that I . . . convinced him that I was right being where I wanted things." Such counsel could hardly be encouraging. Moreover, in the middle of the trial, a process server had entered the courtroom and handed the three Lincoln defendants subpoenas, ordering them to appear before the House Committee on Un-American Activities (HUAC), chaired by the conservative Martin Dies, in April 1940.

Twice before, the HUAC had heard testimony about the relationship between the Lincoln brigade, the Communist party, and the Spanish war. In 1938, while Americans fought on the Ebro front, two deserters, Abraham Sobel and Alvin Halpern, had presented exaggerated and erroneous testimony about

Communist policies in Spain. The next year, the committee summoned two more deserters—William McCuistion and William Ryan—who confirmed the dominance of the Communist party in all brigade affairs. "God knows," said McCuistion two months after the outbreak of World War II, "Hitler and Mussolini can be very little worse than the ruling clique of the Communist bureaucrats and political commissars of war." Among the Lincolns, military desertion served to discredit their testimony. Ryan went on from the hearings to become an articulate anti-fascist, anti-Communist polemicist for U.S. isolationism.

The hearings of 1940 raised the old issues of Communist control and added new ones about the assassination of political prisoners in Spain. Two deserters—McCuistion and John Honeycombe—leveled accusations of arbitrary arrest and shooting of dissidents. Humberto Galleani testified about the harsh treatment of prisoners, including the execution of Paul White. Two parents of deceased Lincoln volunteers—the mother of Vernon Selby and the father of Albert Wallach—brought charges of murder. The veracity of these allegations, as we have seen, remains dubious. Although Wallach may well have been executed for military desertion—there remains no proof—Selby served courageously in battle, and Wolff vividly remembered the night he disappeared during the Great Retreats. Most of the other charges, based on fragments of truth, added little convincing evidence about criminal activities in Spain.

Whatever the claims, however, the HUAC would certainly never find out the truth from the VALB witnesses. During a recess, Wolff called McCuistion "a yellow bastard" and shoved him; he had to be restrained by Capitol police. Anthony DeMaio, accused twice in the testimony of murdering prisoners in his charge, refused to answer most questions directly. He alone of the witnesses sought the protection of the Fifth Amendment. The others—Wolff, Keller, and Cook—answered their inquisitors selectively. Sometimes, they simply lied. Years later Wolff acknowledged that prior to the hearings, the veterans had agreed to conceal certain truths about their political backgrounds. The VALB was then raising money for Spanish refugees and did not want to produce unfavorable publicity. Why did they avoid the Fifth Amendment? "We didn't know anything about the Fifth Amendment," said Wolff. Did they worry about being charged with perjury? "They were stupider than we were."

The government pressure ironically strengthened the VALB's commitment to the party line. "It is no accident that the full power of the District Attorney's office, the Dies Committee, and the FBI is being used to prosecute and persecute," explained David McKelvey White. "The forces that would drag America to Europe's trenches are awake and ready for action." In a series of articles in the *Young Communist Review*, former brigade commissar John Gates observed that the Soviet Union stood as "a socialist island in a sea of hostile capitalism" and suggested that the Russians might do well to form a military alliance with Nazi Germany. (Even Earl Browder flinched at that idea!) "But I was ready to accept that," said Gates many years later. "England and France, the bourgeois democracies, appeared as the main evil." Thus, as the Roosevelt administration moved the nation toward a more interventionist position on behalf of Britain and France in 1940, many veterans participated in the Communist party's American Peace Mobilization campaign to keep the United States out of war. When the president accused Mussolini of stabbing France in the back in June 1940, Gates retorted, "It was you who stabbed Republican Spain in the back. It was you, and the British and French rulers, who provided Mussolini with the dagger that he has now proceeded to plunge into your own backs."

The continuing problems of the Spanish refugees trapped in French concentration camps seemed to confirm the Lincolns' hostile opinion of the Western Allies. During the fall of 1940, the VALB joined with other Spanish relief agencies in raising $300,000 to send an American ship to bring the exiles from French Morocco to Vera Cruz, Mexico. But besides the problems of raising money, the effort encountered opposition from humanitarians and liberals who objected to working with Communists. Eleanor Roosevelt resigned from the project. Then, when the funds became available, the British government refused to allow the chartering of a vessel for the purpose of transporting political refugees. Wolff then led a delegation of six veterans to Washington, D.C., but failed to gain an interview with the British ambassador. While the refugees languished in French territory, rumors spread of violence and severe punishment in the camps. The frustrations of formal diplomacy further eroded the Lincolns' sympathy for the Allied cause. With Spain as their central concern, the veterans thought less of cooperation with the Allies than of getting revenge.

16

The War of Words

N ine men commanded the Lincoln and Lincoln-Washington Battalions," wrote Ernest Hemingway at the end of the Spanish war; four were dead and four were wounded. Milton Wolff, the ninth and last commander, Hemingway described as "alive and unhit by the same hazard that leaves one tall palm tree standing where a hurricane has passed." After their first meeting at the Café Chicote in Madrid, the novelist had come to admire Wolff's brash and undogmatic leadership. When American sculptor Jo Davidson modeled a clay portrait of Wolff at the Hotel Majestic in Barcelona in 1938, Hemingway contributed a text to accompany the figure: "He is a retired major now at twenty-three, and pretty soon he will be coming home as other men his age and rank came home after the peace at Appomattox courthouse long ago. Except the peace was made at Munich now and no good men will be home for long."

Hemingway had already begun to work on a series of Spanish war stories that would blossom into his novel *For Whom the Bell Tolls*, but he paused in the winter of 1939 to write an elegy for the American dead in Spain. The piece, which appeared in the left-wing magazine *New Masses*, evoked both the immediacy of their cause and the timelessness of their sacrifice. "The fascists may spread over the land, blasting their way with weight of metal brought from other countries," conceded Hemingway. "They may destroy cities and villages and try to hold the people in slavery. But you cannot hold any people in slavery." He predicted that the Spanish people would "rise again as they have always risen before against tyranny." But the war's victims, he explained, "do not need to rise. They are a part of the earth now and the earth can never be conquered. . . . It will outlive all systems of tyranny. Those who have entered it honorably, and no men ever entered earth more honorably than those who died in Spain, already have achieved immortality."

Hemingway's grief for the war's victims barely concealed his bitterness at the fall of the Republic. "There is only one thing to do when you have a war," he announced, "and that is win it." Disgusted at the outcome, he plunged his feelings into his novel. By the end of 1939, he had written over 100,000 words. As always, he remained sensitive to criticism. When Alvah Bessie questioned the political function of one of Hemingway's stories, the novelist attacked the "ideology boys," suggesting that "what was wrong with his outfit was too much ideology and not enough military training, discipline or materiel."

Hemingway nonetheless remained friendly with the Lincoln veterans. He encouraged his editor, Maxwell Perkins, to publish Bessie's memoir of the Spanish war, *Men in Battle*. When it appeared in September 1939, the very week Germany invaded Poland, he praised the work as "a true, honest, fine book" and later called it "a damned crime" that Bessie had not achieved commercial success. Meanwhile, Hemingway paid the hospital bills for one veteran's wife, sent money to assist others in need, and shared in the Lincolns' feelings of self-sacrifice. "The people . . . [who] did nothing about defending the Spanish Republic," he complained, "now feel a great need to attack us who tried to do something in order to make us look foolish and justify themselves in their selfishness and cowardice. . . . They now say how stupid it was even to have fought at all." And when Milton Wolff approached Hemingway at his New York hotel for a loan to underwrite a chicken-and-egg farm cooperative for some unemployed veterans, the novelist advanced $400 on his word. It was the last time the two would meet.

By the time *For Whom the Bell Tolls* appeared in October 1940, the camaraderie of the Spanish war had shattered amid the twists and turns of global politics. The novel made no claim to tell the story of the Lincoln brigade. Hemingway focused on a single American volunteer, "Robert Jordan," assigned a special mission to demolish a bridge behind enemy lines. "He fought now in this war because it had started in a country that he loved," wrote Hemingway, with autobiographical candor; "and he believed in the Republic and that if it were destroyed life would be unbearable" for the Spanish people. Working with a band of Spanish guerrillas, Jordan manipulated their strengths and weaknesses to achieve his military objective, and he found a hasty romance with a young woman. But like the novelist, he expressed little interest in politics, beyond a vaguely stated "anti-fascism." For the duration of the war, he would accept "Communist discipline," but only because it promised the best hope of military victory. Indeed, as Hemingway expanded his scope to reveal the Republic's grand military strategy, he depicted the Communist leadership as brutal, callous, and opportunistic. Jordan, the idealistic American, would accomplish his task, but the military bureaucracy would recklessly launch a doomed offensive. Here, Hemingway implied, were the reasons for the collapse of the Republic.

"It was going to be the greatest book," Fred Keller recalled, describing the prevailing sentiment among Lincoln veterans on the eve of the publication of *For Whom the Bell Tolls.* "It was going to vindicate us all. Now somebody was going to tell the true story about why we went to Spain." But instead, the novel touched sensitive political nerves. Not only did the novelist criticize the Communist party leadership; he also suggested that the American volunteers had gone to Spain for ambiguous, adventuristic purposes. Worried about the book's impact on public opinion, the New York veterans held two stormy meetings to evaluate the novel—many had not even read it—and then voted to condemn its message. Twenty-two Lincolns, including Keller and Edwin Rolfe, dissented, and many of them soon brought their personal regrets to Hemingway at his New York hotel. But even Keller signed the formal denunciation, written by Alvah Bessie.

"What emerges from your book," the VALB leadership declared in an open letter to the novelist, "is a picture so drastically mutilated and distorted (by errors of both omission and commission) as to slander the cause for which we fought, which the great majority of the democratic people of the world supported, and which you yourself honorably sustained both by your writing and your personal action." Listing a series of particulars, the Lincolns charged Hemingway with placing all the atrocity scenes on the Republican side; using the real names of Communist leaders, particularly André Marty, the organizer of the International Brigades, and Dolores Ibarruri, solely for purposes of condemning their decisions; and maligning the role of Soviet advisors to the Spanish Republic. Alvah Bessie, in an eloquent but denunciatory review in the *New Masses*, suggested that the novelist was "less concerned with the fate of the Spanish people, whom I am certain that he loves," than with the development of his characters, who, said Bessie, "are *himself*." In a prescient commentary, the critic also warned that Hemingway "will live to see every living and dead representative of the Abraham Lincoln Battalion attacked and slandered because of the great authority that attaches to Hemingway's name and his known connection with Spain."

In the ensuing debate, Milton Wolff, Hemingway's heroic civilian-soldier, stood with his battalion. In a personal letter, he accused the novelist of having been a "tourist" and a "rooter" in Spain. Hemingway promptly countered. "At the time the book deals with you did not know Marx from your ass. What would you like me to have done to aid the cause of the Spanish Republic that I did not do?" he wanted to know, a mounting fury driving his typewriter. "I think you are a prick if that makes it any easier for you to knife your friends in the back. To make it easier just know that the guy you are doing it to knew you, not your clippings, and that now I think you are a prick. . . . I always thought you were a great guy and now I think you are a prick." Within a month, Hemingway had second thoughts, expressing shame for calling Wolff names. "You are not a prick as you know damned well." Yet the novelist had been sorely hurt by the criticism of his book. While asking Edwin Rolfe to pass along some money to another veteran, Hemingway suggested he say that it had been found in the gutter. Vincent Sheean, Wolff's close friend and patron, questioned the Lincolns' need to excoriate the novel. "Except that it is not a C.P. [Communist] book," he exclaimed, "I don't for the life of me see what you've got against it."

More than abstract ideology, however, the denunciation of the novel reflected the immediate political crisis of 1940. Milton Wolff, who helped draft the attack, well understood the primary issues. "We who fought beside them know better than any one else the heroism of the Spanish people," he declared in an urgent appeal for funds to support a rescue ship to aid the Spanish refugees. "We, most of all, know how terribly they now suffer and starve in fascist dominated France, surrounded by bitterly vengeful enemies." Just one day later, Irving Goff transmitted a letter to all Lincoln veterans, requesting a rapid dissemination of the VALB critique of *For Whom the Bell Tolls*, "to undo, as much as possible, the vicious attack" on the Spanish cause. Those two statements were inextricably intertwined. Whatever Hemingway's intentions, the Lincolns could neither afford nor tolerate adverse publicity.

In attacking the novel, the VALB claimed to speak from experience. When the former commissar and ex-Communist Ralph Bates protested that the American volunteers remained ignorant of Spanish affairs and had "existed in a . . . political vacuum" in Spain, Alvah Bessie replied rhetorically, "How better can a . . . group of men get to know a people than in fighting with them, for them, beside them?" One answer came from an unexpected authority: the veteran Morris Maken (a.k.a. Mickenberg), who published a defense of Hemingway's accuracy and anti-fascist credentials. "Anti-Fascist means anti-totalitarian," he asserted, "which is why the Communist bureaucracy had to be dealt with in *For Whom the Bell Tolls*. For it was one of the most poignant and tragic experiences of the men who volunteered for the International Brigade to find out that they could be as greatly defeated by the remote control of the Kremlin as by the nonintervention policy itself." As for André Marty, said Maken, the French Communist was "a menace to any member of the rank and file with self-respect and a love of liberty."

Unlike Maken, most veterans accepted the voice of the Communist party. On the West Coast, Steve Nelson had originally reviewed the novel for the party newspaper *People's World* and drawn favorable conclusions. Although Nelson insisted that Hemingway had exaggerated the role of Soviet Communists in Spain and had distorted the portrait of Marty, he called the work "a monument in American literature." But not for long. Aware of the book's political ramifications, the American Communist party's central committee soon sent Roy Hudson to California to persuade Nelson to write a retraction. "On closer examination," Nelson explained a few months later, "it develops that Hemingway did not tell the truth. . . . Hemingway's people are not a revolutionary people. There is not even a hint of their social motivation." After listing several unfortunate depictions of the war, particularly the failure to distinguish the spontaneous violence of the Spanish peasants from Franco's terror, Nelson concluded that Hemingway was "negative and defeatist." It was therefore no accident, he said, "that this book is hailed in the literary salons of the bourgeoisie."

Such criticism, as all the veterans understood, was part of a larger effort to sway American public opinion about intervention in World War II. While the Roosevelt administration brought the country deeper into the Allied camp, proposing a Lend-Lease measure that would make the United States the "arsenal of democracy," the Lincolns could indirectly oppose this "undeclared belligerency" by attacking Hemingway on a subject they knew best. In February 1941, the former guerrilla soldier Irving Goff led 28 Lincoln veterans in a Peace Motorcade to Capitol Hill to lobby against Lend-Lease. Two weeks later, Milton Wolff followed him to Washington to protest the British refusal to allow a rescue ship to transport Spanish refugees to French Morocco.

The following month, Wolff and Goff, together with John Gates, high-lighted a literary symposium at the Hotel Diplomat in mid-Manhattan that examined the deficiencies of Hemingway's novel. Goff, who like the fictional hero Robert Jordan had worked behind enemy lines, criticized the novelist's ignorance of guerrilla operations. Although one historian has proposed that Hemingway based his fictional account on his own personal experiences with the guerrillas in Spain, Goff's analysis suggests otherwise. "Hemingway did not have an understanding of the nature of guerrilla warfare as being based on the problems of the land," he suggested. The novelist misunderstood the hit-and-run tactics that endeavored to move saboteurs as far as possible from the targets prior to the detonation of explosives. He ignored the crucial political work of the guerrillas. But the main problem, said Goff, was that the author treated the war from "a romantic adventuristic point of view rather than [as] the grim, practical war that it was."

To Milton Wolff, the chief failing of the novel stemmed from Hemingway's fatalism: "There is no hope, no fight, no will in the book." Essentially, said Wolff, Hemingway had misunderstood the character of the Lincoln volunteer. "The Americans there were not of Jordan's type. Those of Jordan's type ended up in Washington at the Dies Committee—McCuistion, Honeycombe and the rest, crying and squealing like rats, so they could wheedle their way into the good graces of the war mongers in America." John Gates, ever the commissar, discussed the book as a product of the conflict between capitalism and communism. "The main enemy of peace and democracy and of the Spanish people," he said, "is right here in America." Most VALB members shared these views. Robert Jordan's lovemaking in an Abercrombie and Fitch sleeping bag, during which his lover, Maria, felt the earth move, became a stock joke, used by the veterans to describe everything from artillery explosions to a bowel movement. "Something moved," explained Irving Fajans in a parody of "Jordanway's" gastric disorders, "but it was not the earth."

This extraordinary resentment toward Hemingway reflected not only the immediate political issues, nor simply personal disappointment with the novelist's views, but more profoundly the alienation of Communists from the cultural mainstream during the period of the pact. Looking back at his poetry of the post-Munich months, Edwin Rolfe offered no apology for his harsh voice, the "bitterness or despair, anger or recrimination" of his words. Instead, he chastised American leaders "who through cowardice, perhaps, or selfishness, or simply myopia, permitted the spread throughout the world of the gangrene to which so many millions of young men are being sacrificed today." To be sure, the veterans expected scorn from right-wingers and conservatives. Believing that American business interests were conspiring to bring the country into a war for profit, they warned, in Alvah Bessie's words, "that fascism is also flourishing here right now." The idea that "America must get ready to go to war and go soon . . . is what our homegrown fascists want us to believe." But now even liberals, especially liberals, had become ideological enemies.

Having completed his autobiographical *Men in Battle*, which described the last days of the Spanish war, Bessie became the theater reviewer for the *New Masses* and used his regular columns to analyze the liberal heresies of the latest cultural fare. "You will not hear any mention of the bombed cities of Germany, the dead children, the blinded men, the people mutilated by bombs dropped by the R.A.F.," he wrote of one anti-Nazi film; "the *mutual* suffering of the working people of both belligerents does not exist." Lillian Hellman's theatrical classic *Watch on the Rhine* exhibited, to Bessie's eye, the same liberal deficiencies. "What she has written," he lamented, "is an anti-Nazi play that . . . has already been misused by those who would like to . . . cajole us into imperialist war under the banner of fighting fascism in Germany." Bessie reserved all his praise for the products of Soviet cinema. "The Russians make pictures about *people*," he announced, "not about streamlined, highbreasted standardized automata who give the total impression of being activated by hidden strings—as indeed they are."

In his contempt for the products of the American mass media, Bessie expressed the orthodox Marxist perspective, but he brought to the ideological barricades a lyricism that was strongest when he was most indignant. At the Fourth Writers' Congress (publicized as the "Congress in Defense of Culture") in June 1941, Bessie drew from the ashes of the Spanish war a "touchstone" for contemporary politics: "If you ask yourself, who were the enemies of Spain," he suggested, "you will know your enemy today." Bessie's litany of conspiracy and betrayal, of governmental calculation and self-aggrandizement, condemned Allied propaganda, which now referred to the British Empire as the "Commonwealth of Nations" and excused the "mistake" of American policies "that raised the cynical embargo against Spain and lowered it for Britain. It was coldly calculated policy," he declared, "and it is still policy—the same policy that admits to our sanctuary the dregs of European nobility . . . , but excludes and hounds and beats and starves and murders the greatest anti-fascist writers (and fighters) of the eastern hemisphere." Bessie acknowledged the defection of some old allies—Vincent Sheean, John Dos Passos, Archibald MacLeish; these, he said, would be offset by those writers and artists who would not abandon "the same fight in which we enlisted the moment we first took up pen or brush to write or paint for the people of our world." Bessie presented the party line, to be sure: he was incisive about the flaws of the Western Allies and uncritical of the Soviet Union. But when he was done, he received a standing ovation; the speech would be published by public subscription, under the auspices of the League of American Writers and the American Peace Mobilization campaign.

The commitment of some Lincoln veterans to the Soviet Union transcended rhetorical posturing and brought them into the murky world of international espionage. At least two Americans who served in the secret special detachment outside Barcelona in 1938 returned to New York and began to cooperate with Soviet intelligence officials. One of them arranged to acquire the passports of American seamen through a veteran who worked for the National Maritime Union, exchanging cash for these documents. He also recruited Lincoln veterans to serve as couriers for a Soviet spy ring, which involved another of his comrades from Spain, Morris Cohen.

Cohen, who became one of the most important Soviet agents of the cold war, was born in New York in 1910. He studied as an undergraduate on a football scholarship in Mississippi, joined the Communist party while a student at the University of Illinois, and worked as an organizer for the YCL in New York prior to his enlistment in the Lincoln brigade under the name Israel Altman. Wounded on the Aragon front in 1937, he was chosen for the special detachment, where he learned radio transmission. "They were thinking of the future," he explained his assignment. "Fascism had to be fought, and the Soviet Union was . . . [the] leading opponent of fascism." After Spain, Cohen began to work for Soviet intelligence in New York. According to documents released by the KGB in 1992, Cohen managed to make contact with a physicist assigned to top-secret atom bomb research, and he arranged to provide scientific information to Soviet agents. Before the plan could be implemented, however, Cohen entered the U.S. Army, where he served in the quartermaster corps. In his absence, Cohen's wife, Lona, journeyed to New Mexico and acquired secret atom bomb information, which she gave to Soviet agents. According to recent testimony, this technical information made it possible for Soviet scientists to accelerate development of an atomic bomb. The Cohens' subsequent role in this project is not known. After his discharge from the army, Cohen took courses at Columbia University and taught elementary school in New York; his wife worked in a public library.

Soon after the arrest of Ethel and Julius Rosenberg on charges of espionage in 1950, the Cohens disappeared. Efforts by the FBI to link them to the notorious spy case did not succeed. But when the FBI seized the Soviet master spy Rudolph Abel in 1957, they found in his possession photographs of the Cohens. Four years later, British authorities arrested 50-year-old Peter Kroger and his wife, Helen, in London on charges of stealing naval secrets, including plans for a British atomic submarine. Although the couple posed as Australian book antiquarians, police found sophisticated espionage apparatus and a radio transmitter in the basement of their home. Upon further investigation, authorities learned that the Krogers and the Cohens were the same people. Sentenced to twenty years in prison, the couple was later exchanged for a British businessman held by the Soviet Union. Lona Cohen died in Moscow in 1992. A lonely Morris Cohen survives in a facility run by the Russian intelligence services. Their willingness to undertake such dangerous, controversial work reflected the ideological fervor of some of the Lincolns. And it

was not very long before U.S. officials were making similar overtures to selected veterans.

"The veterans have special responsibilities," Milton Wolff reminded his
comrades in May 1941. "The American people have learned to respect our
anti-fascist sincerity and political alertness. It is, therefore, already our obligation to take an even more active role in the struggle for peace." But Wolff's
public position, orthodox by Communist standards, conflicted with his private activities. By the spring of 1941, several Lincolns were expressing dissatisfaction with a policy of neutrality while Nazi forces spread through Europe; and although party discipline kept most veterans publicly silent, a few
individuals defied the consensus and enlisted in the U.S. Army. "I was castigated for it," remembered Jack Shafran, who even wore his uniform at antiwar meetings; but he was not expelled from the party. The German invasion
of Yugoslavia in April 1941, aimed in the general direction of the Soviet Union,
aroused further concern about the course of the war. John Gates recalled conversations in the "inner circles" of the YCL about "the potentially anti-Soviet
orientation" of Nazi Germany. "We even felt that the 'unjust character of the
war' was changing, and hence some felt our own policies ought to be changing. But," he emphasized, "it was characteristic of the Communist movement
that while much discussion went on in private, and even in the formal organized committees, little of it was allowed to come before the membership or
be given public expression."

In this period of unstated uneasiness, Milton Wolff received a message from
his friend Dinah Sheean saying that William Donovan, President Roosevelt's
troubleshooter in Europe, requested a private meeting at his office. The next
day, Wolff visited Donovan's chambers on Wall Street. After minimal pleas-
antries, Donovan told Wolff that British intelligence officers, working in the
United States, wanted assistance in establishing contact with resident aliens
from southern and eastern Europe—Italians, Greeks, Yugoslavs, Austrians,
and Hungarians—who would be willing to help the partisan resistance fighters in German-occupied countries. Donovan asked if the Lincoln veterans,
particularly those with language skills, would participate in such an operation. Wolff agreed to find out. He knew that before undertaking such work
individual volunteers would want the sanction of the Communist party. Steve
Nelson referred him to Eugene Dennis, an important party official. After a

brief delay, Dennis gave his consent and assured Wolff that the party would cooperate, provided the scheme was kept secret. According to Wolff, in other words, the highest level of the American Communist party authorized clandestine operations that violated the avowed noninterventionist line.

Secret activities were not unusual in Communist circles. Shortly after the outbreak of World War II, party leaders had feared that their opposition to the Allies might lead to a wave of government persecution, including a ban on the Communist party. To protect the leadership, therefore, party heads decided to create a shadow organization that could function underground. Several Lincoln veterans, including former commissars Steve Nelson and Saul Wellman, conveniently "disappeared" for several months, waiting to resume an active role if the government arrested the regular leadership. "Life on the shelf was closer to a vacation than a harried underground existence," recalled Nelson, who used the time to write a book-length memoir of his experiences in Spain.

The conclusion of the Soviet-Finnish war in March 1940 ended the underground experiment. Soon afterward, however, the party sent guerrilla expert Irving Goff on a mission to investigate pro-fascist "synarchista" organizations in Texas, California, and Mexico. Posing as a newspaper reporter, Goff filed regular reports about these groups with party leaders, but failed in his effort to link them with the right-wing group America First. (Other Communists, according to one veteran, had infiltrated the isolationist group America First to help block aid to the Allies.) Individual Lincoln veterans also accepted special assignments to communicate with Spanish exiles in Latin America or to bring refugees into the United States illegally. Such efforts remained amateurish and anarchic, less the stuff of sophisticated espionage than of blundering, misunderstanding, and foiled connections. "It was the blind leading the blind," admitted Wellman many years later. "But we were not paranoid. The surveillance and harassment of Communists continued during the apparently 'honeymoon' days of the U.S.-Soviet struggle against Hitler."

The party's acceptance of Donovan's overture to Wolff thus represented an audacious departure from its previous distrust. But with permission granted, Donovan introduced Wolff to two British agents who had offices in Rockefeller Center. To Wolff they looked like characters from central casting: one, named Bryce, tall, good-looking, a member of the Tory party; the other, called Bailey, short, heavy, a Labourite. They explained their mission directly. The British needed reliable anti-fascists to place behind enemy lines in Greece, Yugoslavia, and the Balkans. To avoid detection, these men had to be fluent in the local languages, capable of blending into the countryside. They also had to be politically acceptable—that is, party members or at least party sympathizers—so that they could collaborate with the left-wing leadership of the partisan underground. Veterans of the International Brigades, especially those born in eastern Europe or raised in ethnic families, seemed ideally suited to the task.

So, at a time when the Communist party officially opposed American involvement in the war, Wolff started a recruitment program on behalf of British intelligence. With a salary of $80 a week plus expenses and a commercial artist's office in Manhattan as a cover, he began to meet with veterans who had contacts in the ethnic communities of the Northeast. Some of them turned him down; they had ample reasons to distrust the British. But during the next year—well after the United States finally entered the war—Wolff mustered a wide variety of volunteers on the basis of their common experience in Spain. "They trusted me a great deal," he said admiringly. "They were putting their lives on the line because I was asking them to."

On a trip to Detroit, for example, Wolff contacted Mirko Markovicz, formerly commander of the Washington battalion. The Yugoslav American expressed doubts about cooperating with the British, but he introduced Wolff to other ethnic veterans in the area. One recruit was George Delitch, a 40-year-old Yugoslav metal worker who had recently been held on Ellis Island for possible deportation. "If ever there was a rugged-looking character," wrote Wolff, "Delitch is it. His head was built sort of pineapple shape; wide brows . . . dull black hair swept straight back; prominent straight black bushy brows." He had served in the American army and participated in numerous labor struggles before volunteering for Spain. Captured during the Great Retreats, he had also survived as a prisoner of war at San Pedro.

"The work proposed was of the risky variety," Wolff explained, "involving . . . a parachute trip into enemy held territory. It was also risky for a guy like Delitch because Delitch is a Communist . . . because he was going to be under British Army orders and they are not particularly partial towards Communists. But Delitch went right ahead and agreed. After all America hadn't yet reached the shooting stage and he was spoiling to get into battle. . . . So Delitch went ahead and rounded up about twelve of his buddies—coal miners, machinists, seamen, and whatnot . . . and off they went." Dropped into Yugoslavia, these volunteers worked with the partisans under Marshal Tito, himself a former Comintern official who had organized the International Brigades in Paris. Several years later, Wolff met a Croatian who described Delitch's exploits: "blew up more enemy installations in five months than anyone else." After the war, however, the Tito regime charged Delitch with being an American spy; he was executed around 1946.

Before Pearl Harbor, few Lincolns knew about Wolff's activities. While individual veterans chafed at the restraints imposed by the Communist party, the VALB continued to focus on helping former comrades from the Spanish war. When French authorities again announced the closing of the refugee camps and the transfer of Spaniards and International Brigaders to North Africa or, worse, to their homelands in Italy and Germany, the veterans organized another protest delegation to Washington, D.C. "This affair is of no direct concern to our government," responded a State Department official; American citizens were not involved. At the French embassy, a third-ranking official denied the truth of the deportation plan. Later, the veterans learned that this same official had once commanded one of the camps. Such confrontations won scant attention in the mainstream media. But they contributed to a frustration and an anger that defined the Lincolns as outsiders, if not as victims.

This attitude dominated a national convention of Lincoln veterans held in Chicago during Memorial Day weekend 1941. As in most VALB activities of this interwar period, the agenda of this meeting followed the Communists' noninterventionist program, but always placed particular emphasis on the Spanish experience as a rationale and justification for that position. In a blistering keynote address, written by David McKelvey White and delivered, ironically, by Milton Wolff, the veterans indicted Roosevelt for the failure of his foreign policy. The president had supported nonintervention and an embargo; he had backed the appeasement of Hitler and Mussolini; he had ignored the plight of refugees. In this situation the Lincolns bore special responsibilities; their prestige demanded they speak against the administration. "No one [else] can so justly . . . accuse Franklin D. Roosevelt of flouting the expressed wishes and betraying the best interests and welfare of the American people."

Such allegations would bring harsh consequences. The veterans would be called fifth columnists. The government had already commenced the attack: FBI raids, Dies hearings, indictments of individual veterans by local authorities. But the Lincolns, said White and Wolff, had no choice but to demand peace. "We fight against the involvement of our country in an imperialist war from which the great majority of the American people can derive only misery, suffering, and death," they declared. "We stubbornly oppose every move of Roosevelt and the war-mongers in this direction."

Five weeks later, Wolff was saying something quite different: "If need be," he assured a convention of the American Youth Congress in July 1941, "we veterans are prepared to march again." In that brief interval, the whole world had changed. On June 21, 1941, German armies had invaded the Soviet Union; the imperialist war, fought between capitalist nations, had become a war for the survival of the Soviet Union. On the night of the invasion Archie Brown attended an emergency party meeting in San Francisco. Without a formal party statement on the war, some Communists hesitated to endorse aid for the Allies. Brown, at his oratorical best, argued them down. "There was one war," he later said, "and if giving bundles for Britain helped defeat the Nazis that is what had to be done." In New York, veteran George Watt arrived at an emergency meeting early the next morning with John Gates and other YCL leaders. He remembered a single sentiment: "We all felt relief. We felt like we had come home again." Within 24 hours, the American Communist party— and the Veterans of the Abraham Lincoln Brigade—had charted a new course. "This is our war," the Lincolns said. "The war for the destruction of fascism. And we stand ready to volunteer again, our work and if need be our lives."

For the next six months, the Lincolns waged a war of words on the home front, pleading for American interventionism. Veteran Al Prago's pamphlet *We Fought Hitler*, published by the VALB six weeks after the Nazi invasion, ignored their previous position, insisting that the Lincolns had vowed they "would never, never stop fighting . . . against Hitlerism." As German armies blitzed through the Soviet Union, the VALB issued another pamphlet, *Western Front Now!* Written by Milton Wolff, the tract advocated an invasion of the European continent to relieve the eastern front. To those who argued that such an attack was premature, Wolff insisted that "where the social need is urgent and the political will exists, the military means can be found." Indeed, he proposed that the Allies launch their attack in Spain, where a friendly population would surely support their efforts. At a time when Roosevelt was already waging an undeclared naval war in the Atlantic, Wolff demanded even bolder support for the British, and in November 1941 he called for an immediate declaration of war against Hitler's Germany. One month later, his wish had been achieved.

"We who fought the Fascist Axis in Spain proudly volunteer to march shoulder to shoulder with our fellow Americans," Wolff wrote to President Roosevelt on December 8, 1941, "for the final crushing of this menace to the independence and democracy of America and all people." Black veteran Vaughn Love ignored such formalities: "The very next day I went down to volunteer for the army. I didn't ask anybody because I knew that was where I belonged." At last he could assert his independence from the party's nonintervention. "I knew since the end of the war in Spain that we would have to face those bastards ourselves." Nearly all the veterans shared that belief. "We call for National Unity of all anti-fascist forces in support of the war effort," declared the *Volunteer for Liberty*. "The America First Committee—the American Fifth Columnists—must be exposed and treated as traitors to the nation." Behind the spirit of patriotism, nearly two years of noninterventionist rhetoric would be swept away. But the Lincolns, like other prominent Communists, could not so easily dispose of their history.

/7

Premature Anti-Fascists

Ten days after Japanese bombers attacked Pearl
Harbor, former brigade commissar John Gates
stood up at a meeting of the New York Communist party
and announced his enlistment in the U.S. Army. As
enthusiastic comrades rose to their feet, Gates solemnly raised his right hand and recited the Pledge of
Allegiance to the flag of the United States. The ritual
symbolized the Communist party's commitment to the
Grand Alliance against fascism. (A decade later,
Gates's gesture would contribute to the movement to
add the phrase "under God" to the pledge, the assumption being that no authentic Communist would
affirm those words even for purposes of deceit!) For
Lincoln veterans like Gates, America's entry into World
War II abruptly ended nearly two years of political
isolation. "We . . . are proud to give our support to
our government in this hour," declared the *Volunteer
for Liberty*, "as part of the American people."

"I am not a simple kid, hell bent on adventure,"
Milton Wolff explained of his decision to abandon intelligence recruiting for the British in order to enlist
as a private in the infantry. "I am a man who has

something to offer, a special talent . . . with a special reason for offering it, with a special hatred towards some and with a special love towards many. . . . That is why I am here. I just didn't leave a job and a couple of girlfriends, you know." America's entry into the war appealed not only to the political instincts of the Spanish war veterans but also to their self-image as "fighting anti-fascists"; and those who were Communists saw themselves, once again, in the vanguard of warriors.

This feeling of self-importance was reinforced by John Dollard, the distinguished sociologist at Yale University's Institute of Human Relations. As part of the mobilization of academia, Dollard had become interested in evaluating the psychological qualities that produced good soldiers. But his efforts to work with World War I veterans at the American Legion post in New Haven brought disappointing results. In the face of "the dive bomber, the Blitz, and the modern tank," he found, the experiences of the old doughboys appeared largely irrelevant. The veterans of the Spanish war, by contrast, could offer something unique.

So Dollard appealed to the VALB for assistance. With a grant from the Rockefeller Foundation, the approval of the Communist party, and, unbeknownst to the veterans, the consent of the FBI, Dollard interviewed twenty "representative" Lincolns to develop a formal questionnaire. Most responded candidly about their personal experiences, though some showed embarrassment at Dollard's efforts to correlate battlefield valor with sexual activity. The sociologist then drafted a 44-page document that took about five hours to fill out, and he hired Lincoln veteran John V. Murra, a graduate student of anthropology, to administer the survey to three hundred veterans. The study, published under the title *Fear in Battle* in 1943, delineated the varieties of combat stress and offered recommendations for controlling such problems. Praising Dollard's analysis, the army's chief of morale services urged American officers to use the findings in training soldiers.

For the Lincoln veterans, the urge to fight against fascism stemmed from many motives—personal, political, ideological: to seek revenge for Spain; to free the Spanish people from the bonds of Franco; to create a world without war; in the long run, perhaps, to advance communism. More than the average American soldier, they yearned to go into battle, to engage the enemy and destroy him. At a time when popular mythology portrayed the American G.I.

as a civilian in uniform, thinking only of returning home, the Lincolns spoke heroically of fighting until they had scourged the last vestiges of fascism from the earth. "'Home' is the slogan of victory," Wolff observed with dismay; "a stranger slogan never existed—for though . . . men have often fought for home, never did they raise it as a battle cry. It used to be the slogan of deserters. Today it's the cry of fighters—or is it?" Later, in Italy, when he learned that the fascists had executed prisoners of war, including two men he had known in Spain, Wolff said he "didn't cry or get drunk or go into a rage. What for? It's part of the whole thing, isn't it? My hate is with me always; it needs no jolts." This hate, this numbing passion, Wolff shared with many of his comrades from Spain.

Veterans of the Lincoln brigade rallied to the colors after Pearl Harbor. The exact figures remain elusive. Many of the old soldiers had already broken or lost contact with the VALB office in New York. Many bore Spanish wounds that disqualified them from military service, and some were too old to fight. But at the *minimum*, 425 veterans served in the armed forces and about 100 more sailed in the merchant marine. During the course of the war the Lincolns fought on every front—and they died around the world, too: Ben Gardner in France; Joe Hecht in Germany; Larry Lustgarten in the mountains of northern India; Joe Gordon on the frigid Murmarsk run to the Soviet Union; Sid Kurtz and Dave Altman in the jungles of the South Pacific. In all, seventeen were killed in the fighting, four while sailing through combat zones at sea. Too many to count were wounded and maimed or left broken in health. And besides Purple Hearts, they won many decorations for valor—Distinguished Service Crosses, Silver Stars, Bronze Stars, battlefield promotions— probably in disproportionate numbers. For in World War II the Lincolns showed not only remarkable personal courage, but an impressive dedication to the fight. As in Spain, they volunteered for dangerous assignments—as individuals, to be sure, but so often and so repeatedly as to constitute a peculiar fighting breed. Even Harry Haywood, disgraced by his cowardice in Spain, joined the merchant marine at age 45 and then volunteered for the most dangerous voyages to the Soviet Union. In this war, the Lincolns had much to lose, much to gain, much to prove.

Their glory sometimes seemed immeasurable. Herman "Butch" Boettcher, a German-born volunteer who had gone to Spain to serve with the Socialist Debs column, expressed intense bitterness and shame for what had happened to his native land. When news of the Munich conference reached the Lincolns in Spain, his comrade John Rossen recalled,

> Some cursed bitterly
> And flung down their rifles
> Many sank to the ground
> Weeping unashamed tears.
> As for you, Butch
> Only the muscles around mouth and eyes
> Tightened and set
> And more grimly did you bend
> Over the pistol you were cleaning.

As a resident alien of the United States, Boettcher had trouble persuading American immigration officials to allow him to return to his home in San Francisco. But one month after Pearl Harbor he enlisted as a private. "I've always hated dictators," he said. "Now at least we have bullets." Within the year, he was leading forays against the Japanese through the jungles of the South Pacific islands. Widely known as "the one-man army of Buna," he commanded a squad that split the Japanese lines and held a crucial salient for seven days. Boettcher won a promotion to captain as well as the Distinguished Service Cross. *Life* magazine featured his personal exploits. The U.S. Congress passed a special law making him a citizen, but Boettcher missed his award ceremony because he remained in the field training a reconnaissance mission. After recovering from serious wounds, Boettcher led a team behind enemy lines in New Guinea for 57 days. On all patrols he served as point man. Not only did he succeed in dismantling Japanese bridges, but he saved the pieces to reassemble them after the Americans occupied the territory. He also personally captured a Japanese captain on Leyte Island, earning a second DSC plus three Purple Hearts. Commanding still another operation behind Japanese lines, Boettcher died in combat at Leyte in January 1945. He was 35 years old. "The hardest battle for us," he wrote in his last letter to the VALB office, "will be to win the peace, to overcome discrimination, injustice, poverty, insecurity."

Such idealism inspired other Lincoln veterans to perform similarly impressive military exploits. Bob Thompson, among those few who crossed into

Spain twice to fight against fascism, showed his heroism in New Guinea when he swam across an enemy-held river and proceeded to destroy four Japanese pillboxes. He too won a Distinguished Service Cross, and then he shocked a reporter by admitting that his civilian job was "organizer for the Young Communist League of Ohio." Wounded in action and suffering from malaria, Thompson returned home with permanent disabilities. Jerry Weinberg proved less fortunate. As a bombardier on a B-24 Liberator, he said he "always wanted to get back at some of those bastards who strafed us." He participated in the bombing raids on the Ploesti oil fields in Rumania, earning a Distinguished Flying Cross. The action, he said, "made up for" Spain. Forced to land in neutral Turkey, Weinberg might have remained in safe detention. But instead he escaped through Egypt and returned to England to fly again. He died over Germany in 1943. Another Lincoln flyer, former battalion commissar George Watt, parachuted from a stricken B-17 over the Low Countries in 1943, made contact with the Belgian underground, and escaped from German-occupied territory by crossing the Pyrenees into Spain. These are only a few of the stories of extraordinary bravery involving the Lincolns.

The blend of courage and political conviction emerged dramatically in the contribution of Lincoln veterans to the Office of Strategic Services (OSS), led by General William "Wild Bill" Donovan. At Donovan's request, Milton Wolff not only had recruited ethnic veterans to work for British intelligence in 1941, but also had facilitated contact between the State Department and the Communist party in order to establish intelligence networks in Latin America. When the British expressed interest in developing a cadre to work behind enemy lines in the Egyptian desert, Wolff approached the guerrilla fighter he knew best, Irving Goff. On Goff's advice, Wolff invited other Lincoln veterans to participate in the group, including Bill Aalto, Milton Felsen, Mike Jiminez, Vince Lossowski, and Alfred Tanz. One other volunteer also demanded to be enrolled, and Wolff passed the name to the British agents, but in the end they rejected Evelyn Hutchins without explanation, probably because of her sex. "She was furious," Wolff recalled.

Pearl Harbor abruptly terminated the Egyptian scheme. Donovan intervened, turned the project into an American operation, and sent the Lincolns, together with other volunteers, into a training program near Washington, D.C., at what is now Camp David. There they engaged in a vigorous regimen of running, rope climbing, swimming, shooting, parachute jumping, and gymnastics. The Lincolns, the only members of the group with military experience, excelled in these activities. But the presence of so many corporate executives and political conservatives in this OSS outfit greatly disturbed Goff. When Milton Wolff expressed interest in joining the group, Goff protested the influence of "monarchists, royalists, and bankers" and urged him to stay away. Wolff would soon have good reason to regret that advice.

With the Egyptian plans cancelled, Donovan decided to use the Lincoln recruits to develop both an intelligence operation and a paramilitary group to work inside Spain. Hoping to take advantage of Republican guerrilla activities against the Franco regime, Donovan wanted to build an organizational structure and plant ammunition dumps so that Spanish soldiers could be mobilized into action if Germany attempted to move against the British citadel at Gibraltar. Goff, according to the scheme, would enter Spain as a chauffeur for the U.S. ambassador; others would work in various consulates. The Lincolns yearned for this opportunity to fight against Franco, but State Department officials, fearful of jeopardizing the delicate balance of neutrality in Madrid, thwarted the project. Donovan then began scheming for an intelligence operation in Latin America, where the Lincolns might form friendships with Spanish seamen in the port cities. This operation, too, never developed. The Allied invasion of North Africa in the fall of 1942 demanded new orders.

As the only OSS volunteers with guerrilla experience, Irving Goff and Bill Aalto had assumed unofficial leadership of the Lincoln recruits. But just before leaving the United States for duty in North Africa, the two parted ways in a crisis of conscience that spoke volumes about the values—and the limits— of the radical movements of the 1940's. Ironically, Goff and Aalto had experienced their greatest military success in Spain as a team, when they hovered stark naked against the Mediterranean cliffs after liberating a fascist prison. After Spain, they had remained close friends, socializing together and sharing speakers' platforms. One evening Aalto confessed to Goff that he was a homosexual. Goff was startled: "How could a big, athletic guy like that be one of those?" he wondered. The knowledge did not alter his opinion of Aalto's abilities, and Goff recommended Aalto for the OSS. But he apparently felt uneasy about that decision. Goff eventually confided his concerns to the other OSS Lincolns. Determined to verify the rumor, they decided to follow Aalto off the base. One night they observed him entering a honkey-tonk bar in Washington and later saw him leave with his arm around a sailor. After a brief discussion, they reported the situation to Donovan.

The head of the OSS seemed untroubled by the information. But when the Lincolns expressed their doubts, Donovan agreed to remove Aalto from the team and assigned him to a training mission at Camp Meade. Years later, Aalto's roommate, Vince Lossowski, remembered their last conversation: "Bill, I'm sorry for what I did. But I had to do it. Have you ever thought of seeing a psychiatrist?" Aalto, in tears, could only reply: "You don't know what you're talking about."

Six weeks later, while training soldiers in demolition work, Aalto saw someone drop a live grenade and lunged for it. Before he could throw it away, the bomb exploded, severing his arm at the wrist. The accident added to his misery. But Aalto remained close to the veterans. During the war, he attended VALB social functions, where he reportedly drank heavily, and participated in various political activities involving Spain. With the help of his disability payments and the G.I. Bill, he returned to school, studied poetry, published a few pieces in the *New Masses*, and graduated from Columbia University. After the war, the Communist party expelled him for refusing to relinquish his homosexuality. Aalto then traveled in Europe, preferring the company of gay poets (including W. H. Auden). But he himself did little writing, tended toward alcoholism, and frequently became violent. During this period, American intelligence officers approached him in Italy, asking for information about his former associates, including Goff. To obtain compliance, they halted his disability payments; the State Department lifted his passport, forcing him to return to the United States. Aalto steadfastly refused to cooperate (and took pains to assure Goff that he was secure). After Aalto's legal protests, the government restored his disability payments and passport. But then Aalto contracted leukemia. He died in 1958, in his early forties.

The tragedy of Bill Aalto underscored the social prejudices of an earlier generation of radicals. In retrospect, all the veterans involved in the situation expressed remorse at how they had destroyed the life of a good comrade. But their views mirrored the values of American society. Ironically, it was a perspective often shared by the homosexuals in the Left. Several Lincoln veterans admitted to being gay—one former intelligence officer claimed to know at least a dozen in Spain, and probably there were others. One, apparently, was a suicide.

David McKelvey White, son of an Ohio governor and instructor of English at Brooklyn College, had assumed leadership positions in the Friends of the Abraham Lincoln Brigade and, later, the VALB. During World War II, he emerged as a tireless advocate of the Spanish Republic. He gave speeches, wrote pamphlets, and served as a lobbyist to block the admission of Franco's Spain into the newly forming United Nations. But as the war drew to a close, he became troubled by an unsuccessful homosexual affair. According to a close associate, the party also raised questions about his lifestyle, summoning him for discussions. One day in the summer of 1945 White did not come to work at the VALB office. A colleague found him dead in his bed. "The pressure was too much for him," said the person who identified his body. He left behind an envelope with cash for the Lincoln brigade and no note. The VALB announced that White had died of a heart attack at the age of 42. Most veterans never learned the truth of his death. It was an embarrassment best concealed—a failure of the camaraderie for which the Lincolns were so famous.

By the time Bill Aalto started to write poetry with his left hand, however, most veterans of the Lincoln brigade were discovering another form of discrimination, which severely restricted their advancement in the American armed services. The pattern began with the earliest volunteers, among them, ironically, Aalto himself. A private in the U.S. Army at the time of Pearl Harbor, Aalto found himself on a mysterious blacklist that barred him from combat assignments; in fact, "a higher up" had removed him from guard duties at Fort Knox and denied him even the status of corporal. Similarly, John Gates's application for officer training was promptly denied. When his unit prepared for overseas duty, a telegram from the adjutant general's office in Washington, D.C., ordered him transferred into a service group. Intervention by Gates's superior officers—a captain, a major, and a lieutenant colonel—brought no changes. He was assigned to spring cleaning and planting grass. Not until the very end of the war did Gates receive orders to go overseas.

Irving Fajans, by contrast, moved from basic training into officer candidate school at Camp Benning in Georgia. The instructors evaluated his work as outstanding. But the day before graduation, Fajans learned he had been dropped from the program, no explanation given. Two weeks later, the army assigned him to counting linens. In a subsequent interview with military intelligence, he was taunted by such comments as the following: Who had sold him "the bill of goods" that induced him to go to Spain? "We're realists—your saying you went to fight fascism isn't convincing realistically." "What would you do if the United States went to war with Russia?" Thanks to a more liberal policy within the OSS, Fajans, like Aalto, eventually found an alternative assignment.

Other cases of discrimination proved even more bizarre. After being rejected for officer candidate school and for flyer training, Larry Lustgarten was arrested and kept in a guardhouse in New Mexico for a week, allegedly because he had fought in Spain as a pilot under the name Larry Lindbergh. Only after continuous protests through the military bureaucracy did he win the right to fight overseas. He died in a plane crash in India. Jack Lucid, Eugene Morse, and Emil Churchik all found themselves moved from combat groups to Camp Ripley, Minnesota, and assigned to a company of aliens and suspected subversives, whose duties consisted of sorting garbage and collecting scrap metal.

"I hadn't looked forward to being in the Wehrmacht," Lucid wrote of his outfit. "Anti-Semitism is the core of their intellectual processes." These soldiers were not permitted to carry rifles. When Lucid protested to his commanding officer that one of the men was a Nazi, the C.O. replied, "You should talk; you're a goddamned Communist!" Eventually, Lucid managed to transfer into the Rangers and won a Silver Star in Italy. Meanwhile, Robert Colodny gave such good army lectures on Axis penetration of the Western Hemisphere that his colonel became convinced he had participated in that type of subversion. "Don't you know that I was a volunteer in the International Brigades during the Spanish Civil War?" the exasperated Colodny replied. The colonel responded, "What a wonderful cover story." Soon Colodny was transferred under guard to a stockade for political suspects. He ended the war in virtual exile in the Aleutians. Joe Hecht finished first in his class in the medical corps but was not passed. Instead, the army sent him to a hospital in Pennsylvania, where he was assigned to mopping floors and polishing doorknobs. Hecht continued to fight for the right to bear arms at the front. By 1945, he got his wish. "I've been given a rifle, I'm a soldier!" he exclaimed. A few weeks later, the army awarded him a Silver Star in Germany, posthumously.

Milton Wolff, on Goff's advice, had purposely avoided the perquisites of the OSS. He considered himself an infantryman and wanted desperately to participate in the ground war in Europe. Believing that a second front would open during the summer of 1942, Wolff and fellow veteran Gerald Cook enlisted together on the anniversary of the invasion of the Soviet Union. At Fort Dix, an intelligence officer interviewed them about their political views and their involvement in the Spanish war. Then, the two rookies languished at the base, waiting for an assignment to basic training. Inquiries about the unusual delay brought mystified responses, until Wolff mentioned to a clerk that they had been in Spain. "Oh, that's a different story!" exclaimed the friendly sergeant, who finally found their records in a special file. A few nights later, Wolff and Cook sneaked into the office and read their papers. Printed on the corners were the letters "PA." The next day, a clerk explained the initials: "premature anti-fascists." Thus they discovered a euphemism that would become part of anti-Communist rhetoric for the next decade. Service in the Spanish war qualified the Lincolns for that honor.

Wolff and Cook consequently arrived at Camp Wheeler, Georgia, as part of a group of noncombatants, "a batallion of misfits, enemy aliens and suspected Nazis," Wolff lamented. He promptly commenced a series of requests for transfers that would last for two years. After joining a regular unit, Wolff and Cook received permission to enter officer candidate school. But they arrived at Camp Benning just as Irving Fajans was being unceremoniously dropped from the program. Wolff struggled against what he viewed as an inevitable frustration. "I will be number one man in the class," he vowed. "I owe it to the men who once accepted my leadership, who entrusted their lives to me. What else can I do? certainly that little bit." But the abrupt dismissal of Cook a few weeks later undermined his confidence. "The possibility that I have made the greatest blunder of my life is not an easy thing to take lying down," he wrote.

Midway through the course, Wolff's captain summoned him into his office and removed an American flag from a desk drawer. "Is this your flag?" he asked.

"Yes, sir," said Wolff.

"Are you prepared to defend this flag?"

"Yes, sir."

"I don't know what those sons of bitches in Washington are up to," the captain concluded, sliding the flag back into the drawer.

Two weeks later, a special order bounced Wolff from the program, placing him in noncombatant status. His frustrated captain waved a bulging file at Wolff: "Every word of it is in your favor. I have done all I could to keep you here." Wolff immediately began to pull every string he could imagine, including making contact with Dinah Sheean, his private link to General Donovan. Meanwhile, he worked within the army bureaucracy, trying to wrangle a transfer to a service group headed toward Europe. Instead, the army sent him to the West Coast, apparently to exile in the Aleutians (where several other frustrated Lincolns spent the war). In Seattle, Wolff managed to get into a harbor patrol outfit ("I am really too disgusted") and then into a longshoreman's group. Suddenly, his outfit headed toward the East Coast, but not, as it turned out, to the European theater. After nearly three months' travel, Wolff arrived in India, where he was assigned to unloading ships and left to gripe about military inefficiency. He continued to pull strings, gaining a transfer to a combat outfit in Burma. There, at last, two years after he had first enlisted, he got to see action, fighting under General Joseph Stilwell on long-range patrols against the Japanese. And, to his delight, orders from General Donovan finally reached him. He would be joining the contingent of Lincoln veterans he had originally recruited for the OSS in Italy.

The routine discrimination against the Lincolns accentuated the burdens faced by African-American veterans in the ranks. Even before the outbreak of World War II, problems of racism had undermined support for the antifascist effort among American blacks, and Lincoln veterans had agitated to overcome those antiwar attitudes. Despite his ignominious return from Spain, Harry Haywood had coauthored the party publication *Is Japan the Champion of the Colored Races?* in order to counter Japanese propaganda aimed at black audiences. Similarly, veteran Eluard Luchelle McDaniels, working as a cook in the merchant marine, embarked on a one-man crusade to connect the war against fascism with the demand for equal rights.

Having narrowly escaped the Japanese attack on the Philippines in December 1941, McDaniels was sailing home via the Indian Ocean when his ship landed in South Africa. On leave in Durban, McDaniels led his fellow sailors in a sit-down protest at Woolworth's segregated lunch counter. "I sat down there and demanded to be waited on and said I would sit there forever until I got equal rights. And I got them." McDaniels then integrated the local movie theater and led a contingent of black seamen through the streets to demand equal treatment. "We went right down the line, one place after an-other—told them we were Americans sailing a ship to help win a war for de-mocracy and human rights, and demanded to be treated as human beings," he reported. "We didn't threaten or get tough. We talked about the war—talked about their own danger and the importance of people standing together to fight fascism. They served us every place we went. They looked worried and con-fused, but they served us."

Back in the United States, McDaniels headed for his native Mississippi, where he addressed white audiences about the importance of extending civil rights on the home front to reinforce the war effort. "I told them how we have to stand together and build a human brotherhood and they applauded," he remembered. "It made me feel happy. . . . Jim Crow is still on the loose. But it made me feel we're at least pointed in the right direction." Such cautious optimism echoed through the Left. "We know that goose stepping maniacs would carry out with glee jim crow and violation of Negro women," said black veteran Bert Jackson in the *Volunteer for Liberty*. "We also know that death to fascism means a new life for the Negro people."

Where black leaders of World War I had embraced the slogan "close ranks" and reserved their agitation for the indefinite future, blacks of the 1940's adopted the "double V" campaign ("Victory" overseas and at home), de-manding equal rights as a reward for their patriotism. "And we don't need socialism (though it would be nice)," observed Alvah Bessie, "to achieve . . . a mixed brigade of black and white soldiers." Within the army, individual veterans vigorously challenged the segregated system on numerous occa-sions. "As long as the Negro is treated as a second class citizen and falsely pictured by prejudice as naturally inferior to the white," declared the *Volun-teer for Liberty* in the aftermath of race rioting in Detroit, "so long is democ-racy, progress, and victory over tyranny endangered." In California, nurse Ruth Davidow helped organize a strike of the marine cooks' and stewards' union to stop segregated employment practices. Later, she successfully led protests against racial discrimination in a local housing project. "We didn't initiate [the protest]," she recalled, "but we didn't run away from it either. It was a question of standing up or not!" Such efforts, part of a larger rejection of rac-ism in American society during the war, provided an important bridge be-tween the mass protests of the Depression era and the later civil rights move-ment.

The primary victims of military racism—the black soldiers in the ranks—objected bitterly to their second-class assignments. "Not only were we Jim Crowed into Jim Crow units," remembered Crawford Morgan, "but all of the nasty jobs . . . were handed to . . . the Negroes." At Fort Dix, he drew K.P. every day, while veteran Joe Taylor suffered through mosquito control duties—"quite a let down," he said, "when you think those of us who went to Spain *fought* in the army." As they lamented the wastefulness of their service, these volunteers also agitated to overcome white prejudices. Invited to lecture to a group of officers about the battle of Brunete, Walter Garland observed that "it was probably the first time any of them had had a chance to listen to a Negro at all." Later, he developed an improvement in the basic machine-gun sight. And when an M.P. referred to a fellow soldier as a "black bastard," Garland joined in the ensuing fight and was arrested. "However, as a result of some straight talking," he reported, "we were absolved of all 'guilt.'"

Vaughn Love remembered having to contend with a peculiar dilemma: steering a course between "the white officers who were for business as usual, and the Negro troops who thought this was not our war." As chief instructor of a segregated quartermaster unit, Love introduced political lectures to awaken black pride. His talks proved so effective that his commanding officer permitted Love to address white soldiers as well. He also strengthened morale by providing basic military training to a corps normally exempted from such instruction. "I didn't have any military training about the articles of war," he explained, "but I studied it, and studied it . . . and gave it to the soldiers straight." Drawing from his experiences in Spain, Love lectured on defense against tanks and aerial bombardments. He took his men to the rifle range, where they scored the highest marks in the camp; led them on bivouacs; and taught them to dig trenches and build fortifications. But Love knew that, despite his success, the army was holding him back from overseas assignments.

Recent historical scholarship, facilitated by the Freedom of Information Act, reveals that the systematic discrimination against Lincoln veterans in the armed services reflected a deliberate military policy formulated in the War Department against "potentially subversive personnel." That policy effectively prevented lower-level officers and base commanders from intervening to help individual soldiers. It meant that veterans of the Spanish war would be denied commissions and other promotions and would be prevented from going overseas. But during the war, the army firmly denied that such discrimination existed. Thus when the VALB, led by Jack Bjoze, launched a campaign in 1943 to lift the ban on commissions and combat assignments, the military refused to meet with members of the organization. As in most army matters, moreover, official policy appeared to be enforced inconsistently. For the Spanish veterans, the examples of Herman Boettcher and Bob Thompson could certainly prove the loyalty and worthiness of Lincolns who were given the chance to fight. But the War Department used those exceptional cases (and several others) to claim that no discrimination had occurred.

Determined to overcome this stonewalling, Bjoze journeyed to Washington in the spring of 1943 to meet with members of the military affairs committees of Congress and with sympathetic members of the Roosevelt administration. "Our service on the side of democracy in Spain is being held against us," he argued. "We especially request the privilege of serving on the field of battle; a privilege which in most cases is being denied." Responding to his plea, three congressmen—John M. Coffee, Chester Holifield, and Warren Magnuson— drafted letters of inquiry to the War Department, seeking explanations for the evidence of prejudicial treatment. "Demonstrated merit alone is the determining factor," retorted Secretary of the Army Robert Patterson, offering the names of five Lincolns who held commissions. "It appears that deliberate fabrication or rumor is the basis of this [complaint]."

Such deceptions might have stalled the case. But Bjoze also arranged a meeting with syndicated columnist Drew Pearson of the *Washington Post*, who broke the story in April 1943. "The German and Italian armies used the Spanish civil war as a testing ground for modern warfare," he wrote; "but the United States Army has relegated Americans who fought in Spain largely to work battalions." Citing numerous cases of abrupt dismissal from officer training and refusal to give Lincolns combat assignments, Pearson pressed for a change of policy. Within the administration, Secretary of the Interior Harold Ickes supported the Lincolns' appeal. The dam began to break. Although the army explicitly denied that Lincoln veterans had been given second-class status, some individual soldiers now received transfers to combat units and active duty, while others obtained long-thwarted opportunities to become officers. Yet the policy of discrimination never completely ended. Although the War Department rescinded its curbs on "potentially subversive personnel" in January 1944, complaints about sudden removals from combat detail continued to arrive at the VALB office. Whatever the official army policy, individual veterans remained at the mercy of unrelenting superiors.

Government harassment of the Lincolns also occurred on the home front. Two veterans, both sheet-metal workers in defense industries in the Los Angeles area, were summarily placed under armed guard and escorted from their jobs for reasons of "security." FBI agents visited the supervisors of nurse Lini Fuhr, an employee of the Public Health Service, warning of her radical background. She kept her job and continued to speak on behalf of Spain, despite the threat of dismissal. Similarly, the government refused to give veteran George Cullinan a seaman's passport in 1942, explaining that his "whole past record was just 'reeking with communism.'" As Cullinan recounted his conversation with a military intelligence officer, the officer claimed that "I had quite frankly admitted to him that I was a communist. He based this remarkable assumption on the fact that I told him I was proud of having fought against Franco and considered that fight to be the same one we are carrying on today against the axis nations. . . . I told him I would consider myself a traitor to my country today if I turned against the things I fought for in Spain." For such people, the shortage of civilian labor mitigated the hardships of job discrimination. But these wartime policies revealed the government's fundamental mistrust of Spanish war veterans. The cases would set precedents for the postwar period.

The Political War

When Alvah Bessie received a telephone call at his Brooklyn apartment in December 1942, he was thrilled to learn that Warner Brothers movie studio in Hollywood was offering him a job as a screenwriter. Bessie leaped at the chance. He had always wanted to write for the silver screen, and the salary was lavish—$300 a week to start. But whatever his personal ambitions—and they were equally lavish—Bessie had a larger political motive for uprooting himself from his comfortable niche in the New York literary scene.

Since returning from Spain, Bessie had written two books, his war memoir, *Men in Battle* (1939), and the novel *Bread and a Stone* (1941). He had become the drama critic of *New Masses*, and he wrote a regular column under a pseudonym for the *Weekly Review*, published by the Young Communist League. Bessie used both media to articulate his political views, advocating a second front in Europe, urging the desegregation of the armed forces, and supporting women in the military. ("For what the boys who sneer at women's competency are *really* worried about is that women will be less 'feminine'—in other words, less dependent on men . . . will forget 'their place.' . . . And this attitude is part-and-parcel of . . . Hitlerism.") In 1942, he wrote two propaganda pamphlets, *The Soviet People at War*, published by the American Council on Soviet Relations, and *This Is Your Enemy*, the profits of which went for war relief.

Bessie, in short, strove to fulfill his identity as a Communist intellectual, an author who merged literary talent with political ideology. His pieces exuded optimism. "It is a dream come true," he wrote in 1942 of the 25th anniversary celebration of the Bolshevik revolution at Madison Square Garden, in which U.S. officials participated. "Nowhere, at no point, was the voice of Martin Dies or Adolph Hitler heard. . . . The international unity we have shouted for so long is being achieved." Bessie's sympathy for the Soviet Union dovetailed with the prevailing cultural consensus. As part of the war effort, the government's Office of War Information and the major media—magazines, newspapers, radio, and Hollywood movies—cooperated to present a favorable image of the Communist ally to the American public. So it was not particularly unusual the next month for Bessie to receive the invitation from Warner, which promised to expand his literary and political influence.

Bessie's personal agenda soon confronted an unyielding counterforce known as the studio system: it was not so easy for writers to influence the movies. For a script about the Marine Corps, Bessie endeavored to "smuggle" in the character of Herman Boettcher, but got "nowhere fast." In his original screen story for *Objective, Burma*, for which Bessie would be nominated for an Academy Award, he dared to introduce the progressive idea that the Japanese ought to be viewed not as a racial group but as a political enemy. When one frustrated soldier exclaimed, "Japs aren't human; they're animals," Bessie's hero retorted: "There's nothing especially Japanese about this. . . . You'll find it wherever you find fascists. There are even people who call themselves Americans who'd do it. But there are a lot of people who haven't been turned into beasts—and you'll find them in Japan and Germany as well." Nonetheless, Bessie's dialogue vanished from the final script. Bessie concluded that the Hollywood box office remained the prime standard of content: "They would love Uncle Joe [Stalin] if he made them only one million dollars."

Bessie's travails were not atypical. Even as respected a voice as Ernest Hemingway discovered the writer's impotence against the studio system. Paramount's 1943 version of *For Whom the Bell Tolls*, which starred Gary Cooper and Ingrid Bergman, aroused the novelist's ire. Responding perhaps to the

Lincolns' earlier protests, Hemingway expressed indignation at the political naiveté of the Hollywood script, written by Dudley Nichols. Incensed by the corruption of his story, he provided a scene-by-scene critique, declaring that the proposed movie gave "*nothing* of the reason for which a man will die and know it is well for him to die." Lamenting numerous minor errors of fact and inflection, he also argued that the movie should avoid vague political references. Five years earlier, Hemingway's dialogue in the propaganda film *The Spanish Earth* had omitted the term "fascist," lest the movie arouse anti-Republican censors. Now, however, the writer criticized Hollywood for the same obfuscation. Since the United States was "fighting a war against the Fascists," he said, "the enemy should be called the Fascists and the Republic should be called the Republic." Otherwise, American audiences would have "no idea what the [Spanish] people were really fighting for." Hemingway's plea failed to alter the movie. Later, someone asked Dudley Nichols, "Who prevented you from naming the fascists in *For Whom the Bell Tolls*?" The liberal screenwriter replied, "In two words: the fascists."

From the Warner Brothers writers' shack, Bessie loudly joined the debate about the film's political merits. Denouncing a hero who would remark, "This is a war between the Communists and the Fascists, with the poor Spanish people somewhere in the middle," he objected that the Spanish guerrillas were portrayed as "bandits." He complained, too, that the atrocity scene, showing the peasants killing aristocrats and priests, had been "played up in all its horror." To Edwin Rolfe, one of Hemingway's defenders, Bessie said, "he is everything he called Milt—a prick." And he accused Hemingway of preferring money to principle. "Our guys died for the right of Ernie to shit on everything we stood for," Bessie protested. "That's democracy, I guess." Milton Wolff remained equally unforgiving. "Hemingway is not capable of self-deprivation or sacrifice," he maintained. "He will bluster and be heroic . . . but not at a terrible cost to himself. . . . I simply resent a bastard who can do important things in these critical times, sitting on his ass collecting adventure stories . . . to show men how to die—not how to win."

Bessie's confrontation with actor Gary Cooper epitomized his alienation from the Hollywood scene:

"I'm one of the guys you played in the picture," he told Cooper.

"Terrible thing, civil war. Brothers fighting each other."

"It wasn't really a civil war, Mr. Cooper."

"It wasn't?"

"It was a war of invasion on the part of Germany and Italy against the legal government of Spain."

"That so? (Swallows) That's what's so great about this country. . . . A guy like you can go and fight in a war that's none of your business."

Within the year, Bessie would report nervously on the influence of a new organization called the Motion Picture Alliance for the Preservation of American Ideals. "The boys are frankly out to 'drive the Reds out of Hollywood'— to prevent them from slipping Red propaganda into the films—by which they obviously mean propaganda for democracy," he warned in 1944. "It is attempting to terrify producers and writers with the threat of a blacklist of progressives."

Bessie's fears not only proved prescient of the postwar Hollywood Red Scare, but also alluded to the oppressive wartime policies of the federal government toward political dissidents. To FBI director J. Edgar Hoover, the link between the Communist party and the Spanish war made all the veterans suspect of disloyalty. Since many Lincolns remained members of the party, their activities on behalf of Spain reinforced government suspicions about their motives. The logic became circular. Thus the government could interpret opposition to the Franco regime or support for Republican refugees in Mexico as evidence of malicious intent. With the approval of President Roosevelt, moreover, Hoover had ordered the surveillance of all such "subversive activities," which included investigation of propaganda "opposed to the American way of life" and oversight of agitators who aroused "class hatred." The FBI also developed a custodial detention program, which listed "dangerous" individuals who should be arrested in time of emergency. (In 1943, the attorney general ordered the termination of the program, but Hoover, in an act of bureaucratic independence, simply perpetuated the list under another name.) Even as the United States and the Soviet Union cooperated as wartime allies, the federal government built the case for an anti-Communist crusade.

Just five weeks after Alvah Bessie landed in Hollywood, the FBI commenced an intensive surveillance of all his activities that would last for thirty years. J. Edgar Hoover personally noted in 1943 that Bessie was a subject of the bureau's custodial detention program. And the extensive documents in the Bessie file provide a barometer of the government's definition of subversive possibilities. During this period, Bessie remained an active member of the writers' branch of the Communist party, attending meetings and supporting its programs. But what is striking about his thick dossier is Bessie's preoccupation with the issues of the Spanish war (the Republican government in exile, the refugees, U.S. support of the Franco dictatorship) and the FBI's assessment that such interests were dangerous to the American government.

According to the FBI's wartime reports, Bessie had committed several suspicious acts: circulating a petition addressed to President Roosevelt that called for the repatriation of some anti-fascist refugees; sharing a podium with Congressman John Coffee to raise money for the Joint Anti-Fascist Refugee Committee; speaking at a fund-raising benefit for the Spanish underground operating in France; and writing a letter to *People's World* to defend a recent Hollywood movie, *The Fallen Sparrow*, about a Spanish war veteran. To be sure, the FBI observed Bessie engaged in other political work: giving a speech to the International Workers Order about racism in America, in which he warned that race hatred served the interests of the Nazis; addressing the League of American Writers in commemoration of the bicentennial of the birth of Thomas Jefferson and comparing Jefferson's enemies with contemporary fascists; and defending a group of Mexican-American boys who had been railroaded into jail. These public stands mirrored Bessie's communism, but they also reflected a commitment to social justice. Yet Bessie well understood the odds against him. "In America," he wrote soon after Pearl Harbor, "there are . . . men who read our words with fear. Who wait. And you do not have to be a writer, either. Nor do you have to be a Communist. You have merely to be a democrat, a union man, a fighter . . . to have them list your name. To have them deliver you, if they get the chance, into the hands of the people's executioners."

The government's politicization of the war effort had immediate consequences for the Lincoln veterans attached to the OSS. After graduation from the special training program in the fall of 1942, the Lincolns—Goff, Lossowski, Felsen, Jiminez—received the rank of technical sergeants; all other graduates—those bankers and businessmen that horrified Goff—became commissioned officers. Then the OSS ordered them to North Africa. The recent American landings there had liberated thousands of Spanish Republican refugees and former International Brigaders who had originally fled to

French territory in 1939. After years of confinement, these political prisoners wanted to join the war against the fascists; indeed, they expected the Allies ultimately to help them remove Franco from power in Spain.

The OSS Lincolns, because of their experience in the Spanish war, took charge of training the Spaniards to operate behind German lines in North Africa. But now the Lincolns became victims of their noncommissioned status. When Goff objected to leading a reconnaissance mission he considered both dangerous and of no military importance, a major threatened to have him shot. So Goff gathered his crew of Spaniards and penetrated the German lines—to accomplish nothing. A second needless escapade proved more costly. One of the Lincolns, Milton Felsen, was badly wounded by enemy fire and captured in 1943. He spent the rest of the war in German prison camps.

"We didn't care about being officers," Goff recalled. "We just wanted to fight. But we were at the mercy of this military command." Sympathetic officers persuaded Donovan to intercede. Flying to the Tunisian front, he personally gave the three remaining Lincolns—Goff, Lossowski, and Jiminez—field promotions to second lieutenant. He also authorized them to establish a training school in Morocco to prepare a group of Spanish refugees for guerrilla action against Franco. For two months, Goff's group provided instruction in explosives, weaponry, raiding, and physical combat. Then the Spanish volunteers slipped into Spain. But the mission failed. Franco's forces captured them all; none was heard from again.

After the Allied invasion of Italy in 1943, the OSS Lincolns moved to Naples, where Goff's previous experiences in Spain proved a boon for American intelligence. Through conversations with local Communists, he learned that the Italian Communist party had maintained a large underground apparatus, which controlled the railroad unions. Having sabotaged trains in Spain, Goff decided to investigate the possibility of joining forces with the Communist workers. At party headquarters, however, officials appeared dubious about cooperating with the OSS officers—until Goff and Lossowski persuaded them that they had also fought in Spain. (The clincher was Goff's ability to give the street address of the Communist party headquarters in Madrid.) After that, Goff remembered, "all doors were open." OSS leaders in Italy then appointed Goff liaison officer to the Communist party, and the Americans promptly started training programs, using Italian volunteers to wage guerrilla warfare behind the German lines in northern Italy. Goff's infiltration programs parachuted 30 teams of radio operators and meteorologists into enemy-held areas to provide daily weather reports for the Allied air forces.

This unorthodox alliance won the personal approval of General Donovan. "He wanted a modus vivendi because the Communist party was the strongest political force in Italy," Goff recalled. "He wanted to have the relationship crystal clear." In agreeing to Goff's cooperation with the Communists, however, Donovan advised him "to watch out that they don't take advantage of the relationship to advance their own position." Goff replied, "It won't really happen. Their main interest is ousting the Germans and defeating the Italian fascists." Goff remembered that Donovan answered in one word—"okay"— and never again mentioned the subject. The arrangement would later prove extremely controversial, as the U.S. government endeavored to prevent a Communist takeover in Italy at the end of the war, but Goff encountered no problems at the time. "Most people in OSS treated us with respect," he said, "even though they didn't like our political background in the Spanish civil war."

Working with the Italian Communists, Goff built the most effective intelligence operation in northern Italy. With multiple teams of agents behind German lines, he could count on fourteen separate radio reports every day. "We had guerrillas operating on every highway, every railroad, every German convoy. We had the identifications, the material in every car on every highway reported through the network of radios." Once, when a German captive volunteered to assist the Americans, Goff bypassed the objections of the OSS command by clearing him with the Italian Communist party, and then sent the man on a series of parachute missions that climaxed when he captured an overlay map marked with all the German positions in Italy and the military supplies at each one. Since Goff used Communist volunteers, moreover, the cost of these operations remained small. Goff's achievements won high praise from his superiors within the OSS.

The arrangement with the Communist party nonetheless created a serious political crisis. In exchange for their assistance to the OSS, Italian Communists had obtained valuable communication links with the guerrillas. Thus the OSS radios became an important element in the political struggle for the future of the country. The problem emerged in the late autumn of 1944 when British officials, fearful of the growing strength of the Italian Communists and concerned about supplying the underground during the winter, directed the guerrillas to return to their homes and wait to reassemble for a spring offensive in the new year. As Goff later told the story, he disagreed with the plan on military grounds, believing that the guerrillas should remain constantly on the attack. He therefore raised the question with Italian Communist leaders, who shared his concerns. (Like the Italians, the politically astute Goff undoubtedly realized the importance of consolidating Communist gains after the defeat of the fascists, but he did not mention the subject in his oral memoirs.) Party leaders responded by drafting a counterorder to the Communist guerrillas, calling for an all-out offensive as soon as possible. Goff broadcast that message to the underground leader Luigi Gallo (who had also served in the Spanish war under the nom de guerre Luigi Longo).

These transmissions, while permissible under the loose agreement between the Americans and the Italian Communists, produced great concern within the OSS. Challenged by his superior officer, Goff effectively defended the military value of the messages. But the internal investigation continued, including an analysis of Goff's earlier transmissions ("back traffic") to the guerrillas. At issue was whether these messages had abetted Communist attempts to gain supremacy in northern Italy. "On the strength of these messages," concluded the chief investigator, "it certainly would not be possible to take action against Goff under any appropriate Article of War." However, he also advocated "prompt removal of Lieutenant Goff . . . upon completion of active operational duties against the enemy, to insure that he assumes no operational position" with the Italian Communists. Goff's innocence, in other words, offered no assurances that he would avoid pro-Communist political activity in the future.

These issues assumed immediate importance in the United States when a congressional subcommittee announced in March 1945 that it was investigating the promotion of fourteen Communist officers, including the OSS Lincolns. Major General Clayton Bissell, head of army intelligence, defended the appointments, insisting that the men "have shown by their deeds that they are upholding the United States by force and violence." Facing congressional pressure for promoting officers with radical backgrounds, Donovan boldly appeared before the House subcommittee and dismissed the allegations. "These men I've been in the slit trenches with, I've been in the muck with, and I'd measure them up with any men," he declared. "I found that they were not

[Communists]." Despite such assertions, however, the head of the army's counterintelligence in Europe requested that the OSS evacuate the Lincoln officers immediately after the capitulation of German forces in Italy.

In May 1945, therefore, Donovan ordered all the Lincoln officers back to the United States. The decision effectively blocked them from obtaining expected promotions. Donovan hinted privately that they would be used to develop intelligence networks in the continuing war against the Japanese in China. (A Lincoln veteran named George Wucinich, who had worked with the Yugoslav underground, was indeed transferred to China, where he made contact with Chinese Communist forces.) But then Donovan summoned Goff to Washington and explained "very regretfully" that he had "no alternative" but to discharge all the Lincolns from the service. With a $20 million budget request before the Congress, he could ill afford to antagonize the conservative majority that controlled the purse strings.

"But why are my thoughts in another country?" asked Edwin Rolfe, as he learned to fight again in dusty Texas in 1943:

> Perhaps this one will be the last one.
> And men afterward will study our arms in museums. . . .
> But my heart is forever captive of that other war
> that taught me first the meaning of peace and of comradeship.

Whatever their accomplishments in World War II, Lincoln veterans referred frequently to the Spanish war as a benchmark for measuring their experiences. As rookies in basic training, they complained almost universally about the inadequacy of the army's political education programs (and recalled fondly the skill of their commissars). They objected particularly to the pervasive ignorance about the relationship of the Spanish war to the current fight. The battalion officer, wrote one soldier from Fort Bragg, "is a stupid jerk who rabidly snarls that the Lincoln brigade was not fighting for democracy." On many occasions, individual veterans managed to persuade their officers to permit them to give lectures on Spain and usually they expressed satisfaction at their reception.

Once in combat, the comparisons became sharper. "After Espana," observed Larry Cane, in what was a common refrain among the Lincolns, "it's a wonderful feeling to hear and see the planes that roar over our heads all day, and know that they are really 'nuestros.'" The veterans also relished a familiar camaraderie. "I hear the same beefs and remarks we heard and see the same characters we knew," wrote Gerry Cook from France. "We even have a rumor factory—streamlined and run on mass production lines—that would have put Mickenberg's Non-Intervention Committee establishment out of business." Close to the surface, however, lurked an abiding sadness about that first war. While visiting the internment camp that had held the Lincolns prior to their departure from Le Havre in December 1938, Cook surveyed the ruins caused by recent Allied bombardments and "thought of the ease with which it all could have been prevented."

"The swastika will come down at last," wrote Jack Lucid in 1943. "And the boys left in the mountains and in the olive groves can rest easier." The satisfaction of killing fascists, however, never obscured a primary political objective: the liberation of Spain. After the American landings in Morocco and Algeria, the VALB repeatedly petitioned the state and war departments to release anti-fascist prisoners and to allow them to bear arms in the war. "They are patriots, not criminals," the frustrated veterans exclaimed. Criticizing an army policy that paid the refugees wages of fourteen cents a day, Dr. Edward Barsky demanded better treatment "of those men who knew how to fight Hitler in the years our country was asleep."

Endeavoring to keep the Spanish issue in the public eye, the VALB regularly issued press releases and memoranda challenging pro-Franco sentiments. When Archbishop Francis Spellman wrote in *Collier's* magazine that the Spanish dictator had "high ideals," veteran Jack Bjoze protested that American failure to support the Republic had not only contributed "to the temporary defeat" of Spanish freedom but also facilitated "Hitler's plan to conquer the world." A State Department proposal encouraging American participation in an international trade fair in Barcelona in 1944 drew loud criticism. Citing Spanish shipments of tungsten to Germany, the presence of Franco's "Blue Division" in the fight against the Soviet Union on the eastern front, and interference with American commerce in Morocco, the VALB reminded Secretary of State Cordell Hull that "Franco is a partisan of the Axis." Trade with Spain not only undermined the war effort, the Lincolns protested, but also endangered the political objectives of the war. "Is there any American businessman who believes that General Franco will outlast the defeat of his sponsors, supporters, partners-in-crime?" asked the *Volunteer for Liberty* in a revealing comment on the prevailing optimism. "Is there any sense in participating in a Fair organized by men who are bound to go into bankruptcy before this war is over?" Soon afterward, local police arrested several veterans for picketing a visit by Spanish industrialists in Milwaukee.

When "reliable information" about guerrilla insurrections in Spain reached the VALB office in the autumn of 1944, hopes for the liberation of Spain soared. Fighting in the Pyrenees had resulted in the temporary ejection of fascist troops from a few villages, and the Lincolns argued that these victories proved the general dissatisfaction with the Franco regime. Coincidentally, Milton Wolff had inadvertently made contact with the Spanish underground while working in southern France on a mission for the OSS. "Now if that guy de Gaulle doesn't get squeamish . . . the thing will be over with in a hurry," he reported hopefully. "It is a nation [waiting] to be recaptured by its own people." But by then Wolff had grown cautious of his political predictions; too well, he understood the limits of American commitments. "Do we want the people of a country to destroy their own fascists or do we reserve the right for ourselves?" he wondered. "We are committed to the destruction of German fascism, but are we committed to the destruction of Spanish fascism or Polish fascism or Argentinian fascism?" The answer was too obvious to state.

The Spanish uprising nonetheless galvanized the anit-Franco movement at home during the first months of 1945. Cosponsoring a protest meeting that attracted sixteen thousand sympathizers to Madison Square Garden in January, the VALB launched a public relations campaign to win passage of Congressman John Coffee's House Resolution 100, which called for breaking diplomatic relations with the Franco government. Such a policy, they said, would encourage the nations of Latin America to follow the U.S. example, crippling Franco's economy. "The people of Spain do not ask for our armed intervention in their behalf," advised David McKelvey White in a widely circulated pamphlet, *Franco Spain—America's Enemy*. "They ask only that we cease extending our powerful, our invaluable support to their bitter oppressor and our bitter enemy." In the spring, a fund-raising banquet featuring Congressmen Coffee and Adam Clayton Powell at the Commodore Hotel raised

$8,000 to continue the campaign to gain diplomatic recognition for Republican Spain. But by then, the only newspaper to cover the story was the *Daily Worker*.

The silence reflected shifting political winds. At almost the same moment that the New York veterans were listening to after-dinner collection speeches, Lieutenant Milton Wolff was embarking on a mission behind enemy lines near the French-Swiss-Italian border. As he recalled the operation, the cadre of thirty OSS agents consisted mostly of corporate executives in uniform, who were sent to supervise the transition of power at the time of the German surrender; the OSS wanted to prevent the local governments and businesses from falling into Communist hands. Disturbed by the mission, Wolff and his guide split off from the main group, hoping to make contact with partisan leader Luigi Gallo. But a sudden snowfall forced them to abandon the march. Later, Wolff learned that the Germans had captured the other OSS officers.

Wolff subsequently managed to make contact with a group of Spanish guerrillas, who were based near Grenoble. Upon learning of their plans to invade Spain, he wired OSS headquarters in Florence requesting supplies and weapons to support the Spanish action. The return message ordered Wolff to desist. Instead of receiving military aid for the Spaniards, Wolff got a special plane ride back to the American base. Then, even before he could be debriefed, he was taken to an American ship. The other OSS Lincolns were already aboard, waiting for his arrival, and the ship immediately weighed anchor for America. The U.S. government would not endanger its plans for an anti-Communist postwar settlement in Italy.

That spring, the Lincolns on the home front carried the crusade for a free Spain to the founding conference of the United Nations in San Francisco. Working with other pro-Republican groups, David McKelvey White represented the VALB in efforts to prevent the seating of a Franco delegation. Even without the full support of the United States, the coalition succeeded. Franco's government would be barred from the first United Nations sessions. But there the campaign stalled. The Coffee resolution failed to pass in the House of Representatives; the State Department refused to sever relations with Franco. In September 1945, the Lincoln veterans would again issue a call for "V-S Day" and predict the triumphant return of the Spanish Republicans to their homeland. But already they knew that the moment of victory had passed.

*

The conservatism of U.S. foreign policy toward Spain and western Europe coincided with important ideological shifts within the Left. During the war, Earl Browder had led the Communist party in adopting a program of "peaceful coexistence" with American capitalism. In 1944, the party even abolished itself, creating the Communist Political Association to work within the existing two-party system. Putting aside the class struggle, party members embraced organized labor's "no-strike" pledge and, contrary to the preferences of many trade unionists, accepted working conditions that otherwise might have been deemed oppressive. Alvah Bessie's article "Down to the Sea in Tubs" may have criticized the dangerous state of American shipping (the results, he said, of the greed of shipowners); but rank and file members of the National Maritime Union, such as Bill Bailey and Harry Haywood, prudently avoided labor struggles that might disrupt wartime commerce.

The unexpected death of Franklin Roosevelt in April 1945 sent political chills through the ranks. "I felt positively sick," wrote Don Thayer from his army-imposed exile in Alaska, "for immediately there came to me all of the thoughts of what might happen, at least thoughts of what a lot of people are hoping will happen." Jack Lucid, fighting in Germany, spelled out those fears: "The winning of the war will be the prelude to such general confusion on a world scale and such a fucked-up economic and political situation at home that in the general disillusionment and despair obscurantism and reaction will have a field day." Disagreements between the United States and the Soviet Union about the peace accentuated these concerns. Lucid reported listening to German propaganda broadcasts about "the danger of aggression by the Soviet Union." Milton Wolff's hasty removal from southern France provided another early sign of the brewing conflict.

Amidst such consternation, world Communist leaders signaled the American party that the era of accommodation with capitalism had come to an end. In April 1945, an article by the French Communist theoretician Jacques Duclos, read by all as a text from Stalin himself, denounced recent "revisionist tendencies" and summoned a return to the class struggle. Responding to the cue, the American party hierarchy, led by the doctrinaire William Z. Foster and war hero Bob Thompson, pressed Browder to renounce his program. In the ensuing power struggle, a new leadership, committed to the orthodox Leninist formula, forced Browder's expulsion from the Communist party in

July 1945. The decision moved the party in a sectarian direction, just as an anti-Communist crusade was beginning.

Most Lincoln veterans nonetheless viewed these changes with confidence. Milton Wolff, summoned to a meeting with Browder shortly after his return to the United States in 1945, flatly refused to allow the VALB to back the old leadership, pointing to his experiences in the army and OSS as proof of a coming struggle. Veterans like Lucid and Thayer welcomed the purge of "proven opportunists and bureaucrats" who had undermined the militant rank and file. To be sure, an unknown number of Communists followed Browder out of the party; and the reconversion to civilian life—the desire for families, jobs, homes in suburbia—would lure other veterans away from political activity. The VALB mailing list in 1945 numbered "roughly one thousand," according to an estimate made at the time, and included many members who viewed the organization strictly as a fraternal body. But those who remained politically involved—particularly the VALB leadership—usually accepted the party's new militancy. For these Lincoln veterans, the war against fascism had not ended. Spain under Franco symbolized the ultimate failure of the Second World War, and for that miscarriage they held the U.S. government responsible.

19

Red Scares and Blacklists

O n March 10, 1949, the anguished Milton Wolff
paid a call on William C. Dunham, chief of the
Spanish desk at the State Department in Washington,
D.C. The Franco government had recently sentenced
nine Spaniards to death for leading protests against
the regime, and Wolff had come to plead for U.S. intervention to save their lives. A transcription of their
conversation survives.

DUNHAM: "Of course, we do not make representations in the cases of avowed communists. You
wouldn't expect us to, would you?"
WOLFF: "After all, we have a certain responsibility
for the actions of these men. State Department releases . . . and the United States position at the
United Nations, all call for a change in the Franco
government. That is what these men are trying to
bring about. We should support their efforts by more
than just words."
DUNHAM: "All our statements specify 'by peaceful
and orderly means.'"
WOLFF: "They cannot make a change without organizing and belonging to a trade union, a nationalist

group, or a banned political party, and belonging to such a group, or party, is considered an act of violence against the government by Franco."

DUNHAM: "Nevertheless, we cannot and will not intervene except in rare cases."

WOLFF: "Not even in the name of justice? Not even if the case is an obvious frame-up and the death sentence is handed down in a summary court martial?"

DUNHAM: "That is right. But come, they are not summary courts martial. They are military trials and they are not adequately defended, that is true, but they are permitted to make long harangues in their own behalf before being sentenced. Not half so many are being executed these last months as were executed before. [At this point Wolff apparently made an unrecorded comment.] Ha, ha, ha, yes. . . . Maybe there aren't as many left to be shot . . . hah, hah, hah. Yes, I will send a wire to Culbertson in Madrid inquiring about these names. . . . If the men are not communists and haven't blown a bridge or killed anyone, we might make representations in their behalf."

Wolff then turned to the question of the Latin American countries reopening their embassies in Spain, with the approval and encouragement of the United States.

DUNHAM: "Of course! We were against withdrawing the ambassadors in the first place. . . . Never helped any, this withdrawal." . . .

WOLFF: "The withdrawal of ambassadors was a weak move, but it was better than the nothing you all proposed. . . . The thing we want is not a retreat from this weak action, but more positive action—a break in relations." . . .

DUNHAM: "Positively not! We are not going to break relations with Spain. . . . There is no support for such action! . . . No, I don't mean there isn't any anti-Franco feeling . . . but no support for a break. No, I am not sure how much anti-Franco feeling there is in America. Sure I know about the protests . . . mere form letters and cards."

WOLFF: "A signed postcard is a better gauge of public opinion than a Gallup poll. . . . After all, people don't sit down and write letters. . . . They should be paid more attention to."

DUNHAM: "That is interesting, the way you put it I mean. But . . ."

WOLFF: "You mean that is the way it is officially considered?"

No reply.

Dunham then expressed uncertainty about the U.S. position regarding the admission of Franco into the United Nations.

WOLFF: "Well, you are getting everything worked out the way you want it. You blocked, parried and delayed all actions against Franco since 1945 when there was the best possibility to restore the Spanish republic . . . with just this idea in mind. To sweep another tinhorn dictator into the basement along with the other dictators, kings, etc., that you have already collected."

DUNHAM: "You credit us with too much foresight. I am sure that that was not the original plan."

WOLFF: "You couldn't have planned it better."

The conversation ended with Dunham asking Wolff to send him the names of the nine doomed men.

This meeting, presumably like others before it, epitomized the clash of values and assumptions between the administration and the veterans of the Lincoln brigade, a matter of legalism against morality, of calculation against passion; at bottom, it revealed a conflict of ideology. Each side had its own logic. Indeed, what emerged from such confrontations was the utter absence of dialogue, of any sense of responsiveness or the possibility of compromise. Ideological rigidity—the hallmark of the cold war—precluded a generous resolution of the affair.

It was no wonder, then, that the veterans of the Lincoln brigade opposed the foreign policy of President Harry S. Truman. As early as the fall of 1945, just weeks after the end of World War II, the VALB joined the American Committee for Spanish Democracy in picketing the Spanish consulate in New York to demand that Franco be brought to trial as a war criminal. The State Department and the White House, however, preferred to maintain the prewar policy of offering cautious support to the dictatorship. At a time when the Truman administration feared the expansion of Soviet influence and worried about the spread of socialism in Italy, France, even Great Britain, General Franco stood as a bastion of anti-Communist solidarity in the creation of a new Western alliance. "We find ourselves filling the gap left by Hitler and Mussolini," Wolff protested in vain.

Under the leadership of Dr. Edward Barsky, former head of the American Medical Bureau, the Joint Anti-Fascist Refugee Committee continued to send assistance to Spanish exiles and to lobby for political support for a Republican Spain. Veteran Moe Fishman, a dark-haired, dapper man who walked with a limp because of wounds received at Brunete, joined the office staff of the Joint Committee and worked tirelessly with other charitable groups, such as the Unitarian church and the American Friends, to see that shipments of food and clothing reached refugees in France. Some goods even crossed the Spanish border to help victims of the regime. Individual veterans also donated money through a woman named "Red Mary" in New York to support the political work of a clandestine Spanish underground and to provide supplies for the guerrilla resistance to Franco. These were personal "acts of solidarity," Fishman later explained, not a VALB program, but many veterans obviously sympathized with the project.

Through the postwar period, the Lincolns strove to keep the issue of Spain in the public mind. Their activities proved as diverse as their membership. Consider only the year 1946. In January, the VALB directed formal appeals to the president, protesting the sale of aircraft equipment to the Spanish government and proposing a break in commercial and diplomatic relations with Spain; a delegation visited Capitol Hill to lobby against Franco. In February, the veterans launched a letter-writing campaign and petition drive urging the State Department to sever relations with the dictatorship. That month, a VALB convention proclaimed the restoration of the Spanish Republic as its primary goal and voted to subsidize the guerrillas and other veterans of the International Brigades in Europe. Soon the VALB joined with the American Committee for Spanish Democracy to establish a new organization called the Action Committee to Free Spain Now! Milton Wolff served as the campaign director.

During the spring of 1946, the protests continued. First, the VALB organized picket lines outside the Spanish consulates to protest the execution of political prisoners and sent a delegation to the State Department to appeal for changes in pro-Franco policies. Then, in San Francisco and Los Angeles, local veterans organized mass meetings with labor unions and the American Veterans Committee, while a group of veterans in Milwaukee chased a Franco aide from his hotel room. VALB branches in Minnesota, Wisconsin, Detroit, and Chicago began petition and clothing drives on behalf of Spanish refugees. In May, the VALB sponsored an "Oust Franco and Free Spain" rally at New York's Carnegie Hall and held a banquet at the Henry Hudson Hotel to honor the Spanish guerrilla army. Other veterans, backed by the National Maritime Union, picketed the arrival of Spanish ships in American ports. One protest at the Spanish consulate drew two thousand pickets, who burned Franco in effigy. The Lincolns then initiated a postcard protest to the United Nations, urging the end of diplomatic relations with Spain. Newspaper advertisements asked: "Are YOU Still Fighting Fascism?"

All those protests occurred in 1946. During the next year, the Lincolns walked on picket lines, drafted resolutions, signed petitions, and went to jail for protesting outside Spanish consulates. *Franco Spain—A Menace to World Peace* was the title of Milton Wolff's widely distributed pamphlet, which the VALB published in 1947. The veterans continued to sponsor numerous rallies in 1948, including a national tour by Leah Manning, a British Labour M.P. who advocated isolating the Franco government. Seeking the support of the United Nations, the VALB then launched a campaign urging that the Spanish issue be placed on the annual agenda of the General Assembly. Within a year, however, Wolff would report that the Truman administration, despite official acceptance of the 1945 resolution barring the Franco regime from the United Nations, was indeed trying to put Spain on the assembly's agenda— for the purpose of gaining its admission!

In retrospect, one may ask whether the Lincoln veterans opposed American policy toward Spain because they were anti-Franco, anti-fascist or because they were pro-Communist. In the postwar climate, however, the distinction hardly mattered. By 1946, the two threads—Spain and communism—were inseparably interwoven; the reasoning had become perfectly circular. The Truman administration supported Franco *because* he was anti-Communist; his opponents could therefore be dismissed because they were not loyal cold warriors. It is significant, nonetheless, that even anti-Communist Lincoln veterans scorned the Franco regime, and Lincolns who left the Communist party remained hostile to U.S. policy toward Spain.

In any event, the VALB's pro-Communist leadership did not limit its criticism of Truman to the issues of Spain. Thus the 1946 VALB convention endorsed the administration's conciliatory secretary of commerce, Henry Wallace, over the cold warrior secretary of state, James Byrnes, and demanded the end of military support for Chiang Kai-shek in China. "Two wars against fascism have enabled us to tell a fascist from a democrat," declared the VALB leadership a few months later, protesting the enunciation of the Truman Doctrine against communism in Turkey and Greece. By May Day of 1948, the veterans were marching in their accustomed first rank in the annual left-wing parade carrying a list of discontents that included Truman's proposed Universal Military Training, the Taft-Hartley "slave labor law," and other ingredients of anti-Communist policy. The VALB did not take a position on the 1948 presidential election, but many veterans, Communist and non-Communist alike, backed Henry Wallace and the Progressive party.

Using the slogan "Make Democracy Work," Lincoln veteran Irving Goff had dared to violate the laws of Louisiana by arranging racially mixed political meetings during Wallace's 1948 presidential campaign. As the Communist party's district organizer in New Orleans, Goff had encouraged black voter registration, agitated on behalf of black prisoners, and jeopardized his life on several occasions by ignoring southern racial customs. But a minor traffic accident involving two other party members, one white, the other black, forced Goff to defend himself before the central committee on charges of disrespect to the black driver. "No one accused me of any racist or chauvinist act or words," he later explained of his two-day interrogation; "nobody accused me of not fighting. They *did* accuse me of not fighting hard enough against racism that existed." After further investigation and numerous hearings, the party finally exonerated Goff of wrongdoing, but the prolonged fight forced his reassignment. The imbroglio epitomized the Communist party's crusade against any vestige of "white chauvinism." But the result showed both the folly of the accusations and the willingness of white Communists to endure personal humiliation in the name of party discipline.

Heightened awareness of race problems reflected the growing rigidity of the Communist party amidst the tensions of the cold war, a scrupulosity that disguised the party's irrelevance to most African Americans. In the postwar climate of ideological struggle, Communists discarded a program of racial integration and reaffirmed the doctrine of black nationhood. Harry Haywood, still hoping to rehabilitate his position in the party, resurrected the old agenda in a series of theoretical articles that appeared in the party journal *Political Affairs* in 1946. Using recent statistics, he reiterated the importance of gaining land reform in the black belt of the South as a precondition for black self-government. In his book *Negro Liberation*, Haywood linked the oppression of American blacks to the Truman administration's "imperialist" foreign policy, chiding the State Department for demanding "free elections" in the "people's democracies" of eastern Europe while sanctioning the disenfranchisement of blacks in the South.

Haywood's ideas, garbed in Marxist rhetoric, made few inroads within the larger black community. Indeed, the strident two-pronged campaign—in favor of black self-determination and against even unconscious prejudice—reflected the party's distance from the mainstream of African-American protest. "So isolated did we become from Negro life," John Gates later recalled, "that when the U.S. Supreme Court in May 1954 handed down its historic decision on school desegregation, we were taken completely by surprise. This prime issue was not even a central point in the party's program at the time." The party eventually acknowledged that the campaign against white chauvinism constituted an "error of nationalism," the treatment of racial issues outside the context of the class struggle.

Most Lincoln veterans, however, had not waited for the Communist party or the Supreme Court to oppose racial injustice. Even in this era of racial quiet, Spanish war veterans carried on the fight against discrimination. Milton Wolff served as campaign director for the Civil Rights Congress (postwar successor of the International Labor Defense) and raised funds on behalf of black defendants, including the "Trenton Six" and Mississippi's Willie McGee, charged with committing race-related crimes. Other Lincolns led crusades to end discrimination in employment and housing. Through the 1940's and 1950's, blacks served on the VALB executive board and shared responsibility for veterans' affairs. Such activities would provide a direct continuity with the civil rights protests of the next decade.

During the cold war, however, civil rights issues had less to do with race than with political beliefs. Five months after the end of World War II, in January 1946, Dr. Edward Barsky and other executives of the Joint Anti-Fascist Refugee Committee received subpoenas to appear before the House Committee on Un-American Activities (HUAC). As part of an investigation of pro-Communist groups, HUAC also demanded a full accounting of the Joint Committee's financial transactions, including the names of all donors and recipients. On legal grounds, the request raised the issues of the confidentiality of political records and free speech. (Since the First Amendment forbade Congress from enacting legislation that would infringe the freedom of speech, and since the purpose of congressional investigations was ostensibly to provide information to enact such legislation, opponents of HUAC claimed the investigation had no constitutional basis.) More specifically, the summons imperiled the safety of Spaniards who were beneficiaries of American donations. Barsky announced that the Joint Committee would refuse to comply with the HUAC demand.

VALB leaders well understood the issue and the danger: the attack on the refugee aid committee was intended to reinforce American support of the Franco dictatorship. A cartoon published in the *Volunteer for Liberty* showed Generalissimo Franco answering a telephone: "Am I an anti-Communist? You're forgetting Congressman—I was a member of the Axis!" Describing HUAC as "pro-Franco, pro-Fascist," Lincoln veterans decried its chilling effect on the fundraising effort to help Spanish refugees, but they could only watch in anger as Congress voted in 1947 to hold the Joint Committee's executive board in contempt. Ten members of the committee, including the novelist Howard Fast, were sentenced to three months in jail; Barsky, because of his leadership, earned a six-month term. After an unsuccessful legal battle that lasted for three years, Barsky served five months in federal prison. The New York State Medical Committee then suspended his medical license for another six months because he had been convicted of a crime. Barsky's appeal of the suspension reached the U.S. Supreme Court in 1954, where he learned that a state "has the broad power to establish and enforce standards of conduct within its borders relative to the health of everyone there." Justice William O. Douglas's dissent offered the only balm: "When a doctor cannot save lives in America because he is opposed to Franco in Spain, it is time to call a halt and look critically at the neurosis that has possessed us." Barsky was just the first Spanish war veteran to face the government's wrath.

Since many members of the VALB worked actively in the labor movement, the passage of the Taft-Hartley Act in 1947, prohibiting Communists from holding union office, provided fresh ammunition to attack individual veterans. Indeed, during the postwar witch-hunts, as in the military during World War II, service in Spain constituted prima facie evidence of subversive leanings. Thus in November 1947 the "League for Justice" in Cleveland, Ohio, issued a pamphlet announcing that "Stalin's Pet Commissar Rules Ohio U[nited] E[lectric] Members." Based on dubious testimony from Representative Dies's HUAC hearings seven years earlier, the league charged former commissar Fred Keller with subverting the labor movement. "It is sickening and revolting," the league wrote of Keller's record in Spain, "but it is better that you become informed and nauseated as an American and act while you still have time than to remain in ignorance and health until you become a Soviet slave." The pamphlet also denounced Keller's wife, Ruth Davidow, for having "nursed your wounded soldiers with communism at Crile General Hospital." Keller claimed that he had never joined the Communist party, but in the climate of the cold war, red-baiting polemics could not be overcome. Nor could Keller deny his participation in the Spanish war. Similar allegations eventually affected dozens of Lincoln veterans, who lost their jobs and faced occupational blacklists. When veteran Robert Colodny wrote in 1947 that "the intellectual night is fast setting in, and activity in favor of Spain may cost one his livelihood," he was forecasting his own fate.

"We were not only premature anti-fascists," Milton Wolff said with disgust, "but we were the premature victims of McCarthyism." In December 1947, Attorney General Tom Clark implemented Truman's anti-Communist executive orders by releasing a formal list of "subversive" organizations. Careful readers could find the Lincolns listed alphabetically in two places: as the Abraham Lincoln Brigade and as the Veterans of the Abraham Lincoln Brigade. Another entry named the Joint Anti-Fascist Refugee Committee. With this list the government and the private sector obtained grounds to discriminate against and persecute members of groups "suspected of disloyalty." One month later, the Justice Department ordered the VALB to register officially as a foreign agent, specifically as the representative of the underground trade unions operating in Spain. The order also required the veterans to submit all membership lists, financial records, correspondence, and public statements. Penalties for noncompliance could reach five-year jail terms and fines of $10,000. Vowing to resist "all attempts to place the chains of fascism" on the American people, a group of veterans hastily removed the VALB's office records to a farmhouse in Connecticut and burned the lists of members and donors as well as other potentially embarrassing material. "The only reason for this request," VALB secretary Jack Bjoze assured the veterans, "is to cripple the anti-Franco movement in this country."

The sense of encirclement intensified. In 1948, the U.S. Supreme Court rejected the appeals of Dr. Barsky and other members of the Joint Committee, effectively denying First Amendment protections against government investigations of political activity. That summer, the administration indicted the executive board of the Communist party for violating the 1940 Smith Act, which prohibited conspiracies to overthrow the government by force and violence. With two Lincoln veterans, Gates and Thompson, among those charged, the VALB rallied to the defense, helping to organize picket demonstrations outside the federal courthouse at Foley Square. And when, during the trial, Gates justified his falsification of a passport application to go to Spain in 1937—"to fight on behalf of democracy," he said, "to prevent war from coming to the United States"—the Lincolns asked the court to respect "the moral grounds" of his action.

Government repression soon threatened to stop the VALB's political work. With limited funds—an emergency appeal in 1948 drew $1,235 from 61 veterans—the Lincolns had to spend their resources defending their organization. "Bad news awaited me here," Wolff wrote to his wife from New York one Monday morning in 1949. "We cannot get a license for a street collection anymore and now they are moving to ban all the 'front' organizations from public halls and places!" Activities on behalf of Spain inevitably waned. "It is indeed fortunate that the American people are . . . superior to their organizations or parties," Wolff wrote optimistically in February 1950; "otherwise we should have had war and fascism in this country a long time ago." Three months later, Wolff was less confident. In a series of rulings, the Supreme Court had rejected Barsky's final appeals, upheld the anti-Communist provision of the Taft-Hartley labor act, and ruled that the Communist party represented a conspiracy to overthrow the government by force and violence.

"When I'm faced with this kind of thing," said Wolff, "the opening door to fascism—I get slightly worried." In another week, he would have more to add to the tally of worrisome actions: the arrest and planned deportation of two officials of the International Workers Order; the Supreme Court's rejection of appeals by two South Carolina blacks allegedly framed on murder charges;

the trial of West Coast Communists; Secretary of State Dean Acheson's promise to support the French in the Vietnam war in exchange for France's support
of a rearmed Germany; the incarceration of Communist party secretary Eugene Dennis (who just nine years before had given Wolff permission to recruit
Communists for British intelligence); and President Truman's threat to use
the atom bomb again "if." "These are just the highlights," exclaimed Wolff;
"all this big stuff is having its effect down below."

"Strange characters call at night," Wolff told Edwin Rolfe, "and wage a
war of nerves." In 1948, the *Volunteer for Liberty* reported that Communists
and non-Communists alike had been receiving "official and unofficial visits
from a variety of organizations"—a euphemism for the presence, indeed the
omnipresence, of police agencies and the FBI. Ever since the raids on the
VALB offices in 1940, the FBI had maintained files on the veterans' organization and many of its members. During World War II, the FBI had placed
many Lincolns on a list of "individuals deemed most dangerous" to the national security, who would be summarily arrested in time of national emergency. As the anti-Communist campaign intensified, so did the FBI's scrutiny
of the VALB leadership. Sometimes federal investigators sought specific information: they approached veterans in the streets, at their homes, or in their
places of employment. Often, however, the FBI simply endeavored to intimidate radicals, harassing them with late-night visits and telephone calls.

Of the hundred-odd veterans interviewed for this book, *none* had been exempted from an FBI inquiry, not even the apolitical or anti-Communist. Indeed, one purpose of such investigations was to find "friendly" witnesses who
might testify to the subversive intent of their former comrades. One April
morning in 1953, an FBI agent arranged to find a seat on a Connecticut com-
muter train next to Milton Wolff, who was on his way to take painting classes
at the Art Students' League in New York. After introducing himself, the agent
engaged Wolff in a conversation about the dangers of communism. They spoke
about the arrest of atom bomb spies, the Korean War (Wolff called it "something of a military W.P.A."), and various political issues. Although the VALB
commander denied that "the Communists [were] a threat to the internal security of the United States," he did express minor disagreements with the party
line, leading the agent to conclude that Wolff "is not a well-disciplined Communist Party member." The two parted at Grand Central Station, as the agent

put it, "in a very friendly manner." One month later, the agent telephoned Wolff to request another interview in the near future, explaining that he was being transferred to another region. Wolff asked if the agent was being moved because of his failure to convert him. The agent suggested Wolff not exaggerate his own importance, to which the Lincoln veteran replied: "That's what I've been telling you that you've been doing!" Despite the banter, Wolff would remain on the FBI's "most dangerous" list for another twenty years; indeed, his name would be forwarded to the Secret Service, responsible for protecting the life of the president.

FBI appearances at the workplace were especially nefarious. Nurse Lini Fuhr, for example, lost her civil service job as a public health nurse in Los Angeles in 1947. When ex-Communist Elizabeth Bentley named Fuhr as her party recruiter in highly publicized testimony before Congress, the former Spanish volunteer could barely find any employment. She moved to New Mexico, but another FBI visit caused her to lose her job once again. Back in California, a blacklist prevented Fuhr from finding anything but the most menial nursing work, and even then she was fired after an FBI inquiry. Finally, in 1949, she moved to Mexico, where she offered her skills to a remote rural population. Numerous other veterans provided testimony of a similar pattern of job discrimination. The FBI also infiltrated the VALB office in New York, using an unidentified informer to locate individual veterans. Such surveillance aggravated the prevailing climate of fear.

"Part of that fear," Wolff would say many years later, "was fed by the party's 'Cry Havoc!!' The idea that war was just a trigger finger away and fascism coming through the window. This sort of rhetoric didn't help steel the spines of their own people, much less those of liberals." But Wolff's contemporary letters attest to very practical and prudent reasons to fear the efforts of the FBI and the courts. "The trend cannot be mistaken as a passing half-hearted attack on labor, the CP, and all progressive forces," he claimed. "It is an attack on the Bill of Rights. . . . It seeks to achieve the conditions at home that will make an aggressive war possible abroad."

The outbreak of the Korean War in 1950 and the imprisonment of the national board of the Communist party convinced many left-wing veterans that war between the United States and the Soviet Union was inevitable; and if such a war was imminent, they reasoned, so was fascism; and then, according to that logic, the next step would be the illegalization of the Communist party. "If this attack upon communists for what they think is not defeated," John Gates warned a gathering of the VALB in 1951, "a period of thought control will be initiated in America. . . . Today those who rule our nation are determined to outlaw even the very thought of peace." The arrest and conviction of Julius and Ethel Rosenberg for transmitting atom bomb secrets to Soviet spies accentuated such fears. Among the few palpable "exhibits" of political views introduced at their trial was a cardboard collection can that read "Save a Spanish Republican Child." "That shook a lot of people up," remembered Vaughn Love.

Forced on the defensive, and keenly aware that the first victims of fascism in Nazi Germany had been Communists and trade unionists, the party resolved to protect a remnant of its leadership. "Whenever the party entered a period of militancy as against popular front government," Gates later explained, "whenever it felt the direct threat of government persecution or prosecution, it went underground." A few Lincoln veterans had participated in such a program during the Soviet-Finnish war in 1939–40. Ten years later, the party asked several veterans to prepare for another underground. Among them was George Watt, former commissar of the Lincoln battalion, who had relied on the underground resistance in Belgium and France to escape from Nazi-occupied Europe during World War II. Summoned by the party's general secretary, Eugene Dennis—who conducted their conversation on yellow pads to avoid government bugs—Watt agreed to create an apparatus capable of hiding a cadre of Communist leaders. The underground would not only protect Communists from arrest, but also enable the party to function as a political entity. Such a project required an extensive support system: safe houses, drivers, and couriers, as well as places to store printing machinery, radios, and automobiles. Eventually, about two hundred leaders and eight hundred support people became involved in the operation. The party classified some as "operative but unavailable," others as totally unavailable, and still others as living in "deep freeze." And a few, such as Bob Thompson, jumped bail and became fugitives.

Since the underground demanded proof of the utmost loyalty to the party, a considerable number of Lincoln veterans, having demonstrated their reliability in battle, qualified for this work. Indeed, some of them were uniquely qualified. When Watt attempted to arrange the escape of Smith Act fugitive Gus Hall through Mexico in 1951, he asked the former guerrilla fighter Irving

Goff to scout the terrain and find an appropriate point to cross the Rio Grande. After much maneuvering, Hall made his way into Mexico, only to be arrested there by FBI agents who had been advised of his arrival. Similarly, the FBI arrested World War II hero Bob Thompson in the California mountains after two years in hiding. He eventually served five years and one month in jail.

Such celebrated captures proved exceptional and, according to one fugitive, were deliberately arranged to serve particular political purposes. Former commissar Saul Wellman had gone underground in the summer of 1951 but continued to function as a party leader. After several months, he realized that the FBI knew exactly where he was; they followed him, but made no effort to arrest him. Perhaps they were hoping to be led to other Communist fugitives. (The FBI files of another veteran show clearly that the agency had hesitated to make an arrest on exactly those grounds, only to lose the fugitive when he made a routine change of identity and whereabouts.) But Wellman linked his own arrest in the fall of 1952 to election-campaign accusations that the Democrats were soft on Communists. His "dramatic" capture, he claimed, aimed more at headlines than at legal retribution.

Archie Brown managed to avoid arrest for over four years. In 1946, he had run for governor of California on the Communist party ticket, gathering over 20,000 write-in votes. After the CIO expelled his union, the International Longshoreman's and Warehouseman's Union, because of Communist influence, Brown became state labor director for the Communist party. But when the U.S. Supreme Court ruled in July 1951 that party leaders convicted under the Smith Act had to go to jail, he accepted an assignment in the underground. "There's no great romance in the underground," he later conceded. "We had to learn what to do. There were no blueprints; there were no rules." Making frequent moves, using assumed names, avoiding contact with his family, finding occasional menial labor, Brown functioned as a shadow leader. "We were always on the defensive," he recalled. "That was the big problem: How to defend the party. How to defend the unions. How to defend our families." He spent most of his time doing research on labor issues and took credit for influencing local legislation. He attended rare meetings with other underground leaders, some of them fellow Lincoln veterans. Meanwhile, the FBI installed a 24-hour surveillance on his family, though the Browns managed to have three brief reunions in four years. Not until the celebrated "thaw" in the cold war in 1955 did Brown feel secure enough to surface.

"Hindsight," he later admitted, "shows us that . . . our judgment about the oncoming of fascism was wrong. There was a threat, all right, but it wasn't to the extent we thought." Worse, the underground strategy seemed to confirm government accusations that the Communist party and its various "front" organizations indeed constituted a conspiracy rather than a bona fide political movement. In this way the Red Scare fed upon itself. Most Communist leaders later viewed the underground experience as a disaster.

The threat to the VALB moved closer with passage of the McCarran Internal Security Act in 1950. The law obliged members of Communist-front organizations, designated by the attorney general's list to include the VALB, to register with the federal government as agents of a foreign power. Penalties for noncompliance included imprisonment and heavy fines. As a precaution against indictments, the VALB executive board promptly resigned, leaving Milton Wolff, the national commander, and Moe Fishman, the executive secretary, as the only officers.

"The progressive movement . . . has been knocked for a loop by the un-americans, the terror and the shrinkage of available funds," reported Alvah Bessie from Hollywood; "and in my pessimistic opinion it will be worse before it is better." Fear of government reprisals, together with the disappearance of veteran activists underground, greatly weakened anti-Franco organizations. VALB leaders complained about the difficulty of mustering the membership for political work. Outside New York, the VALB posts ceased to function. Although individual veterans might gather for social or political purposes, organized activity on behalf of Spain and the Spanish refugees virtually came to an end. Fund-raising became a tremendous burden. Yet VALB leaders struggled to implement an agenda of helping members and agitating for a free Spain. "No Jail for Franco's Foes," read picket signs, as a solitary line of veterans paraded outside the White House gates on the day Dr. Barsky went to jail in June 1950.

Two months later, the news from Washington underscored their distance from the administration. Continuing to build an anti-Communist coalition in Europe, the State Department announced on August 2, 1950, the approval of a sizable loan to the Franco government. That day, angry Lincoln veterans joined an antiwar demonstration in New York's Union Square to protest the betrayal of anti-fascist ideals. Veteran Bill McCarthy, who had struggled since

Spain to overcome the stigma of his mental collapse, perched on a lamppost above the parade and shouted peace slogans, until police and firemen brutally kicked him into submission and then charged him with disorderly conduct. "I know in my heart that the spark that sent you to Spain to fight fascism is still there," he wrote to fellow veterans from his hospital bed.

Worse news followed swiftly. The Dominican Republic, acting, in Moe Fishman's words, "as a front for the U.S. State Department," had placed the question of recognition of Franco's Spain on the United Nations' agenda. Amidst cold war polemics, the anti-fascist alliance of World War II had lost all meaning. In this hostile environment, the VALB could only try to mobilize public opinion against the proposal, but already the veterans were preoccupied with other political struggles. A dozen years after Franco entered Madrid, Spain had slipped from the nation's conscience.

The Trials

When former brigade commissar Steve Nelson moved to Pittsburgh, Pennsylvania, in 1948 to assume leadership of the regional Communist party, a local newspaper published a personal welcome: "Whatever Steve Nelson's assignment to Pittsburgh might involve, one thing is certain, it won't be in the interests of democracy, American style." Two years later, at about midnight of August 31, 1950, Nelson and his wife returned from the movies to find two detectives outside their house. Flashing badges, the police pushed Nelson into the back of a squad car and drove him to a downtown jail. The charge: sedition against the state of Pennsylvania.

Thus commenced a six-year ordeal that saw Nelson shunted from county jail to state prison, from state jurisdiction to federal court, from guarded hospital rooms to solitary confinement. Bails rose and fell; the media screamed for his head. Nelson could not find a lawyer to defend him. To compound his problems, Nelson was arrested a second time and held with fellow veteran Irving Weissman for violations of the Smith Act. Once an armed man entered his hospital room and threatened to kill him. In 1952, a Pennsylvania court convicted Nelson of sedition and imposed a twenty-year prison sentence. The state supreme court eventually overturned the decision, but the state prosecutor carried an appeal to the U.S. Supreme Court. In 1956, the high court denied the constitutionality of state sedition laws. Meanwhile, a federal court convicted Nelson under the Smith Act in 1953; three years later, the Supreme Court overturned that ruling as well.

"The American warmongers," Milton Wolff protested in 1951 about a rash of arrests of Lincoln veterans, "are trying to implant the idea that it is un-American to be anti-Franco—and to paralyze the anti-Franco movement by sending its leaders to jail." In the May Day parade that year, the Lincolns marched with placards linking the cases of Nelson, John Gates, and Bob Thompson with the plight of the thousand strikers recently jailed by Franco in Barcelona. Twenty-two veterans also attended the American Peace Crusade in Chicago that summer, urging diplomatic negotiations to end the Korean War and opposing the American alliance with Franco.

Passage of the Walter-McCarran Immigration Act of 1950 had provided the federal government with additional grounds for harassing foreign-born veterans of the Lincoln brigade. Frank Bonetti, Willy Busch, and Felix Kusman found themselves on trial as undesirable aliens and subject to deportation. After years of litigation, only Busch had to leave the country. In another cause célèbre, Allan McNeil, former commander of the American training base in Tarazona under the nom de guerre Major Allan Johnson, faced deportation hearings in Pittsburgh, despite his claim that he had been born in the United States. "The attempt of our government to go to bed with butcher Franco . . . requires that they silence all opposition to their pro-fascist drive," he complained. Central to the case against McNeil was the testimony of two disaffected Lincoln veterans: William Harris, a deserter, described as a research specialist in anti-Communist activities for the American Legion; and Robert Gladnick, himself a recently naturalized citizen, who traced his hatred of Communists and the VALB to his experience with Russian officers in Spain. Despite McNeil's conviction by immigration officials, the case lingered in the courts for thirteen years, halted only by the defendant's death in 1966.

By 1953 dozens of Lincoln veterans had been hailed before various courts of law to face inquisitions about their political activities; among the grounds for suspicion was their service in Spain. The VALB responded by forming a

Committee to Defend Lincoln Veterans, headed by Dr. John Simon, once a frontline medic in Spain, to raise money for legal defense and to challenge the political attack on civil rights. "We start from the anti-Franco premise," Moe Fishman explained the committee's strategy to Alvah Bessie, "then develop that into . . . a defense of our comrades, repeal of the Smith Act, fight against political persecution."

For the VALB, the legal issues facing individual veterans remained inseparable from their political position on Spain. In the spring of 1952, for example, Dr. Simon headed a delegation of nine veterans who visited the White House to appeal for amnesty for the Lincolns in prison. Since President Truman was away in Florida, however, they had to settle for a meeting with a Secret Service officer. ("This local Gestapo apparently is empowered to talk officially and to otherwise act as a high government functionary," observed one of the veterans.) Afterward, the same group went to the State Department to protest death sentences given to strikers in Barcelona and to ask the government to work for their release. The delegates also objected to a planned visit to New York by the mayor of Madrid. The government made no formal response, but by the end of the year, Fishman could tally at least two successes: the mayor did not come to New York; and an American ballet troupe did not travel to Spain.

Such meager accomplishments did not ease the pressure on the veterans. In June 1953, a subcommittee of the Senate Judiciary Committee, headed by Indiana's conservative William Jenner, opened hearings on subversion in government and subpoenaed several Lincoln veterans who had served in the OSS. Among them was George Wucinich, who had won a Distinguished Service Cross fighting behind enemy lines in the Balkans. Adopting a truculent attitude, Wucinich scoffed at the committee's counsel: "You may have a paratrooper's haircut, but I don't believe you earned it." Although not a member of the Communist party, Wucinich took the Fifth Amendment on that question, stating simply, "I am an irate citizen." The committee got nowhere in attempting to link Wucinich with the Steve Nelson case or other so-called subversives. Other OSS Lincolns who were called as witnesses, including Wolff and Irving Fajans, took the Fifth Amendment rather than risk citations for contempt of Congress or perjury. They also cited an "oath of secrecy," taken during wartime, not to divulge matters relating to military intelligence.

Indeed, though Barsky had failed to gain protection under the First

Amendment guarantee of free speech, many witnesses found shelter under the Fifth Amendment, which protected a person from self-incrimination. Such defenses, however, did not offer security from public institutions that demanded the signing of loyalty oaths. At the University of California at Berkeley, veteran Robert Colodny had earned a master's degree and a doctorate in history and was working as a teaching assistant in 1950 when he was summoned before a committee on tenure, which was investigating teachers who refused to sign a mandated loyalty oath. "Have you written or published anything which could be construed as espousing communist doctrines?" the chairman inquired. Colodny referred them to his master's thesis ("A Study of the Foreign Genesis of the Franco Regime") and his dissertation ("The Struggle for Madrid"), and then recited a quote from the seventeenth-century French minister Jules Mazarin: "Show me six sentences written by the most innocent of men, and I will show you six reasons to hang him." Colodny's historical arguments had little impact. The university cancelled his contract.

As he looked for another position, the historian discovered that his college placement file included not only the usual transcripts and letters of recommendation, but also material from the files of the FBI. A decade later, Colodny would face charges that his lectures at the University of Pittsburgh expressed subversive opinions. In that case, the FBI forged letters of complaint and threatened his students. He also had to respond to subpoenas from the Senate Internal Security Subcommittee and the HUAC. Other academics among the Lincolns, in such diverse fields as biology and anthropology, faced similar problems of harassment and persecution. The geneticist Clement Markert received a temporary suspension at the University of Michigan for taking the Fifth Amendment before the HUAC. But perhaps because of his candor and unusual brilliance, the faculty supported him and overcame the administration's ruling. Markert eventually proceeded to Yale, where he became head of the biology department.

In May 1953, the new Eisenhower administration brought the witch-hunts closer to the veterans' lives when the Subversive Activities Control Board, an executive tribunal created three years earlier by the McCarran Act, notified the VALB that the organization faced investigation as a Communist front. An unfavorable ruling would force the veterans to register as a subversive group. "That we should be singled out," the VALB office advised the veterans with no small exaggeration, "is a tribute to the effectiveness of the anti-Franco, anti-fascist activities we are conducting."

Such inflated opinions had to yield to worse news five months later when the White House announced the signing of a mutual assistance pact with the Franco regime. Soon afterward, the opening of an exhibition of Spanish handicrafts and the appearance of a Spanish theater group in New York ostensibly suggested the advantages of normal relations between the two countries. The VALB countered with protest leaflets and a demonstration on opening night. The efforts carried no weight. "Now the wheel of history has made a full turn," objected Robert Colodny in a fund-raising appeal for the Spanish refugees. "To have been the mortal enemy of the United States is rewarded by the grant of hundreds of millions of dollars. To have fought Spanish and international fascism is a crime."

Is It Subversive to Be Anti-Franco? asked a VALB pamphlet as the Lincolns confronted the Subversive Activities Control Board (SACB) in the spring of 1954. In the lexicon of the cold war, the idea of a "popular front"—indicating a common cause among various groups—had been transmogrified into the notion of a "Communist front," which was defined as a false facade behind which the party pulled the political strings. The federal government would charge that the "parallelism" between the VALB and the Communist party on political issues demonstrated conspiratorial intent. Yet precisely because many VALB leaders remained active Communists, such manipulation was surely unnecessary. Some members of the VALB executive board, such as Earl Browder's driver, veteran Harold Smith, probably served as conduits of information between the two organizations. But as a political entity, the VALB made its decisions independent of party leaders. Indeed, the most prominent Lincoln veterans in the Communist party—Bob Thompson, John Gates, Steve Nelson, George Watt, Saul Wellman—remained aloof from VALB activities, except in the most unusual circumstances. "We didn't go to the party for picket lines and demonstrations," explained Jack Bjoze, executive secretary of the VALB through most of the 1940's. Only twice, in his recollection, did the VALB seek explicit advice from the Communist party about particular policies: first, about whether to cooperate with Professor John Dollard's study of fear in battle; and second, about how to handle the rehabilitation and erratic behavior of veteran Robert Raven. Otherwise, the veterans' organization and the party remained distinct both financially and politically.

From the government's perspective, however, Communists who formed separate groups still remained subject to the discipline of party edicts. Lacking an independent will or purpose, they were part of a Communist conspiracy. To some extent, that view could apply to the VALB. Certainly the Communist leadership in the VALB used the veterans' platform to affirm party positions. But that congruence did not mean that the party ordered the VALB to follow a particular line. As Communists or as veterans, the Lincolns could reach a position on their own and sometimes, particularly with Spanish affairs, they did so ahead of the party leaders. Very rarely, as in the case of *For Whom the Bell Tolls*, did the party advise its members on how to vote in VALB affairs. And even that advice was not always taken; some good Communists, like Edwin Rolfe and Edward Barsky, opposed the party and supported Hemingway. Moreover, most of the veterans' business was conducted in open forums, where non-Communists participated equally. (By the late 1940's, the VALB had established an open-door policy toward ex-Communists.) Indeed, had the VALB confined itself strictly to questions involving Spain, the allegations might have had less credibility. But because the Lincolns, Communist and non-Communist alike, saw American policy with Spain as part of the larger cold war strategy—which, indeed, it was—they extended the VALB agenda to include non-Spanish issues. "We took positions," Milton Wolff later admitted, "that we had no business taking. Anything that was anti-fascist we were into."

The argument about the VALB's status as a front organization therefore hinged on whether the relationship between the Lincolns and the Communist party was institutional or ideological. The former scarcely existed; the latter appeared self-evident. But would the SACB accept that distinction?

Opening arguments before the SACB commenced in May 1954. Wolff and Fishman, the VALB's only remaining executive officers, worked closely with attorney Homer Clay, a raw-boned Kentuckian who had once sympathized with Republican Spain, personally knew a few Lincoln volunteers, and now offered his services pro bono. Clay was not especially political, but he believed fervently in the constitutional protections of free speech and due process. Throughout the hearings, he would challenge the introduction of innuendo and hearsay evidence, forcing the board to adhere to traditional rules of law. In his first statement he requested a dismissal of the case, arguing that the VALB had not been charged with breaking any laws and had offered no hint of subversion or treachery against the United States. In response, the government charged that the Communist party had already been proven a subversive organization by the SACB and that after 1939 "orders went from the Communist Party National Committee and Communist Party functionaries . . . to the Veterans of the Abraham Lincoln Brigade and its Posts, to inform [them] in order that they would be in absolute accord with the policies of the Communist Party." The panel quickly rejected Clay's motion.

The first government witness was John Lautner, a former Communist official who had recently been expelled from the party on charges of being a government informer; indeed, just prior to his expulsion he had been taken to a basement in Cleveland, stripped naked, and terrorized by party officials, including a couple of Lincoln veterans. In his testimony, Lautner established the government's main argument: that the Communist party had supported the Lincoln brigade in the 1930's and had encouraged the formation of the VALB after the Spanish war. He also stated that party leaders had cooperated with VALB officers in taking public positions. The veterans had picketed the Smith Act hearings at Foley Square in 1949, Lautner said, "under Party direction and Party control." Lautner proceeded to name nineteen veterans who held positions in the Communist party. In this way, the government tried to develop the idea of "parallelism" between the party and its various "fronts." The next three witnesses added little in that direction; instead, they simply verified that the VALB had donated material to the New York Public Library, kept funds in a regular bank account, and procured city licenses to solicit donations on the streets of New York.

The testimony of William Herrick (known in Spain as Bill Harvey) offered a different kind of information, based on personal experience. Raised in the radical movement in New York—as a boy he had joined the Communists' Young Pioneers and later the Young Communist League—Herrick had worked with a party group in the furriers' union before volunteering with the first Americans to go to Spain. His responses stressed the intimate connection between the Communist party and the Lincoln recruits. Despite the rhetoric of the Popular Front, said Herrick, "we understood and all communists understood that that meant the ultimate control of the Communist party." He recalled discussions among the volunteers, indicating "that we knew we were going to fight for the Communist party." Herrick also remembered that the men "discussed that we were going into the heat of battle; that we would be hardened revolutionists; and when we came back we would be in the forefront of a revolutionary struggle in our own country." On the basis of such memories, the government would later argue that the Communist party had intervened in Spain with dual motives: publicly, to fight fascism; secretly, to build a cadre of militant revolutionaries.

At the core of Herrick's account, however, lay a saga not so much of political subversion as of corruption and evil. He testified about the abrupt removal of men from the trenches in Spain "for breach of party discipline," implying that they had subsequently been assassinated or placed in particularly dangerous positions where they would be killed in battle. Wounded in one of the first encounters, on February 23, 1937, Herrick had been evacuated to a hospital and spent the remainder of his time in Spain in convalescence. But he had not escaped the scrutiny of a Comintern official, who boasted of killing "Trotskyite Fascists" and who terrorized Herrick into spying on fellow patients. (Years later, Herrick offered additional details, which also rationalized his testimony to the SACB: "I was informed on twice in Spain for what were deemed party infractions, once by a Lincoln comrade and so-called friend, Ruby Kaufman, and once by my nurse and lover, the first causing me little harm, the second costly to me in terms of dignity and honor.")

After his return from Spain, Herrick stated, the Communist party had instigated the formation of the VALB (he did not mention that he had run for treasurer of the veterans' organization in 1937). But though his disillusionment with the party had increased, Herrick recalled, he hesitated to leave because of serious medical problems and personal attachments. Only after the signing of the Nazi-Soviet pact in 1939 had he repudiated the party publicly, and that step had cost him his job with the furriers. Although he had flirted with the Independent Labor League of America, a "revolutionary Marxist organization," the group had disbanded in 1940 because, as Herrick put it, "there was no role for revolutionary Marxism in a country like the United States."

Despite his forthright anticommunism, Herrick felt decidedly uncomfortable about appearing before the SACB. "I felt guilty, sick. I felt I was going to puke on myself. I felt terrible," he later admitted. "I was brought up in the Communist party. I was doing the unforgivable." Interestingly, Herrick was forced by the VALB defense to divulge more than he had intended. In his opening testimony, he had referred to specific individuals he had known in Spain. Under cross-examination, Homer Clay asked him to name other volunteers. Herrick did so hesitantly. Then, in a curious strategy, the defense urged him to identify Lincoln volunteers who belonged to the Communist party. The transcript of the hearing reveals the witness's obvious discomfort. Indeed, he began by naming dead volunteers; but under the defense's pressure, "a few names," in Herrick's words, "slipped through." Asked many years later to explain that peculiar defense strategy, Fishman and Wolff suggested that by forcing Herrick to name names, they hoped he would introduce information that could be refuted by other witnesses; but no refutation followed.

However biased in his conclusions or exceptional in his experience, Herrick appeared to tell the truth as best he remembered it. (Like most witnesses, he made some obvious errors of fact.) But he knew exactly the harm he had produced. "I felt very badly about it," Herrick later stated; "and I've never felt right about it." Nonetheless, he had testified not against friends, he insisted, but against avowed enemies. His primary motive, he would admit, was a desire for revenge: the party had taken away his job in 1939. "It was pure and simple—getting mine back. . . . And from vengeance," he also confessed, "you can only get pain."

The government's next witness, Morris Maken (a.k.a. Mickenberg), felt no such compunctions. Where Herrick had been subpoenaed before the SACB, Maken gladly volunteered to retaliate against the former comrades who had expelled him from the party. His quarrels had already prompted him to become part of the anti-Communist struggle. After leaving the party and the VALB, he had served in the U.S. Army in World War II, and then resumed his career as an organizer of textile workers. He had also joined the American Veterans Committee, hoping that group would become a liberal alternative to the American Legion and the Veterans of Foreign Wars. Within the AVC, the cold war soon provoked a contest for power between liberals and Communists. In the end, the veterans' group voted to prohibit members of the Communist party; and to prove its sincerity, the AVC moved to expel John Gates in 1948. When the former commissar protested such unconstitutional procedures, Maken offered to describe Gates's own disregard of due process in expelling him from the VALB. His testimony was not needed; the AVC purged Gates from the ranks. But, meanwhile, the *Daily Worker* published a story, later reprinted in the *Volunteer for Liberty*, that Maken had deserted from the International Brigades in Spain. Maken sued both the author of the story, veteran Bernard Rubin, and Gates, then editor of the *Daily Worker*, for libel. And many years later, they indeed retracted their statements.

Maken, by reason of politics and temperament, had no desire to mince words with the SACB. His testimony emphasized the arrogance and incompetence of the Communist leadership in running the brigades. He depicted the irrational promotion of officers such as Oliver Law. He remembered having to censor reading material that made "any unfavorable references to the [Soviet Union] and the international Communist movement." He reported the execution of Paul White and denied that White had been court-martialed. Most relevant, he described how his expulsion from the party complicated his acceptance into the VALB in 1938, requiring him to obtain special clearance. He exhibited no hesitation in identifying veterans as Communists or otherwise embarrassing his former comrades. So it was somewhat surprising when, in the course of his cross-examination by Homer Clay, Maken interrupted the hearing to ask the SACB panel if the name of his employer, the Textile Workers of America, CIO, could be deleted from the record. "We do a lot of our work in the South," Maken explained, "and we face very serious difficulties at the hands of employers who are reactionary and unscrupulous in their counter-propaganda to unionism. . . . People in the South are fearful and primitive. They . . . cannot differentiate . . . between an active Communist and an ex-Communist." The SACB recessed to consider his request, then denied it.

Four other veterans provided testimony about Communist influence in Spain and in the VALB. Edward Horan (a.k.a. Palega), an informant for the Chicago police and the FBI since 1940, declared that the local VALB regularly received orders from the Communist party and consistently followed the party line. Robert Gladnick, who had cooperated with the FBI as early as 1940 and had testified in the McNeil deportation case, stressed the power of Soviet agents in Spain and attacked the VALB's subservience to communism. As an example, he cited the veterans' picketing of the French consulate in New York in 1940 to protest conditions in the refugee camps, which, he said, "helped to stab France in the back." A deserter named William Harris told the board about the secret mission of Commissar John "Robbie" Robinson, who had journeyed from Spain to the Soviet Union in 1937 to report on the military situation on the Aragon front. In his cross-examination of Harris, Milton Wolff would label the story "so fantastic in nature" as to discredit the testimony; yet other veterans have subsequently corroborated its truth.

Harris also introduced the issue of the VALB's aid to the Spanish underground in the 1940's, but on cross-examination admitted his ignorance about the dispersal of food, clothing, and medical supplies sent to refugees and other war victims in Europe. Leo Hecht, the last Lincoln to testify for the government, had been incarcerated in Spain for seven months for attempted desertion. He had also been arrested upon his return to New York for passport violations. (Hecht may have been the only Lincoln formally charged with such crimes; a Brooklyn grand jury voted not to indict him.) A seaman like Harris, Hecht told an elaborate story about Soviet intelligence that had nothing to do with the VALB, but that implied some secret relationships. Although Hecht had participated in VALB functions, he explained that recently he had "experienced a complete change . . . in my ideological political beliefs."

Besides these veteran informers, the government also introduced testimony from other "experts" in Communist affairs. Most notorious was Harvey Matusow, who mixed fact, fantasy, and hearsay evidence into a web of intrigue, linking the VALB to the political controversies of the 1940's. He charged, for example, that because Lincoln veterans had learned "street fighting and riot participation" in Spain, the party had recruited them as bodyguards for the black entertainer Paul Robeson after riots in Peekskill, New York, in 1949 jeopardized his life. Such statements, wholly untrue, fed the theory that the Spanish war had been a training ground for revolutionary cadres. But then, in a remarkable conversion, Matusow repudiated his testimony and the SACB exempted it from consideration. More damaging was the impact of Louis Budenz, former editor of the *Daily Worker*, who specifically named party leaders who had directed VALB programs. He mentioned the creation of the "Browder Brigade" in the summer of 1941, a program in which the Lincoln veterans volunteered to build the circulation of the party newspaper. He also claimed that VALB leaders had reported to the national committee and that the VALB constitution had been approved by the party's highest political body. Other witnesses, including ex-Communists and police detectives, added a mishmash of evidence showing that the VALB and individual veterans took the same positions as the Communist party on a multitude of issues.

After hearing sixteen government witnesses, Homer Clay moved for a dismissal of the case. He pointed out that the VALB had dissolved itself as a corporation in 1952 and no longer existed as a legal entity to register with the SACB. He observed that only 33 veterans had been named as Communists and that those who were party organizers had been operating in that capacity prior to the creation of the VALB. While acknowledging that some veterans, such as Steve Nelson, had been promoted in the party because of their work in Spain, he insisted that those few instances remained independent of the VALB. The evidence, he argued, showed that the party neither controlled the VALB financially nor dictated instructions to its members. Finally, he emphasized that every parallel action between the Communist party and the VALB had been legal and appeared "perfectly consistent with the overall purposes of the organization."

In response to Clay, the government's attorney, Robert Purl, offered a long rebuttal, suggesting alternative interpretations of the evidence. He added, moreover, that the issue of Communist influence in Spain remained important because that country had inordinate influence in Latin America. Clay's request for a dismissal was denied.

The VALB opened its defense in September 1954. Milton Wolff began with a blunderbuss attack on the Eisenhower administration's friendship with Franco's Spain, arguing that the SACB's reexamination of the Spanish war served only to justify current American foreign policy, which, he said, "is determined to rewrite history in such a fashion as to accommodate the alliance and its purposes." The government attorney promptly objected to the speech and the SACB ordered the remarks removed from the record. Wolff, forced to mute his voice, insisted nonetheless that the inquiry served primarily "to revile the legally elected government of Spain in order that this administration may, in better conscience, embrace Franco." The hearings attempted, he observed, "to make anti-Franco synonymous with anti-American." He cited a peculiar coincidence: Senator Pat McCarran, "the father of the law under which we are being heard," had been a recent guest of General Franco. The veterans, Wolff admitted, did not expect to win their case. But to register with the board was equivalent to admitting subversion and treason; and to enter no defense meant accepting "the characterization of our anti-fascism as subversive." The Lincolns had no alternative, he said, but to fight.

Their first witness, General José Asensio of the Spanish Republican Army,

had a Spaniard's pride in his country's independence. He not only denied that
the Spanish Republic took orders from any other government or political party,
but also claimed to have himself conceived of the idea of using political commissars in the army. Furthermore, his testimony equated the presence of Soviet officers in Spain with the United States' wartime military mission in Valencia under Colonel Fuqua. Government objections to his statements created
a whirl of controversy, and he was soon dismissed from the stand.

The next VALB witness was Evan Biddle Shipman, a wealthy, European-
educated non-Communist veteran who made his living as a horse-racing
columnist. A friend of Ernest Hemingway, he had gone to Spain as an ambulance driver and then served in the Washington battalion at Brunete. His
presence, designed to offset the stereotyped view of working-class revolutionaries, deemphasized the role of the party in controlling the political views of
the volunteers. The government cross-examination appeared perfunctory.

Crawford Morgan, a machine gunner in Spain and a veteran of World War
II, spoke about the motives of the black volunteers. "I, being a Negro," he
said about his desire to enlist with the Lincolns, "I had a pretty good idea of
fascism, what fascism was, . . . and I got a chance to fight it there with bullets." Morgan contrasted the Jim Crowism of the World War II army with the
equality of the International Brigades: "I was treated like all the rest of the
people were treated," he said, "and when you have been in the world for quite
a long time and have been treated worse than people treat their dogs, it is
quite a nice feeling." With such logic, Morgan appeared to be no dupe of some
Communist recruiter. When the government attorney questioned him about
the threat of fascism in the United States, Morgan simply described the dis-
advantages of being a black man in America: his difficulty in getting a job as
a printer because of his race; the residential problems of Harlem, where he
lived; and the threat of lynching in his native North Carolina. These facts, he
said, were signs of "fascist tendencies." As for his own political views, Morgan took refuge behind the Fifth Amendment.

Milton Wolff, the VALB's last major witness, keenly understood the problems of self-incrimination, perjury, and contempt. His direct testimony focused on the military aspects of the war, avoiding the issues of commissars
and deserters. He insisted that the political position of the VALB frequently
reflected the unique lessons of Spain rather than the doctrines of the party
line. Thus the VALB's support of the Soviet Union during its war with Finland

in 1939–40 derived from the pro-fascist policies of the Finnish embassy in Madrid three years earlier; that "common knowledge," Wolff remarked, he had learned from Ernest Hemingway. Similarly, he maintained that the VALB's attitude toward postwar Spain followed not so much the Communist party line as the statements of the United Nations.

Under cross-examination, Wolff proved a cautious witness. "Having failed to touch our case as presented by us," he reported, "the government counsel in collaboration with the [SACB] panel has resorted to a diversion. . . . They are going into matters wholly irrelevant and immaterial to this case." Such a strategy, he believed, left him open "for a contempt citation or a perjury rap." Moreover, with enough Fifth Amendment answers, the government might move to strike all his testimony. Yet Wolff's relationship to the party remained so ambiguous—he had never joined technically, but he enjoyed complete access to the leadership—that he dared not expose himself to a demand to name names. About his own Communist connections, therefore, he took the Fifth Amendment several times. Still, the government attorney drew inferences from Wolff's many public appearances at Communist-sponsored functions. By showing that the VALB continued to take political stands—opposition to the McCarran Act, for example—the government denied that the organization had dissolved itself.

The final arguments, heard in December 1954, reiterated the main lines of testimony. In summing up the case, the government listed 33 veterans who held significant party offices, suggesting that these leaders assured that the VALB adhered to the party position. Homer Clay, in his rebuttal, used the same data to deny the government claims. Observing that only 33 names had been introduced, he stressed the lack of ideological conformity within the organization. Non-Communists, even apolitical people like Shipman, would be wrongly associated with subversion if the SACB were to condemn the VALB. "Was Maken or Mickenberg dominated when he came back and went into the VALB?" he wondered. "Was he dominated or controlled? Can you imagine a more indomitable character than Mickenberg?" Besides, Clay said, those 33 Communist functionaries had been in the party before the Spanish war, absolving the VALB from its alleged role as a training ground for new cadres. Most important, he reminded the board that all the VALB's activities had been open and entirely legal.

*

While the veterans waited for the preliminary findings, the government's case against the Joint Anti-Fascist Refugee Committee took the ultimate toll. In 1950, the leadership had gone to prison. Then the U.S. Treasury Department had filed a claim to collect $315,000 in back taxes. Such legal actions drained the committee's finances and distracted it from political efforts. No longer did members have time or money or energy to devote to relief work for Spanish refugees. In March 1955, the Joint Committee announced its dissolution. "The Eisenhower administration has achieved two 'victories,'" explained a frustrated board. "It has succeeded in giving millions of American taxpayers' money to Franco. It has forced the JARC to cease its efforts to send aid and comfort to the [Spaniards] . . . Franco drove out of their native land." Within a few years, Spanish exiles and American liberals would form a new American Committee to Aid Spanish Democracy and the Lincoln veterans would become major supporters. But the demise of the Joint Committee symbolized the futility of defying the federal government during the cold war.

In this political climate, the SACB rendered the expected recommendations about the VALB in May 1955. As Wolff had predicted, the board regretted that the use of the Fifth Amendment had "precluded full cross-examination of highly pertinent . . . testimony." Nonetheless, the SACB concluded that the veterans' organization "throughout its existence has been and is substantially directed, dominated, and controlled by the Communist Party of the United States and is primarily operated for the purpose of giving aid and support to the Party and the world Communist movement." In accepting the government's reasoning, the board pointed to four basic points of evidence. First, because "a substantial number of the persons" active in the VALB also participated in the Communist leadership, the Communist party "has guided and directed the internal affairs" of the veterans' group. Second, the VALB received support, financial and otherwise, from the Communist party; third, the veterans aided and supported the party. Finally, the board cited the evidence of parallelism: the VALB "never knowingly has deviated from the views and policies advanced by the Communist party."

The ensuing 250-page report elaborated on those basic contentions. Summarizing the role of the Communist party in Spain, the board concluded that members of the Lincoln brigade had recruited, trained, and operated as Soviet agents. After the war, the board found, the VALB had performed a variety of functions for the party, not the least of which was criticism of American foreign policy relating to Spain. The board also denied that anti-Franco activities had been stigmatized as pro-Communist: "Anti-fascist activity," it asserted, "does not afford a sanctuary from this [McCarran] Act, in which another brand of alien totalitarianism can operate without revealing its true purposes." In short, the SACB accepted the government's case uncritically. It made no distinctions between ideology and institutions; it condemned Communists and non-Communists alike. The VALB, it ruled, was indeed a Communist-front organization.

In September 1955, the VALB presented final arguments against the recommendation, but that month the veterans focused on an equally ominous development: Franco's Spain had formally applied for admission to the United Nations. "This fascist leopard has not changed a single spot," Wolff protested to Henry Cabot Lodge, the U.S. ambassador to the United Nations. Even "expediency," he charged, which had rationalized the 1953 pact for war bases in Spain, did not justify altering the diplomatic status of the Franco regime. But the Eisenhower administration and the General Assembly thought otherwise, and Spain entered the United Nations that fall. VALB protests made no difference.

Nor did Homer Clay's arguments influence the SACB. In December 1955, the board ordered the VALB to register with the government under the terms of the McCarran Act. For the veterans, it was another failure, another defeat, another betrayal of the cause of Spain. It was another opportunity to surrender. But that was also something the Lincolns would not accept. Two months later, the VALB petitioned the courts for a formal review of the SACB order, setting in motion a series of legal rulings that would be decided a decade later, as we shall see, by the U.S. Supreme Court.

The prolonged legal complications of the SACB case, however, had shaken the foundations of the VALB. Other government harassment burdened the ranks. In 1955, the Veterans Administration added insult to injury by cancelling the disability pensions of World War II veterans convicted under the Smith Act; three Lincolns—Bob Thompson, Saul Wellman, and Robert Klonsky—fell into this category. (Wellman, who had been seriously wounded in the Battle of the Bulge, received a bill of over $9,000 for back payments.)

Other Lincoln veterans found themselves subpoenaed by the HUAC or summoned before similar anti-Communist agencies in the states. Most refused to cooperate and found legal protection in the Fifth Amendment.

After the outbreak of the Korean War, the Coast Guard routinely screened Communists from maritime jobs, taking away employment from the many seamen and waterfront workers who had fought in Spain. Bill Bailey, hero of the *Bremen* protest, abruptly found himself ashore without the prospect of a job. Black veteran Eluard Luchelle McDaniels, once a seafaring cook, literally starved for want of an income. "It is about 6 o'clock in evening," he wrote one day in 1954, "and I hasn't had breakfast yet. . . . I have two pennies to my name, no food in the house, and don't know if and when I will be able to get any." The Coast Guard policy "is not just political," he insisted, "but more racial discrimination than anything else." Such personal problems plagued dozens of Lincoln veterans, effectively preventing them from undertaking political work.

Their impotence percolated upward. By the autumn of 1956, the VALB faced the basic question of perpetuating its existence. The SACB hearings had drained its financial resources; the unfavorable ruling had frightened the membership. The organization's inability to affect U.S. policy toward Spain was particularly galling. "Shall we continue an organization which was founded . . . to influence our fellow Americans—and can no longer do so?" asked Wolff and Fishman in a candid letter to their comrades. "Shall we continue an organization whose only present role is to defend itself against government attacks? Shall we continue to ask for funds from faithful supporters who are pressed by more immediate appeals from all sides?" The answer, the two concluded, was that the VALB should be dissolved.

Most veterans disagreed. At a crowded meeting in New York in November 1956, man after man stood up to avow the importance of fulfilling promises made in Spain nearly two decades earlier. They said that Lincoln veterans should never abandon the Spanish people or surrender the fight against Franco. Sympathizing with the problems of the VALB leadership, new voices offered to head the battered organization. Maury Colow, expelled from the Communist party in 1952 for suggesting a more flexible analysis of American conditions, now volunteered to serve as executive secretary. Implicitly, he promised some independence from the party line. Bolstered by the enthusiasm of his comrades, Fishman agreed to remain as the organization's treasurer. Wolff would stay as national commander, though for personal reasons he would soon be replaced by Steve Nelson. And, as if to seal those commitments, some five hundred veterans and friends gathered at a New York hotel three months later to celebrate the twentieth anniversary of the birth of the Lincoln brigade and to affirm what became an annual call to the colors: "Next year, in Madrid!"

The Politics of Culture

Political pressures against radicalism, dissent, and nonconformity raised special problems for Lincoln veterans who worked as creative artists. Even before the formal blacklisting (and the informal "graylisting") associated with the McCarthy era, the broadcast networks, Hollywood studios, magazines, and publishing houses started to put a damper on politically sensitive material. Lincoln veteran Milton Robertson, who had won prizes during World War II for such radio stories as "Ballad for Herman Boettcher" and "Hitler Meets Abe Lincoln," learned in 1946 that the networks in New York would not even read his scripts about the Spanish war, much less broadcast them. Edwin Rolfe, who had moved to Hollywood after a medical discharge from the army in 1943, encountered similar difficulties in placing a collection of short stories about his experiences in Spain. "In L.A.," he wrote in his 1945 novel *The Glass Room*, "murder was always splashed over page one; it got triple-A priority over everything except anti-Russian propaganda." Indeed, the book's plot hinged on the threat of a fascist takeover in southern California.

The anti-Communist mood, harbinger of the postwar Red Scare, became palpable during a bitter strike of Hollywood screen-writers in 1945. The studios took the opportunity to dismiss dissident writers. Among those fired was Alvah Bessie, author of the year's Oscar nominee for best original story (*Objective, Burma*). "Workers for Spain are automatically Red," he complained. "I certainly feel much better about a free Spain than I do about freeing our own country."

Bessie's notion of creative freedom, however, remained constricted by Communist discipline. A few weeks after Warner Brothers dropped Bessie's contract, screenwriter Albert Maltz published an essay in the *New Masses* en-titled "What Shall We Ask of Writers?" The article aroused Bessie's ire. For in questioning the axiom that "art is a weapon," Maltz had dared to protest the party's preference of ideological conformity over artistic creativity. "An artist can be a great artist without being an integrated or a logical or a progressive thinker on all matters," Maltz suggested. "Writers must be judged by their work, and *not* the committees they join." The proposal brought a quick and angry counterattack from the West Coast Communist intelligentsia. "No," shouted Alvah Bessie, in a rebuttal in *New Masses*. "We need more than 'free' artists. We need *Party* artists. We need artists deeply, truly and honestly rooted in the working class who realize the truth of Lenin's assertion that the abso-lute freedom they seek 'is nothing but a bourgeois or anarchist phase.'" Within weeks, Maltz bowed to his critics and published a retraction of his heretical views.

Edwin Rolfe, unlike Bessie, expressed sympathy for Maltz, an old friend from New York. Rolfe, to be sure, clung to an orthodox Marxist view of the role of the proletarian artist and writer: "It is not a question," he said, "of who—as individuals—are the leaders or pathfinders, but rather in which class their roots are sunk." But Rolfe also possessed a personal compassion that enabled him to transcend strict party edicts. Earlier, he had ignored requests that he sever relations with Vincent Sheean and Ralph Bates because of their criticism of the party line. Now, without altering his political allegiances, he argued "that good writing cannot be measured against the rigid yardsticks of good intentions or basic Marxist clarity alone." To Rolfe, a working-class writer remained, after all, a worker; he could never understand why radical organi-zations often expected writers to waive their rights to royalties, while they scrupulously insisted on paying the printers and the bookbinders. And precisely because creativity involved hard work, Rolfe distrusted ideological criteria for judging artistic endeavor.

What the party needed, Rolfe told a meeting of left-wing writers, was fewer conferences and more creative energy. Writers needed the same "sense of exaltation and dedication to work which a Spanish or Greek guerrilla gets out of his struggle against Franco or against King George-Paul-Truman." In time, ironically, Bessie would come to accept Rolfe's position. Badgered by party editors to "be 'as correct' as possible," often denied publication even in the party press, Bessie would argue in the midst of the McCarthy period that "we are the ONLY people who can afford to tell the truth, or engage in controversy, and I think we should do both."

By then, however, Bessie had paid for his political loyalties. As one of the Hollywood Ten—along with Albert Maltz—he had been summoned to Washington, D.C., by the HUAC in October 1947 and had declined to answer questions on grounds of the First Amendment. In an unpublished article (rejected by the party's *Mainstream* magazine), Bessie compared his anxiety at the ordeal to the fear of battle—cramps, sweaty palms, dry mouth—"because you know that this is the enemy; the same enemy in different uniform, speaking your native tongue." Hustled from the chambers before he could read a statement into the record, Bessie had intended to link the congressional inquiry to the destruction of the Spanish Republic. The idea that support of Spain "was and is subversive, un-American and Communist inspired" was, he said, a "lie originally spawned by Hitler and Franco." When the U.S. Supreme Court refused to rule on the First Amendment defense, Bessie went to jail for contempt of Congress in 1951. He served eleven months in Texarkana, Arkansas. During that time, all he could write (besides a limited number of letters to his family, his lawyers, and a single Lincoln veteran) was a cluster of "poems to the free world."

The long legal fights, the political chill, the economic consequences of the blacklists—all provided the background for yet another controversy within the VALB about the place of Ernest Hemingway in the literary canon of the Spanish civil war. As part of their defense against charges of subversion, the Lincolns had planned to publish a series of books that would document their anti-fascist commitments, raise funds, and publicize their current predicament. Veteran Irving Fajans now proposed that the VALB produce a literary anthology of poetry and prose about Spain. The veterans hoped to reach a broader constituency, to create, at least on a literary level, a new Popular Front. No one could have anticipated the resulting uproar.

Alvah Bessie, who signed on as Fajans's coeditor, framed the problem simply by asking the VALB office whether the anthology should include writers "who were once good and are now lousy." Bessie certainly wanted to include Hemingway's moving eulogy to the American dead in Spain, but he proposed that the work be paired with the veterans' public criticism of *For Whom the Bell Tolls*. Rolfe, resuming the position he had held in 1940, argued against publishing the attack on the novel; the "half-dead dog" would interfere with using Hemingway's other work. Besides, he observed, the novelist was still considered a progressive writer by Soviet critics. Bessie acquiesced in that judgment and listed the eulogy in his projected table of contents. Rolfe, meanwhile, protested the exclusion of the former Communists Ralph Bates and Tom Wintringham, insisting that only "excellence of material should guide us . . . ; unless, of course, the authors have turned out to be out-and-out fascists." Hemingway, for his part, was not so sure he wanted his name linked with the VALB. When Milton Wolff appealed to him for moral support, citing the impending imprisonment of Bessie and Barsky, Hemingway offered little consolation. "You guys sort of bought this anyway," he said. "You hired out to be tough and then somebody gets hit and says you can't do this to me." Although Hemingway considered Barsky "a saint," he thought Bessie "to be a jerk on the best day he ever lived."

Such quibbles escalated when the French poet Louis Aragon announced he would withhold permission to publish his works unless he had assurances that the anthology would include the writings of Dolores Ibarruri and exclude those of Ernest Hemingway because of his insults to André Marty. Bessie promptly advised the veterans to ignore Aragon's request: "Maybe even he can understand that conditions and attitudes here are different." But the argument assumed greater importance when the French veterans of the International Brigades endorsed Aragon's position. Behind the scenes, moreover, the French Communist party supported Aragon. Their endorsement, which appealed to international class solidarity, persuaded the American Communist party—in what was virtually an unprecedented move—to intervene directly in VALB affairs.

At a stormy meeting of the VALB executive board, such prominent party veterans as John Gates and Irving Goff urged compliance with the French position. They insisted that including Hemingway "would be 'scabbing on the Spanish people,'" that the *Daily Worker* would condemn the project, that trading Hemingway for Aragon would provoke an international scandal. On the other side, Irving Fajans, the originator of the anthology, threatened to resign as executive secretary of the VALB if Hemingway was dropped. Gates, exercising his prestige as a member of the Communist party's central committee, finally convinced the board to adopt an unhappy compromise, leaving the ultimate decision to Louis Aragon. Accordingly, the veterans sent a copy of their critique of Hemingway's novel to France, offering to include it in the anthology along with the novelist's other work; if Aragon rejected that proposal, the veterans would publish only the critique.

A few weeks later, a boisterous meeting of Lincoln veterans in New York reexamined the question. Dr. Edward Barsky, still facing prison for his contempt conviction, stressed Hemingway's support of the Spanish Republic and pleaded for his inclusion in the anthology. Gates spoke, as before, for the Communist party. Then, in open session, a majority of the veterans voted to exclude Hemingway. Fajans promptly resigned as secretary of the VALB and as editor of the book. But the war of words continued. From California, both Bessie and Rolfe decried the idea of publishing Hemingway and condemning him in the same volume. Both pleaded for a reconsideration of the value of Hemingway's name in assisting the Spanish underground and the veterans themselves.

Milton Wolff took the opposite position. On behalf of the VALB executive board, he assured the French veterans "that we owe you all a hearty vote of thanks for pointing out the incorrectness of the steps we were about to take." Bessie chided Wolff for perpetuating "a grave political and cultural error" and pleaded that no other writers be dropped. Yet the VALB office continued to evaluate the political bona fides of other authors, relying on the British veterans for approval of European writers. Some writers, like Herbert Matthews, were excluded temporarily (apparently because he supported aspects of the cold war), only to be restored on second thought. In the end, the deletion of Hemingway remained most blatant.

The Heart of Spain, as the anthology was titled, appeared in 1952, self-published by the VALB because no commercial publisher would accept it.

The final version omitted not only the work of Hemingway but also the VALB's condemnation. As editor, Bessie coolly measured the inadequacies of *For Whom the Bell Tolls*: "The novel in its total impact presented an unforgivable distortion of the meaning of the struggle in Spain. Under the name and prestige of Hemingway, important aid was thus given to humanity's worst enemies." Meanwhile, the editor illogically protested another literary censorship—the refusal of United Artists to permit a reprinting of the anti-fascist screenplay *Blockade*, by John Howard Lawson, one of the Hollywood Ten.

Numerous writers on the Left, including Rolfe, scorned Bessie's rationalizations. Lillian Hellman protested what she considered "censorship" and withdrew permission to include her works in subsequent printings (though, in the end, there would be none). Wolff, in turn, took the opportunity to chastise Hemingway for his ungratefulness toward the Spanish people. "Hemingway gave an eager and receptive world *For Whom The Bell Tolls*," he told Hellman, "and thereby struck a blow against the very spirit that had nurtured him." Yet the exclusion of Hemingway remained a matter of discomfort even to him. In their private correspondence, Bessie and Wolff frequently commented on the worthiness of Hemingway's activities and writings, joked about his failed marriage to Martha Gellhorn, and speculated about his lack of political convictions.

Nor did the quarrel cease. For the controversy between Ernest Hemingway and the Lincoln brigade constituted no mere literary debate. The argument hinged, rather, on questions of responsibility. To what extent had the Lincolns participated in a Communist terror in Spain? Did their commitment to the Republic justify political persecution at home? And for their part, the Lincolns demanded greater accountability from Hemingway for the plight of the Spanish people under Franco. To what degree had Hemingway's novel contributed to pro-Franco sentiment in the United States? Should the novelist have spoken more boldly against U.S. postwar friendship with the last fascist dictator? These moral questions made accommodation virtually impossible.

"I don't know one damned thing about Marty," Wolff assured Herbert Matthews 25 years later, referring to Hemingway's prime villain. "And *that's* significant." Whatever the machinations of the Communist party in Spain, Wolff argued, the Lincoln volunteers had fought and died primarily as anti-fascists. Moreover, Lincoln veterans felt keenly their obligations to comrades killed in Spain. Those Americans who, in Hemingway's poignant phrase, had entered

Spanish earth offered no solace to the war's survivors—just the opposite, in fact. Their sacrifice created a sense of responsibility, something that journalists and novelists like Sheean and Hemingway would never face.

That was why Wolff remained so unforgiving of Hemingway. "He was a 'tourist' in Spain," Wolff wrote to Bessie in 1981, "a voyeur who darted in and out of the action as it pleased him. . . . Which is not to say Ernest Hemingway was not on our side. He was. And his contribution was considerable. . . . But his commitment was not as ours." Unlike the Lincoln veterans, Wolff told another comrade, Hemingway "was free to choose where to go, when to go, when not to go. . . . In other words his commitment was such that he could write For Whom the Bell Tolls without taking into account what was truly best for la causa." The result, Wolff asserted, was that for Hemingway "the essence of commitment to the struggle did not exist." Yet when Alvah Bessie prepared a second anthology to commemorate the 50th anniversary of the Spanish war in 1986, he placed Hemingway's work at the beginning of the book. And not a single Lincoln veteran questioned its appearance.

Many writers, painters, and musicians who had served in the Lincoln brigade had assumed a responsibility to commemorate the anti-fascist struggle in their work. During the anti-Communist crusade, however, their sympathy for the Spanish Republic exposed them to government harassment and private blacklists. At the same time, their creative aspirations often put them at odds with the political rigidity of the Communist party; for many, it became impossible to reconcile their individualism with ideological orthodoxy. Feeling stifled, numerous creative workers on the Left sought a haven in Mexico. The Hispanic culture evoked memories of Spain, and the political climate was more liberal. Mexico had not only supported the doomed Republic, but also welcomed Spanish refugees. And, not to be underestimated, the cost of living there was relatively low.

Conlon Nancarrow had returned from Spain an angry man. One of the last Americans to cross into France, he had spent eight excruciating days in a refugee concentration camp. After returning to America, he felt outrage at the government's antagonism toward the Lincoln veterans. When the State Department refused to reissue his passport in 1940, Nancarrow opted for self-exile in Mexico City. That uprooting set the background for a remarkable career in musical composition.

Born in Texarkana, Arkansas, in 1912, Nancarrow had studied classical trumpet, learned to play jazz, and devoured the five-cent Socialist "Little Blue Books" published by Haldeman-Julius. His formal education included a brief stay at the Cincinnati Conservatory of Music, before he moved to Boston to study counterpoint with the composer Roger Sessions. During the Depression, he found work with the WPA, first as a conductor, then as a composer of theater music. In Spain, Nancarrow served with an anti-aircraft battery. One comrade observed his intellectual restlessness, calling it "a rebellion against the ivory-tower work of our contemporary classicists." Later, as an expatriate in Mexico (he became a Mexican citizen in 1956), Nancarrow could indulge his nonconformity—personal, political, aesthetic. His geographical isolation from the musical mainstream reinforced his personal seclusiveness, encouraging an eccentric interest in polyrhythm and multiple tempos. But he could seldom find musicians willing to play—or capable of playing—his complicated compositions.

Nancarrow, in any case, detested the idea that each performance inevitably involved a reinterpretation of his musical work, and he searched for a form that would assure the preservation of his peculiar originality. He found the answer in the mechanical player piano. Returning to New York in 1947—his only visit to the United States before his belated discovery by the music world in the 1980's—Nancarrow bought a player piano and a hand-operated punching machine on which to compose piano rolls. The result was some incredibly innovative music, some of it too difficult ever to be played by human hands. In that format, he developed rhythms and musical lines of tremendous intellectual complexity, but which still expressed feelings of wild exuberance.

It took months, sometimes years, for Nancarrow to complete a ten-minute composition; after twenty years' labor, the duration of his composed music amounted to about five hours. Yet the unconventional music eventually found an appreciative audience. In 1981, he received a prestigious MacArthur Foundation "genius" grant—$300,000—and this brought Nancarrow's work into public view for the first time. (The U.S. government, which had earlier refused him a visa because of his "subversive" background, now consented to his return, even though Nancarrow refused to renounce his political views.) A series of concerts brought renown around the world. But, true to Nancarrow's nonconformity, such "performances" required audiences to listen to recordings of his compositions because the player pianos were too unwieldy to transport. "It's all there," insisted the laconic composer. "The other is just nostalgia about hearing things 'live!'" In 1992, the American Academy and Institute of Arts and Letters elected Nancarrow as a "Foreign Honorary Member."

Such stubborn individualism played a lesser role in the musical career of another Lincoln veteran, Lan Adomian, who also found exile and creative encouragement in Mexico City. Born the son of a Jewish cantor in the Ukraine in 1906, Adomian had survived the extreme poverty caused by World War I and the Russian revolution. "Adomian"—the composer's translation of his Jewish name—meant red wine, the wine of even the poorest, he said. He immigrated with his family to New York in 1923. The next year he won a scholarship to study the viola at the Peabody Conservatory in Baltimore and then another to pursue composition under Reginald Morris at the Curtis Institute of Music in Philadelphia.

Returning to New York just as the Depression struck, Adomian joined other unemployed musicians in the Symphony Without Conductors, which provided him an opportunity to write serious compositions, including sonatas and a piano concerto. In 1930, he became friends with Hall Johnson, the black composer and choral director, whose Harlem chorus brought African-American folk music and spirituals to national attention. Adomian attended the weekly rehearsals, developing an interest in ethnic music that would last the rest of his life. Sensitive to his own roots, he wrote serious working-class compositions and helped form various bands and choruses, whose concerts were broadcast on network radio.

The call of Spain interrupted Adomian's career. Given his left-wing, Jewish sensibilities, he later explained, he felt obliged to stand against the fascist threat. "I had a blank page in my life," he said, "and it had to be filled." Later he would dedicate his Spanish Symphony (1960) to a fallen comrade, Jim, "and all the Jims of this small world who fought in Spain to fill the blank pages and who remain in Spanish soil." The Spanish war introduced Adomian to diverse working-class and national songs, and he became intrigued with developing the symphonic potential of everyday music. In Spain, he found time to compose a cycle of songs to accompany the poetry of Miguel Hernández and José Pla y Beltran. (His second wife, a Spaniard, learned this music inside fascist prisons years before she set eyes on the composer.) Back in America, Adomian resolved to become a serious composer; but to his surprise, he found that for two years the trauma of the war prevented him from writing what he envisioned.

While struggling with his muse, Adomian worked as a copyist, played in orchestras, and wrote incidental music for radio broadcast. He also drafted scores for U.S. Navy propaganda films, for which he won a commendation. But a 1943 work setting to music the words of a Pablo Neruda poem, "Song of Love for Stalingrad," aroused political criticism, and his network cancelled the broadcast of the piece. Adomian continued to write for the theater—Konstantin Simonov's *Red People*, Hemingway's *Fifth Column*, productions of *Carmen* and *Peer Gynt*. These activities finally enabled him to overcome his writer's block. By 1951, he had completed 21 compositions.

The coming of the Red Scare soon put Adomian out of work. As a Lincoln veteran, his name appeared on the blacklists that excluded suspected Communists from the entertainment industries. Without income and facing family pressures, he welcomed an opportunity to conduct a series of Mozart concerts in Mexico City. Other work followed, and in 1956 Adomian became a Mexican citizen. He continued to write extensively—eight symphonies, an opera, four cantatas, and many other works for large orchestras and chamber groups— and he established a reputation, winning prizes and honors from around the world. Many of his works reflected his enduring political conscience, particularly his sensitivity to themes of the Jewish holocaust. About his Spanish Symphony he said, "I focused on the constant scream of oppressed Spain," not just the war or its aftermath, but "the roots of a permanent tragic Spain . . . the eternal Spain." As for his involvement in the Spanish war, "it was a decision I never regretted, in spite of all the problems it created for me later." Still nostalgic for New York, Adomian died in exile in 1979.

Even relatively apolitical Lincoln veterans, such as the novelist James Norman Schmidt, found in Mexico a refuge from government harassment. Raised in a conservative Catholic family in Chicago, Schmidt went to Paris to study art but ran out of funds, and he found work as a reporter for the *Chicago Tribune*'s Paris bureau. The position gave him a close vantage point from which to observe the rise of fascism in Europe. He was in Germany the day Hitler came to power; he witnessed street riots by French fascists in 1934. He also covered the revolt of Asturian miners against the right-wing Spanish government in October 1934, reporting on the brutal suppression led by General

Franco. Three years later, Schmidt returned to Spain, intending to write articles about the war, but the activist role of André Malraux persuaded him to enlist in a French anti-aircraft battery.

After the withdrawal of the International Brigades in 1938, Schmidt remained in Madrid to broadcast English-language news programs beamed at the United States. There, he witnessed the very last days of the war, managing to flee the besieged city in March 1939 just before the arrival of Franco's troops. After a harrowing escape to Marseilles—where he was briefly jailed—Schmidt returned to Chicago, joined the staff of the Communist newspaper *Midwest Record*, and enrolled in the Communist party—but only for a short time. "I got disillusioned very fast," he later said; "the party was too didactic and I was much more interested in the anarchist movement with which I was more in tune." With the outbreak of World War II, he became a freelance writer with the nom de plume James Norman. His work drew frequently on the Spanish war, and he wrote two thrillers about the Japanese invasion of China, dedicating the first, *Murder, Chop Chop*, to Irving Goff and Bill Aalto, "guerrilleros extraordinary." After serving in the army during World War II, Schmidt resumed his writing, mostly pulp-magazine fare, and published several stories about heroes returning to Spain to rescue anti-fascists. With the coming of the cold war, however, the FBI began to make frequent visits. Schmidt decided to move to Mexico in 1951.

The Spanish war remained an unsettling inspiration, and Schmidt mined the experiences of his last days in Spain in a haunting autobiographical novel called *The Fell of Dark*, which was published in 1960 and became a bestseller in Europe. Set in Madrid and Valencia during March 1939, the book chronicled the desperate efforts to rescue the defeated anti-fascist leaders from the imminent arrival of Franco's army. Among his heroes was a character modeled on Malcolm Dunbar, the English chief of staff of the Fifteenth Brigade, who had returned to Spain as a newspaper correspondent to spirit Spaniards aboard the rescue ship *Erika Reed*. "Whatever bravery he had was collective," wrote Schmidt of the journalist turned military volunteer. "He could be brave or foolish or frightened because he shared it with others." Yet Schmidt expressed a distinct detachment from collective ideology—"the doctrines of the churches, of the social scientists," which, he said, "are essentially totalitarian in their affirmation of social destiny and their denial of the true individual." Schmidt returned to the United States in 1965, taught literature at

Ohio University, and wrote several books of fiction and nonfiction. He died in 1983.

Spain also haunted the imagination of another talented Lincoln novelist, William Lindsay Gresham, reinforcing a restless eccentricity that both terrified and inspired him. Born in 1909 into a southern family that spoke mournfully of the Confederate lost cause, he had moved to New York at the age of eight. Even as a boy, he saw himself as a loner, creative yet unlovable, and he gravitated to the odd carnival atmosphere at Coney Island. In his early twenties, he graduated into the bohemianism of Greenwich Village. Lanky, bespectacled, and charming, he sang folk music in an artsy nightspot. After a stint in the Civilian Conservation Corps, he returned to the city, met and married a wealthy woman, and determined to become a writer.

Amidst the cultural ferment of the 1930's, Gresham joined the Communist party. "We taught paranoia," he remarked ruefully in 1950, "and called it Political Education." When a close friend died at Brunete, Gresham went to Spain and served with the Anglo-American artillery battery for fifteen months. He was never promoted, he later boasted, never disciplined, and never fired a shot. "I only realized long after," he admitted, "that in my subconscious I had probably got the Spanish Civil War mixed up with the War Between the States!" Comrades remembered him "huddled over a glass of wine," wearing a "Trotsky-like beard" and, no matter how hot the weather, "wrapped in his poncho and with a scarf around his neck." One of the volunteers, "Doc" Holliday, had worked in a carnival, and Gresham interrogated him endlessly about the tricks of the trade. Gresham was one of the last Americans to leave Spain, and he came home, as he put it, "to the bitterness of a lost war, a light attack of tuberculosis, and a long nightmare of neurotic conflict." His marriage collapsed; he drank heavily. Finally, in despair, he attempted to hang himself in a closet, but the hook pulled loose from the wall and he came to consciousness on the closet floor, alone.

A friend introduced Gresham to psychoanalysis, which provided a mental ballast, and he agreed to leave the Communist movement until he recovered. Meanwhile, he met and married a remarkable young writer, Joy Davidman. Working as a freelance writer and editor, Gresham published several stories and articles, and he continued to frequent the bar at the Dixie Hotel, a hangout for carnival workers. In 1946, his obsession crystallized in his first novel,

Nightmare Alley, which explored the creepy characters who inhabited the midways. Purchased by Hollywood for $60,000—it would be made into a successful movie starring Tyrone Power—the book catapulted Gresham into fame and fortune.

He remained troubled and uneasy, prone to drink and rage, simultaneously depressive and violent. An adulterous affair nearly wrecked his marriage. For his wife, the experience wrought a religious conversion, completing her rejection of Communism and launching a spiritual career. Initially, Gresham followed her into the faith. While completing a second successful novel, *Limbo Tower*, set in a tuberculosis ward, in 1949, he became deeply interested in Christianity and joined the Presbyterian church. He described his spiritual awakening in a widely touted series of articles. "Baptized an Episcopalian, raised an agnostic, in turns a Unitarian, a hedonist, a stoic, a Communist, a self-made mystic, and an eclectic grabber after truth," he wrote at age 40, "I had at last come home."

But not for long. While his wife pursued her religious interests, ultimately divorcing Gresham and marrying the English theologian and spiritualist C. S. Lewis, Gresham lapsed into alcoholism. He had to sell his estate to meet his income taxes. He dabbled with Dianetics, Zen, the tarot, Yoga, and I Ching, and he continued to write both fiction and nonfiction about a variety of subjects, including magicians and carnivals. "Writing is one hell of a way to make a living," he assured a fellow veteran from Spain. "I sometimes think that if I have any real talent it is not literary but is a sheer talent for survival. I have survived three busted marriages, losing my boys, war, tuberculosis, Marxism, alcoholism, neurosis, and years of free-lance writing. Just too mean and ornery to kill, I expect." Gresham later joined Alcoholics Anonymous and resumed a stable, secular life. Interested in physical fitness, he published *The Book of Strength* in 1961. But the next year he was diagnosed with cancer, and he saw no reason to suffer. One day, he checked into the Dixie Hotel under an assumed name and committed suicide.

The frustrations of the radical writers and composers formed part of the Spanish war's legacy. Like the party organizers and militant trade unionists, they were not prepared to renounce their political views, even when they despised the dogma of the Communist party. Yet as artists, performing individual work, they lacked a community of supporters. However fine their creative merit, they faced a cold war climate that deprived them of an audience. Often they had to struggle merely to survive, and their output remained on the fringes of cultural taste. Unlike the radical intellectuals of the 1930's, they had lost their place in history.

Alienated Artists

The price of creating art in an unfriendly environment was frustration, poverty, and obscurity—
burdens that weighed heavily on the many cultural
workers who had served in Spain. What is striking,
then, is how many Lincoln veterans persisted in artistic careers, despite the political, economic, and psychological perils. That their names are often unfamiliar speaks less about their talent and creativity than
it does about the difficulty of surmounting cultural
obstacles. If art is a measure of a society's prevailing
predicaments, the work of these Lincoln veterans illuminates the problems of creative expression in the
era of the cold war consensus.

No veteran anguished more about the tensions between political responsibility and creative individualism than the poet Edwin Rolfe. Plagued by repeated heart attacks in the 1940's, he suffered doubly
in the "witch-hunt atmosphere" that prevented him
from working even when he was healthy. For a time,
it seemed that Warner Brothers would produce his
thriller *The Glass Room* (coauthored with Lester Fuller)

and feature Humphrey Bogart and Lauren Bacall in leading roles; but then
the studio cancelled the project. Rolfe found incidental work in Hollywood,
wrote verse for the award-winning documentary *Muscle Beach*, and sold treat-
ments and scripts for several pictures. But the dearth of opportunity sapped
his spirit and self-confidence.

"It's not so much gloom I feel as a sense of powerlessness in the face of so
many things that happen," he wrote in 1951, "small things that . . . keep
breaking up careers and homes and people." Numerous friends fell into the
snags of the "snoopers," as he called the HUAC investigators; at least twice,
he was named as a Communist during the 1951 hearings in Hollywood. The
next year, he received a subpoena to appear before the committee. The news
aggravated his apprehensions, ruined his concentration, and then a series of
legal postponements prolonged the ordeal. Finally, on the basis of his health,
he obtained an indefinite delay.

Rolfe's poetry traced the political course of his time, though he found it
increasingly difficult to see his work published. His most brilliant poem about
the Spanish war, "Elegia," a song to Madrid, appeared in the United States in
a privately financed volume of poetry, *First Love*, in 1951:

> Wandering, bitter, in this bitter age,
> I dream of your broad avenue like brooks in summer
> with your loveliest children alive in them like trout. . . .
> Now ten years have passed with small explosions of hope,
> yet you remain, Madrid, the conscience of our lives.
> So long as you endure, in chains, in sorrow,
> I am not free, no one of us is free.

Amidst the ubiquitous attacks on the Left, Rolfe grieved at the defection
of former allies. "What will you do, my brother, my friend," he asked in "Ballad of the Noble Intentions," "when they summon you to their inquisition?
. . . When they threaten your family's food instead?" Those who succumbed
to fear or to blandishments, he said, "resigned from the living." In "Little Ballad
for Americans—1954," one of his last poems, he depicted an oppressive world
of omnipresent informers, wiretapping "in living-room, in auto, in bed," with
"stoolies" planted in kindergartens, where "no person's really trustworthy until
he's dead." His own convictions never wavered; nor did his irony and wit. As

he put it in a piece called "Idiot Joe Prays in Pershing Square and Gets Hauled in for Vagrancy":

> Let us praise,
> while time to praise remains
> the simple bullet . . .
> we who have made
> and used napalm
> and casually—
> alone among all men—
> dropped on Man
> the only atom bomb.

"Personal depression inevitable these days," he wrote in the winter of 1954. "The longer I live, the less I want to make history; would be satisfied with a good living. But the big *and* the little escape me." Three months later, on May 24, 1954, Edwin Rolfe died of a heart attack. He was 44. "Permit me refuge in a region of your brain," he wrote in the posthumously published "Bon Voyage":

> carry and resurrect me, whatever path you take,
> as a ship creates its own unending wake
> or as rails define direction in a train.

A poet, Edwin Rolfe stated, "writes out of compulsion far more than desire. He writes out of a morass, a jungle of memories, experience, feelings, and impressions which are more often unconscious than conscious." Such was the case with another Lincoln veteran, Ramon Durem, who turned to poetry late in life to articulate a transformation of consciousness that could be expressed in no other way. Durem had gone to Spain in 1937 with a group of students from the Berkeley campus of the University of California. But he was hardly an ordinary undergraduate. Born in Seattle, Washington, in 1915, he had run away from home at fourteen, joined the navy while underage, and sailed as a telegrapher until a falling hatch cover permanently damaged his leg. Already a radical, he settled in California and was arrested once for picketing the importation of Japanese silk. On his way to Spain, he had to throw away a leg brace in order to climb the Pyrenees; at Brunete, a bullet in his bad leg put an end to his fighting. While recuperating at Villa Paz, he fell in love with an American nurse, Rebecca Schulman. When she became pregnant, they married in Spain (and later named their daughter Dolores, after La Pasionaria). After the war, they moved to California, where Durem tried to unionize farm workers; but in 1940, he fell afoul of the local un-American committee and went to prison for violating the state's anti-syndicalist laws.

The shift in the Communist party line after World War II abruptly altered Durem's perception of the radical cause. Without explaining why, he had always been particularly sensitive to racial issues. His wife remembered Durem's indignation at the manufacture of blond dolls, which he considered inappropriate playmates for black children. "I hoped that by building left-wing organizations without respect of color," he later wrote, "we could do away with the rank injustice in the [United] States." The Communist party's decision to cease coalition work with other civil rights groups frustrated Durem's expectations. "I discovered that even the white radicals," he said, "were not interested in a radical solution to the Negro Question." Durem's resentment became a personal preoccupation—an obsession, even—based, it would turn out, on a circumstance of birth he had kept secret from everyone, including his family.

"I am descended from a mixed family," he would later write, "but my appearance is that of a white man." Indeed, with blue eyes and pale skin and the slightest kink in his hair, Durem had passed his entire life as a white; some who knew him well, including his wife, even doubted the literalness of his black ancestry. But about his cultural orientation he became militantly clear. Whatever his bloodlines—and because he never knew his mother they remain uncertain—Durem began to live as an African American. He left his wife and family, married a black woman, and participated fully in black community life. "I am the same black as Walter White," he said, referring to the light-skinned leader of the NAACP. But instead of seeking racial integration, Durem emerged from the white world as a black nationalist, full of fury at the oppression of his people. "I lived many years thinking to teach the American white man," he wrote. "I discovered that the task is to kill him!"

His compulsion erupted in poetry. Starting around 1950, Durem channeled his anger into short, tight poems that exposed the hypocrisy of white society. "Some of my best friends are white boys," he conceded in "Broad-minded":

> When I meet 'em
> I treat 'em
> just the same as if they was people.

"My hope is that my poems will play some role in arousing that righteous anger and fury and willingness to die," he declared, "without which no people wins its liberty." His first published pieces appeared in black journals, such as the radical *Crusader*, as well as *Phylon* and *Venture*. They caught the attention of Langston Hughes, who had met Durem in Spain. Hughes included his poetry in an anthology, *New Negro Poets*, and tried to find Durem a publisher. But poetry remained primarily an avocation, a cathartic expression of indignation. "The merit in my poems," he said, "lies in the fact that I was the first negro in the United States, in modern times, to embrace the nationalistic approach and reject the 'all men are brothers' school which wants to win over the white man by appealing to his good nature. . . . All men are brothers— but the white man's name is Cain."

His vision, fueled by the terror waged against the civil rights movement of the 1950's, remained uncompromising. In a poem addressed "To the Pale Poets," he decried the prevailing literary sensibility:

> I know I'm not sufficiently obscure
> to please the critics, nor devious enough.
>
> . . .
>
> You deal with finer feelings,
> very subtle—an autumn leaf
> hanging from a tree—
>> I see a body.

Other works focused on particular political crimes. The murder of Emmett Till, a black teenager killed for whistling at a white woman, agonized him. He used that atrocity, in a prose poem directed to President John F. Kennedy, to condemn the killing of a Cuban child by American bombs during the invasion of the Bay of Pigs in 1961. In other works, he snapped at the Beat poets, chiding them for their self-indulgent comforts and reminding them that "there were no hypes at Stalingrad / and Malcolm X is real!" In a funny poem, "Award," he offered a gold watch to the FBI agent who had followed him for 25 years, in effect enabling Durem to support the man, clothe his wife, assure his children's college education. Durem moved to Mexico, hoping to shield his children from white racism, but economic necessity forced a return to Los Angeles. There he died of cancer at the age of 48 in December 1963. He left behind fifty or sixty poems. A posthumous collection, entitled *Take No Prisoners*, provides ample testimony of his unrelenting radicalism.

The invisibility of an American poet like Ramon Durem followed a tradition of dissident artists; but "the non-existent man," as Alvah Bessie called himself, reflected the specific political culture of postwar America, which would haunt Bessie's imagination for the rest of his life. Having taken his stand on the First Amendment—and failed—Bessie entered a painful, terrifying world of marginal employment and economic insecurity. Given the drastic turns of fortune in his background—affluent childhood, rural starvation during the Depression, Hollywood riches—the latest twist in his circumstances, "to be skidded out of the economic system on your backside," aroused Bessie's deepest anxieties. The facts could be seen in his financial ledgers, in which he kept a record of every penny he earned. During the war years at Warner Brothers, he made $300 a week. After his layoff in January 1946, he still claimed a weekly paycheck of $600, but for shorter terms of employment; his annual income exceeded $14,000. But in 1947, the year of the HUAC hearings, his income dropped nearly in half to $7,000; the next year, it fell to $3,000; and in 1949 it totaled $4,614.

With high legal expenses, a wife and young daughter, child support of his two sons, and a middle-class lifestyle to which he had grown accustomed, Bessie became dependent on loans and donations from friends and sympathizers; and he accepted every occasional assignment, no matter how paltry the payment. The need for money demeaned him, exacerbating his irascible temperament, which often offended his benefactors. The situation did not improve after his prison sentence. Unable to find any work in the Los Angeles area, Bessie finally landed a job as assistant editor of the longshoreman's union newspaper in San Francisco, run by Harry Bridges. Four years later, an economic squeeze forced his dismissal. He found work as a lighting technician and off-stage announcer at a popular nightclub, the hungry i. But quarrels with his employer shortened his tenure. By the mid-1960's—Bessie was then in his late fifties—he had returned primarily to freelance writing.

His material situation, while comfortable by working-class standards, nonetheless aggravated Bessie's sense of self-sacrifice. He had "been persecuted," he said, "for accepting (or being said to accept) ideas." All his subsequent words—and Bessie was a prolific writer—addressed that basic injustice. Some of his writing was plainly political: addresses to benefit the Spanish refugees; articles that challenged the U.S. rapprochement with Franco; speeches in support of his jailed comrades from the Lincoln brigade. He wrote hundreds of book reviews for the Communist party newspaper *People's World*, usually under a pseudonym (and once even praised his own work as "a rather special piece"). His subjects ranged from history and contemporary politics—Nazi concentration camps, the Rosenberg case—to movies and belles lettres, particularly Soviet fiction and Beat literature, which he loathed. "The Beatnik," he declared, in a statement perhaps typical of the Old Left view of cultural dissent in the 1950's, "not only rejects the . . . capitalist class (and its workings—poverty, oppression, war) but . . . the working class as well . . . , the endless struggle of workers for minimum security." Such opinions, which scarcely changed over the next quarter of a century, kept Bessie's name in print in small magazines and local newspapers in northern California, as political and literary fashions came and went.

Bessie's primary obsessions, however, were Spain and Hollywood. In his writing and in his life, the two remained tightly knit. Thus he believed that if he could clarify the good motives that led him to volunteer in the Lincoln brigade in 1938, then he could validate (and vindicate) his position before the HUAC nine years later. (Then, too, he might achieve the literary recognition—and the royalties—he felt he deserved.) He expressed these themes most clearly in what is probably his best novel, *The Un-Americans*, published in 1957 by the sympathetic editor of a small press. In the pattern of screenplay cuts, Bessie moved the narrative between events in Spain, many of them historically accurate, and the government investigation of a Communist Lincoln veteran in 1947, the year of his own confrontation with the HUAC. That narrow time frame underscored the psychological proximity of the two crises. Despite stylistic clumsiness, the novel captured the frustrations of the witch-hunts. As Bessie had feared, however, his book received little attention. He then produced a nonfiction version, *Inquisition in Eden*, which appeared in 1965 to few reviews.

The failure of these books illuminates the tragedy of Bessie's literary career. For all his talent—and Bessie was a skilled, endearing narrator—he could never transcend his didacticism or the pleading of his personal cause. He would write three other books—*The Symbol*, a Hollywood novel based loosely on the career of Marilyn Monroe; *Spain Again*, an autobiographical account of his return to Franco's land; and *One for My Baby*, a fictional version of his adventures at the hungry i. All would reflect those same shortcomings. Each, moreover, suffered from the choppy structure of the screenplay format; each, in this way, reflected Bessie's desire to get back to (if not at) the Hollywood studio system that had discarded him. The critical results: minimal reviews, many of them unfavorable, and disappointing sales. These, in turn, provoked Bessie's frustration and aroused his anger. In the end, his indignation kept him alive politically, but sapped his creative juices. It was entirely characteristic of the man that at the time of his death in 1985 he was embroiled in a legal case against his own publisher for the inadvertent shredding of unsold copies of his last novel. (The publisher settled one day after he died.) And he was editing *Our Fight*, a collection of stories written by his comrades in the Lincoln brigade.

Bessie's fixation on the political inquisition of the 1950's mirrored, almost literally, the concerns of another Lincoln veteran turned novelist, William Herrick, who focused, by contrast, on the totalitarian threats that justified the persecution of Communists. Having testified against the VALB to the SACB—having experienced some particle of guilt or shame for his appearance—Herrick became obsessed with the need to preserve his version of the Spanish war. A court stenographer by profession, he knew much about words, little about the craft of writing. "I always wanted to write," he said. "So I started writing and couldn't stop." His first effort, a novel about the Lincoln volunteers, originally titled "Sad-Faced Heroes," passed through numerous unsuccessful drafts. Herrick had so much to say, so deep an anger, he could not bring himself to cut and edit. Stymied, he broke from the subject and wrote another partially autobiographical novel, *The Itinerant*, which was published in 1967. It too sprawled and rambled, tracing the erratic adventures of a young radical during the Depression. Among other themes, the overwritten book expressed Herrick's contempt for political zealotry—"all the manipulators, all those who thought of themselves as molders of human destiny."

Herrick returned to the Spanish novel and took it through seven drafts before it appeared as *Hermanos!* in 1969. Heralded as the bridge between Hemingway's *For Whom the Bell Tolls* and Orwell's *Homage to Catalonia*, the work told a grim story of ruthless Communist ideologues manipulating the Spanish crisis purely for the benefit of Stalin and the Soviet Union. "It was discipline which was the Party's genius; discipline which made its politics viable," wrote Herrick. "To remold billions of men required discipline and will." From its conspiratorial origins, the Lincoln battalion served in the book as a seedbed for political intrigue and assassination. With cynical and incompetent party leaders in command, the idealistic volunteers marched needlessly into olive groves of slaughter, while survivors behind the lines betrayed friends and principles for the higher claims of the party's dialectics. In this world of self-deceiving moral corruption, the victims fell as battlefield casualties, were betrayed by their lovers, and ultimately died at the hands of the very revolution they proclaimed. "The chicaneries, the venalities, the murderous bloodletting," one comrade remarked, "are only interludes in the grand design."

Herrick wrote as a novelist, to be sure, but he insisted that his work should stand as history. In chronicling the experiences of the American volunteers, he barely fictionalized the men he had known at Jarama. His working-class heroes were friends from New York: Joe Gordon, Doug Roach, Robert Gladnick. Merriman became "Prettyman"—and then, after the debacle of February 27th, "Murderman," as some had actually called him in Spain. Mickenberg ("Mack Berg") remained the spokesman of the rank and file, "their voice against the incompetence of their commanders, the arrogant stupidity of their political commissars." Although Herrick had been shot in the neck before he had witnessed much fighting, he drew on the stories he had heard while convalescing (like his hero, "Jake Starr") in the hospital at Murcia. These details created a plausible authenticity. His dialogue rang true; he understood the hopes and anxieties of the common soldiers. Thus his description of Oliver Law ("Cromwell Webster") as a coward and a drunkard who was killed by his own men transcended its novelistic function. Indeed, Herrick would repeat the story as historical fact to a newspaper reporter, provoking angry rebuttals from Lincoln veterans who remembered Law differently. Such criticism sim-

ply confirmed Herrick's judgment that the veterans were ready "to lie, prevaricate, perjure themselves in order to protect the pseudohistory and manu-
factured myths about the Americans in the XV brigade." He never doubted
his own sources or questioned the selectivity of his memory.

Herrick proceeded to write seven other novels, many of them examining
the minds of old revolutionaries. Just as Alvah Bessie's work revealed a
preoccupation with the consequences of Spain, so in Herrick's novels the
characters relived the traumatic experiences of the author. *Shadows and Wolves*,
published in 1980, placed an old fascist general, the assassin of Federico García
Lorca, on a collision course with his revolutionary son determined to avenge
the death of the poet. The general, who had fought against the Americans at
Jarama, admired their courage—"proof," said Herrick, "that adherence to a
fanatic faith can overcome rational thought and lack of fire power." Yet instead of violent confrontation, the novel ended with forgiveness and reconciliation, the same healing that had enabled Spaniards to restore a republic after
the death of Franco.

Love and Terror, which appeared in 1981, similarly juxtaposed a gang of
young radicals—terrorists in West Germany—against three former Communists of an older generation. Here exaggerated Oedipal conflicts, not uncom-
mon in Herrick's fiction, precluded an accommodation. Once again, the novelist returned to the issues of the Spanish war, developing a character based
on Robert Gladnick (and himself), who had testified to a government committee about his former comrades. "Sure I testified," said "David Grad." "I
wanted a place to tell the truth under oath. Gave names. Why not? I was graduated from the greatest Informer College the world's ever known—the C.P."
Claiming that his words had cost no one a job ("When a Communist talks about
blacklisting, I laugh in his face"), Herrick's hero denied any feelings of guilt:
"They're left fascists, why pussyfoot about it." A third novel, *Kill Memory*,
published in 1983, explored the frightened memories of an old woman, once
a party nurse in Spain, who had placed her political beliefs above her love for
a wounded American patient (the author in real life).

Herrick attempted through such works to describe the metamorphosis from
a young revolutionary, prepared to die for a Communist dream, to an older
middle-class citizen, hostile to ideological illusions. But his words remained
angry, his voice self-righteous. "Yes, we gave all of our lives," he said of the

Communists who volunteered for the International Brigades. "That was our greatest strength and our greatest weakness. For in giving all of your life, you fight to the death, but you also yield up all of your brain and your heart and your morality. You are not a free man." Herrick's tone betrayed a certain defensiveness. He admitted that if he had known in the 1950's that he would become a novelist, he might never have testified before the SACB, might have saved his words for the printed page, might have averted the awkwardness he still felt. "If you hear a man squeaking about the truth," he warned in his 1990 novel, *Bradovich*, "you know immediately it's his own truth he wants to hear about, not yours or anyone else's."

While the polemics of the Spanish war persisted in the creative writing of its participants, the conflict also nourished a broader humanitarian concern among many artists who had served in the ranks. Several painters returned from Spain with a commitment to express their political outlook in an aesthetic context. "My paintings have always been political," explained Anthony Toney, an artist who had gone to Spain after studying at the Beaux-Arts in Paris. During a career that spanned nearly sixty years, Toney experimented with a variety of styles and techniques, choosing manifestly political subjects—the turmoil of the 1960's, for example, or the antiapartheid movement—to evoke a response in the viewer. "I think that I am fiddling while the world burns," he admitted. "I think I'm a failure at being able to persuade people through my painting. It's too subtle." In the end, he feared, the images of the mass media would prevail.

Joseph Vogel, once an activist in New York's Artists Union, also grappled with the problem of communicating social and political ideas in nonrepresentational language. "You . . . find sentimentality or false romanticism," he complained of popular art. "The fake sunset: The sunset exists, it's magnificent, but what it's reduced to is a five and ten cent store mentality of pure association." Like Anthony Toney, Vogel continued to paint against the grain and to exhibit his art in New York galleries.

Such artistic compulsions dramatically changed the life of Irving Noachowitz, another Lincoln veteran, who worked under the name Norman. Born in 1906 in Poland, he had immigrated to New York as a teenager, become a barber, married, and moved to California in the 1930's. As a member of the Young

Communist League, he had volunteered for Spain in 1938, arriving in time to experience the horrors of the retreats and the pounding of the Ebro offensive. Alvah Bessie would later write, ungenerously, of Norman's naiveté:

"'Comrades,' he said. 'Do I understand you retreated and threw your guns away?'

"'Yeh,' they said.

"'But comrades,' he said, 'that's cowardice. Don't you realize how difficult it is for the Government to get arms? Don't you realize that it's impossible to retreat from Fascism . . . ?'

"'Haul your ashes,' said an Italian-American with an amusing handle-bar mustache. His name was Joe Bianca."

"I had no choice," said Norman many years later of his involvement in the Spanish war. "I was young, active, and I had to go. It was the most rewarding and the greatest experience in my life. I learned the most. I learned how any side, right or left, can be unbelievably cruel. I never, never knew to what high degrees people could spend time, energy, intelligence, and money to tear each other apart." Spain, in short, put an end to his activist career. He returned to southern California bruised and numb. Severely depressed by the war, he would sit motionless on a deck outside the room he rented in a private home. "I wanted to go to a monastery," he later explained, "one of those where you can't talk, just so I wouldn't have to discuss what I saw. So I wouldn't have to speak of the horror of war." The housekeeper, an older woman named Sonia Robbins, watched his silence with dismay. One day, to pull him out of himself, she brought him a box of children's paints. Norman, as much in therapy as in awe, had found his medium.

"What I was doing seemed very silly and very trivial," he said later of his work as a barber. Hoping to resolve his personal crisis, he isolated himself on Catalina Island, bought a box of watercolors, and made some tentative paintings. A sympathetic commercial artist recognized Norman's talent. They formed a study group, shared models, discussed the elementary problems of doing art. In 1940, Norman felt confident enough to seek a formal education and entered the California School of Fine Arts in San Francisco.

One of his first efforts was an oil painting of the burial site of Joe Bianca on Hill 666, a grisly picture that he gave to Bill Bailey, who had dug the grave. He had his first exhibition at the Tom Mooney Art Gallery of the California Labor School in 1940. "With unflinching truth he depicts the horrors and stupidities of war," observed one critic. His pencil drawings were described as "bitter commentaries on war and on society shattered by war." In 1945, Norman traveled to Mexico, where he was influenced by the mural paintings of José Orozco. He went to New York to study drawing with Reginald Marsh and anatomy with Robert Beverly Hale at the Art Students' League. He then returned to northern California, adopting a frugal lifestyle that permitted him to survive as a part-time barber, full-time artist.

Norman, small in stature, preferred large canvases worthy of his vast vision. "I comprehend history as a fast moving mass of humanity driven by a historic momentum that is blind and hungry," he wrote expansively in 1950. "Most people are caught up in history and are unable to act on what even enlightenment or intuition reveals to them they *should* do." To capture that feeling, he painted huge skyscraper cities, then filled each window frame with unique elements of a person's life. A seven-foot watercolor entitled *Big City* soon aroused the indignation of San Francisco's most prominent art patrons. Looking closely at some of the window scenes, an alert security guard at the DeYoung Museum detected what appeared to be a house of prostitution. The museum promptly banned the work on grounds of obscenity. Local artists rallied to Norman's defense, to no avail. "Essentially," Norman insisted, "it is a religious picture, in the Dante tradition." In the end, the brief imbroglio brought him more attention than he would receive for the next 25 years.

Norman continued to produce large canvases that depicted the terrible impersonality of modern life, showed the evils of militarism, and confronted the specter of annihilation. Such fare did not bring him the professional recognition he desired—and deserved—although he realized that his somber mood hardly appealed to a materialistic culture. When left-wing critics praised his anticapitalist images, however, Norman denounced their efforts to use his work for propaganda. "Let all politicians of the right and of the left," he advised in 1956, "keep their bloody hands and scheming minds out of the field of art."

Norman's criticism of the cold war consensus nonetheless marked him as a dissenter. One large work, called *The Cross Road*, compared contemporary life to the transitional time between the fall of the Roman Empire and the rise of Christendom; in his own times, he saw high-rise buildings and feverish tempos contrasting with human blindness and empty stomachs. A large triptych, *The Human Condition*, showed helmeted rows of identical warriors, but each with individualized faces, abandoning agonized souls above them and masses of ignored protesters below. *Crucifixion*, a thirty-foot magnum opus purchased by San Jose State University in the mid-1970's, brought some recognition of Norman's unrelenting warnings about an impending disaster. "That is what is good about art," he said. "It is an answer to death. It is the only thing that can prolong earthly remembrance, the continuation of the human that did it." That, surely, was Norman's profound response to the tragedy of Spain: the realization that the same threads that suspended the corpses of friends and enemies from the branches of the olive trees—an image that haunted him forever—held all life in tenuous embrace. "We are faced with so much that is unknown, so many unanswered questions," he remarked, "so we hope for the best and create illusions. . . . I try to go beyond illusions." Norman died in 1989.

Norman's dark vision contrasted with the wonderful, exuberant masses of people that filled the large canvases of Ralph Fasanella, another self-taught painter who emerged from the Lincoln brigade. Both men shared a visual imagination that saw anguish in the impersonality of contemporary urban society; but where Norman remained pessimistic about the future, Fasanella celebrated the passion of street life, the plain joy of watching a baseball game, and the courage of political dissenters and labor leaders who defied their oppressors. In the tiny details of his cityscapes, he portrayed less the desperation of Norman's characters than the affirmation of individual difference. Interestingly, the two painters never met—indeed, neither knew of the other's existence. Yet as Norman's experience in Spain drew him toward foreboding conclusions about modern civilization, so Fasanella's feisty style reflected the tenacity of an irrepressible survivor.

Born on Labor Day 1914 to Italian parents in New York's Greenwich Village, Fasanella struggled against the burden of poverty from his first breath. His father was an iceman, overworked, underpaid, frustrated by the failure of his American dream, and he shared his misery with the rest of the family. Ralph, from the age of eight, worked on his father's ice wagon, a job he detested. "I was a little boy. I didn't want to work on the wagon lugging that ice. I wanted to play with the kids." His mother worked as a button-hole maker in a factory, where she acquired an interest in socialism. But her son seemed incorrigible, and after he ran away from home a few times, the family sent him to a Catholic protectory that was run like a prison. Ralph was nine years old. "I was always being punished by the Brothers," he recalled. "Even when we were allowed to play games, some kids were always doing penance against the wall. That was me."

The Depression introduced the teenager to another school of hard knocks. His father disappeared, leaving the family impoverished. Unable to find work, Ralph joined the Unemployed Councils; later he entered the Young Communist League in the Bronx and participated in his first protest demonstrations. His mother supported these steps, even bade him farewell at the dock when Fasanella sailed for Spain in 1937. He was short, broad, and tough; earthy and obscene; and Fasanella easily won friends and respect from his comrades in the Regiment de Tren. "Fasanella is a little New York Italian guy," wrote one midwesterner to his wife. "He taught me a lot about what youth from beer joints, pool rooms and corner gangs feel. (You should hear me swear now.)" Everyone remembered Fasanella introducing the term "ballbreaker," which "caught on like swing music" and, in the hands of Dave Thompson, a jazz critic before the war, became the theme of "The Ballbreakers Blues": "And then we have this mother's cunt who says it's tougher at the front / We've got the ball-breakers blues." The leisure that allowed the truck drivers to invent songs also encouraged serious intellectual discussions. From his college-educated comrades, Fasanella began to glimpse a larger world of literature, history, music, and art.

Despite his popularity, Fasanella's quick temper brought him into conflict with a commanding officer who was attempting to establish military discipline. Fasanella vehemently protested the changes, considering gestures like saluting a sign of incipient fascism. The officer ordered him into an artillery division at the front. Convinced that he was being sent to his death, Fasanella swore to get revenge, and he wangled a pass from his new unit to take his case to the inspector general, Luigi Gallo, in Barcelona. But when he could not find Gallo at the office, Fasanella impulsively boarded a British ship that was sailing to Oran. His desertion never dampened Fasanella's political ideals. Even aboard the ship that returned him to New York, he managed to organize a seaman's strike, which won better food, beer, and American cigarettes. Nor did his departure offend many of the veterans. He had not fled the war in cowardice or jeopardized his comrades. So after Spain, Fasanella returned to the party and to the labor movement.

Fasanella was 30 years old, working as a union organizer for the United

Electrical Workers in 1944, when he began to develop peculiar pains in his fingers, a kind of tension that compelled him to rub his fingertips across table tops. He finally picked up a pencil, grabbed some paper, and sketched a pair of shoes lying in the corner. "After that," he said, "I started to draw everything in sight."

Fasanella continued to work for the union, but now he had trouble keeping his mind on the job. "I couldn't listen to the meetings on how to run a union," he recalled. "All I could do was sit and sketch the faces of the members." Sent to organize a shop in Ohio, he became more interested in painting it. He finally asked for a leave of absence, bought a stock of paints and canvas, and started producing bright-colored pictures of the urban scenes he knew so well—stickball games, tenements, churches—and the characters that inhabited the city's streets. When a friend suggested he take his works to a gallery, he expressed surprise, but he felt even more amazement when he sold them. "I was very belligerent," he remembered. "I told them, 'either a picture is good or not so don't beat around the bush with me. I don't give a damn.'" But the act of painting consumed him; he could not have held a job if he wanted to. Fortunately, his family agreed to stake him. In 1947, he had his first one-man show, and the critics praised his "social primitive" style.

"I try to catch the detail—lace curtains in the winds, Captain Midnight on the newsstands—so as not to lose the essence of what I'm trying to say," he explained of his early works. "The thing I want to paint about is the modern tempo; I want to show that today, the streets still run in both directions, but faster." Fasanella's fascination with the details of urban life reflected a continuing interest in politics. His 1948 painting *May Day* celebrated a labor heritage that included Sacco and Vanzetti, Eugene Debs, and the varieties of the American working class.

Fasanella's art, above all, expressed his roots in the culture of America's workers. *Dress Shop* captured the monotony of his mother's labors and paid homage to the women killed in the Triangle fire of 1911. *Iceman Crucified* portrayed the agonies his father had suffered. He painted scenes of union halls, bench workers in a machine shop, commuters on the subways of New York. He celebrated the working-class leisure experience—the street festivals of Little Italy, sidewalk socializing, and especially baseball, with scenes that ranged from pickup games in the gutters to the brightly lit Yankee Stadium at night. He loved the feeling of the neighborhood; his crowded street scenes reflected the perspective of a pedestrian. He also explored the political culture of these ordinary citizens. *Death of a Leader* evoked his deep personal loss at the sudden death of Vito Marcantonio in 1954; *Gray Day* and *McCarthy Period* expressed his revulsion at the execution of Julius and Ethel Rosenberg, which he had protested in Washington, D.C., in front of the Supreme Court. A few years later, *American Tragedy* offered a heartfelt indictment of a society he held responsible for the assassination of President Kennedy.

By the early 1970's, a time when Americans were rediscovering the virtues of blue-collar culture—hard hats, Archie Bunker, Studs Terkel's *Working*—the slick *New York* magazine found Ralph Fasanella, then 58, working in a Bronx gas station. The editors put him on the cover and proclaimed, "He may be the best primitive painter since Grandma Moses." A book followed, *Fasanella's City*, illustrating his colorful imagination. It brought the kind of fame and acceptance that every artist might want (the stuff Irving Norman lamented he never got). But, ironically, the notoriety deflected Fasanella's genius. He lost his ability to concentrate. At the suggestion of some friends, Fasanella resolved to return to his roots in the labor movement, opting for Lawrence, Massachusetts, site of the famous "Bread and Roses" strike of 1912. There, he lived on a subsistence level at the YMCA for three years while painting the history of the textile industry. The result, a series of large, detailed, brightly colored canvases, revealed his remarkable empathy for an earlier generation of American workers. And the painter obviously relished the popularity of his achievement. Jamming his elbow into the ribs of a comrade from the Lincoln brigade, he said one day with a laugh, "You didn't think stupid Ralph'd get these paintings in museums!"

The popular creativity of Ralph Fasanella, the loneliness of Irving Norman, the bitterness of Alvah Bassie, the justifications of William Herrick, the angry visions of Ramon Durem, the wry wisdom of Edwin Rolfe—these expressions revealed some of the complicated legacies of the Spanish war, consequences that reached beyond simple categories of radical or reactionary, liberal or conservative. For Spain touched at the consciousness of its participants, affected their minds and hearts deeply and forever. And just as the Lincoln volunteers went to Spain with a multitude of backgrounds and possibilities, so they returned—those lucky few—to build careers and articulate values that encompassed the experiences of the war. What remained striking about all these creative artists—even Herrick, the apostate—was their continuing commitment to a world of human decency and social justice and their concomitant belief that their work as artists would hasten the fulfillment of those hopes. "I am against oppression, suppression *anywhere in the world*," said Alvah Bessie late in life; "I am also against fascists." To the end of their days, the artistic veterans of the Lincoln brigade shared that credo and added their voices to a continuing struggle.

Bridging Old Left and New

Abe Osheroff, bushy-haired, stocky, and tough, had given all of his considerable energies to the Communist party for most of his forty years when Soviet leader Nikita Khrushchev's dramatic denunciation of Stalinism reached his ears in 1956. Osheroff had always been a party loyalist. Wounded at Belchite, he had returned to New York to become a low-level party organizer. During the Red Scare, a friend in the Justice Department had warned him of his forthcoming arrest, and Osheroff had immediately fled into the Communist underground, but he had missed his contact. For the next three years he had survived on his own, changing his identity and whereabouts every six months.

By the time Osheroff felt safe enough to surface, the Communist party was in disarray. Claiming a membership of 75,000 in 1945, it had dwindled to 22,000 a decade later. The reasons were manifold: the unprecedented prosperity of the American working classes after World War II; ideological skirmishes within the party, which produced numerous defections and expulsions; frustration at Soviet policy in the cold war; and, not least, the success of the anti-Communist crusade in isolating radicals from the political mainstream.

Like many Lincoln veterans, Osheroff could not evade the implications of Khrushchev's revelations. Steve Nelson, who chaired the meeting at which American Communists first heard Khrushchev's tale of Stalinist atrocities, remembered people weeping in the audience. "This is not the reason why I joined the party," he exclaimed. "From now on we have to reject this; we have to make our own decisions; there are no more gods." As the party attempted to redefine its position and salvage its membership, Lincoln veterans assumed an important role in the acrimonious debates. This prominence indicated their continuing stature within party circles; it also showed how dedicated many veterans remained to the Communist standard that had led them to Spain twenty years earlier. Indeed, two Lincolns on the party's national committee emerged as leaders of rival factions: Bob Thompson, who identified with the old leadership; and John Gates, who argued strenuously for adjusting Communist principles to suit American conditions. Gates, editor of the *Daily Worker*, even published editorials condemning the Soviet invasion of Hungary in 1956.

For the first time in its 37-year history, the party was permitting candid discussion of its basic premises, but ironically the weakening of the orthodoxy further eroded loyalty and support. As the spirit of unity collapsed, party membership dropped from 17,000 in 1956 to less than 5,000 at the end of the next year. And many of the remnants proved to be FBI agents and informants. Although no Lincoln veteran ever admitted to serving as a government spy, declassified government documents indicate that at least one man in New York and another in the Los Angeles area provided information to the FBI about veterans' activities; perhaps there were others. In any event, the factionalism, recrimination, and government pressure destroyed the Communist party as a political force.

Although some Lincoln veterans remained stalwart Communists, the disintegration of the party loosed many from a lifetime's moorings. "I am floating," lamented Alvah Bessie about his new status as "an unaffiliated radical" in 1957. "We stand no chance of acceptance," he acknowledged, "until such time as we can rehabilitate ourselves . . . as individuals (in whatever trade or craft we operate) and prove that we *are* part of the mainstream of American life, instead of fancying ourselves in the 'vanguard' of a class that has rejected us." As an independent writer, Bessie retained some limited outlets for his radical views.

Abe Osheroff, a carpenter by trade, groped for a similar opportunity. In a teary farewell speech to the party leadership, he explained his need to resign; he was thanked by another Lincoln veteran who spit on his face. Within a month Osheroff had closed his affairs in New York and headed for Los Angeles. He had no goals, no expectations. But he remained an activist, at least by temperament, and he continued to search for a cause. For a while Osheroff did some neighborhood organizing, and then he made a commitment to the civil rights movement.

Other Lincoln veterans who left the Communist party wanted no more causes. The political odyssey of Lincoln commissar John Gates revealed a familiar accommodation to liberal reformism. "I am no longer a Communist," he declared in resigning from the party in 1958, "but I am convinced that American life needs an effective and courageous radicalism." Gates began by seeking alliances with Socialist groups, but he found that their own sectarianism precluded an agreement. Reluctantly, he withdrew from political work. He resumed his education, earned a degree in economics, and attended graduate school briefly before obtaining a job as a research assistant for the International Ladies Garment Workers Union, headed by the staunch anti-Communist David Dubinsky.

During the 1960's, Gates rejected his radical vision—not just the Communist party, but the premises of Marxist analysis. He became a liberal Democrat, supporting the civil rights movement, Lyndon Johnson's Great Society, and the Vietnam War. "I am an anti-Communist," he declared in 1970. "I will do anything I can to defeat it anywhere in the world." At Dubinsky's prodding, Gates received a presidential pardon from Richard Nixon in 1970, restoring the civil rights lost as a result of his conviction under the Smith Act. As he faced retirement twenty years later, Gates looked back with pride and satisfaction at the practical accomplishments of his career, gaining compensation benefits for union employees. "I'm doing now for individuals what I used to do for humanity," he said. "Now I help individuals and let humanity take care of itself." He died in 1992.

Most Lincoln veterans fell somewhere between Osheroff and Gates in terms of their ideological commitments. Like the frustrated carpenter, most did not publicly reject their socialist principles; like Gates, though, they found alternative activities in union or professional affairs. Steve Nelson went back to full-time carpentering. Others returned to school or moved to California to start afresh. Still others found occupations that were compatible with their social ideals. Thus while many Lincoln veterans stayed in the Communist party, the large exodus of veterans weakened their commitment to organized activities. The VALB was a casualty of that shift. A small core of dedicated leaders, many of them party members, kept the veterans' organization afloat, but just barely. "A guy gets mail if he wants, and he does something about it if he wants," remarked Moe Fishman about the loosening of old relationships.

Although the VALB breathed a sigh of relief in 1958 that "the mass hysteria days of McCarthyism may be over," few doubted that its remnants would "take some fighting to overcome." Still tainted by the guilt-by-association rulings of the SACB and the attorney general's list of subversive organizations, the veterans remained prey to anti-Communist crusaders. Indeed, if Dr. Edward Barsky and Alvah Bessie were among the first postwar victims of the HUAC, other Lincoln veterans, such as Robert Colodny and Milton Cohen, proved in the 1960's to be among the last. Both succeeded in thwarting the committee's probes. Yet when World War II hero Bob Thompson died in 1965, the secretary of the army refused to permit his burial at Arlington National Cemetery. The VALB supported a legal case, which forced the Pentagon to reverse its decision.

Meanwhile, the VALB's judicial appeal of the SACB ruling crawled through the federal courts. In October 1962, 25 veterans journeyed to Washington, D.C., to hear attorney Louis Boudin present oral arguments before the U.S. Court of Appeals, urging dismissal of the obligation to register as agents of a foreign power. At issue, he maintained, was whether a "front" organization—so defined by the role of Communists in its formation—enjoyed the protections of the First Amendment. Two months later, the court ruled two to one that the VALB indeed constituted a subversive group. "It is clear," declared the appellate judges, "that the struggle between the Republican government and the rebel forces was basically between Fascism (led by Franco and the Spanish Fascist Party) and Communism (supporting the Republican government.)"

Such historical judgments reflected the cold war dichotomies. "For the first time, American judicial credence is given to the pretext used by Hitler and Mussolini to destroy the democratic government of Spain," protested Moe Fishman. "We will not allow the case . . . to be used to distort history. . . . We are determined not to allow this lie to go unchallenged." And so, by October 1964, the VALB case stood before the U.S. Supreme Court. As presidential candidates Lyndon Johnson and Barry Goldwater contested the gravity of the Communist peril, the high court would not belittle the danger of internal subversion; but neither would the justices tolerate the witch-hunting zeal of the previous decade. Prudently, the Court found a middle ground, voting to overturn the SACB ruling, but not on the merits of the VALB claims. Instead, the justices stressed the antiquity of the available evidence: "On so stale a record we do not think it is either necessary or appropriate that we decide the serious constitutional questions." Dissent came from three liberal justices, William O. Douglas, John Harlan, and Hugo Black, all of whom wanted to adjudicate the broad legal issues of the McCarran Act, which seemed, as Black put it, "a wholesale denial of . . . the constitutional heritage of every freedom-loving American."

In avoiding the fundamental questions, the Court remanded the case to the Department of Justice, which had the option of seeking fresh evidence. But Attorney General Nicholas Katzenbach promised in 1965 to suspend the litigation. Yet when the VALB appealed for a dismissal before the SACB, he reneged and recommended the matter be placed in an inactive file. Four months later, the attorney general had still failed to introduce new motions, permitting the Supreme Court to cancel the registration order. Fishman called the result "a complete vindication of our thirteen-year fight against a law we considered unconstitutional from the beginning."

The Lincolns did not rest on their laurels. Soon the VALB filed papers seeking to have the attorney general's list of subversive organizations declared illegal. Bureaucracy again intervened, stalling the proceedings. Six years later, however, Richard Nixon's attorney general, John Mitchell, directed the SACB to remove the Abraham Lincoln brigade from the list of subversive organizations, since it had been extinct since 1939. Several months later, a federal court of appeals ordered the attorney general also to remove the Veterans of the Abraham Lincoln Brigade from that list, ending 25 years of legal harassment. During that time, no criminal charges had been brought against the VALB, nor had the organization been accused of violating any law. The Lincolns had been maligned and punished for harboring deviant political beliefs.

By then, the political commitments of most Lincoln veterans had evolved into a series of individual activities, some public, some private, some over-lapping with the concerns of other veterans, some idiosyncratic. Such choices might be deeply ingrained or simply fortuitous. But to a remarkable degree, Lincoln veterans embroiled themselves (or were embroiled) in almost every significant political movement of the postwar period. Although most acted as individuals, their efforts remained congruent with the values and ideals that had motivated them to fight in Spain. Many, consequently, managed eventually to persuade other veterans, or even the VALB, to endorse their work. Taken collectively, their concerns demonstrated the persistence of a radical tradition, a continuity between the protests and principles of the Old Left of the Depression era and those of a generation associated with the "New Left" and the political controversies of the 1960's and 1970's.

Veteran Archie Brown had made no secret of his Communist affiliations. Serving publicly as a party leader, running as a Communist candidate for statewide office, the popular waterfront organizer had spent four lonely years in the underground. Brown responded to the Khrushchev revelations of 1956 by praising the party's self-correcting process. As a longshoreman and trade unionist, he had no doubts that the capitalist system oppressed the American worker more than any errors of the party line. In 1959, he ran as the Communist candidate for supervisor in San Francisco and pulled 33,000 votes. Brown's militancy made him a prime target when the HUAC arrived in California to gather evidence of Communist subversion in May 1960. Subpoenaed before the committee, Brown prepared a formal statement, intending to take the Fifth Amendment in response to the questioning.

As the hearings opened, however, crowds outside objected to a partisan seating arrangement that excluded most HUAC critics from the courtroom. The documentary film *Operation Abolition* captured the moment Brown yelled "Get out of town!" and then joined the throng in singing "The Star Spangled Banner." "Open the doors," he chanted five times into the microphone. "What are you afraid of?" And as the police dragged him from the podium, ripping his coat, Brown could be heard saying, "Watch this Americanism in action!"

Meanwhile, police and firemen turned on the angry spectators, many of them students at the nearby colleges, and literally washed them down the marble steps of city hall.

The *San Francisco Chronicle*'s reporter on the scene, George Draper, had served in the ambulance corps in Spain. Virtually apolitical, he had recently violated what he considered professional objectivity—for the one and only time in his career, he said—by speaking against the execution of Caryl Chessman in May 1960. As he entered the San Francisco courthouse a few weeks later, Draper recognized some of the student activists who had shared his opposition to capital punishment. His report vividly described their singing what would become an anthem of the decade: "We shall not be moved." Ironically, Draper had no idea that his shipmate from the journey to Spain, Ruth Davidow, and her husband, veteran Vernon Bown, were among the 52 people arrested that afternoon on charges of disturbing the peace.

While news of the HUAC confrontation flashed around the country, Archie Brown faced the committee again the next day and tried to read his statement into the record. Angered by his intransigence, the committee ordered his ejection from the proceedings. Unlike the defendants of the 1940's, Brown avoided a citation for contempt. More important, the unexpected protest heralded a new era of radical dissent. Although the government claimed that Communists had organized the demonstrations (that was the central theme of HUAC's *Operation Abolition*), the protesters were more often liberals who perceived the investigation as a threat to civil rights. Such attitudes stimulated a political awakening on American campuses and led directly to the Free Speech demonstrations at the Berkeley campus of the University of California. As for Archie Brown, he continued to be reelected to the executive board of Local 10 of the International Longshoreman's and Warehouseman's Union, headed by Harry Bridges.

Brown's popularity, however, placed him in violation of the Landrum-Griffin Act of 1959, which forbade Communists from holding union office. Indeed, the non-Communist leadership of the ILWU had supported his candidacy—though Brown was elected on a secret ballot—as a way of challenging government intervention in internal union affairs. In 1961, federal agents arrested Brown at work, and Attorney General Robert F. Kennedy announced that he would be the first person charged with violating the new law. "I think it had to do with the fact that the Committee got its lumps at City Hall," Brown told reporters. In indicting Brown, the government claimed that Communist control of labor unions would produce "political" strikes based on non-economic grounds. But in the ensuing trial, prosecutors objected to evidence about Brown's participation in two political walkouts—a protest against unloading a Nazi ship in 1938 and a refusal to load scrap iron onto a ship headed for Japan in 1941. The defense, moreover, explicitly denied the "political" strike threat, arguing that the ILWU's democratic constitution prevented any one person from calling a strike. The judgment nonetheless distilled into a single question of law: was Brown both a Communist and a union official? On those narrow grounds the jury found him guilty. But a federal court of appeals overturned the verdict, and the U.S. Supreme Court sustained that ruling, holding that the relevant portion of Landrum-Griffin was an unconstitutional bill of attainder.

Brown remained a tireless organizer on the San Francisco waterfront, concerned about immediate working conditions and larger questions of American policy. Following the right-wing coup d'état in Chile in 1973, he helped create a local trade union coalition which supported a commercial boycott of that country, interfered with arms shipments to the right-wing regime, and provided material aid to Chilean dissidents. Brown then brought the issue to the Bay Area post of the VALB, sparking "Hands Off Chile" protests led by the Lincoln veterans. A decade later, Brown helped initiate a union boycott of cargo from South Africa, one of the first American efforts to exert economic pressure against the apartheid system. Convinced of the inevitability of class struggle, Brown never abandoned his identity as a plain worker, a trade unionist no less than a Communist. He died in 1990.

Cold war passions also shaped the veterans' response to Fidel Castro's revolution in Cuba. One veteran arrived in Havana two days after the successful coup in July 1959 and reported optimistically to the VALB office about "the universal enormous enthusiasm of Cubans for the Castro regime and its programs." More skeptical was the account of Sam Romer, one of the few Socialists to serve with the Lincolns, who visited Cuba as a reporter for the *Minneapolis Tribune* in 1959. In a perceptive series of articles, Romer warned that Castro was no friend of the United States. When the premier visited New York to address the United Nations General Assembly in 1960, however, the VALB privately appealed to him to include a reference to Spanish political prisoners in his speech. Castro's positive response and warm public references to the

Lincoln brigade underscored their common anti-fascist background. Such sentiments prompted individual veterans to offer assistance to the Cuban revolution.

Ted Veltfort, an ambulance driver in Spain and a skilled electronics engineer, had wearied of the professional blacklist that limited his employment in California's nascent Silicon Valley; and he did not wish to work on the military projects that dominated American electronics. "To construct something new—a socialist society," he recalled, Veltfort moved to Cuba in 1961. During the missile crisis the next year, Veltfort garbed himself in army fatigues, carried a gun, and prepared to defend the island against an American invasion. But most of his activities were more mundane, tapping his talents in economic planning, electronics production, and teaching applied physics at the University of Havana. A surge of Cuban nationalism persuaded him to return to the United States in 1968. Nurse Ruth Davidow also brought her professional skills to Havana, drafting a public health program to control the spread of infectious diseases. With the fear of an American invasion, she, too, prepared to resume her old role as a combat nurse. "I felt like I was coming home," she later said, "like Spain again. There was a feeling of closeness because we were being attacked."

"All of the situations and struggles I have participated in throughout my life have stemmed pretty much from the same reason I went to Spain," remarked Vernon Bown: "my extreme dislike, and yes, hatred of oppression. . . . I've always felt a kinship with the oppressed." Thus Lincoln veterans like Bown responded enthusiastically to the rebirth of the civil rights movement in the 1950's. Usually, some problem of local concern—segregated housing or job discrimination—forced a private decision to become involved. Sometimes, as in the 1930's, individuals self-consciously resolved to participate in the changes sweeping the country. The impulse to take action had never waned. "When I've felt strongly about something," Abe Osheroff explained, "I've felt a terrible need to do something about it or suffer a loss of self-respect."

While working as a truck driver in Louisville, Kentucky, in the spring of 1954, Vernon Bown noticed a newspaper story about community protests against a black family that had purchased a house in an all-white neighborhood. As threats of violence continued, Bown volunteered to live in the house to discourage further attacks. It was a bold act, a fact that became more apparent a

few weeks later when Bown returned to his native Wisconsin for a family reunion and so missed a dynamite explosion that severely damaged the structure. Segregationist officials promptly attributed the violence to a Communist
plot to instigate racial turmoil. Bown became a prime suspect when a search
of his room produced so-called Communist literature. "I have gradually come
to the conclusion that Negro people have been pretty badly treated in this
country," he explained to a grand jury that investigated the bombing. "I believe that colored people . . . should have the same rights as anyone else." For
expressing such opinions, Bown was held in jail on a high bond—which no
one in Louisville would post—for six months on charges of sedition. The
prosecutor based the allegations, ironically, on the theories of black self-determination articulated by Harry Haywood. "My freedom was gone. My job
was gone," Bown recalled. "There was nothing left but to fight." But not until
the U.S. Supreme Court ruled in 1956 in the Steve Nelson case that state sedition laws were unconstitutional did the state of Kentucky drop the charges
against Vernon Bown.

Abe Osheroff had been looking for a cause ever since leaving the Communist party. In the early 1960's, he began small fund-raising activities in the
Los Angeles area for the militant Student Nonviolent Coordinating Committee, but he felt that he was acting more like a liberal than the radical he knew
himself to be. As a builder, he believed he could contribute something tangible for southern blacks, and he developed the idea of constructing a community center in the heart of the Mississippi black belt. With the encouragement of black activist Robert Moses and the Council of Federated Organizations, Osheroff selected a site at Mileston in Holmes County, Mississippi, and
began building a cultural center in 1964. Whites greeted him with placards
that said "White Nigger" and dynamited his car.

"I was in a foreign country," Osheroff later remarked, drawing an analogy
to Spain. "I had gone abroad, so to speak, to fight in a foreign cause." The
carpenter kept a shotgun in his toolbox and a .38 at his waist. (He also reported his whereabouts to the local FBI; the agent told him he had been looking for Osheroff a decade earlier during his years in the underground!) No
further violence occurred, but for Osheroff, the experience of living with constant fear and triumphing over bigotry and hate ultimately compelled him to
reevaluate his career. "It suddenly came home to me that Spain was not the
highest peak in my activist life," he confessed after a reunion with other civil

rights workers in 1990. "It has to do with love. In Spain we loved and were beloved by the Spanish people, but inside the Brigades it was ideology, not love which dominated. In Mississippi, we loved and were loved by black people, *and we loved each other* in a movement free of ideology."

Ruth Davidow made a similar pilgrimage to Mississippi in 1966. When the Medical Committee for Human Rights sought volunteers to implement a nutrition evaluation of preschool children under the Head Start program, Davidow devoted three months to teaching local blacks how to acquire adequate health care. Emphasizing her professional standing rather than her political beliefs, she also persuaded the state department of health to provide vaccinations for 1,500 rural children. Davidow's sojourn in Mississippi, like Osheroff's, represented part of a larger commitment to social justice. Back in California in the late 1960's, she worked with drug-damaged children of the counterculture. "Youth were being destroyed just like the ones in Vietnam— a whole generation of youth destroyed through lies, distortions," she explained, discussing her decision to establish a health clinic in the Haight-Ashbury section of San Francisco. "I compared them to me when I was younger," she remembered. "Things were much clearer. There was a Depression; you could see the economics. . . . It was much harder for these kids to understand what was wrong. That's why they went inward."

Davidow's involvement with young people sometimes brought inordinate demands. In 1969, the American Indians who occupied Alcatraz Island to protest centuries of mistreatment summoned her to provide medical care for their besieged community. "You put your money where your mouth is," they demanded. "I didn't dare not go," she recalled. For over a year, she attended to their medical needs—pregnancies, illnesses, drug-related problems, suicides. Often, she was the only white person on the island. There she witnessed the tragedy of forlorn and wasted lives, a mental suffering that exhausted her own energies. Yet, like Osheroff, Davidow continued to seek opportunities for creative dissent: agitating for the homeless, helping AIDS patients, and fund-raising to send a health unit to Nicaragua.

"Call them the 'Bakers Dozen,'" said Moe Fishman of the twelve veterans who paraded through Harlem beneath the VALB banner to support the voting-rights march in Selma, Alabama, in 1965; "because that is about the number we can consistently turn out for any action." Although the VALB seldom spoke officially about civil rights, most veterans expressed their sympathies through other organizations. Black veterans participated in the struggle on local levels: Jimmy Yates, a leader of the Greenwich Village NAACP, supported food and clothing drives for Mississippi; Eluard Luchelle McDaniels led black protesters to city hall in Sacramento, California, to demand sidewalks for their muddy streets. But this older generation of black militants, nurtured in the theories of class conflict, did not always accept Martin Luther King's doctrine of passive resistance. "I didn't go around with those people because I would probably have gotten into trouble," explained Vaughn Love. "I'm not a passive person. I wished them well but I would not have turned the other cheek."

The rise of "Black Power" in the late 1960's raised objections of another sort. Harry Haywood, still a revolutionary theorist, saw the slogan as a fulfillment of his forty-year-old thesis. He now predicted "the growing consciousness of the Afro-American masses that they are an oppressed nation whose road to freedom and equality lies through taking political power into their own hands." Yet Haywood chastised the Left for failing to link black consciousness with the needs of white workers to forge a multiracial class alliance. After sixty years of militancy, Haywood could only hope that the next black explosion, whenever it occurred, would do better. He died in 1978, clinging to that wistful vision.

For radicals like Vaughn Love, however, Haywood's intellectual gymnastics avoided more practical issues. "You must try and get into mainstream America, for this is where we belong," he insisted. "Where is the black power when you don't have a job? You [must] work in the system and with people who are going in your direction." Love's rejection of black separatism paralleled Haywood's criticism of traditional Marxists for failing to support Black Power. Both, at bottom, were defending the values of racial integration; both respected the relationship between class and power. Both articulated the legacy of the Old Left in racial affairs. During the next decade, the VALB would denounce the South African regime, support economic boycotts, and send medical aid to antiapartheid groups. And Love, who died in 1990, lived to see that the cause of Spain—"the battle against racism and fascism," as he put it—also embraced "the fighters for South African freedom."

*

It was as soldiers, however, that the Lincoln veterans most clearly shared a collective identity, and the cause they embraced most fervently in the 1960's was opposition to the war in Vietnam. Maury Colow, a navy veteran of World War II, helped create the antiwar group Veterans for Peace to stand against the American Legion and the Veterans of Foreign Wars—"to show that veterans of World War II, wearing their old uniforms, were opposed to the Vietnam war," he explained; "to [answer] the hooting on the sidelines of people who were yelling 'cowards, yellow-bellies, reds.'"

Like many antiwar demonstrators, Colow criticized the American soldiers in Vietnam, but when two young veterans arrived at the peace office and expressed opposition to the war, he saw the opportunity to organize a separate group. In this way, with the organizational experience of older veterans and some funding from Veterans for Peace, a younger generation of dissenters formed the Vietnam Veterans Against the War. As an antiwar leader, Colow acted independently of the VALB, though he persuaded the executive board to appoint him as a delegate to Veterans for Peace. With such credentials, Colow attended numerous peace conferences, demonstrations, and picket lines. "Wherever I went," he recalled, "I was announced as a Lincoln brigade veteran, and those guys . . . reacted in the most beautiful heartfelt manner."

Such prestige had political potential. Colow pleaded with the VALB to take a formal stand against the war, arguing that "Vietnam is the Spain" of the 1960's. "Are we, the premature anti-fascists of yesterday to become the old silent men of today?" he asked. "Will the record show . . . that the Lincoln veterans of 1966 remained silent when their country committed genocide? I don't think so." But some veterans questioned the propriety of affirming any positions on issues other than Spain and warned that politicization of the VALB had already estranged numerous veterans, perhaps even a majority. Colow persisted. "When every ladies tea society is taking a position on Vietnam, I propose we act with the same courage," he declared. "The hour is late, and it is already embarrassing. . . . It means letting our kids and the youth of today know where we stand."

These antiwar sentiments rebounded even from Spain. On May Day 1967, Spanish students in Madrid, Barcelona, and Salamanca protested U.S. intervention in Vietnam, provoking bloody police reprisals. Three American students, including Roberta Alexander, the daughter of a Lincoln veteran, were expelled from the country. Such repression drew VALB pickets to the Spanish

tourist office in New York, where the Lincolns also protested the gift of an
aircraft carrier to the Spanish government. "Let Franco know," read a leaflet,
"that democratic Americans support the struggle against fascism in Spain!"

Still the VALB hesitated to speak on Vietnam. In a speech before a veterans' gathering in 1967, historian Robert Colodny invoked the lessons of history to goad the VALB into action. "The same power elites which have maintained the hangman's regime of General Francisco Franco," he reminded them,
"now sustain with blood and fire the military junta in Saigon." Moved by the
historical analogy, the veterans voted to publish Colodny's address as an inexpensive pamphlet, *Spain and Vietnam*, to support the antiwar movement.
Three months later, as protesters prepared for a massive march on the Pentagon, the VALB executive board formally resolved to join the demonstration.

On October 15, 1967, a day memorialized in Norman Mailer's *Armies of
the Night*, the Lincolns rallied behind banners that proclaimed "Spain Yesterday, Vietnam Today" and asked "How Many Guernicas, LBJ, Will Your
Bombers Destroy in Vietnam Today?" Seventy-five veterans, wearing black
Spanish berets, converged on Washington as part of a half-million demonstrators demanding peace in Vietnam. To their surprise, these middle-aged
protesters found they enjoyed a special stature among a younger generation
of radicals. As the veterans marched near the end of the long parade toward
the Lincoln Memorial, word spread through the throngs that the Lincoln brigade was coming and, as Moe Fishman reported, "a path opened up through
the crowd as if by magic. To the applause of many of the young people present, we made our way in a single file. We got flowers and kisses. . . . You
could spot many a tear." Not since the farewell parade in Barcelona in 1938
had the veterans found such wholehearted support.

The antiwar movement of the 1960's thus served as a vital connection between the Old Left and the New. "Your generation now faces *its* Spain," Professor Colodny advised his university students who had come to watch the
feature movie *To Die in Madrid*. "If you have tears to shed for the million dead
of the Spanish Republic," he said, "save them. Shed them for the million dead
of Vietnam. And if you feel moved to praise the courage of the defenders of
Madrid, save that praise too. Save it for the young men of your own generation
who shared with you the agony of Vietnam and who resist the war." After thirty
years of anti-Communist red-baiting, the Lincoln brigade had recaptured a
youthful audience.

24

The Death Watch

Few veterans would have predicted the renaissance of the Lincoln brigade in the 1960's. During the summer of 1961, the 25th anniversary of the outbreak of the Spanish war, a score of silver-haired veterans journeyed to East Germany to attend the only official celebration of the fight against fascism in Spain. Most were in their mid-forties and fifties, and they were glad to meet long-lost comrades, hoist drinks, pay homage to the dead, and hear Dolores Ibarruri's farewell address translated into German. For the majority of Spanish war veterans, however, the formal reunion hardly mattered. Of approximately one thousand surviving Lincolns, the VALB office knew the whereabouts of less than half, and many of them desired no relationship with their comrades. "They are kept apart by the usual hindrances of distance, age, and dimming memories, such as might bother even an American Legion post," observed a magazine reporter. "But they are further sundered by a growing political reticence."

Still reeling from the Red Scare, VALB officials tried to rebuild an organization based on the "common bonds of comradeship" and the "unity of divergent viewpoints" that had brought them together in Spain. But the quest for a specific program or cause continued to elude them. Communists and ex-Communists hesitated to cooperate on any plan of action. "We've had our problems and difficulties which have militated against living up to our tradition," Moe Fishman acknowledged in a letter to the veterans in 1958. But he reminded his comrades "that Spain still suffers and the good fight has not yet been won." Perhaps, he suggested, "it is time we considered renewing some anti-Franco activities in a modest way."

A few weeks later, Fishman received just what he was looking for—an issue that would quickly galvanize the veterans into action. Without prior warning, a letter arrived at the VALB office from a former member of the executive committee, Leoncio Pena, a Spaniard who had once lived in New York. During the Spanish war, Pena had fought against Franco in his native Asturias; after the fascist victory there, he had escaped in a small boat through the Bay of Biscay to rejoin the Loyalists fighting in Catalonia. At the end of the war, he had traveled from France to Haiti and then to Cuba, and from there he had entered the United States illegally in 1941. Arrested by immigration authorites, Pena was interned on Ellis Island, but a Spanish refugee committee gained his release. The U.S. Army promptly drafted him, and Pena accepted this opportunity to continue his war against fascism. On Okinawa, he won a Bronze Star as well as two Purple Hearts; his service also earned him U.S. citizenship. In the immediate postwar years, Pena edited an anti-Franco newspaper in New York called *Liberación*, served on the VALB executive board, wrote numerous articles on Spanish affairs, and acted as a liaison between Spanish exiles in America and the underground in Spain. Around 1948, however, Pena stopped attending VALB meetings and disappeared.

Ten years later, the letter to Fishman revealed his whereabouts. He was writing from a prison in Burgos, Spain, having been sentenced in 1958 to twenty years for clandestine activities against the Franco regime. The Lincolns immediately launched a campaign for his freedom. Based on Pena's military record in World War II, they contacted an American veterans' group, which in turn pressured the State Department to send a consul to visit him in prison, one of the few times the U.S. government intervened directly on behalf of a political prisoner in Spain. (It turned out that Pena had lost his citizenship because he failed to report to the consulate in due time.) Through its inquiries, the VALB also learned that Pena could receive personal parcels addressed to him in prison. Fishman, who for years had organized direct aid to Spaniards as a member of the Joint Anti-Fascist Refugee Committee, promptly assembled a package of food and clothing and sent it to the prisoner. To his surprise, the parcel arrived safely. Thus commenced a regular packet service between the VALB office and numerous political prisoners in Franco's Spain, a small but steady traffic that would last for nearly twenty years. Perhaps because of his U.S. support, Pena obtained his freedom in 1964, after serving more than six years in jail. He went into exile in France, where he continued to work with the anti-Franco underground. Not until the mid-1970's would Pena safely return to Spain.

The ordeal of Leoncio Pena testified to the strength of the fascist dictatorship long after most Americans considered the issues of the 1930's dead and buried. Lincoln veterans could not forget so easily. The oppression of political prisoners in Spain resonated with the domestic persecution of the cold war: the jailing of Barsky, Bessie, Gates, Nelson, Thompson, Wellman, Watt, and so many other veterans charged and convicted by various government agencies. And the multitude of prisoners in Spain demonstrated, even to those who might doubt, Franco's continuing suppression of his people. "Spain is still the question that all liberal, progressive Americans can unite on," explained the VALB's renamed newsletter, *The Volunteer*, in summoning the veterans back to the ranks in 1959. "We can do a terrific job on the question of political prisoners."

The increasingly liberal climate of the early 1960's encouraged the renewal of VALB activities. After the reunion in East Germany in 1961, Lincoln veterans in northern California revived the local post, dormant for at least seven years, and began to hold regular meetings. Yet with the SACB rulings still under appeal, such gatherings posed some risk. When the Communist newspaper *People's World* carried a story about an annual dinner reception in northern California, the national VALB formally protested that no such local chapter existed, nor did the veterans hold annual affairs. "This is an important legal question," the national office declared, because the newspaper article might one day appear in court "as *the* evidence of an 'underground' organization." Similarly, the Los Angeles VALB acknowledged "a resurgence of activity," but carefully deleted last names from their report. (The California veterans also objected to a compilation of a Lincoln brigade roster.) Amid this climate of fear, veterans in other areas remained unorganized. Some rebuffed any connections with former party comrades. Others simply did not identify their political work as VALB activity, though, as Milton Wolff observed, "apparently many of them are doing good things as just plain joes."

The 25th anniversary of the Lincoln brigade created an opportunity for a revival. Celebrated in February 1962 with a "Fight Back" luncheon in New York, the affair attracted fifteen hundred supporters and widespread news coverage. There, the veterans appealed to President John F. Kennedy to "seize the imagination of the world by urging Franco to grant amnesty" for the six thousand political prisoners in Spain. The audience promptly donated $2,500 to assist the campaign. Delighted by the support, few paid attention to fifteen pickets carrying placards that read "Red Animals Inside," "Abe Lincoln Brigade Murdered Nuns." But the HUAC promptly accused the Lincolns of collecting money for Spain's underground Communist party and voted to refer such criminal violations to the Department of Justice. Appearing before the committee, Moe Fishman denied these charges, insisting the funds served only "to alleviate a tiny bit of suffering." And when a congressman requested a list of donors, Fishman asked tartly, "Are you acting as an agent for the Franco government in trying to get their names?" There the matter rested.

Despite the lingering fear of government retaliation, Lincoln veterans continued to agitate against the Franco dictatorship. The VALB sent modest sums and clothing to those in jail and to their families outside; they held small demonstrations at Spanish tourist offices and consulates. At the New York World's Fair of 1964, 150 veterans staged a demonstration on the anniversary of the Franco uprising and demanded political amnesty for Spanish prisoners. At the doors of the Spanish exhibition, the blind Robert Raven presented a formal petition, asking that "another treasure be added to the many in your pavilion—democracy." Other veterans picketed a Spanish ship in New York harbor to protest government terror against striking miners in Spain, reminding the White House that "not all Americans are on the side of our government's friendship with the Franco regime."

Such efforts seldom reached the mainstream media; they had no effect on American foreign policy. In 1968, as the Johnson administration moved to renew the executive agreement that gave the United States military bases in Spain in exchange for economic and military support, the veterans organized protests around the country. "Make No Vietnam in Spain," stated the placards. But the White House did not read the signs. Two years later, the Nixon administration renewed the executive pact.

"Hasta pronto!" ("Soon!") It was Abe Osheroff, the carpenter, who brought the phrase to the attention of the VALB. While the veterans could draw little solace from the course of U.S. policy, the news from Spain sustained their hopes. As Franco aged and younger workers and students became restive under his regime, Osheroff reported that the new slogan and salutation was a sign of political ferment; the end of the dictatorship seemed imminent. Still, he was haunted by a puzzling, inescapable question: "How does Franco stay in power?"

Osheroff decided to see for himself. The question of returning to Spain had haunted the veterans for decades. Most had vowed never to touch Spanish earth until the restoration of a Republican government assured a victory over the fascist conquerors. Alvah Bessie had expressed contempt for the premature return of Ernest Hemingway in 1953 and again in 1959, when the novelist investigated the bullfighting scene for *Life* magazine. Yet some veterans found the thought of retracing the steps of their youth irresistible. And Bessie himself had put aside his scruples in 1967 to participate in the making of a film, *Spain Again*, about the return of an American volunteer. He recalled a feeling of "instant schizophrenia . . . thinking of himself alternately as an international *agent provocateur*—and as a fink." Osheroff suffered no such pretensions. But he, too, intended to make a film, a statement of his personal involvement with Spain for 35 years.

"It was all so different from anything I expected," he reported. "Spain was caught up in the bustle of the twentieth century." People on the street assured him of their contentment; except for some bullet-scarred buildings, there were no signs of the war. But when he returned to Belchite, site of the great Republican victory on the Aragon front in 1937, Osheroff saw to his shock that the town had been preserved as a ruin. Standing where he had witnessed the death of his closest friends—Danny Hutner, a lawyer who had once worked for the FBI; the sculptor Paul Block; the seaman Wallace Burton—Osheroff asked, "Can it be your dreams died here?" Aroused by what psychologists might call "survivor guilt," Osheroff realized he was seeking, as he put it, "my own validation." He resolved to probe deeper. From conversations with construction workers, he learned more about paltry wages and the low standard of living, as well as the existence of underground labor unions known as "workers' commissions" that staged illegal strikes. With the help of other dissidents, he arranged interviews with former political prisoners and with discontented students. "The fight for freedom is alive and well in Franco Spain," concluded Osheroff. "Despite the heightened repression, the struggle against the dictatorship and U.S. intervention is better organized and stronger . . . as the crisis of the Franco succession approaches."

Despite the varieties of dissent inside Spain—the same multiple interests that had bedeviled Republican politics in the 1930's—Osheroff found an underlying unity of demands: "no dictatorship, no monarchy, an end to American intervention." This last point provided the keystone of his movie. Appealing to the growing opposition to U.S. global power in the 1960's, Osheroff attacked American economic and military aid in propping up another faltering dictatorship. "It will go on," he warned, "as long as we permit our leaders" to exercise unrestrained power. Like Vietnam, Spain had become an American problem. "Is there no other way?" he pleaded. "Must all our dreams turn into nightmares?"

Released in February 1974, Osheroff's *Dreams and Nightmares* won prizes at the Cannes and New York Film Festivals, and it bolstered the veterans' campaign to support political prisoners in Spain. By the early 1970's, the VALB's annual reunion dinners were raising thousands of dollars to send assistance to the families of political prisoners in Spain. In 1973, the arrest of ten Spanish labor leaders—the so-called Carabanchel Ten—who were charged only with holding a meeting of the national coordinating committee of workers' commissions, focused the veterans' protest against the plight of anti-Franco dissidents. VALB posts in New York, Los Angeles, and San Francisco staged street demonstrations at the Spanish consulates and tourist offices to demand amnesty.

Ironically, the continuing repression in Spain fueled the Lincolns' optimism about the inevitable end of the dictatorship "through retirement, death or the action of the Spanish people." Franco's brutality, they argued, proved the fragility of his power. "Your murder yesterday of five heroic antifascist Spaniards," wrote Alvah Bessie in an open letter to "El Puto" (male whore), following the execution of five Basque revolutionaries, "signed the death warrant of your putrescent regime." *The Volunteer* regularly carried analyses of Spanish politics, speculating anxiously about post-Franco prospects. In the wake of the Watergate scandals of 1974, moreover, the U.S. Senate asserted its right to approve the executive agreement with Spain when it came up for renewal the next year. Joining with the U.S. Committee for a Democratic Spain, the VALB lobbied actively in Congress and held public demonstrations around the country to protest the treaty. Unable to influence Gerald Ford's administration, however, the Lincolns saw another American president make a commitment to Franco. Their hopes shifted to a death watch; the dictator could not live forever.

The long, slow death of Generalissimo Francisco Franco brought immeasurable relief to the Americans who had fought for a lifetime against his regime. When the final word came in November 1975, more than one Lincoln veteran broke open a bottle of Spanish champagne to celebrate. "But my crystal ball goes cloudy," exclaimed Alvah Bessie, "when I ask it 'What then?'" The end of the dictatorship aroused fresh tensions about the future of Spain. As Lincoln veterans braced for another civil war or worried about the rise of a new dictator, they scrutinized the Spanish news for signs of fascist tendencies or signals of popular rebellion. The expected explosion did not come. As the Spanish government moved slowly but steadily in a democratic direction, freeing prisoners, legalizing dissident parties, including the Communists, calling free elections, even permitting the return to Spain of that gallant symbol of resistance, Dolores Ibarruri, the historical drift appeared optimistic for the first time in forty years. The absence of retribution on either side underscored the powerful desire for reconciliation in Spain. Finally, the Lincolns felt free to state the obvious: "The evidence is undeniable!" proclaimed *The Volunteer* in 1978. "The war is truly over; peace is in the hands of the Spanish people."

One last obligation remained. With the creation of a more democratic government in Spain, the Lincolns wanted to return to the land that had nourished their dreams, inspired their sacrifice, and taken from them the flower of their youth. They wanted to pick up the broken threads. At first, they made pilgrimages alone; later they traveled in small groups, clusters of gray-haired veterans touring the old battlefields and reliving distant memories. "And wherever we went," wrote Milton Cohen of a group of eight that returned in 1977, "we were greeted, literally, with open arms." For Milton Wolff, the journey "began and ended with flowers. And love." He could still see "cruel battle scars" on the walls of old buildings, "but everywhere on this day," he said, "the streets are lined with flowers, the red and gold banners of Catalonia bold in the sun everywhere, and smiling people—no longer in the black dress we remember—waving banners and flowers at the passing buses—smiling, singing." Treated as celebrities, if not exactly heroes, the Lincolns absorbed the gratitude and the affection of the Spanish people, shared wine and food, gave justification for a lifetime's commitment to something so much more than a political abstraction. "The road to democracy is rough but it will be followed," observed Bill Susman, "and our love for Spain requited."

The journey back to Spain inevitably meant a turn inward as well. "How strong the feeling of nostalgia—a gray bitter sadness," reported William Herrick. The veterans revisited old haunts, sites of glory and terror, searched for a familiar café or an overgrown grave or a lost lover. And something unexpected happened to many of the Lincolns: Alvah Bessie, flying over the Pyrenees, suddenly crumbled in tears; the irreverent, wisecracking Nick Pappas visited the olive groves where his brother had died forty years earlier and abruptly "cried like a baby"; Bill Susman sat silently on a bench in the Plaza de Cataluna in Barcelona, "and I wept without knowing why, and still don't."

They grieved for all that might have been, would never be. "The Spanish people were our brothers. Our sisters. Our parents," exclaimed Irving Weissman, who stood in awe before the ruins of Belchite. "We all understood that, the forty thousand of us who came from every corner of Europe and the Americas. . . . We came to deliver the future as a gift to the world."

The world had not accepted the offer, however, and the return to Spain forty years later demanded a reconciliation with that terrible reality. Milton Cohen and his comrades made a full tour of the battle sites—"places where each of us had left so much of ourselves behind." In the Sierra Pandols, they found Hill 666, target of incredible bombardments, "where we fingered the ruined rock and felt once again the beating as of hearts entombed beneath the soil." And when they were done, Cohen said, they experienced a sense of completion. "A part of our lives had finally been rounded out—that part belonging to war and defeat and dedication," he said.

For forty years Lincoln veterans had carried the burden of their failure. Their grief for the dead had never been assuaged, and the longevity of Franco's regime mocked their efforts to claim even symbolic victory. During the intervening years, many comrades had died or vanished from the ranks. Now the vision of a democratic Spain offered a touch of comfort; the books, at last, were being closed—or nearly so. "Before we went to Spain," admitted Milton Cohen, "I assumed there was little we could do for Spain any longer—and nothing Spain could do for us." Having ventured back, however, he was less willing to cut the cord. Spain, he speculated, might still welcome support as the country moved toward democracy. And for the Lincolns, the transformation of Spain would symbolize the rebirth of a dream.

So the veterans flocked back to Spain. Marion Merriman Wachtel, one of the two American women to serve in the brigade, stood alone on a hot afternoon at the base of a yellow hillside near Gandesa and wondered anew what had happened to her husband, Robert Merriman, the first military commander of the Lincoln battalion. Evelyn Hutchins, the other woman, considered the new political environment "absolutely amazing." Alvah Bessie viewed Franco's immense mausoleum in the Valley of the Fallen, built by slave labor during the dark years of the dictatorship, and concluded wryly that the huge marble stones served to keep the body interred forever. Mel Anderson walked through the dark streets of Barcelona, retracing his footsteps to a familiar apartment doorstep, rang the bell, and found himself holding his old sweetheart in his arms. These were the satisfactions of outliving the horror.

In October 1986, the 50th anniversary of the creation of the International Brigades, dozens of Lincoln veterans journeyed to Madrid for a reunion with comrades from around the world. Once again they toured the battlefields, shook hands with courteous Spanish officials, and saluted the defiant spirit that had kept anti-fascism alive in Spain. Finally, in a huge auditorium in Madrid, they were dazzled to see 90-year-old Dolores Ibarruri, still vibrant and intense. Forty-eight years earlier, she had spoken of this moment. "We shall not forget you," La Pasionaria had promised the departing Lincoln brigade on another bittersweet October day in 1938, "and when the olive tree of peace puts forth its leaves again, entwined with the laurels of the Spanish Republic's victory—come back! . . .

"Come back to us. With us those of you who have no country will find one, those of you who have to live deprived of friendship will find friends, and all of you will find the love and gratitude of the whole Spanish people who, now and in the future, will cry out with all their hearts: Long live the heroes of the International Brigades!"

Now she was a wisp of a woman, bony and nearly blind. She made no speeches to mark the occasion. Instead, she stood on a stage before the veterans, clasped her hands to her black dress, and sang a song of victory. "We are all grateful to them," she would say in 1989, one year before her death at age 93, "because they fought to give our country freedom and happiness."

After this ceremonial homecoming, few Lincolns would return to Spain again. Many were too old and frail to make the journey. For most, there was no longer any need. What had begun half a century earlier as a crusade to stop fascist aggression had proved a noble failure; fascist aggression had been stopped everywhere *but* in Spain. "A thousand years from now," asserted historian Robert Colodny, professor emeritus at the University of Pittsburgh, "the scholars will discover that it was my generation's sacrifice which prevented fascist flags from flying over Washington and Moscow." In Spain, by contrast, democracy had slipped through the back door just as Franco exited from the front. Somehow, in the recesses of the fascist dictatorship, the Spanish people had kept the fires of liberty alight. Lincoln veterans, who for four decades had given every particle of moral and material support possible, could share the satisfaction of their courage, their tenacity, their victory. Through all those years of darkness, they had seen and spoken and struggled. "You can go proudly," La Pasionaria had told them in words which still echoed in their hearts. "You are history. You are legend."

Old Radicals, New Causes

Spain does not end the story of the Lincoln brigade. Just as most volunteers of the 1930's had
participated in other movements for social justice so
the veterans continued to seek causes that reaffirmed
their anti-fascist principles. Spain, in this way, became a prototype and a precedent for involvement in
El Salvador, Nicaragua, and South Africa. On a deeper
level, this political activity had become a matter of
habit. After fifty, sixty, even seventy years of commitment to radical dissent, Lincoln veterans had come to
view political agitation as the surest measure of personal fulfillment and the value of a life's work.

By the mid-1970's, the Lincolns had acquired a
certain respectability, not only among young radicals
but among liberal dissenters of more moderate stripes.
Their annual reunions became crowded extravagan-
zas, jumping in attendance from a few hundred at the
beginning of the decade to over a thousand by the end.
These ceremonial events, marked by political speeches
and left-wing entertainment, served as successful fund-
raisers, enabling the VALB to send tens of thousands
of dollars to political dissidents around the world. Such

popularity could be attributed to the changing historical climate—the waning of the cold war and the anti-Communist crusade. But equally important in altering the texture of the VALB was the aging of the membership. As more veterans reached their mid-sixties and retired from their jobs, they found in the veterans' group an arena for political work and social interaction. In returning to VALB activities, however, many brought new agendas that would shake the organization to its foundations.

The long-awaited collapse of the Franco dictatorship had created a crisis of identity. Without a common foe, Lincoln veterans no longer felt obliged to suppress the political antagonisms that had been festering within the VALB for years. Indeed, the membership quickly polarized into Communist party members and ex-Communists who distrusted their former comrades. The quarrels, reminiscent of the sectarian struggles of the 1930's, threatened the organization's survival.

The issues were ideological, matters of principle and conscience, but the style of argument appeared hysterical, if not puerile. One debate raged over whether a group of Polish Jewish veterans (the Botwin company in Spain) had forfeited their old-age pensions by migrating to Israel. (The Communists backed the Polish government; the non-party members, charging anti-Semitism, urged compensation for their fellow veterans.) Another argument erupted over the custody of the brigade's military archives. (The Communists claimed sole possession; the VALB demanded the release of all historical material. An unhappy compromise was finally reached.) When Steve Nelson published an op-ed article in the *New York Times* to oppose renewal of the treaty with Franco in 1975, Communists trounced the former commissar for omitting any reference to the role of the party in the Spanish war.

Animosity became so severe that each group lobbied aggressively for political control and organized slates of candidates. When a non-party faction won decisively in Los Angeles, party members boycotted post meetings, while the anti-Communist majority rejected the idea of "unity" if that meant bringing party people into administrative positions. "Total 'control' is now in non-[Communist] hands," observed veteran Pete Smith, "but [their] methods . . . [are a] mirror image of [the Communists]!! Same manipulation, same cliquishness. . . . Same slander and paranoia and overreaction."

To break the impasse, Milton Wolff, one of the few veterans who had continuously identified with the VALB, proposed the adoption of a formal constitution. Accordingly, in 1979 a national convention of one hundred veterans proceeded to accept a four-point program that defined the political limits of the organization. First, the veterans reaffirmed their commitment to a Republican Spain and promised to continue to provide assistance to anti-fascist Spaniards. Second, they reiterated their opposition to fascism anywhere else in the world—"our only ism," as Wolff put it, "is anti-fascism"—but agreed to confine their activities only to those cases where the veterans could reach a consensus. (That decision tacitly represented a defeat of the Communist membership, for the VALB had historically adopted broad positions that converged with the party line, but as the anti-Communist John Gates observed, the agreement also prevented the VALB from taking a stand that contradicted the party!) Third, the veterans accepted responsibility for preserving their historical record. The VALB thus became a major supporter of a non-profit organization, the Abraham Lincoln Brigade Archives (ALBA), which began building an archival collection at Brandeis University; West Coast veterans established a collection at the Berkeley campus of the University of California. Finally, the veterans resolved to take care of each other. Some had done well in their careers and gave generously to political causes and to their comrades, but poverty, illness, and isolation were not unfamiliar problems to people who often lived outside the security of mainstream careers. To a remarkable degree, less fortunate Lincolns could expect support from their fellow veterans. With these four points settled, at last, the VALB could return to the political struggles of their waning years.

"Me," roared Alvah Bessie at the beginning of the 1980's, "I am FURIOUS that good people I know are dying right and left, and the Nixons, the Carters, the Fords and the Ronniebaby Reagans march merrily on, enriching themselves at our expense and trying to work up a war they confidently think they can win and which will eliminate Communism." The election of Ronald Reagan served as a catalyst for mustering resistance to the conservatism that emanated from the Republican White House. By then, the survivors of the Lincoln brigade numbered fewer than four hundred—a tally that grew smaller each month—and illness, physical impairment, and bereavement slowly circumscribed their political activities. But at a time when elderly Americans of all political persuasions demanded recognition of their value and experience, the old activists were not about to abandon a lifetime's tradition of dissent and protest. To the contrary, their dwindling numbers added a sense of urgency to the political work.

Four months after Reagan's inauguration, thirty veterans were marching in Washington, D.C., to protest American intervention in El Salvador. Along the route, a new sentiment lightened their steps: as the Lincolns paraded, other marchers and onlookers spontaneously broke into applause, paying homage to the radical tradition they embodied. It would prove a recurring phenomenon. Some anti-Communist veterans questioned such political stands. But the New York post twice voted unanimously to assert opposition to Reagan's foreign policy, and the Lincolns in California raised over $50,000 to help Salvadoran refugees and to provide medical aid for the victims of U.S.-backed military attacks.

During the 1982 campaign for a nuclear freeze, the VALB joined the opposition to the administration's Star Wars strategy. That spring, more than sixty Lincolns marched in the largest peace demonstration in the nation's history as over half a million people congregated in New York's Central Park. Parading beneath banners that read "No More Guernicas, No More Hiroshimas," the veterans received enthusiastic applause whenever the parade line turned a corner. Spectators of all ages broke into their ranks to embrace them, to thank them, and, as one veteran put it, "to marvel that we were still alive." At the park gates, the happy crowd rose for a standing ovation. "Wow!" yelled an amazed teenager, capturing the feeling of surprise and awe. "They made it!" In San Francisco, the local veterans gained inordinate attention from spectators and media as they carried a flag first given to the volunteers by a Spanish seamstresses' union in 1938. "We are marching now under the same banner," said Milton Wolff, "for the same ideals, without weapons, for a ban of weaponry and killing, for a world without war."

Such idealism even inspired some aging veterans to commit themselves anew. Among the reborn activists was Reuben Barr, the ex-Wobbly, onetime prisoner of war in Spain, who had withdrawn from political work in 1940, raised a family, and then in his early eighties reclaimed the radical heritage of his youth. "Rest a while, comrade," he advised Alvah Bessie about the frustrations of the moment, "and like me, you'll return, refreshed and rejuvenated." Despite his advanced age, Barr reentered the burgeoning peace movement with enthusiasm and hope. To protest the development of the MX missile in 1983, he joined with two other Lincoln veterans—Bill McCarthy and Frank

Brown—in nonviolent demonstrations at the Lawrence Livermore Laboratory in California. All three were arrested and spent eight days in jail, where they taught younger demonstrators the old working-class songs. McCarthy died soon after this protest, but Barr became a fixture at local demonstrations, marching for miles beneath the VALB banner. In 1985, he was again arrested for protesting the University of California's investments in South Africa. "We have to do our fighting right here," he declared five years later. "There's no use being discouraged because victory is ours if we fight for it." Barr was 90—and still marching. He died in 1993.

This spirit of defiance climaxed when the Reagan administration intensified attacks against the Sandinista regime of Nicaragua in the mid-1980's. Old radicals who traveled there to witness the triumph of socialism experienced, in the words of veteran Lou Gordon, "the most dramatic deja-vu imaginable. I was suddenly transported back to Spain, 1937 Spain." Struck by the similarity of terrain and language, several veterans commented on other signs that evoked the earlier war—colorful wall posters, bombed streets and buildings, armed soldiers, male and female, and the ubiquitous streamers stretched above cobblestone streets that proclaimed the very motto of the Spanish Republic, Dolores Ibarruri's "No pasaran." Veteran Bob Reed, who visited Nicaragua as part of the Seattle-Managua sister city project in 1984, observed more ominous parallels to Spain: "the involvement of big foreign powers." To many veterans, the United States had assumed the interventionist role of Germany and Italy fifty years earlier. "In the United States during the Spanish war the cry was 'Lift the Embargo!'" said Reed; "now it seems to me that 'Hands Off Nicaragua' is very appropriate."

Former ambulance driver Ted Veltfort, who had provided engineering expertise for Castro's Cuba in the 1960's, visited Nicaragua twenty years later to restore the country's damaged television broadcasting equipment. While touring the provinces, he noticed serious shortages of hospital equipment, ranging from bandages and medicine to light bulbs and vehicles. Back in California, Veltfort proposed that the VALB embark on an ambulance supply project similar to the national campaigns of the 1930's. Building coalitions with other organizations, the Lincolns launched a national fund-raising drive to send ambulances to Nicaragua. By 1984, they had raised enough for two ambulances (at $17,000 each); the next year, they funded seven more; and by the end of the decade, the VALB had sent twenty ambulances, as well as spare parts and a mechanic to provide instruction for repairs. "It was natural for us to go in and help," explained Milton Wolff. "Just as the people of Spain voted to come out of the dark ages, so have the people of Nicaragua. We went to Spain to stop the aggressors and avert World War II. And we were right. We could have stopped them in Spain. And what happened in Spain is happening in Central America. Once again, we've got to stop the aggressors. Only this time, we are the aggressors."

Abe Osheroff, who had built a community center in Mississippi twenty years earlier, now organized a labor crew, including his two sons, to construct private housing in a remote peasant village. "I'm going to Nicaragua not simply to build houses," he explained, "but to register my protest against the Reagan policy," to show the Nicaraguan people "that there is another America that cares and is opposed to U.S. intervention." He proceeded to construct fifty dwellings. For Osheroff, these tangible contributions provided a fundamental continuity with the rest of his life's work.

Ted Veltfort discovered, however, that while VALB ambulances might save the lives of the sick and the wounded, military attacks against hospitals by the U.S.-backed Contras often forced the abrupt curtailment of all medical services. He soon persuaded the veterans to endorse another fund-raising drive to send electrical generators for use at Nicaraguan medical centers. After Hurricane Joan devastated the impoverished country in 1988, the VALB again organized campaigns to send food, clothing, and medical supplies. Two years later, they funded a wheelchair center in Managua, run by handicapped Nicaraguans, to repair equipment for the maimed victims of the war; and they sent additional assistance for a care facility for mothers and children. Other beneficiaries of VALB support included a water-pumping project in Nicaragua, a medical program for opponents of apartheid in South Africa, and children's clinics in Cuba.

The enthusiastic public response to the ambulance project reinforced the Lincolns' commitment to political dissent, but their appeal apparently tapped some hidden memory within the presidential psyche, permitting the commander in chief to use the Lincolns as a historical justification for the very policies they abhorred. Seeking to validate his support of the Contra rebels in 1984, President Reagan assured a group of news reporters that such extralegal military efforts reflected "a well-established tradition in our country" that dated to the Lincoln brigade and the Spanish war. Then, in a remarkable comment, he added, "The individuals that went over there were, in the opinion of most Americans, fighting on the wrong side." The statement, given the public opinion polls of the 1930's, was patently false. More seriously, it suggested that in aligning with the Spanish Republic against Franco and his fascist allies, the Lincolns had backed "the wrong side." Undeterred by history or logic, Reagan repeated that assessment on other occasions. The Lincolns' protests failed to alter the president's opinion.

The controversy involved much more than President Reagan's distorted view of the past. For Lincoln veterans the issue involved the most basic element of their identity: their place in history. Often maligned in their youth, attacked by the government during their middle years, they understood in their old age the necessity of defending their past in order to perpetuate a meaningful legacy. When the VALB campaigned in the 1980's for World War II veterans' benefits, few expected the measure to pass in Congress. But the idea that the Spanish war constituted the first battle of "one war, the Great War Against Fascism," seemed important to proclaim and defend. For then American participation in the Spanish war could be seen not as a radical aberration in an isolationist decade, but as a realistic analysis of the world situation, a forerunner and an essential component of World War II, which most citizens agreed was a just and worthy undertaking. During the 50th anniversary of the Spanish war in 1986, the VALB participated in dozens of programs around the country to commemorate their anti-fascist tradition.

These historical activities represented more than a nostalgic urge for times past—just the opposite, in fact. For beneath all the ceremonial rhetoric and sentimental reminiscence, the Lincolns looked to history not for understanding, but for vindication. Literary critic Malcolm Cowley, who had journeyed to Spain during the war to attend a writers' conference in Valencia, touched a sore nerve when he published a "lament" for the Lincoln brigade in 1984. "In spite of all the youth and promise that went into the [brigade]," he observed, "only a few of the veterans were to have distinguished careers in art or scholarship or industry. Not one of them . . . was ever elected or appointed to public office. They were to remain victims . . . for the rest of their lives."

Cowley's view outraged the survivors—first, because it seemed to denigrate those who did have distinguished careers in a variety of callings; and second, because it assumed criteria that most Lincoln veterans would have rejected. In choosing to go to Spain as soldiers, they had stepped beyond the safety and comfort of traditional institutions. After the war, to be sure, some veterans had returned to that security. (No one knows how many Lincoln veterans disappeared into the American mainstream—two or three hundred, at the least; when Carl Geiser conducted research on former prisoners in the 1980's, he located several veterans who never knew the VALB existed!) More typical, however, were those who remained committed to social justice and political struggle. Working in labor unions, professional groups, or community projects, they viewed themselves not as "victims," but as fighters carrying on the principles of their youth.

That commitment appeared to many veterans far more important than any particular accomplishment. Thus the appearance in 1984 of an inspiring documentary film about the brigade called *The Good Fight* provoked intense discussions about the historical lessons of their experience. When, in the last scene of the movie, Abe Osheroff posed the haunting question "Can you ever win the good fight?" other veterans criticized what they considered his defeatist tone, the suggestion that the war and its sacrifices had been futile. "The Good Fight," Osheroff responded, "is the committed response to all forms of human suffering, exploitation and injustice. It is not episodic, but rather an ongoing process," of which the Spanish war was but one part. "It may be comforting and helpful to believe in a future ultimate victory," he explained, "but it is not required." The fight itself, the conversion of principled outrage into communal activity, the sharing of effort and responsibility, created feelings of love that transcended the pain and loss of political or military defeat. "Rare indeed," Osheroff reminded his comrades, "is the Lincoln veteran who regrets his participation in the glory of that epic struggle."

For men and women who viewed their lives as a seamless pattern of idealism and struggle, the soul-searching of old age inevitably aroused disagreements about the verdict of history. Invited to address a 50th anniversary symposium on the Spanish war at the Smithsonian Institution, former commissar George Watt used that prestigious forum to challenge the popular view of the Lincoln brigade as a monolithic organization, "our ideas and beliefs . . . frozen at that time and place."

Watt proceeded to bare his soul. As a former Communist cadre, who admitted that "breaking with the party was the most traumatic episode of my life," Watt emphasized that the same ideological fervor which inspired the Lincolns to volunteer to fight in Spain also led them to adopt a noninterventionist stand during the period of the Nazi-Soviet pact, which, he argued, "damaged our credibility among the American people as genuine anti-fascist fighters." Those errors may have belonged to the past, he conceded; but the failure of popular histories like *The Good Fight* to explore this aspect of the radical experience obscured "an important object lesson on the pitfalls of blind, unquestioning faith in any movement, no matter how worthy the objectives." In acknowledging such mistakes, Watt also confronted the darker side of the Spanish war—those "negative and seamy . . . power struggles among conflicting ideologies, parties, and factions on the Republican side." Responding to Orwell and other anti-Communists, Watt maintained that the Lincolns remained innocent "of this secret war within the war," unaware of assassinations or executions; but, he declared, the Americans had participated in the "political war" against the so-called Trotskyists. The history of the Lincoln brigade, he suggested, demanded an honest consideration of such unpleasant truths.

Watt's sober reappraisal drew instant cross fire. One angry veteran dismissed him as a "disillusioned old [radical] fighting ancient, sectarian battles and spreading demoralization and pessimism." Moe Fishman, a leading architect of many of the VALB's policies, protested that the Smithsonian speech attributed to the Lincolns the very things the SACB and HUAC could never prove in court: that the VALB remained merely a "front" organization of the Communist party, incapable of reaching independent positions. Fishman expressed no regrets about either the VALB's support of noninterventionism in 1939 or its reversal two years later; both stands, he said, reflected a majority view of the membership. He emphasized, moreover, the existence of "an anti-fascist ideology," distinct from communism, which had informed the Lincolns' politics on many issues. Citing "fifty years in the trenches," Milton Wolff denied that the veterans had squandered their credibility among leftists, as Watt had charged; instead, the VALB had proved to be one of the few left-wing groups to survive the ravages of the McCarthy period. Besides, as all, including Watt, agreed, the Lincolns had not participated in the infamous atrocities in Spain.

The rancorous debate revealed not only the touchiness of the issue, but a more uncomfortable reality: as Watt put it in rebuttal, "We as a group are not

the way we were." Of course—and this was central to their collective identity—the Lincolns had little trouble reaching agreement on many basic issues. Only two or three veterans objected publicly to the ambulance campaign for Nicaragua or disagreed with the condemnation of apartheid and the
advocacy of nuclear disarmament. About such matters the VALB leadership
could easily build a consensus. Similarly, nearly all veterans shared—or even
hoarded—feelings of pride about their earlier commitment to Spain. But
questions involving the Communist party or, by extension, the Soviet Union,
easily produced quarrels, suspicion, bitterness, and fury. The VALB rule that
only subjects of general agreement could reach the agenda served to mute
and mask fundamental oppositions.

These contentions had their roots in the 1950's, in the bitter debates about
the relevance of communism to American conditions. Thirty years later, in a
world of changing global politics, they assumed a new importance. As the
transformation of the Soviet Union and eastern Europe forced the Lincolns to
reappraise contemporary questions of self-determination and international
rapprochement, the changes also required a reassessment of personal opinions and loyalties. Most Lincoln veterans, including even the strident ex-
Communists, had remained optimistic about the advantages of a socialist society. "If we had socialism, everybody would be better off," asserted black
veteran Vaughn Love in a statement typical of the Lincolns' sentiments in the
late 1970's. "You don't need to exploit human beings, you don't need to degrade a whole segment of the population in order for some people to live in
luxury." A decade later, most veterans believed the old ideology had failed;
newer alternatives had not yet emerged.

Having devoted their lives to political dialectics, the old radicals labored
to understand the changes that abounded. Lincoln veterans who remained in
the party, such as Archie Brown, rejected the spreading criticism of the Marxist
class struggle. "The working class is growing in numbers, does learn, and is
only beginning to fight back," he declared. "It is precisely the false theory
that the working class is dying out . . . that makes it easy to sell the class
collaborationist program." Others tried to separate the party organization from
socialist theory. "Because socialism has been distorted in the countries where
the Communists have come to power," George Kaye asked defiantly in 1984,
"does that mean that everything we did and stood for was wrong?" Half a dozen
years later, however, as Kaye prepared for his death, the revolutions of east-

ern Europe brought tears to his eyes. "They are rejecting my generation of revolutionaries," he said. Then, in a revealing comment, he added: "We are going to have to begin all over again." Kaye's union brother, Bill Bailey, felt the same way. Criticizing the governments of eastern Europe "for pissing on Karl Marx's grave," he expressed hope that socialism might yet be reborn.

So did Steve Nelson, the 90-year-old ex-commissar. The collapse of communism in Europe, he said, showed the failure of "democratic centralism" and the bureaucracy of revolution; but the dream lived. "Socialism in the long run is inevitable," he insisted, citing the inability of private enterprise to protect natural resources. He envisioned a socialism within democratic structures—perhaps a coalition of labor unionists, environmentalists, feminists, and other exploited groups. "The class struggle wasn't invented by Marx," agreed Ed Bender, who had helped create the Lincoln brigade in 1936. "And it won't disappear because socialism did not work in the Soviet Union."

Whatever their ideological prejudices, the Lincolns agreed that a resolution of their concerns about the economy, war, and social justice would not take place in their lifetime. "We ain't got the answers," admitted Archie Brown in his last public appearance. "The answers are going to be made by young people and middle-aged people that are growing up. . . . They are going to become the new activists," he explained, "because they are going to get bit in the ass." For Brown, the continuation of economic exploitation assured the perpetuation of class struggle. Ruth Davidow also took the long view. "Throughout history there have been people who have taken the road of justice to fight for other people," she said. "And when we go I am convinced that the young people we are so worried about will do their thing."

The struggles of the Lincoln veterans thus formed part of a continuing history of dissent and protest, a radical tradition that challenged the structure of power and defied the American consensus. Half a year after his speech, Archie Brown was dead of cancer; but already Ruth Davidow, Milton Wolff, Reuben Barr, and many of the other surviving veterans were marching in San Francisco to protest the American war against Iraq. And in New York, Moe Fishman rallied nine old men, who rose at 2:00 A.M. to catch a 5:30 bus to Washington, D.C., to voice their objections. "Don't forget I am 75 and one of the young ones," Fishman remarked. "We'd have had more naturally if it were held in New York City."

*

"I knit and someone rips," said Ruth Davidow in a homey metaphor that spoke less of the futility and frustration of leftist activism than of the feelings of pride and continuity that went with it. "You make progress slowly; it's a long historical process. And nothing is won forever unless you fight for it." But first an activist had to overcome the fear that paralyzed dissent. "When I went to Spain, I put my life on the line," Davidow expalined. "Nothing I ever had to decide again was that drastic. After that I'd say to myself, 'Is this as difficult as going to Spain?' And it isn't." So after Spain, she worked for the labor movement, for the party, for the VALB; she went to Cuba and to Mississippi and to Alcatraz Island in San Francisco Bay. "Each time you take a position you're less fearful," she advised. "Each time you learn how to control your life."

For the Lincoln veterans, the precedent of Spain encouraged commitments to causes that went far beyond their original agenda. "Because the world has changed in more than only political ways," explained Irving Weissman in *The Volunteer*, "our own morality must today go beyond the limits that we once considered sufficient." Social and economic problems, the stuff of Marxist dialectics, remained serious issues, he said, but there were also larger questions involving nuclear weapons and environmental contamination, threats to all people, all societies, indeed to the planet. "We veterans," proposed Weissman, "although only a modest contingent, must grasp the hands of other people of good will and go with them into these current battles." From the vantage point of old age, such visions offered obvious satisfactions.

For most veterans of the Lincoln brigade, the experience in Spain had defined their entire lives: given friends, made enemies, forged a fundamental identity. But the survivors did not dwell in the past. "Spain was only one battle," observed Milton Wolff; "World War II was only one battle, what's going on in Central America, South Africa, the Middle East now is another battle, and we're into those things." After Spain, the Lincolns had continued to grow, most of them anyway; and as Milton Wolff said of his enduring activism: "Struggle is the elixir of life, the tonic of life. I mean, if you're not struggling, you are dead."

Reference Matter

A Note on Sources

The largest collection of source material on the Abraham Lincoln brigade resides in the Abraham Lincoln Brigade Archives at Brandeis University. It includes the office records of the Veterans of the Abraham Lincoln Brigade (VALB) as well as material relating to individual veterans. The newly opened Russian Center for the Preservation and Study of Recent Historical Documents (Rossiiskii tsentr khraneniia i izucheniia documentov noveishei istorii) in Moscow is a goldmine of previously unused source material about the International Brigades. Other valuable depositories are at Adelphi University; the Bancroft Library at the Berkeley campus of the University of California; the Hoover Institution on War, Revolution and Peace at Stanford University; and the Marx Memorial Library in London. Published guides to other archives are Sibylle Fraser and Alison Ryley, "The David McKelvey White Collection," *Bulletin of Research in the Humanities* 87 (1986–87): 269–350, which describes the holdings of the New York Public Library; and Cary Nelson and Jefferson Hendricks, *Edwin Rolfe: A Biographical Essay and Guide to the Rolfe Archive* (Urbana, Ill., 1990), which lists some of the papers at the University of Illinois. Since some of the privately held material I used was subsequently donated to one of these libraries, the notes that follow cannot always provide up-to-date locations. My own material will be deposited with the ALBA papers at Brandeis.

Notes

The following abbreviations are used in the notes:

AU   Adelphi University, Garden City, New York

BU   Brandeis University, Waltham, Massachusetts

CU   Columbia University, New York City

DW   *Daily Worker*

HI   Hoover Institution on War, Revolution and Peace, Stanford, California

MML   Marx Memorial Library, London, England

Moscow Russian Center for the Preservation and Study of Recent Historical Documents (Rossiiskii tsentr khraneniia i izucheniia documentov noveishei istorii), Moscow

NA   National Archives, Public Records Group 59, followed by call numbers

NYPL   New York Public Library

Ph   Privately held

SACB   Subversive Activities Control Board Hearings, "Attorney General of the United States vs. Veterans of the Abraham Lincoln Brigade," microfilm

UCB   Bancroft Library, University of California at Berkeley

UI   University of Illinois, Champaign, Illinois

VALB   Veterans of the Abraham Lincoln Brigade

Prologue

Page   1   "They did not smile": Irving Weissman, "The Return," *Massachusetts Review* 19 (Autumn 1978); reprinted in Alvah Bessie and Albert Prago, eds., *Our Fight: Writings by Veterans of the Abraham Lincoln Brigade* (New York, 1987), 316–18, 324.

3   "Because of the intensity": Don MacLeod, audiotape [1984], UCB.

3   "We, all of us": Edwin Rolfe to Mary Rolfe, Sept. 12, 1938, Rolfe MSS, UI.

4   "a bad wound": Edward E. Stanton, *Hemingway and Spain* (Seattle, Wash., 1989), 150.

4   "We were naive": MacLeod, audiotape [1984], UCB.

4   "If you lose": Carlos Baker, ed., *Ernest Hemingway: Selected Letters 1917–1961* (New York, 1981), 498.

4   "lost the war": Milton Wolff to Alvah Bessie, Aug. 15, 1981, Bessie MSS, Ph.

5   "Say of them": Genevieve Taggard, *The Long View* (New York, 1942), 40; originally published in *New Masses* 38 (Mar. 4, 1941): 12.

Chapter 1

Page   10   "one glimmer of hope": Edward Bender interviews, June 5, 1989, Nov. 7, 1991.

10   "a doomed city": Dan Kurzman, *Miracle of November: Madrid's Epic Stand, 1936* (New York, 1980), 18.

11   "We shall know": Hugh Thomas, *The Spanish Civil War* (New York, 1961), 318.

11   "The Popular Front": Ibid., 143.

14   "History was going": Alfred Kazin, *Starting Out in the Thirties* (Boston, 1965), 82.

15   According to historian: Robert Rosenstone, *Crusade of the Left: The Lincoln Battalion in the Spanish Civil War* (New York, 1969), app. A; see also Edwin Rolfe, *The Lincoln Battalion* (New York, 1939), chap. 1.

15   Russian archives: Fond 545, opis 3, file 455; opis 6, file 845–46, Moscow; Leonard Levenson, "U.S. Communists in Spain: A

Profile," *Political Affairs* 65 (Aug. 1986), table E; Danny Duncan Collum, ed., *African Americans in the Spanish Civil War* (New York, 1992), part 2; Frances Patai to author, May 24, 1991.

16   1,249 Communists: Levenson, "U.S. Communists"; fond 545, opis 6, file 846, Moscow.

16   A survey: John Gerassi, *The Premature Antifascists: North American Volunteers in the Spanish Civil War, an Oral History* (New York, 1986), 3; Patai to author, May 24, 1991.

17   "I think I resented": James Benét interview, Sept. 15, 1989.

17   "Yes, Ma": Hyman Katz to mother, Nov. 25, 1937; Hyman Katz to Aunt Sophie, Feb. 9, 1938, box 8A, VALB MSS, BU; see also Aaron Katz, "Letters from the Front in Spain," *Jewish Currents* 40 (Apr. 1986): 5–9, 32.

18   an inordinate proportion: Albert Prago, "Jews in the International Brigades in Spain," *Jewish Currents Reprint*, Feb. 1979, 4–6, 16–17; see also Gerassi, *Premature Antifascists*, 3–4.

18   "I had read": Vaughn Love interview, Apr. 7, 1978.

18   eighty African Americans: Robin D. G. Kelley, "This Ain't Ethiopia, but It'll Do," in Collum, ed., *African Americans*, 5–57.

18   "I saw in the invaders": *People's World*, Feb. 13, 1939, 3.

19   two-thirds and three-quarters: Fond 545, opis 3, file 455, Moscow; Levenson, "U.S. Communists."

Chapter 2

Page 21   "to keep his feet": Reuben Barr interviews, Nov. 1, Nov. 11, 1989; Reuben Barr, unpublished memoir, Ph.

24   Edwin Rolfe: Bernard Fishman interview, June 2, 1989; Leo Hurwitz interview, June 15, 1989; see also Cary Nelson and Jefferson Hendricks, *Edwin Rolfe: A Biographical Essay and Guide* (Urbana, Ill., 1990).

25   "forbidden pipes": Edwin Rolfe, "The Pattern of Our Lives," in *To My Contemporaries* (New York, 1936), 28–30.

25   "America": "The New Magazine," *DW*, Mar. 12, 1927, 2.

25   "What the Communist": *DW*, July 26, 1927, 6.

26   "dogged sullenness": *DW*, Nov. 19, 1927, 4.

26   "Disorderly Conduct": *DW*, Aug. 13, 1927, 2.

26   "when that was": *DW*, Oct. 22, 1927, 7.

27   "Slowly, relentlessly": *DW*, Apr. 26, 1928, 6.

27   "I have heard": *DW*, June 22, 1929, 6.

27   "twilight sleep": *New Masses* 4 (Apr. 1929): 21.

28   "Now . . . we were just": Harry Haywood, *Black Bolshevik: Autobiography of an Afro-American Communist* (Chicago, 1978), 33.

29   "It came to me": Ibid., 1, 83.

29   "Garveyism": Harry Haywood, "The Theoretical Defenders of White Chauvinism in the Labor Movement," *Communist* 10 (June 1931): 503.

30   "When we sang": Haywood, *Black Bolshevik*, 132.

30   "an historically developed": Irving Howe and Lewis Coser, *The American Communist Party: A Critical History* (Boston, 1957), 206.

31   "To contend": Haywood, "Theoretical Defenders," 505–6.

31   "looked toward the future": Frederick Lewis Allen, *Only Yesterday* (New York, 1931), 226.

32   "Today our party": Howe and Coser, *American Communist Party*, 175.

32   "The radical on the soap-box": Allen, *Only Yesterday*, 254.

32   "Youth forever stays": "Song for Youth!" *DW*, May 20, 1929, 6.

Chapter 3

Page 34   "When I got": Ruth Fisher, "Coming of Age in the 30s: An Era of Radicalization," Master's thesis, Goddard College, 1981, 4–5.

35   "With the present breakdown": Irving Bernstein, *The Lean Years* (Boston, 1960), 425.

35   "The Failure of Wisdom": Caroline Bird, *The Invisible Scar* (New York, 1966), 58.

36   Communist party issued: Harvey Klehr, *The Heyday of American Communism: The Depression Decade* (New York, 1984), 14. See also Fraser M. Ottanelli, *The Communist Party of the United States: From the Depression to World War II* (New Brunswick, N.J., 1991).

36   "I remember clear": *DW*, Nov. 10, 1937, 6; see also Peter Car-

roll, "Steve Nelson: Good Fight Fighter," *In These Times*, May 20, 1992, 4.

36 "I saw the logic": Steve Nelson, James R. Barrett, and Rob Ruck, *Steve Nelson: American Radical* (Pittsburgh, Pa., 1981), 69, 78.

37 "Comrades, keep your heads": Ibid., 82.

39 "militant alliance with": Harry Haywood and Milton Howard, *Lynching* (New York, 1932), 15.

39 "It had a cleansing": Harry Haywood, *Black Bolshevik: Autobiography of an Afro-American Communist* (Chicago, 1978), 357.

39 "I went to Spain": *City Collegian*, Nov. 6, 1980, carton 5, UCB.

39 "played the role": Harry Haywood, "The Scottsboro Decision," *Communist* 11 (Dec. 1932): 1069, 1071.

40 an exhaustive address: Haywood, *Black Bolshevik*, 426–34.

40 74 blacks: Mark Naison, *Communists in Harlem during the Depression* (Urbana, Ill., 1983), 68.

40 "The Struggle": Harry Haywood, "The Struggle for the Leninist Position on the Negro Question in the U.S.A.," *Communist* 12 (Sept. 1933): 888–901.

40 "I always felt": Vaughn Love interview, Apr. 7, 1978; see also James Yates, *Mississippi to Madrid* (Seattle, Wash., 1989).

41 "If the generation": John Gates, *The Story of an American Communist* (New York, 1958), 16; see also Milton Felsen, *The Anti-Warrior: A Memoir* (Iowa City, 1989).

41 the YCL grew steadily: Klehr, *Heyday*, 307.

42 "a new world": Gates, *Story of an American*, 17, 24–25, 26.

43 "there was always": Milton Wolff, interview with Maria Brooks, videotape [c. 1988], Ph.

43 "forced labor camps": Klehr, *Heyday*, 204.

43 "That was the first time": Wolff, interview with Maria Brooks, videotape, Ph.

44 "At least for": Milton Wolff, autobiographical notes, Ph.

45 "We never won": Archie Brown interview, Nov. 25, 1985.

46 "The nights were cold": *Volunteer for Liberty* 2 (Sept. 17, 1937): 13.

46 Robert Merriman: Marion Merriman and Warren Lerude, *Amer-*

ican Commander in Spain: Robert Hale Merriman and the Abraham Lincoln Brigade (Reno, Nev., 1986), 17–38.

47   "I became sort of ": Esther Silverstein Blanc interview, Nov. 1, 1989.

Chapter 4

Page 49   "Communism is twentieth-century": Harvey Klehr, *The Heyday of American Communism: The Depression Decade* (New York, 1984), 191.

49   "We began to feel": Maurice Isserman, *Which Side Were You On? The American Communist Party During the Second World War* (Middletown, Conn., 1982), 259, n. 13.

51   "Socialist, Communist—all": *DW*, June 2, 1934, 3.

51   "Holmesburg," he wrote: Ben Gardner to Alice, Feb. 25, 1938, UCB.

51   "Turn this sailing": *DW*, July 24, 1935, 2.

51   Bill Bailey: Bill Bailey interview, Jan. 9, 1990; see also Bill Bailey, *The Kid from Hoboken* (San Francisco, 1993).

52   "There were 1300": "Letters from Spain," *Connexions* (Santa Barbara, Calif.) 10 (Aug. 1987): 25.

52   "no enthusiasm": Bailey interview, Jan. 9, 1990; see also *The Good Fight*, documentary film, 1985.

53   "a pirate ship": *DW*, Sept. 7, 1935, 1.

54   "Hands Off Ethiopia" parade: Harry Haywood, *Black Bolshevik: Autobiography of an Afro-American Communist* (Chicago, 1978), 448–57.

55   "the contacts weren't": Vaughn Love interview, Apr. 7, 1978.

55   "in fact as well": Richard D. Mandell, *The Nazi Olympics* (New York, 1971), 71; see also Peter Carroll, "Irving Jenkins: Olympic Contender," *In These Times*, July 22, 1992, 4.

56   "husky, blond young": *DW*, July 3, 1936, 3. Also valuable is Bernard Danchik's scrapbook, Danchik file, BU.

57   "I didn't worry": Dorothy Tucker interview, June 26, 1991.

57   "The rumbling of cannon": *DW*, Aug. 20, 1936, 2.

57   "shooting out": Francis A. Henson, "An American in Spain," *Presbyterian Tribune*, Nov. 26, 1936, 8.

57   "Each time a nest": Danchik scrapbook, Danchik file, BU.

57   "The speed and externality": Muriel Rukeyser, "Barcelona, 1936," *Life and Letters Today*, Autumn 1936, 30–31.

58   "colorful procession": Danchik scrapbook, Danchik file, BU.

58   "the fighting dead": Rukeyser, "Barcelona, 1936," 33.

58   "You came to see": Muriel Rukeyser, "Barcelona on the Barricades," *New Masses* 20 (Sept. 1, 1936): 11.

59   "If they weren't": Danchik scrapbook, Danchik file, BU; see also Jenny Chakin Berman interview in *The Good Fight*.

59   "The Spanish people": *DW*, Aug. 5, 1936, 1–2.

59   American policy: see Douglas Little, *Malevolent Neutrality: The United States, Great Britain, and the Origins of the Spanish Civil War* (Ithaca, N.Y., 1985).

60   "irresponsible members of left-wing": Richard P. Traina, *American Diplomacy and the Spanish Civil War* (Bloomington, Ind., 1968), 61.

60   United Committee in Support: *DW*, July 29, 1936, 1.

61   "There is no civil": *DW*, June 18, 1937, 2.

61   "I am . . . a soldier": *DW*, Oct. 9, 1936, 1.

61   Leo Fleischman: *DW*, Dec. 29, 1936, 2.

61   Ethel Rosenberg sang: Robert and Michael Meeropol, *We Are Your Sons: The Legacy of Ethel and Julius Rosenberg* (Boston, 1975), 159–60.

61   "The legality of the [Spanish]": James Benét, "Some Friends of Spain in New York," *New Republic* 89 (Nov. 11, 1936): 44.

62   "aid one or the other": Little, *Malevolent Neutrality*, 262.

62   "thoroughly legal": Traina, *American Diplomacy*, 82, 165–68.

Chapter 5

Page 64   word of recruitment: Edward Bender interviews, June 5, 1989, Nov. 7, 1991.

65   "They seemed very": SACB, 703–16; fond 545, opis 6, file 948, Moscow.

65   A survey of 1,745: Fond 545, opis 3, file 455, Moscow. See also Robert Minor to Comrade Alfredo, Apr. 15, 1938, explaining that the Americans lacked military experience because there was no

compulsory service in the U.S. Minor, the highest American Communist leader in Spain, denied Marty's allegations: "It would be quite unfair to say that the XV Brigade was defeated, not by the fascists, but by the Americans within it." Fond 545, opis 6, file 948, Moscow.

66   "On this issue": Bender interviews, June 5, 1989, Nov. 7, 1991; see also Edwin Rolfe, unpublished notes, BU.

66   Bill Bailey: Bill Bailey interview, Jan. 9, 1990.

67   "This is it": SACB, 721.

68   "we were going there": SACB, 486.

68   American Medical Bureau: Edward K. Barsky and Elizabeth Waugh, "The Surgeon Goes to War," unpublished memoir, BU.

69   "This is a battle": *From a Hospital in Spain* (New York, 1937), 28–29.

69   "Somehow all at once": Barsky and Waugh, "Surgeon," 17.

69   "Someone from the nurses": *San Francisco Chronicle*, Feb. 10, 1977, 22.

69   "I felt I *had*": Lini DeVries, *Up from the Cellar* (Minneapolis, Minn., 1979), 174, 189.

69   "a slender chocolate": Langston Hughes, *I Wonder as I Wander: An Autobiographical Journey* (New York, 1956), 382.

70   "I always had to": Interview no. 17, June 1942, John Dollard file, BU.

70   "I explained to them": Barsky and Waugh, "Surgeon," 29.

71   "I thought it": Leland Stowe, "Evelyn the Truck Driver," *Harper's* 178 (Feb. 1939): 279–80.

71   "When the crisis": Saul Wellman interview, Oct. 21, 1990.

71   1,745 American volunteers: Fond 545, opis 3, file 455, Moscow. See also Leonard Levenson, "U.S. Communists in Spain: A Profile," *Political Affairs* 65 (Aug. 1986), table E.

72   Justus Kates: NA 852.2221/463.

72   Durward Clark: Box 2, no. 65, Sandor Voros MSS, AU.

72   "for united front": Bill Sennett to Gussie, June 29, 1937, UCB.

72   Hans Amlie: Robert Merriman diary, Ph.

73   "I, the Socialist": *DW*, Aug. 6, 1937.

73   "Spain faces its": Gil Green, "Spain at Gettysburg," *New Masses* 31 (Oct. 27, 1936): 8.

73   "Tall as Lincoln": Ernest Hemingway, "Milton Wolff," in Jo Davidson, *Spanish Portraits* (New York, n.d.).

73   "Any democratic": Allen Guttmann, *The Wound in the Heart: America and the Spanish Civil War* (New York, 1962), 41.

73   "The revolution that is": Burnett Bolloten, *The Spanish Revolution: The Left and the Struggle for Power During the Civil War* (Chapel Hill, N.C., 1979), 94.

74   "For the first time": Gene Wolman to family, June 22, 1937, carton 1, UCB.

74   "I would have": Wallace Burton to Millie Bennett, Aug. 12, 1937, Bennett MSS, HI.

75   "If we sit by": Hyman Katz to mother, Nov. 25, 1937, box 8A, VALB MSS, BU.

Chapter 6

Page 76   "When a Communist": André Malraux, *Man's Hope*, tr. Stuart Gilbert and Alastair Macdonald (New York, 1968), 318.

76   "It is good": André Malraux, "Help Spain!" *7rtfront* 3 (1937): 8.

77   A survey of prominent: *Writers Take Sides* (New York, 1938).

77   "with notions of sacrifice": Valentine Cunningham, ed., *Spanish Front: Writers on the Civil War* (New York, 1986), 256; see also John Miller, *Voices Against Tyranny: Writing of the Spanish Civil War* (New York, 1986); and Allen Guttmann, *The Wound in the Heart: America and the Spanish Civil War* (New York, 1962).

77   "see what the boys": Carlos Baker, *Ernest Hemingway: A Life Story* (New York, 1969), 383.

77   "a dress rehearsal": Carlos Baker, ed., *Ernest Hemingway: Selected Letters 1917–1961* (New York, 1981), 458.

77   "I was in Paris": Alvah Bessie, ed., *The Heart of Spain* (New York, 1952), i–ii.

78   "If fascism creeps": *Volunteer for Liberty* 1 (Sept. 13, 1937): 4.

78   "Spain is fighting": Malcolm Cowley, "To Madrid," *New Republic* 92 (Aug. 25, 1937): 64; see also ibid., 92 (Sept. 22, 1937): 181.

78   "Undoubtedly the famous": *Washington News*, Nov. 1937, microfilm, NYPL.

78   "It still": William White, ed., *By-Line: Ernest Hemingway* (New York, 1967), 266.

79   "A writer who will not": Ernest Hemingway, "Fascism is a Lie," *New Masses* 23 (June 22, 1937): 4.

79   "writers, artists, sculptors": *New Masses* 5 (Jan. 1930).

79   "to assist in the development": *DW*, May 4, 1932, 32.

79   Phil Bard: Walt Carmon, "Phil Bard: American Artist," *International Literature* 5 (Nov. 1934): 80–84.

80   "the revolt of youth": Mildred Rackley Simon interviews, Sept. 25, 1989, Apr. 6, 1991.

81   "slammed across the head": *Artfront* 2 (Jan. 1937); see also Gerald M. Monroe, "Artists on the Barricades: The Militant Artists Union Treats with the New Deal," *Archives of American Art Journal* 18 (1978): 20–23.

81   "We won": Walter Grant to Charlotte, Dec. 10, 1936, Prisoner of War MSS, BU.

82   "every attempt to": *Partisan Review* 1 (Feb.–Mar. 1934): 2.

82   "put into verse": Edwin Rolfe, "Poetry," *Partisan Review* 2 (Apr.–May 1935): 37, 42.

82   "a play, or a poem": Edwin Rolfe to Bernard Fishman, Dec. 4, 1936, Rolfe MSS, UI.

83   "If you were here": Edwin Rolfe to Mary Rolfe, Sept. 4, 1937, Rolfe MSS, UI.

83   *To My Contemporaries*: Edwin Rolfe, *To My Contemporaries*: (New York, 1936), 59, 64.

84   "We'll watch you": Alvah Bessie, Apr. 14, 1934, Bessie MSS, Ph.

84   "a gift": *New Masses*, Jan. 27, 1942, articles scrapbook, Bessie MSS, Ph.

85   "If you want": Alvah Bessie to David Bessie, May 10, 1983, Bessie MSS, Ph.

85   good short stories: see *Alvah Bessie's Short Fictions* (Novato, Calif., 1982).

86   "opportunity to continue": Alvah Bessie, *Dwell in the Wilderness* (New York, 1935), jacket copy.

86   "For the first": Speeches miscellaneous, 1948, Bessie MSS, Ph.

86   "inverted sentimentality": Book reviews scrapbook, Bessie MSS, Ph.

86   "When art departs": *Brooklyn Eagle*, Mar. 25, 1934, book reviews scrapbook, Bessie MSS, Ph.

87   "communism, fascism, and the need": Book reviews miscellaneous, Dec. 1935, Bessie MSS, Ph.

87   "liberals who have felt": *Brooklyn Eagle*, May 31, 1936, book reviews scrapbook, Bessie MSS, Ph.

87   "who have . . . seen": *Fight*, Oct. 1936, book reviews scrapbook, Bessie MSS, Ph.

87   "He is that rare": *Brooklyn Eagle*, Mar. 7, 1937, articles scrapbook, Bessie MSS, Ph.

88   "I came to know": Speeches miscellaneous, 1948, Bessie MSS, Ph.

Chapter 7

Page 91   "War," wrote Edwin Rolfe: Edwin Rolfe, "City of Anguish," in *First Love* (Los Angeles, 1951), 19.

92   "he didn't look": Box 9, folder 5, Millie Bennett MSS, HI; Robert Merriman diary, Ph.

93   "since he is": NA 852.221/Merriman. For a negative view of Merriman, see Cecil Eby, *Between the Bullet and the Lie* (New York, 1969), 32–33; but see also Marion Merriman and Warren Lerude, *American Commander in Spain: Robert Hale Merriman and the Abraham Lincoln Brigade* (Reno, Nev., 1986); and Louis Fisher, *Men & Politics: An Autobiography* (New York, 1941), 403.

94   numbered about one hundred: Box 2, no. 72, Sandor Voros MSS, AU.

94   "We received a royal": Fond 545, opis 3, file 468, Moscow.

94   Alfred Tanz: Alfred Tanz interview, Nov. 27, 1989.

94   anti-aircraft battery: Vince Lossowski, "Battery Record," Pete Smith MSS, BU.

96   "Most officers from": Anna Louise Strong papers, box 15, folder 9, Bennett MSS, HI; see also Arthur H. Landis, *The Abraham Lincoln Brigade* (New York, 1967), 28–30.

96   "Comrade, you are": Saul Wellman interview, Oct. 21, 1990.

96   "The main role": John Gates, "The International Brigades," box 69, Burnett Bolloten MSS, HI.

96   "the ones who": Vaughn Love interview, Apr. 7, 1978.

97   "naughty children": Confidential diary, Ph.

98   Walter Grant: Prisoner of War MSS, BU.

99   "Lookee, boss": Box 9, folder 5, Bennett MSS, HI; William Herrick interview, Aug. 23, 1990.

99   "cracked up": Merriman diary.

99   "none working": Box 2, no. 72, Voros MSS, AU.

99   "feeling punch-drunk": Edwin Rolfe, *The Lincoln Battalion* (New York, 1939), 50.

99   "We could have broken": Merriman diary; see also Merriman and Lerude, *American Commander*, 101, 104.

100   "Some kind of attack": Strong papers, box 15, folder 9, Bennett MSS, HI.

100   "We waited without": Merriman diary; see also Merriman and Lerude, *American Commander*, 107–8.

101   "nobody there": Sid Levine interview, Feb. 14, 1990.

101   "Our men advanced": Robert Merriman to Martin Hourihan, Mar. 1, 1937, box 2, no. 72, Voros MSS, AU.

101   "I don't know": Edwin Rolfe, unpublished notes, BU.

102   263 men: Box 2, no. 72, Voros MSS, AU.

102   "idiotic": Robert Rosenstone, *Crusade of the Left: The Lincoln Battalion in the Spanish Civil War* (New York, 1969), 48.

102   "The Americans had": *New York Times*, Apr. 23, 1937.

102   "from a military": Strong papers, box 15, folder 9, Bennett MSS, HI.

102   "a complete success": Rolfe, *Lincoln Battalion*, 57.

103   "to have it": Merriman diary; Merriman and Lerude, *American Commander*, 111.

103   "In Spain": Edward K. Barsky and Elizabeth Waugh, "The Surgeon Goes to War," unpublished memoir, BU, 22, 2.

103   "a very feeble": *From a Hospital in Spain* (New York, 1937), 12–13.

104   "It was an ordinary": Harry Wilkes to Evelyn Ahrend, Apr. 12, 1937, box 37, Spanish Refugee MSS, CU.

104   "I cut through": Lini DeVries, *Up from the Cellar* (Minneapolis, Minn., 1979), 207; Lini Fuhr to Ida, Mar 15, 1937, box 13, Spanish Refugee MSS, CU.

104   "None of us": Barsky and Waugh, "Surgeon," 8.

104   "There's nothing impersonal": *DW*, Apr. 17, 1937, 3.

105   "We are going": *From a Hospital in Spain*, 8.

105   "was appalled at": *The Volunteer* 7 (July 1985): 4–5.

105   "We hugged him": Rolfe, unpublished notes, BU.

105   Martin Hourihan: Fond 545, opis 3, file 453, Moscow.

106   Alex McDade: Fond 545, opis 3, file 473, Moscow.

Chapter 8

Page 107   "More clearly than": *Let Freedom Ring!* (Los Angeles [1937]).

107   "It was a highly": SACB, 832.

107   "The level of political": Edwin Rolfe to Mary Rolfe, July 2, 1937, Rolfe MSS, UI.

108   "The cause enveloped": Saul Wellman interview, Oct. 21, 1990.

108   "as a Communist": Fond 545, opis 6, file 844, Moscow; see also opis 6, file 852, and opis 3, file 448.

108   Hilliard Bernstein: Hilliard Bernstein to Pete Smith, June 26, 1980, Pete Smith MSS, BU.

109   "wobbly outlook": John Cookson, interview with Sandor Voros, Sept. 26, 1937, box 1, Voros MSS, AU; Harry Fisher interview, Mar. 17, 1990.

109   "They twice refused": Joe Dallet to mother, Mar. 19, 1937, Dallet file, BU.

109   "We felt terrible": Bill Wheeler interview, Nov. 15, 1989.

109   "order one drink": *Volunteer for Liberty* 1 (Aug. 13, 1938): 6.

109   "We all ought": *Let Freedom Ring!*

110   "nothing is more": Edwin Rolfe to Mary Rolfe, July 7, 1937, Rolfe MSS, UI.

110   "The fight for": Carton 1, UCB.

110   "I am more of a pacifist": Feb. 16, 1938, carton 1, UCB.

111   "the honor to be": Ben Gardner to Alice, July 5, 1937, UCB.

111   "They do it": Rolfe to Mary Rolfe, July 7, 1937, Rolfe MSS, UI.

111   "We shared common": SACB, 616, 727, 736, 740, 750, 770–71.

112   "In the battalion": Paul Wendorf to Sandor Voros, Dec. 15, 1937, box 3, no. 111, Voros MSS, AU.

112   "Here we were": SACB, 771–73.

114   "He was an accomplished": Confidential to author; "Trial of Wattis," box 3, no. 88, Voros MSS, AU; Marion Merriman, diary, Ph.

114   "You can say": SACB, 774.

115   "Go fuck yourself ": Martin Hourihan, interview with Sandor Voros, box 3, no. 84, Voros MSS, AU.

115   "Single Command": Robert Merriman diary, Ph.

115   "The [political] commander": *DW*, June 1937.

115   "When the battle": William Herrick, *The Last to Die* (New York, 1971), 100–101.

115   "When we were": Edwin Rolfe, "First Things First," Rolfe MSS, UI.

116   "Fear is normal": John Dollard, *Fear in Battle* (New Haven, Conn., 1943), 12, 8–9, 17–18, 20, 22, 54, 62.

117   "I had bad": Leland Stowe, "Evelyn the Truck Driver," *Harper's* 178 (Feb. 1939): 281, 286.

117   "I just wouldn't": Dollard file, BU.

118   "A soldier who": Dollard file, BU; Fond 545, opis 6, file 850, Moscow.

118   "Dear": Box 15, folder 4, Millie Bennett MSS, HI.

118   "It is not bravery": Ben Iceland, "The Big Retreat," Alvah Bessie and Albert Prago, eds., *Our Fight: Writings by Veterans of the Abraham Lincoln Brigade* (New York, 1987), 229.

118   "new man": Bill Bailey, interview with Maria Brooks, audiotape, Ph.

118   "The war has ripped": *New Masses*, Sept. 13, 1938, Rolfe MSS, UI.

119   "there's my self-respect": Barney Baley diary, UCB.

119   "I wanted . . . to": Alvah Bessie notebooks, Ph.

119   "To change the world": William Herrick, *Hermanos!* (New York, 1969), 100.

120   "but primarily . . . to": Sidney Kurtz to Wilson Morris, Nov. 19, 1937, Jan. 13, 1938, David M. White MSS, NYPL.

120   "Men ran and": Merriman diary.

120   "I lost my nerve": SACB, 1497.

120   James Harris: William Pike interview, May 8, 1990; Merriman diary.

121   "The men had": SACB 1498.

121   Dr. Pike could help: Pike interview, May 8, 1990; Paul Margolis, "Dr. Pike's Spanish War," unpublished major project, Bard College, 1976, Ph. See also John Tisa, *Recalling the Good Fight: An Autobiography of the Spanish Civil War* (South Hadley, Mass., 1985), 106–8.

122   "in great danger": *Foreign Relations of the United States: Diplomatic Papers, 1937* (Washington, D.C.), 1: 482–84.

123   "Here at the frontier": James Neugass, "Before Battle," in Alvah Bessie, ed., *The Heart of Spain* (New York, 1952), 177–79.

Chapter 9

Page 124   "It was so dark": Alvah Bessie, *Men in Battle* (New York, 1939), 21.

125   "Most of the guys": Milton Wolff interview, June 1942, John Dollard file, BU.

125   "Paciencia, paciencia": Edwin Rolfe, *The Lincoln Battalion* (New York, 1939), 80.

125   "I remember the screaming": Abe Osheroff, "The *City of Barcelona*," in Alvah Bessie and Albert Prago, eds., *Our Fight: Writings by Veterans of the Abraham Lincoln Brigade* (New York, 1987), 85.

125   "What I'll never": Rolfe, *Lincoln Battalion*, 84.

126   Tom Mooney: Box 3, no. 119, Sandor Voros MSS, AU.

126   MacKenzie-Papineau battalion: Robert Merriman diary, Ph.

126   "He sure knew": Wolff interview, June 1942, Dollard file, BU.

127   "I felt that": Steve Nelson, James R. Barrett, and Rob Ruck, *Steve Nelson: American Radical* (Pittsburgh, Pa., 1981), 187–88.

128   "a tremendous success": Edwin Rolfe, unpublished notes, BU.

128   "the lice were": Paul Burns to Pete Smith, Feb. 5, 1977, carton 1, UCB.

128   "prevent the enemies": Burnett Bolloten, *The Spanish Revolution: The Left and the Struggle for Power During the Civil War* (Chapel Hill, N.C., 1979), 160.

129   "A strange and wonderful": George Orwell, *Homage to Catalonia* (Boston, 1955), 127.

129   "Soldiers giving their": Jerry Warren to Bernie Danchik, May 22, 1937, Danchik file, BU.

129   "damn fools": *DW*, Aug. 6, 1937, 2.

129   "mythical Debs Column": *DW*, Oct. 17, 1938, 4.

129   "contemptible few pigmies": Hans Amlie, "An Open Letter to the Socialist Party," box 15, folder 1, Millie Bennett MSS, HI.

130   "Trotskyist treason": *DW*, Oct. 31, 1938.

130   "The American working": Ben Gardner to Alice, Feb. 9, 1938, UCB.

130   "a school for the training": *DW*, Aug. 10, 1937, 8.

130   "Our purpose throughout": Nelson et al., *Steve Nelson*, 187.

130   "this was a man": SACB, 787.

130   "If we have": *DW*, June 23, 1937, 3.

131   "You can't stick": Milton Wolff to Art Landis, n.d., Landis file, BU.

131   "I have been": *DW*, Nov. 10, 1937, 6.

131   "We're making a complete": Nelson et al., *Steve Nelson*, 207–8.

131   "He knew every": *DW*, Nov. 10, 1937, 6.

131   "a very good": SACB, 781.

132   "I took things": William Sennett oral history, UCB, 95; William Sennett interview, Sept. 5, 1990.

132   "He imposed discipline": William Sennett to Art Landis, May 31, 1965, carton 2, UCB.

133   "I felt ashamed": Harry Haywood, *Black Bolshevik: Autobiography of an Afro-American Communist* (Chicago, 1978), 472.

133   "Harry's downfall": Steve Nelson interview, Dec. 16, 1989.

133   "a package . . . in": Ernest Hemingway to Edwin Rolfe, Apr. 13, 1950; see Cary Nelson and Jefferson Hendricks, *Edwin Rolfe: A Bibliographical Essay and Guide* (Urbana, Ill., 1990), 92.

133   "KAYOING MYTH": *Volunteer for Liberty* 2 (Aug. 13, 1938): 6.

133   "I wouldn't be": Danny Duncan Collum, ed., *African Americans in the Spanish Civil War* (New York, 1992), 147.

133   "had come to": Langston Hughes, *I Wonder as I Wander: An Autobiographical Journey* (New York, 1956), 354.

133   "I would rather": *People's World*, Feb. 9, 1938, 5.

133   "what we were fighting": *People's World*, Jan. 13, 1941, 1, 4.

134   "I felt like a": SACB, 3211.

134   "Folks over here": Langston Hughes, "Postcard to Alabama," *Volunteer for Liberty* 2 (Apr. 9, 1938): 4.

134   "As we approached": David Smith interview, Mar. 17, 1990.

134   "coward and shit": Edwin Rolfe diary, Rolfe MSS, UI.

135   "When I suggested": Hughes, *I Wonder*, 355–56.

135   "the brave Negroes": *DW*, Oct. 12, 1937, 2.

135   "malicious rumors": Haywood, *Black Bolshevik*, 490, 493.

135   "Hero of the Jarama": *DW*, Apr. 17, 1937, 3. The current Law controversy burst into print with Paul Berman's interview of William Herrick in the *Village Voice*, July 22, 1986. In reconstructing Law's career, I have interviewed and corresponded with numerous Lincoln veterans, including Herrick and some of Herrick's sources.

136   "We came to wipe": *DW*, Apr. 17, 1937, 3.

136   "Good record as officer": Fond 545, opis 3, file 448, Moscow.

137   "The idea was that": Steve Nelson interviews, June 9, Dec. 17, 1990.

137   "not an honor": Fond 545, opis 3, file 451, Moscow.

137   "Restore the whites": SACB, 791–92.

137   "he did not": David Smith to author, May 1991.

138   "The commander of": Martin Hourihan, interview with Sandor Voros, Aug. 26, 1937, box 3, no. 4, Voros MSS, AU.

138   "incompetent commander": SACB, 1006.

138   "Law was cowardly": Confidential interview, 1990.

138   "He was the first": Harry Fisher, interview with Jerry Fischman, c. 1970, transcription, Ph; Harry Fisher interview, Mar. 17, 1990. See also Arthur H. Landis, *The Abraham Lincoln Brigade* (New York, 1967), 206–7.

Chapter 10

Page 140   "All of a sudden": Philip Detro, interview with Sandor Voros, Aug. 25, 1937, box 2, no. 71, Voros MSS, AU.

140   "We were tickled": Milton Wolff interview, June 1942, John Dollard file, BU.

141   "The boys were": *Columbus Citizen* (Ohio), Oct. 1937.

141   "Everybody suddenly became": Detro, interview with Sandor Voros, Aug. 25, 1937, box 2, no. 71, Voros MSS, AU.

141   "Don't be alarmed": Wolff interview, June 1942, Dollard file, BU.

141   "All night there": *The Book of the XV Brigade* (Madrid, 1938), 145–47.

142   "I grit my teeth": *DW*, Nov. 10, 1937, 6.

142   "Constant threat of sudden": Esther Silverstein, "Nursing in Modern Warfare," unpublished paper, Ph.

143   "We dug our faces": Arthur H. Landis, *The Abraham Lincoln Brigade* (New York, 1967), 220.

143   "The men and things": "William B. Titus Memorial," BU.

143   "A deep silence": Steve Nelson, "It's Time to Tell," unpublished paper, Ph.

144   "The men felt": Box 1, no. 71, Voros MSS, AU.

145   "There were murmurs": Steve Nelson, James R. Barrett, and Rob Ruck, *Steve Nelson: American Radical* (Pittsburgh, Pa., 1981), 224–25.

145   "All along the road": *Let Freedom Ring!* (Los Angeles [1937]).

145   "There he was": Wolff interview, June 1942, Dollard file, BU.

146   "Men became hysterical": William Pike interview, May 8, 1990.

146   "The fascists beat": *Letters from the Trenches* (New York, 1937), 25–26.

146   "there are a lot": Leland Stowe, "Evelyn the Truck Driver," *Harper's* 178 (Feb. 1939), 281.

146   "'At's a real": *Buffalo News*, Aug. 27, 1938.

146   "went off the deep": Fredericka Martin to Pete Smith, Dec. 29, 1981, Pete Smith MSS, BU.

147   "My ears keep": *New York World Telegram*, Nov. 3, 1937.

149   "a blue eyed southerner": NA 852.2221/495.

149   "mixed motives": *Chillicothe Gazette* (Ohio), Sept. 22, 1937; Milton Weiner interview, Jan. 30, 1990.

150   "a very vicious": David M. White to Hans Amlie, Dec. 31, 1938, Millie Bennett MSS, HI.

150   "a childish kick": *St. Louis Post-Dispatch*, Dec. 3, 1939.

150   "Naturally I went": Hamilton Tyler, "The Pilgrimage of Evan Cade," unpublished MS, Ph.

151   "a negative experience": Carton 2, UCB.

151   "not so much ashamed": Malcolm Cowley, "To Madrid," *New Republic* 92 (Oct. 6, 1937): 236.

151   "All this was very": Martha Gellhorn, "Visit to the Wounded," *Story* 11 (Oct. 1937): 59.

151   "There was never enough": Edwin Rolfe, "Elegia," in *First Love* (Los Angeles, 1951), 89

152   "and no visiting": Landis, *Lincoln Brigade*, 328.

152   "the good guys": Ernest Hemingway, *The Fifth Column* (New York, 1969), 139–40.

152   "Ernest is quite": Milton Wolff to Ann Lenore, 1937, Wolff MSS, UI. Herbert Matthews of the *New York Times* reached the same conclusion: "Ernest Hemingway is great-hearted and childish, and perhaps a little mad"; Herbert L. Matthews, *The Education of a Correspondent* (New York, 1946), 95.

153   "I just wanted": Hemingway, *Fifth Column*, 175.

Chapter 11

Page 155   "Haggard bad looking": Robert Merriman diary, Ph.

156   "We had to": Steve Nelson, James R. Barrett, and Rob Ruck, *Steve Nelson: American Radical* (Pittsburgh, Pa., 1981), 228.

156   "What am I going": Arthur H. Landis, *The Abraham Lincoln Brigade* (New York, 1967), 288.

157   "with orders I": Merriman diary.

157   "It doesn't yet": Millie Bennett to J. H. Abramson, Sept. 12, 1937, box 2, folder 6, Bennett MSS, HI.

157   "would not come": *Columbus Citizen* (Ohio), Oct. 1937.

158   "This war they": Joseph Starobin, *The Life and Death of an American Hero: The Story of Dave Doran* (New York, 1938), 33, 36.

159   "What other American": Nelson et al., *Steve Nelson*, 238–39.

159   "Since I have": *Hemingway Review* 7 (Spring 1988): 48.

160   remarkable meeting: interviews and correspondence with Abe Osheroff, George Watt, Irving Weissman, and Saul Wellman. See also Fond 545, opis 3, file 441, Moscow. Such party meetings were rare, but not unknown. In one case, party leader Robert Minor attacked Dr. Barsky for two days for his political and personal behavior in Spain.

160   "It was like": Nelson et al., *Steve Nelson*, 197.

160   "than to beat": Joe Dallet to mother, May 31, 1937, Dallet file, BU.

161   "anti-leadership": Abe Osheroff interview, July 20, 1990.

161   "He was trying": Steve Nelson interview, Apr. 29, 1990.

161   "a last confession": Merriman diary.

162   "It demonstrated that": Irving Weissman to author, Nov. 1, 1990.

162   "Earlier discussion": Abe Osheroff to author, Oct. 26, 1990.

162   Colonel Copic: Percy Ludwich interview, May 25, 1993.

162   "One of their men": Abe [Sasson], carton 2, UCB.

163   "It seems": Merriman diary.

163   "Both professed to be": NA 852.2221/604.

164   "He is a man": NA 852.2226/18.

164   "off on [the] wrong": Merriman diary; NA 852.2221/583; Ben Kassmap, "Second Day at Quinto," box 2, no. 71, Sandor Voros MSS, AU; Maury Colow interview, Mar. 15, 1991.

164   "Sad bunch": Merriman diary.

165   "This court is not": Fond 545, opis 2, file 199; opis 3, files 441, 451, Moscow.

165   "They're trying to": *Letters from the Trenches* (New York, 1937),

21. The issue of saluting was a recurring problem. See fond 545, opis 3, files 433, 451, Moscow.

165   "arbitrary and dictatorial": *Socialist Appeal*, Sept. 9, 1939, 2.

165   "always attacking": Harry Fisher interview, Mar. 17, 1990.

166   "my own father": Edwin Rolfe diary, Rolfe MSS, UI.

166   "go fuck himself": Landis, *Lincoln Brigade*, 390–91.

167   "Where I come": Fred Keller interview, Nov. 14, 1989.

167   "I froze up": Irving Goff, interview with Jim Carriger, audiotape, Ph.

168   "We weren't a raiding": *Rochester Evening News*, Feb. 15, 1939.

169   "Spain's Valley": Edwin Rolfe, *The Lincoln Battalion* (New York, 1939), 158.

169   "With a few": Landis, *Lincoln Brigade*, 360.

169   "When I first": *DW*, Mar. 30, 1938, 2.

169   "Take it standing": Agnes Detro to Millie Bennett, June 30, 1938, box 2, folder 31, Bennett MSS, HI.

170   "We stayed there": Rolfe, *Lincoln Battalion*, 180.

Chapter 12

Page 171   "There's machine gun": *Chicago Times*, Mar. 9, 1939.

172   "they would be able": Edwin Rolfe, *The Lincoln Battalion* (New York, 1939), 197.

172   "Whatever the cost": Ibid., 198.

173   "precious individualism": Alvah Bessie, *Men in Battle* (New York, 1939), 53, 74–75, 82–83, 113.

174   "That was a painful": Clement Markert, interview with John Gerassi, May 26, 1980, transcription, BU.

174   "through the dark": Rolfe, *Lincoln Battalion*, 212.

174   "We shall fight": *New Orleans Picayune*, Mar. 25, 1938.

174   "We looked back": Bessie, *Men in Battle*, 126.

175   "He is young": *New York Times*, Apr. 12, 1938.

175   "as conscientiously": Rolfe, *Lincoln Brigade*, 220.

175   "I am suffering": Carl Geiser, *Prisoners of the Good Fight* (Westport, Conn., 1986), 40–41; for statistics, see 259.

176   "Each man was": SACB, 3468.

176   "jittery": Stan Junas interview, audiotape, UCB; Edward Palega to David M. White, Aug. 3, 1939, box 7A, VALB MSS, BU; NA 852.2221/Sachs, David/27.

176   "Bullets, shells, bombs": Douglas Taylor to mother, n.d., Ph.

176   "For the first time": Edward Deyo Jacobs to father, Apr. 2, 1937, Ph.

177   "There's nothing more": Saul Wellman, interview with Blaine Taylor, "War's Earliest Round," *Military History*, Feb. 1989, 39.

177   "It was considered": Newsclips, carton 5, UCB.

177   "The circumstances around": Interview no. 7, John Dollard file, BU.

178   "It is hard": Frances Vanzant to Helen Veltfort, Feb. 26, 1938, Ph.

178   "We had the feeling": *DW*, June 29, 1938, 7.

178   "I began to realize": Ruth Davidow interview, in Petra Lataster-Czisch, *Eigentlich Rede Ich Nicht Gern Über Mich* (Leipzig, Ger., 1990), translation by Lenore Veltfort, Ph; Ruth Davidow interview, Oct. 25, 1989.

178   "It was a hellish": William Pike interview, May 4, 1990.

179   "I was trembling": Bill McCarthy, interview for *The Good Fight*, transcription, BU; Bill McCarthy to Milton Wolff, Aug. 16, 1985, UCB.

180   "extremely nervous": *New York Times*, Apr. 8, 1938.

180   "My experience in Spain": *Detroit Free Press*, June 26, 1938.

181   "The Chairman": House Committee on Un-American Activities, *Hearings Before a Special Committee on Un-American Activities*, 75th Cong., 3d. sess., Aug. 18, 1938, 741.

181   "an unmitigated lie": *New Masses*, Sept. 13, 1938; *DW*, Sept. 10, 1938.

181   "comradeship was something": Aug. 23, 1938, box 4, VALB MSS, BU.

181   "Sobel did very": Robert Rosenstone, *Crusade of the Left: The Lincoln Battalion in the Spanish Civil War* (New York, 1969), 303.

181   Paul White: Bill Bailey, interview with Jerry Fischman, May 20, 1970, audiotape, Ph; Bill Bailey interview, Jan. 9, 1990.

182   "After Belchite": Fond 545, opis 6, file 1012, Moscow.

183   "I couldn't bear": Confidential interview, 1990.

183   "wipe out": Rosenstone, *Crusade*, 309–10.

184   Harry Wilkes: Ken Graeber to Fredericka Martin, Oct. 6, 1970, Martin MSS, BU; Fredericka Martin to Pete Smith, 1982, Pete Smith MSS, BU; Adolph Ross interview, July 28, 1992.

184   three Finns: Ross interview, July 8, 1992.

184   "a purely American": NA 852.2221/661, /704, /706.

185   "a tall handsome": Sandor Voros memoir, Apr. 1939, box 2, no. 55, Voros MSS, AU, 41.

185   "my smart Jew": NA 852.2221/704.

186   "after being brutally": NA 852.2221/Wallach/29.

186   Fifty years later: Anthony DeMaio to Milton Wolff, July 1988, Ph.

186   "The general, the banker": Harry Melofsky to Julius Blickstein, Apr. 27, 1937, BU; Vaughn Love interview, Aug. 23, 1990.

186   "A communist for years": Harry Melofsky to Julius Blickstein, Apr. 1, 1937; Meloff memorial, BU.

186   "the gay, lovable": Box 3, no. 73, Voros MSS, AU.

187   "He groaned and moaned": Milton Wolff, "The Spanish Graduates," unpublished memoir, UI.

187   "Cousin Bernie disappeared": Harry Melofsky to Julius Blickstein, July 30, Aug. 29, 1937, BU.

187   May Day: Confidential interview.

187   "claimed total ignorance": Fond 545, opis 3, file 453, Moscow.

Chapter 13

Page 189   "You built this": Vincent Sheean, *Not Peace but a Sword* (New York, 1939), 65.

189   "But for the benefit": Alvah Bessie diary, Ph.

190   "demoralization great": Alvah Bessie notebooks, Ph, 25, 46–47, 50.

190   "Arise, and seek": Gerald Quiggle notebook, carton 2, UCB.

190   "Today we accept": *DW*, May 31, 1938, 7.

190   "veterans company": "Problems of the Veterans Company," box 1, Sandor Voros MSS, AU.

191   "I felt very": SACB, 794.

191   "It was politically": John Gates interview, Oct. 16, 1989.

191   "If you can't": Alvah Bessie, *Men in Battle* (New York, 1939), 192.

191   "I became intolerant": John Gates, "International Brigades," box 69, Burnett Bolloten MSS, HI.

191   Mickenberg waited: Harry Fisher interview, Mar. 17, 1990.

192   "reactionary press": Bessie, *Men in Battle*, 54, 194.

192   "The sound of an explosion": Edwin Rolfe to Leo Hurwitz, Mar. 17, 1938, Rolfe MSS, UI.

192   "But he had": Bessie, *Men in Battle*, 150.

192   "You can't kill": Barney Baley diary, UCB.

193   "If it is any": James Lardner to mother, May 3, 1938, BU.

193   "steel rods": George Watt interview, Nov. 9, 1990.

194   "a big imposing": Gates interview, Oct. 16, 1989.

194   "bitterly satirical": SACB, 1080, 862.

195   "Bad. Trotskyist": Fond 545, opis 6, file 948, Moscow.

196   "was responsible only": Confidential interviews.

196   "must have operated": Steve Nelson interview, Dec. 16, 1989.

196   "I had power": Confidential interviews.

197   "detached service": Confidential interviews.

198   "But they were human": Bessie, *Men in Battle*, 194.

198   "Before another day": Edwin Rolfe, *The Lincoln Battalion* (New York, 1939), 256–57.

198   "the remarkable thing": Milton Wolff to Don MacLeod, Sept. 12, 1980, carton 1, UCB.

199   "All day, hour after hour": Bessie, *Men in Battle*, 289.

200   "Their planes came": Rolfe, *Lincoln Battalion*, 288–89.

200   "the slightest sort": Edwin Rolfe to Mary Rolfe, Sept. 22, Oct. 3, 1937, Apr. 7, 1938, Rolfe MSS, UI.

201   "We didn't go": *Manchester Union* (N.H.), Aug. 14, 1937.

201   "Not only must": *DW*, Oct. 6, 1938, 1.

201   "We had hoped": Clement Markert, interview with John Gerassi, May 26, 1980, transcription, BU.

201   "felt the shame": Carton 3, UCB.

201   "We have learned": *Volunteer for Liberty* 2 (Nov. 7, 1938): 9.

202   "I felt that": Milton Wolff interview, Apr. 13, 1988.

202   "That feeling of loss": Abe Osheroff interview in *The Good Fight*, documentary film, 1985.

202   "mentally, psychologically": Archie Brown interviews, Jan. 31, 1986, July 30, 1990.

202   "Men dying in battle": Edwin Rolfe, *First Love* (Los Angeles, 1951), 66.

202   "I hear you sobbing": *Volunteer for Liberty* 1 (Aug. 9, 1937): 3.

202   "clarity and understanding": *Volunteer for Liberty* 2 (Aug. 6, 1938): 8.

202   "I was politicized": Ruth Davidow interview, Oct. 25, 1989.

203   "I had never realized": Walter Schuetrum, "A Letter from Spain," Oct. 6, 1937; Dec. 27, 1937, Ph.

203   "I hate fascism": *Milwaukee Journal*, Nov. 3, 1938.

203   "It was only": William G. Ryan, "I Fought in Spain," *Scribner's Commentator* 11 (Dec. 1941): 8.

203   "I had already": SACB, 1523.

203   "opportunist": William Herrick interview, Aug. 23, 1990.

204   "The great majority": Joe Gordon to William Herrick, Dec. 14, 1937, Ph; SACB, 558.

204   "That was the sense": *People's World*, Nov. 22, 1955.

204   "corner . . . that is": Edwin Rolfe diary, Rolfe MSS, UI; Rolfe, *First Love*, 29.

204   2,800 volunteers: Adolph Ross to author.

205   "After a time": Archie Brown to Hon Brown, Oct. 31, 1938, Ph.

205   "They gave up": Alvah Bessie, ed., *The Heart of Spain* (New York, 1952), 345–47.

Chapter 14

Page 210   "The church was": Ruth Davidow interview, Oct. 25, 1989.

210   "So much blood": Alvah Bessie, *The un-Americans* (New York, 1957), 136.

211   "more cops than": Milton Wolff interview, Apr. 13, 1988.

211   "You can be": James Benét, "Return from Spain," *New Republic* 96 (Nov. 2, 1938): 356.

211   "The war of bullets": Edwin Rolfe, *The Lincoln Battalion* (New York, 1939), 312.

212   "They were willing": *People's World*, Sept. 29, 1938, 3.

212   over 1,500 Americans: VALB, Proceedings of the Third Na-
       tional Convention, mimeograph, Ph.

213   "the place depressed": Barney Bailey diary, UCB.

213   Robert Raven: Box 7, VALB MSS, BU.

213   "who returned in": *DW*, Aug. 2, 1938, 5.

214   "The veterans are": VALB, Proceedings.

214   "Now I know": Fred Keller to Ernest Hemingway, May 31, 1939,
       Hemingway MSS, John F. Kennedy Library, Boston, Mass.

215   "sincerely believing that": Milton Wolff to War Department, Mar.
       30, 1939, UI.

215   "These men are": *DW*, Feb. 2, 1939, 5.

215   "Wish I could": Baley diary.

215   "Otherwise," he recalled: Barney Baley interview, Sept. 27, 1990.

215   "learned the hard way": Barney Baley, *Hand Grenades* (Los An-
       geles [1942]), 45.

216   "I didn't feel": Wolff interview, Apr. 13, 1988.

216   "We have maintained": VALB, Proceedings.

217   "Ray buggered off": Marion Merriman to Millie Bennett, July 6,
       1938, Bennett MSS, HI.

217   "American Communists": Robert Gladnick MSS, AU.

217   "My basic philosophy": David Smith interview, Feb. 9, 1990.

217   "didn't want": Clement Markert, interview with John Gerassi, May
       26, 1980, transcription, BU.

218   "I had no idea": Reuben Barr interview, Nov. 1, 1989.

218   "Guerrilla warfare still": "Report on International Volunteers in
       French and Spanish Prisons," Apr. 13, 1940, Releases, Radio
       Addresses, etc., 3, NYPL.

219   "I was entertained": Lini DeVries, *Up from the Cellar* (Minne-
       apolis, Minn., 1979), 235.

219   "the peace and anti-fascist": *DW*, Dec. 8, 1937, 2; Dec. 20, 1937,
       3.

220   "It is hard": *DW*, Dec. 24, 1937, 2; Jan. 11, 1938, 2; Jan. 18,
       1938, 2.

220   "a friendly democratic": VALB to Franklin Roosevelt, Feb. 13,
       1938, Releases, Radio Addresses, etc., 3, NYPL; *Washington
       Post*, Feb. 14, 1938; *DW*, Feb. 15, 1938, 4.

221   "The Spanish people": *DW*, Jan. 3, 1939, 2.

221   "carrying banners without": *People's World*, Mar. 27, 1939, 3.

221   "It is hard": *People's World*, Feb. 11, 1939, 5.

222   In the summer: Robert Taylor interview, 1990; Taylor miscellaneous papers, Ph.

222   "Veterans of the A.L.B.": *Volunteer for Liberty* 3 (Feb. 1941): 4.

223   "Most of the men": SACB, 3594.

223   "Our work here": Ben Richman to Winifred Bates, Sept. 5, 1940, carton 2, UCB.

Chapter 15

Page 225   "unfit for human habitation": Claude G. Bowers, *My Mission to Spain* (New York, 1954), 408.

225   "Everyone slept on": Herbert L. Matthews, *The Education of a Correspondent* (New York, 1946), 185–86.

225   "Spanish comrades are": Sid Kaufman, "The Flight," Alvah Bessie and Albert Prago, eds., *Our Fight: Writings by Veterans of the Abraham Lincoln Brigade* (New York, 1987), 295.

225   "will fight you": *Socialist Appeal*, Aug. 15, 1939, 1.

225   "undermining . . . confidence in": *Volunteer for Liberty* 1 (Oct. 1939): 3–4.

226   "slander and provocation": VALB, Proceedings of the Third National Convention, mimeograph, Ph.

226   "I was staggered": Saul Wellman interview, Oct. 21, 1990.

226   "The USSR is": James Benét, "Why Doesn't Russia Go To War?" *New Republic* 100 (Oct. 11, 1939): 272.

226   "the pact was": Clement Markert, interview with John Gerassi, May 26, 1980, transcription, BU.

226   "I justified it": Milton Wolff interview, Apr. 13, 1988.

227   "Hitler's plans against": John Gates, "The Nature of this War," *Young Communist Review* 4 (Oct. 1939): 4.

227   "This is not": *Volunteer for Liberty* 1 (Oct. 1939): 1–2.

227   "We learned our": Joseph North, "No Pasaran: 1940," *New Masses* 24 (Jan. 9, 1940): 9–10.

227   "If Milton Herndon": *Volunteer for Liberty* 2 (May 1940): 4.

228   "I am no": *Socialist Appeal*, Sept. 9, 1939, 4.

228   "Break with the party": *Socialist Appeal*, Oct. 6, 1939, 2.

229   "Hero in Spain": *Jewish Daily Forward*, Dec. 20, 2939, 7; William Herrick interview, Aug. 23, 1990; SACB, 543–45.

230   "The majority of us": *New Republic* 102 (Feb. 19, 1940): 249.

230   "Soldados": *Volunteer for Liberty* 1 (Dec. 1939): 1.

230   Robert Taylor: [Ernest Goodman], *FBI Detroit* [Detroit, 1940]; Ernest Goodman, "The Spanish Loyalist Indictments: Skirmish in Detroit," *Guild Practitioner* 36 (Winter 1979): 1–13; Robert Taylor, miscellaneous documents, Ph.

231   "It doesn't matter": *DW*, Feb. 8, 1940.

232   "I believed Spain": Richard Dunlop, *Donovan: America's Master Spy* (Chicago, 1982), 193; see also Corey Ford, *Donovan of OSS* (Boston, 1970), 83; Milton Wolff interviews, Apr. 13, Sept. 13, 1988, Feb. 22, 1989.

232   "tried to tell": Milton Wolff to Ann, Apr. 21, 1940, UI.

233   "God knows": House Committee on Un-American Activities, *Investigation of Un-American Propaganda Activities in the United States*, 76th Cong., 3d sess. (1940), vol. 13, 6707.

233   "We didn't know": Milton Wolff interview, Feb. 4, 1990.

234   "It is no": "Report on International Volunteers," Apr. 13, 1940, Releases, Radio Addresses, etc., 3, NYPL.

234   "a socialist island": John Gates, "Soviet-German Military Pact?" *Young Communist Review* 5 (Feb. 1, 1940): 13; John Gates interview, Oct. 16, 1989.

234   "It was you": John Gates, "The Stab in the Back," *Young Communist Review* 5 (July 8, 1940).

Chapter 16

Page 235   "Nine men commanded": Ernest Hemingway, "Milton Wolff," in Jo Davidson, *Spanish Portraits* (New York, n.d.).

236   "The fascists may": Ernest Hemingway, "On the American Dead in Spain," *New Masses*, Feb. 1938, reprinted in Alvah Bessie and Albert Prago, eds., *Our Fight: Writings by Veterans of the Abraham Lincoln Brigade* (New York, 1987), 23–24.

236   "There is only": Carlos Baker, ed., *Ernest Hemingway: Selected Letters 1917–1961* (New York, 1981), 476.

236   "a true, honest": Ernest Hemingway, "Preface," in Gustav Regler, *The Great Crusade* (New York, 1940), x; Baker, ed., *Ernest Hemingway: Selected Letters*, 499, 480–81.

237   "He fought now": Ernest Hemingway, *For Whom the Bell Tolls* (New York, 1940), 163.

237   "It was going": Fred Keller interview, Mar. 4, 1990.

237   "What emerges from": *Volunteer for Liberty* 2 (Dec. 1940): 2.

238   "less concerned with": *New Masses*, Nov. 15, 1940, 27–28.

238   "At the time": Ernest Hemingway to Milton Wolff, ca. Dec. 1940; reprinted in *American Dialogue* 1 (Oct.–Nov. 1964): 11.

238   "Except that it is": Vincent Sheean to Milton Wolff, Oct. 1940, UI.

238   "We who fought": Milton Wolff to Mr. Littauer, Nov. 27, 1940, carton 3, UCB.

239   "to undo": Irving Goff to veterans, Nov. 28, 1940, carton 3, UCB.

239   "existed in a": *New York World Telegram*, Dec. 2, 1940.

239   "Anti-Fascist means": *New York World Telegram*, Dec. 14, 1940.

239   "a monument in": *People's World*, Oct. 30, 1940, 5; Feb. 12, 1941, 5.

239   "Hemingway did not": Irving Goff, "Masterpiece or Potboiler: Symposium on 'For Whom the Bell Tolls,'" Ph. For a different view, see William Braasch Watson, "Investigating Hemingway," *North Dakota Quarterly* 59 (Winter 1991): 38–68.

241   "Something moved": *Volunteer for Liberty* 3 (Mar 1941): 4.

241   "bitterness or despair": Edwin Rolfe, "Preface," 1944, Rolfe MSS, UI.

241   that fascism is": *New Masses*, Aug. 20, 1940.

241   "You will not": Theater scrapbook, Jan. 14, 1941, Bessie MSS, Ph.

241   "What she has": Ibid., Apr. 15, 1941.

241   "The Russians make": Film scrapbook, Mar. 18, 1941, Bessie MSS, Ph.

242   "If you ask": *New Masses* 40 (July 1, 1941): 2.

242   Morris Cohen: Morris Cohen interviews, May 26, June 2, 1993. Louise Bernikow, *Abel* (New York, 1970), 19–20, 198–99, 269–72; Ronald Radosh and Eric Breindel, "Bombshell," *New Republic* 204 (June 10, 1991), 10–12; Edward Lending, "Morris Picket . . . Nee Morris Cohen," unpublished paper, Ph; *New Times* (Moscow) 16 (1991): 37–40; *Washington Post*, Oct. 4, 1992, 1.

244   "The veterans have": Scrapbook, UI.

244   "I was castigated": Jack Shafran interview, May 8, 1990.

244   "inner circles": John Gates, *Story of an American* (New York, 1958), 80.

244   Milton Wolff: Milton Wolff interviews, Apr. 13, Sept. 13, 1988, Mar. 29, 1989. This evidence has been corroborated by interviews with other volunteers, including Irving Goff. For a garbled version of Wolff's activities, see Harvey Klehr and John Haynes, "The Comintern's Open Secrets," *American Spectator*, Dec. 1992,

245   "Life on the shelf": Steve Nelson, James R. Barrett, and Rob Ruck, *Steve Nelson: American Radical* (Pittsburgh, Pa., 1981), 251; Irving Goff, interview with Jim Carriger, audiotape, Ph.

245   "It was the blind": Saul Wellman interview, Oct. 21, 1990.

246   "They trusted me": Wolff interview, Sept. 13, 1988.

246   "If ever there": Miscellaneous notes, UI; see also Carl Geiser, *Prisoners of the Good Fight* (Middletown, Conn., 1986), 168.

247   "This affair is": *Volunteer for Liberty* 3 (May 1941): 3.

247   "No one [else] can": Typescript, UI.

248   "If need be": *DW*, July 6, 1941.

248   "There was one": Archie Brown interview, Jan. 31, 1986.

248   "We all felt": Maurice Isserman, *Which Side Were You On?* (Middletown, Conn., 1982), 104.

248   "This is our": *Western Volunteer*, July 1941, 2.

248   "would never, never": Albert Prago, *We Fought Hitler* (New York, 1941), 3.

248   "where the social need": Milton Wolff, *Western Front Now!* (New York, 1941), 7, 14.

249   "We who fought": Box 10, VALB MSS, BU.

249   "The very next": Vaughn Love interview, Apr. 7, 1978.

249   "We call for": *Volunteer for Liberty* 3 (Dec. 1941): 2–4.

Chapter 17

Page 250   John Gates: John Gates, *Story of an American* (New York, 1958), 82–83; see also George Charney, *A Long Journey* (Chicago, 1968), 126.

250   "We . . . are proud": *Volunteer for Liberty* 4 (Jan. 1942): 2.

250   "I am not": Milton Wolff to Ann, June 27, 1942, UI.

251   "the dive bomber": John Dollard, *Fear in Battle* (New Haven, Conn., 1943), 7.

252   "'Home' is the slogan": Milton Wolff to Ann, July 19, 1944, UI.

252   "didn't cry": Milton Wolff to Ann, Sept. 25, 1944, UI.

252   425 veterans: Adolph Ross to author, Oct. 1990.

253   "Some cursed bitterly": *DW*, Feb. 24, 1945.

253   "I've always hated": *Yank*, Mar. 2, 1945.

253   "The hardest battle": *Volunteer for Liberty* 4 (Feb. 1944): 9.

254   "organizer for the Young": *New York World Telegram*, Jan. 7, 1943.

254   "always wanted to": Jerry Weinberg, May 8, 1942, July 9, 1943, World War II letters, BU.

254   George Watt: George Watt, *The Comet Connection* (Lexington, Ky., 1990).

254   Milton Wolff: Milton Wolff interview, June 9, 1989.

255   Irving Goff and Bill Aalto: Irving Goff, interviews with Jim Carriger, audiotape, Ph.

256   "Bill, I'm sorry": John Gerassi, *Premature Antifascists: North American Volunteers in the Spanish Civil War* (New York, 1986), 211–12; see also Milton Felsen, *The Anti-Warrior: A Memoir* (Iowa City, Iowa, 1989), 87–89.

256   The tragedy of Bill Aalto: James Schuyler interview, Oct. 19, 1989; James Foss, "William Aalto: A Hero of the Left," unpublished paper, BU.

257   "The pressure was": Sophie Pitney interview, Dec. 2, 1989.

257   "a higher up": William Aalto to Irving Goff, Mar. 8, 1942, World War II letters, BU.

258   "the bill of goods": Irving Fajans to Jack Bjoze, Apr. 25, 1943, World War II letters, BU.

258   "I hadn't looked": Jack Lucid to Archie Brown, Oct. 14, 1942, Ph.

258   "Don't you know": Robert Colodny, "An American Dark Age: Echoes and Memories," 1988, unpublished paper, Ph.

258   "I've been given": Alvah Bessie, "Joe Hecht, American," *New Masses*, May 29, 1945.

259   "Oh, that's a": Milton Wolff to Ann, July 29, 1942, UI.

259   "a battalion of": Milton Wolff to Ann, Aug. 15, Dec. 20, 1942, Jan. 8, 1943, UI.

260   "I sat down": *People's World*, Apr. 29–30, 1942.

261   "We know that goose": *Volunteer for Liberty* 4 (Jan. 1942): 12.

261   "And we don't need": *Weekly Review*, Aug. 4, 1942.

261   "We didn't initiate": Ruth Davidow interview, Oct. 25, 1989.

262   "Not only were we": SACB, 3211.

262   "quite a let down": Joe Taylor, May 17, 1943, World War II letters, BU.

262   "it was probably": Walter Garland, Aug. 8, 1942, World War II letters, BU.

262   "the white officers": Vaughn Love interview, Apr. 7, 1978.

262   "potentially subversive personnel": Maurice Isserman, *Which Side Were You On?* (Middletown, Conn., 1982), 181. See also Kai Bird, *The Chairman: John J. McCloy—The Making of the American Establishment* (New York, 1992), 185–86.

263   "Our service on": Jack Bjoze to Military Affairs Committee, Apr. 1943, Alleged Discrimination file, BU.

263   "Demonstrated merit alone": Robert Patterson to Rep. John M. Coffee, Apr. 28, 1943, Alleged Discrimination file, BU.

263   "The German and Italian": *Washington Post*, Apr. 14, 1943.

264   "whole past record": George Cullinan, Jan. 5, 1944, World War II letters, BU.

Chapter 18

Page 265   "For what the boys": Bill Root [Alvah Bessie], *Weekly Review*, Dec. 22, 1942.

266   "It is a dream": *New Masses*, Nov. 17, 1942.

266   "smuggle" in the character: Alvah Bessie to Edwin Rolfe, Mar. 23, 1943, Rolfe MSS, UI.

266   "Japs aren't human": Bernard F. Dick, *Radical Innocence: A Critical Study of the Hollywood Ten* (Lexington, Ky., 1989), 109; see also Alvah Bessie, *Inquisition in Eden* (New York, 1965), 80–81.

266   "They would love": Alvah Bessie to Edwin Rolfe, Apr. 13, 1943, Rolfe MSS, UI.

267   "*nothing* of the reason": Ernest Hemingway to Donald Friede, Mar. 16, 1942, Ph.

267   "Who prevented you": Alvah Bessie, "Blockade," *The Screenwriter*, June 1943, 23, articles scrapbook, Bessie MSS, Ph.

267   "This is a war": Alvah Bessie to Edwin Rolfe, July 22, 1943, Rolfe MSS, UI.

267   "Hemingway is not capable": Milton Wolff to Edwin Rolfe, June 2 [1942?], Rolfe MSS, UI.

267   "I'm one of the guys": Bessie, *Inquisition*, 103–4.

268   "The boys are": *New Masses*, Mar. 7, 1944.

268   ordered the surveillance: Richard Gid Powers, *Secrecy and Power: The Life of J. Edgar Hoover* (New York, 1987), chaps. 7–8; Alvah Bessie, FBI files, Ph.

269   "In America": *New Masses*, Jan. 6, 1942.

270   "We didn't care": Irving Goff, interviews with Jim Carriger, audiotape, Ph. See also Anthony Cave Brown, *The Last Hero: Wild Bill Donovan* (New York, 1982), 706–20.

272   "have shown by their": Maurice Isserman, *Which Side Were You On?* (Middletown, Conn., 1982), 239, 290; Brown, *Last Hero*, 711.

273   "But why are": Edwin Rolfe, *First Love* (Los Angeles, 1951), 91.

273   "is a stupid": Saul Birnbaum, Aug. 21, 1942, World War II letters, BU.

273   "After Espana": Larry Cane, June 11, 1944, World War II letters, BU.

274 "I hear the same": Gerry Cook, July 9, Dec. 13, 1944, World War II letters, BU.

274 "The swastika will": Jack Lucid to Archie Brown, Christmas 1943, Ph.

274 "They are patriots": *DW*, Feb. 7, 1943.

274 "of those men": Press release, Mar. 29, 1943, carton 4, UCB.

274 "to the temporary": Oct. 26, 1943, Releases, Radio Addresses, etc., 1, NYPL.

274 "Franco is a": Apr. 17, 1944, Releases, Radio Addresses, etc., 2, NYPL.

274 "Is there any": *Volunteer for Liberty* 6 (May 1944): 2.

275 "Now if that": Milton Wolff to Ann, Nov. 3, 1944, UI.

275 "The people of Spain": David M. White, *Franco Spain—America's Enemy* (New York [1945]), 22.

277 "I felt positively": Don Thayer to Edwin Rolfe, Apr. 17, 1945, Rolfe MSS, UI.

277 "The winning of ": Jack Lucid, Apr. 15, Apr. 26, 1945, Ph.

278 "proven opportunists and": Don Thayer to Edwin Rolfe, Sept. 8, 1945, Rolfe MSS, UI.

278 "roughly one thousand": *Volunteer for Liberty* 8 (Apr. 1946): 8.

Chapter 19

Page 279 "of course, we": Report on Interview with William C. Dunham, State Department, with Milton Wolff, Mar. 10, 1949, State Department folder, carton 4, UCB.

282 "We find ourselves": Milton Wolff speech, 1945, Releases, Radio Addresses, etc., 1, NYPL.

282 "acts of solidarity": Moe Fishman interview, June 14, 1989.

284 "Two wars against": *Volunteer for Liberty* 9 (Mar. 1947): 1.

284 "No one accused": Irving Goff, interview with Jim Carriger, audiotapes, Ph.

284 rigidity of the Communist party: See Joseph R. Starobin, *American Communism in Crisis, 1943–1957* (Cambridge, Mass., 1972).

284 Harry Haywood: Harry Haywood, *Negro Liberation* (New York, 1948), 162.

285   "So isolated did": John Gates, *Story of an American* (New York, 1958), 108.

285   Joint Anti-Fascist Refugee Committee: JARC folder, carton 4, UCB; see also Howard Fast, *Being Red* (Boston, 1990), 143, 173.

286   "Am I an anti-Communist?": *Volunteer for Liberty* 10 (1948): 2.

286   "pro-Franco, pro-Fascist": *Volunteer for Liberty* 6 (Apr. 1946): 6.

286   "has the broad": Martin F. Shapiro, "Medical Aid to the Spanish Republic During the Civil War," *Annals of Internal Medicine* 97 (July 1982): 122.

287   "Stalin's Pet Commissar": League for Justice, *Stalin's Pet Commissar Rules Ohio U E Members* (Cleveland, Ohio, 1947). According to commissariat records, Keller was not a member of the Communist party when he fought in Spain; see fond 545, opis 6, file 846, Moscow.

287   Robert Colodny: Robert Colodny to Nan Green, Mar. 14, 1947, box 24, MML.

287   "We were not only": Peter Carroll, "War Stories," *Image Magazine, San Francisco Examiner*, Apr. 13, 1986, 31.

287   "all attempts to place": *Volunteer for Liberty* 9 (Dec. 1947): 1.

288   "The only reason": *Volunteer for Liberty* 10 (1948): 3.

288   "to fight on behalf": Box 6, box 7A, VALB MSS, BU.

288   "Bad news awaited": Milton Wolff to Ann, Jan. 24, 1949, UI.

288   "It is indeed": Milton Wolff to Ann, Feb. 21, 1950, UI.

288   "When I'm faced": Milton Wolff to Ann, May 9, May 11, 1950, UI.

289   "Strange characters call": Milton Wolff to Edwin Rolfe, Apr. 8, 1952, Rolfe MSS, UI.

289   "official and unofficial": *Volunteer for Liberty* 10 (1948): 1.

289   "something of a military": Milton Wolff, FBI file, Ph.

290   Lini Fuhr: Lini DeVries, *Up from the Cellar* (Minneapolis, Minn., 1979).

290   "Part of that fear": Milton Wolff to Alvah Bessie, Apr. 10, 1981, Bessie MSS, Ph.

290   "The trend cannot": Wolff to Ann, May 11, 1950, UI.

291   "If this attack": Alvah Bessie, ed., *The Heart of Spain* (New York, 1952), 478.

291   "That shook a lot": Vaughn Love interview, Apr. 7, 1978.

291   "Whenever the party": Peter L. Steinberg, *The Great 'Red Menace': United States Prosecution of American Communists, 1947–1952* (Westport, Conn., 1984), 77.

291   George Watt: George Watt interview, Nov. 9, 1990.

292   Saul Wellman: Saul Wellman interview, Oct. 21, 1990.

292   "There's no great": Ann Fagan Ginger, *The Relevant Lawyers* (New York, 1972), 137–38; Archie Brown interview, July 3, 1989.

293   "The progressive movement": Alvah Bessie to Milton Wolff, Jan. 12, 1949, UI.

294   "I know in my": *Volunteer for Liberty* 11 (Aug. 1950): 2.

294   "as a front": Ibid., 1.

Chapter 20

Page 295   "Whatever Steve Nelson's": Steve Nelson, James R. Barrett, and Rob Ruck, *Steve Nelson: American Radical* (Pittsburgh, Pa., 1981), 319.

296   "The American warmongers": March 27, 1951, box 4, VALB MSS, BU.

296   "The attempt of": Allan McNeil to Moe Fishman, June 5, 1953, box 6, VALB MSS, BU.

297   "We start from": Moe Fishman to Alvah Bessie, Feb. 19, 1952, box 18, VALB MSS, BU.

297   "This local Gestapo": *Volunteer for Liberty* 13 (Apr. 7, 1952).

297   "You may have": U.S. Senate Judiciary Committee, *Hearings on Interlocking Subversion in Government Departments*, 83d Cong., 1st sess., June 11, 1953, 703, 705.

298   "Have you written": Robert Colodny, "An American Dark Age," unpublished paper, Ph.

298   "That we should": May 20, 1953, box 4, VALB MSS, BU.

299   "Now the wheel": Spanish Refugee Aid folder, carton 4, UCB.

299   "We didn't go": Jack Bjoze interview, May 8, 1990.

300   "We took positions": Milton Wolff interview, Mar. 29, 1989.

301   "orders went from": SACB, 43.

301   "under Party direction": SACB, 143.

301   "we understood and all": SACB, 487.

302   "I was informed": William Herrick statement, Feb. 1988, Ph.

302   "revolutionary Marxist": SACB, 689.

302   "I felt guilty": William Herrick interview, Aug. 23, 1990.

304   "any unfavorable references": SACB, 834.

304   "We do a lot": SACB, 1110.

304   "helped to stab": SACB, 1550.

305   "so fantastic in nature": SACB, 2194.

305   "experienced a complete": SACB, 2580.

305   "street fighting and": SACB, 1719.

306   "perfectly consistent with": SACB, 2876.

306   "is determined to": SACB, 2931, 2939, 2942, 2964.

307   "I, being a Negro": SACB, 3203, 3211, 3281.

308   "common knowledge": SACB, 3598.

308   "Having failed to": Milton Wolff to Alvah Bessie, Oct. 1, 1954,
       Bessie MSS, State Historical Society, Madison, Wis.

308   "Was Maken or": SACB, 4642.

309   "The Eisenhower administration": *Dispatcher* (San Francisco),
       Mar. 4, 1955, 3.

309   "precluded full cross-examination": SACB, 3–4, 6, 244.

310   "This fascist leopard": *Volunteer for Liberty* 16 (Oct. 1955): 3.

311   "It is about 6": [Eluard] Luchelle McDaniels to Wallace and Connie
       Putnam, Mar. 13, 1954, archives from the estate of Wallace Put-
       nam, Ph.

311   "Shall we continue": Nov. 1956, Dec. 2, 1956, Feb. 9, 1957,
       box 4, VALB MSS, BU.

Chapter 21

Page 313   Milton Robertson: *DW*, May 20, 1946, 11.

313   "In L.A.," he wrote: Edwin Rolfe and Lester Fuller, *The Glass
       Room* (New York, 1946), 79.

314   "Workers for Spain": Alvah Bessie to Milton Wolff, Sept. 21, 1946,
       UI.

314   "What Shall We": Albert Maltz, "What Shall We Ask of Writ-
       ers?" *New Masses*, Feb. 12, 1946.

314   "No," shouted: *New Masses*, Mar. 12, 1946.

314   "It is not": Edwin Rolfe, [1947?], Rolfe MSS, UI.

314   "that good writing": Edwin Rolfe, speech to *Mainstream* Conference, Rolfe MSS, UI.

315   "be 'as correct' ": Alvah Bessie to Milton Wolff, Nov. 8, 1953, Bessie MSS, State Historical Society, Madison, Wis.

315   "because you know": Speeches, Bessie MSS, Ph.

316   "who were once": Alvah Bessie to Irving Fajans, Mar. 13, 1949, box 18, VALB MSS, BU.

316   "half-dead dog": Edwin Rolfe to Irving Fajans, Mar. 14, 1949, box 18, VALB MSS, BU.

316   "excellence of material": Edwin Rolfe to Irving Fajans, Nov. 2, 1949, box 4, VALB MSS, BU.

316   "You guys sort": Ernest Hemingway to Milton Wolff, May 7, 1950; reprinted in *American Dialogue* 1 (Oct.–Nov. 1964): 13.

316   "Maybe even he": Alvah Bessie to Irving Fajans, Feb. 3, 1950, box 18, VALB MSS, BU.

317   "would be 'scabbing' ": Irving Fajans to Alvah Bessie, Feb. 10, 1950, box 18, VALB MSS, BU.

317   "that we owe": Milton Wolff to French comrades. Mar. 6, 1950, box 18, VALB MSS, BU.

317   "a grave political": Alvah Bessie to Milton Wolff, Mar. 30, 1950, box 18, VALB MSS, BU.

318   "The novel in": Alvah Bessie, ed., *The Heart of Spain* (New York, 1952), vi–vii.

318   "Hemingway gave an eager": Milton Wolff to Lillian Hellman, Aug. 1, 1952, box 18, VALB MSS, BU.

318   "I don't know": Milton Wolff to Herbert Matthews, Aug. 8, 1975, UCB.

319   "He was a 'tourist' ": Milton Wolff to Alvah Bessie, Aug. 15, 1981, Bessie MSS, Ph.

319   "was free to choose": Milton Wolff to Joseph Brandt, Feb. 15, 1980, UCB.

319   "the essence of commitment": Milton Wolff to Herbert Matthews, Aug. 27, 1975, UCB.

319 Conlon Nancarrow; Kyle Gann, "A Biographical Sketch," un-published manuscript, Ph; *Newsweek*, Sept. 13, 1982, 96; *Washington Post*, Jan. 25, 1984, B3.

320 "a rebellion against": Box 1, David M. White MSS, NYPL.

321 "It's all there": *New York Times*, June 28, 1981, sec. 4, 17–18.

321 "I had a blank": Lan Adomian, *La Voluntad De Crear*, (Mexico City, 1981), 2:98–99, 139.

323 "I got disillusioned": John Gerassi, *Premature Antifascists: North American Volunteers in the Spanish Civil War* (New York, 1986), 168; Robert Whealey, notes on James Norman Schmidt, audio-tape, Ph.

323 "Whatever bravery he had": James Norman, *The Fell of Dark* (Philadelphia, 1960), 100, 187.

324 "We taught paranoia": *Newsweek*, Feb. 20, 1950, 70.

324 "I only realized": Jack Pearl, "Inside Saga," *Saga* 18 (June 1959): 4.

324 "huddled over a glass": *Volunteer for Liberty* 12 (May 1990): 18.

325 "Baptized an Episcopalian": *Newsweek*, Feb. 20, 1950, 70; see also Lyle W. Dorsett, *And God Came In* (New York, 1983), 49–78.

325 "Writing is one": William Gresham to Sid Kaufman, June 9, 1955, Ph.

Chapter 22

Page 327 "witch-hunt atmosphere": Edwin Rolfe to Bernard Fishman, Jan. 16, 1948, May 2, 1951, Rolfe MSS, UI.

328 "Wandering, bitter": Edwin Rolfe, "Elegia," in *First Love* (Los Angeles, 1951), 87–88.

328 "What will you do": Edwin Rolfe, *Permit Me Refuge* (Los Angeles, 1955), 20–22.

328 "in living-room": Edwin Rolfe, "Little Ballad for Americans—1954," Rolfe MSS, UI.

329 "Idiot Joe Prays": Rolfe, *Permit me Refuge*, 23.

329 "Personal depression inevitable": Edwin Rolfe to Ruth Fishman, Feb. 18, 1954, Rolfe MSS, UI.

329   "Permit me refuge": Rolfe, *Permit Me Refuge*, 46.

329   "writes out of compulsion": Edwin Rolfe, speech to *Mainstream* conference, Rolfe MSS, UI.

329   Ramon Durem: Ray Durem, *Take No Prisoners* (London, Paul Breman, 1971); Rebecca Durem interview, Jan. 27, 1991.

330   "I hoped that": Ray Durem, "Posthumous Preface," in *Take No Prisoners*, 3.

331   "Some of my best": Durem, *Take No Prisoners*, 11.

331   "To the Pale": Ibid., 18.

332   "there were no": Ibid., 20.

332   "the non-existent man": *Contact* (Sausalito, Calif.) 2 (Oct. 1960): 90.

333   He had "been": Ibid.

333   "a rather special": *People's World*, Nov. 3, 1960.

333   "The Beatnik": *People's World*, July 5, 1958.

334   "I always wanted": William Herrick interview, Aug. 23, 1990.

335   "all the manipulators": William Herrick, *The Itinerant* (New York, 1967), 137.

335   "It was discipline": William Herrick, *Hermanos!* (New York, 1969), 22, 208, 295.

336   "to lie, prevaricate": William Herrick to Randall "Pete" Smith, Jan. 11, 1987, Ph.

336   "proof," said Herrick: William Herrick, *Shadows and Wolves* (New York, 1980), 85.

336   "Sure I testified": William Herrick, *Love and Terror* (New York, 1981), 56–57.

336   "Yes, we gave": William Herrick statement, n.d., Ph.

337   "If you hear": William Herrick, *Bradovich* (New York, 1990), 4.

337   "My paintings have": "Verbal Self-Portrait: An Interview with Anthony Toney," *Political Affairs* (Sept. 1985): 17–18; Anthony Toney, interview with Paul Cummings, Aug. 3, 1976, Archives of American Art, Washington, D.C.; Anthony Toney interview, Oct. 19, 1990.

337   "You . . . find sentimentality": Joseph Vogel, interview with Betty Hoag, Jan. 5, 1965, Archives of American Art, Washington, D.C.

338   "'Comrades,' he said": Alvah Bessie, *Men in Battle* (New York, 1939), 84.

338   "I had no choice": Irving Norman, interview with John Marlow, *Currant* 1 (Apr.–May 1975): 36–37.

338   "What I was doing": Irving Norman, interview with Michael Bell, Mar. 5, 1988, Archives of American Art, Washington, D.C.

338   "With unflinching truth": Marion Cotton, May 22, 1940, Norman file, Oakland Museum, Oakland, Calif.

339   "I comprehend history": *Comprehension* 1 (Summer 1950).

339   "Essentially," Norman insisted: Newsclip, 1950, Norman file, Oakland Museum, Oakland, Calif.

339   "Let all politicians": Statement, Apr. 20, 1956, Norman file, Oakland Museum, Oakland, Calif.

340   "That is what": Norman, interview with John Marlow.

340   "I was a little": Nicholas Pileggi, "Portrait of the Artist as a Garage Attendant in the Bronx," *New York*, Oct. 30, 1972, 37–45. See also Peter Carroll, "Ralph Fasanella," *Smithsonian Magazine*, August 1993.

341   "Fasanella is a little": William Sennett to Gussie, Nov. 9, 1937, carton 1, UCB.

341   "ballbreaker": Miscellaneous file, carton 2, UCB.

342   "After that": *PM*, Sept. 28, 1947; Patrick Wilson, *Fasanella's City* (New York, 1973); Ralph Fasanella interviews, Oct. 2, Oct. 5, 1989, May 7, 1990.

342   "I am against": Alvah Bessie to Eva, Mar. 1, 1974, Bessie MSS, Ph.

Chapter 23

Page 345   Abe Osheroff: Abe Osheroff interview, July 20, 1990.

346   "This is not": Maurice Isserman, *Which Side Were You On?* (Middletown, Conn., 1982), 250.

346   "I am floating": Miscellaneous papers, Alvah Bessie MSS, Ph.

347   "I am no": John Gates, *Story of an American* (New York, 1958), 192.

347   "I am an anti-Communist": John Gates, interview with Jerry

Fischman, 1970, audiotape, Ph; John Gates interview, May 8, 1990.

348   "A guy gets": Brock Brower, "The Abraham Lincoln Brigade Revisited," *Esquire*, Mar. 1962.

348   "the mass hysteria": *The Volunteer*, Apr. 1958.

348   "It is clear": Moe Fishman, statement on U.S. Court of Appeals, Dec. 26, 1963, UI; *The Volunteer*, Mar. 1964.

349   "On so stale": U.S. Supreme Court, no. 65, Oct. term, 1964; reprint, UCB.

349   "a complete vindication": *The Volunteer*, Apr.–June 1966, 1.

350   "Get out of town!": Archie Brown in *Operation Abolition*, documentary film, 1960.

351   "We shall not": *San Francisco Chronicle*, May 14, 1960, 1; Vernon Bown to author, Mar. 14, 1991.

351   "I think it has": *San Francisco Chronicle*, May 25, 1961, 4.

352   "the universal enormous": *The Volunteer*, Nov. 1959, 4.

352   Sam Romer: *Minneapolis Tribune*, Apr. 6, 1959, 1; Aug. 17, 1964.

352   United Nations: Joseph Brandt, Sept. 24, 1960, box 4, VALB MSS, BU.

353   "To construct something new": Ted Veltfort interview, Sept. 17, 1990.

353   "I felt like": Ruth Davidow interview, Mar. 3, 1990.

353   "All of the situations": Vernon Bown to author, Mar. 4, 1991.

353   "When I've felt": *Los Angeles Times*, Mar. 28, 1985, sec. 5, 25.

354   "I have gradually": Anne Braden, *The Wall Between* (New York, 1958), 119.

354   "I was in a": Abe Osheroff, interview for *The Good Fight*, transcription, BU.

354   "It suddenly came": Abe Osheroff to author, July 28, 1990.

355   "Youth were being": Ruth Davidow interview, Oct. 25, 1989.

355   "Call them the": Moe Fishman to Art Landis, Mar. 15, 1965, Landis MSS, BU.

356   "I didn't go": Vaughn Love interview, Apr. 7, 1978.

356   "the growing consciousness": Harry Haywood, *Black Bolshevik: Autobiography of an Afro-American Communist* (Chicago, 1978), 630, 635.

356   "You must try": Vaughn Love interview, Apr. 7, 1978; Vaughn
       Love, "Spain was a love affair," in [Joseph Brandt], *Black Amer-*
       icans in the Spanish People's War Against Fascism (New York
       [1978]), 26.

357   "to show that": Maury Colow interview, Oct. 6, 1990.

357   "Wherever I went": Maury Colow, interview with Judy Montell
       for *Forever Activists*, documentary film, 1991.

357   "Vietnam is the Spain": *The Volunteer*, Oct.–Nov. 1966, 1.

358   "Let Franco know": Box 12, VALB MSS, BU.

358   "The same power": Robert Colodny, *Spain and Vietnam: The Fight*
       for Freedom (New York, 1967), 2–3.

358   "a path opened": Box 12, VALB MSS, BU.

358   "Your generation now": *The Volunteer*, Spring 1970, 1–2.

Chapter 24

Page 359   "They are kept": Brock Brower, "The Abraham Lincoln Brigade
           Revisited," *Esquire*, Mar. 1962.

359   "common bonds of": *The Volunteer*, Apr. 1958.

360   "We've had our": Nov. 5, 1958, box 4, VALB MSS, BU.

360   Leoncio Pena: Moe Fishman interview, June 14, 1989.

361   "Spain is still": *The Volunteer*, Nov. 1959, 4.

361   "This is an important": VALB to *People's World*, Feb. 23, 1963,
       box 4, VALB MSS, BU.

361   "a resurgence of": *The Volunteer*, Nov. 1959.

362   "apparently many of": Milton Wolff to Alvah Bessie, Apr. 9, 1968,
       State Historical Society, Madison, Wis.

362   "seize the imagination": *The Volunteer*, Mar. 1962.

362   "to alleviate a tiny": *New York Times*, July 30, 1963.

362   "another treasure be": *The Volunteer*, July–Aug. 1964, 2.

362   "Make no Vietnam": *The Volunteer*, Sept.–Oct. 1968.

363   "Hasta pronto!": *The Volunteer*, Apr. 1972.

363   "How does Franco": Abe Osheroff in *Dreams and Nightmares*,
       documentary film, 1974.

363   "instant schizophrenia": Alvah Bessie, *Spain Again* (San Fran-
       cisco, 1975), 23.

363   "It was all": Osheroff in *Dreams and Nightmares*.

364   "The fight for": *The Volunteer*, Apr. 1972.

364   "through retirement, death": *The Volunteer*, Dec. 1972.

364   "Your murder yesterday": Peter Carroll, "Spain and Spain Again," *San Francisco Bay Guardian*, Oct. 24, 1975, 21.

365   "But my crystal": Alvah Bessie to author, Oct. 24, 1975.

365   "The evidence is": *The Volunteer* 1 (1978): 1.

365   "And wherever we": *Spain Revisited* (New York [1977]).

365   "began and ended": *The Volunteer* 1, no. 3 (1978): 1.

366   "The road to democracy": *The Volunteer*, Mar. 1977, 5.

366   "How strong the feeling": William Herrick, "Going Back to Spain," *New Leader* 60 (Jan. 3, 1977): 9.

366   "cried like a baby": *New York Times*, Sept. 28, 1977.

366   "and I wept": *The Volunteer*, Mar. 1977, 5.

366   "The Spanish people": Irving Weissman, "The Return," *Massachusetts Review* 19 (Autumn 1978); reprinted in Alvah Bessie and Albert Prago, eds., *Our Fight: Writings by Veterans of the Abraham Lincoln Brigade* (New York, 1987), 325–26.

366   "places where each": *Spain Revisited*.

367   "absolutely amazing": Ibid.

367   "We shall not": Alvah Bessie, ed., *The Heart of Spain* (New York, 1952), 347.

368   "We are all grateful": Dolores Ibarruri interview, June 3, 1988.

368   "A thousand years": Robert Colodny to author, Feb. 9, 1991.

Epilogue

Page 370   op-ed article: "Lincoln Brigade Recalled," *New York Times*, Feb. 12, 1975; see also *Daily World*, Mar. 1, Mar. 15, Mar. 21, 1975.

370   "Total 'control' is": Pete Smith to William Herrick [1980?] Pete Smith MSS, BU.

371   "our only ism": *The Volunteer* 2 (1979).

371   "Me," roared Alvah: Alvah Bessie to Eva, Oct. 12, 1981, Bessie MSS, Ph.

372   "to marvel that": *The Volunteer* 4 (Nov. 1982): 1–2.

372   "We are marching": Ibid., 12.

372   "Rest a while": *The Volunteer* 5 (June 1983): 14.

373   "We have to do": Ruth Davidow, "Premature Anti-fascists—Circa 1990," videotape, Ph.

373   "the most dramatic": *The Volunteer* 5 (Dec. 1983): 11.

373   "the involvement of ": *The Volunteer* 6 (Oct. 1984): 20.

374   "It was natural": Peter Carroll, "War Stories," *Image Magazine, San Francisco Examiner*, Apr. 13, 1986, 31.

374   "I'm going to": *Los Angeles Times*, Mar. 28, 1985, sec. 5, 25.

375   "a well-established": *New York Times*, May 10, 1985, A11.

375   "one war": *The Volunteer* 3 (1981): 8.

375   "In spite of ": Malcolm Cowley, "Lament for the Abraham Lincoln Battalion," *Sewanee Review* 92 (July 1984): 347.

376   "The Good Fight": *The Volunteer* 6 (Oct. 1984): 17.

376   "our ideas and beliefs": *The Volunteer* 9 (May 1987): 7.

377   "disillusioned old": *The Volunteer* 9 (Nov. 1987): 20.

377   "an anti-fascist": Ibid.

377   "We as a group": *The Volunteer* 10 (Apr. 1988): 4.

378   "If we had": Vaughn Love interview, Apr. 7, 1978.

378   "The working class": *The Volunteer* 5 (Dec. 1983): 18.

378   "Because socialism has": *The Volunteer* 6 (Apr. 1984): 16; George Kaye interview, Nov. 28, 1989.

379   "for pissing on": Bill Bailey interview, Jan. 9, 1990.

379   "Socialism in the long": Steve Nelson, Edward Bender interviews, Dec. 15, 1989.

379   "We ain't got": Davidow, "Premature Anti-fascists."

379   "Throughout history": Ruth Davidow interview, Feb. 13, 1991.

379   "Don't forget I": Moe Fishman to author, Feb. 4, 1991.

380   "I knit and someone": Davidow interview, Feb. 13, 1991.

380   "Because the world": *The Volunteer* 11 (May 1990): 6.

380   "Spain was only": Milton Wolff, interview with Judy Montell for *Forever Activists*, documentary film, 1991.

Index

In this index "f" after a number indicates a separate reference on the next page, and "ff" indicates separate references on the next two pages. A continuous discussion over two or more pages is indicated by a span of page numbers, e.g., "57–59." *Passim* is used for a cluster of references in close but not consecutive sequence.

Library of Congress Cataloging-in-Publication Data

Carroll, Peter N.
    The odyssey of the Abraham Lincoln Brigade : Americans in the
Spanish Civil War / Peter N. Carroll.
        p.   cm.
    Includes bibliographical references (p.   ) and index.
    ISBN 0-8047-2276-5 (cl.)   ISBN 0-8047-2277-3 (pbk.)
    1. Spain—History—Civil War, 1936–1939—Participation, American.
2. Spain. Ejército Popular de la Republica. Brigada Internacional,
XV. 3. American—Spain—History—20th century. I. Title.
DP269.47.A46C37   1994
946.081—dc20
93-21131   CIP   Rev

⊗ This book is printed on acid-free paper.